CANDY

CANDY

A

Century

of

Panic and Pleasure

Samira Kawash

ff Faber and Faber, Inc.
An affiliate of Farrar, Straus and Giroux • New York

Faber and Faber, Inc.
An affiliate of Farrar, Straus and Giroux
18 West 18th Street, New York 10011

Copyright © 2013 by Samira Kawash
All rights reserved
Printed in the United States of America
First edition, 2013

Library of Congress Cataloging-in-Publication Data
Kawash, Samira, 1963–
    Candy : a century of panic and pleasure / Samira Kawash. — First edition.
      pages   cm
    Includes bibliographical references and index.
    ISBN 978-0-86547-756-8 (hardback)
    1. Candy—Social aspects.   2. Candy—United States—History.
    3. Candy industry—United States—History.   I. Title.

GT2868.2.U6K39 2013
394.1'2—dc23

2013020053

Designed by Abby Kagan

Faber and Faber, Inc., books may be purchased for educational, business,
or promotional use. For information on bulk purchases, please contact
the Macmillan Corporate and Premium Sales Department at 1-800-221-7945,
extension 5442, or write to specialmarkets@macmillan.com.

www.fsgbooks.com
www.twitter.com/fsgbooks • www.facebook.com/fsgbooks

1   3   5   7   9   10   8   6   4   2

To my family

Contents

CANDY

1 ◎ Evil or Just Misunderstood?

It all started with the Jelly Bean Incident.

My daughter was three years old, and she loved jelly beans. A baby fistful of the brightly colored morsels was just about the biggest prize she could imagine, and at one tiny gram of sugar per bean, it seemed to me—her caring, reasonably attentive mother—to be a pretty harmless treat. So it was with the best of intentions that we decided one day to bring some jelly beans to share for her playdate at Noah's house.

Noah's mom, Laura, stocked their pantry with normal kid stuff—Popsicles and juice boxes and Teddy Grahams—so I didn't think much about offering the jelly beans. But Laura seemed taken aback: "Well, he's never really had that before . . . I suppose it couldn't hurt."

Couldn't hurt? Could she really believe I was harming my child, and threatening to harm hers, by holding out a few tiny pieces of candy? But greater condemnation was to follow. Her husband, Gary, had been listening to the exchange and with a dark glare in my direction he hissed at Laura, "Oh, so I guess you'll start giving him crack now too?"

He might as well have shouted in my face, "Bad mother!" I was stunned—it was just a few jelly beans, after all.

I had already promised my daughter she could have some candy—and to be honest, I like jelly beans too—so we snuck out to the patio to enjoy our illicit treat. As we ate, though, I couldn't help but think, *What if I'm wrong?* Candy is certainly not a "healthy" snack. But there I was, letting my three-year-old eat the jelly beans, encouraging her, even. My own mother wouldn't have let me have them, that's for sure—my childhood home was a no-candy zone. Maybe I *was* a bad mother.

This moment was when I first started paying attention to candy, and especially to the ways people talk about eating or not eating it. Just about everyone agrees that candy is a "junk food" devoid of real nutrition, a source of "empty calories" that ruin your appetite for better things like apples and chicken. But empty calories alone couldn't account for a reaction like Gary's, which made it seem like it was just a skip and a hop from the innocence of Pixy Stix to the dangerous and criminal world of street junkies.

And it isn't just Gary who sees candy as some kind of juvenile vice. Once I started paying attention, I noticed that a lot of stories out there suggested disturbing connections between candy and controlled substances. In 2009, *The Wall Street Journal* broke the news that middle school kids were freaking out their parents by inhaling and snorting the dust from Smarties candies; YouTube "how to" videos were all the rage for a few months.[1] Even more worrisome were exposés in 2010 on Detroit television stations about proto-alcoholic teens sneaking "drunken gummy bears" into homerooms and movie theaters.[2] And it can't be an accident that "rock" can be either candy or crack; "candy" was used as a euphemism for cocaine as early as 1931.[3] In the spring of 2012, actor Bryan Cranston offered talk-show host David Letterman a taste of "blue meth," the superpotent methamphetamine that drives the action in the AMC hit drama *Breaking Bad*. It wasn't real methamphetamine, of course, just a sugar prop, but candy maker Debbie Hall, who created the TV version, quickly started selling the ice-blue rocks in little drug baggies to fans at her Albuquerque shop the Candy Lady.[4]

Hall's creation is just a novelty gag, but there are some people who think that the sugar it's made from is as harmful as the meth it's imitating. Addiction researchers warn that the tasty pleasures of candy, cakes, potato chips, and the rest of the sweet, fatty indulgences we fondly know as "junk food" light up the same brain receptors as heroin and cocaine. A team at Yale showed pictures of ice cream to women with symptoms of "food addiction" and found that their brains resembled the brains of heroin addicts looking at drug paraphernalia.[5] The idea of food addiction has become part of the national anti-obesity conversation; even Kathleen Sebelius, U.S. secretary of health and human services, announced in May 2012 that for some people, obesity is the result of "an addiction like smoking."[6]

The belief that craving a sugar fix is the same thing as jonesing for a hit of something stronger depends in large part on one's definition of "addiction." Representatives of the food industry tend to favor a more narrow designation. A study funded by the World Sugar Research Organization concluded in 2010 that although humans definitely like to eat sugar, the way we eat it doesn't strictly qualify as addiction.[7] On the other hand, Dr. Nora D. Volkow of the National Institute on Drug Abuse warns that "processed sugar in certain individuals can produce . . . compulsive patterns of intake."[8] Compulsion isn't quite addiction, but there are even more alarming reports of research at Princeton and the University of Florida, where "sugar-binging rats show signs of opiatelike withdrawal when their sugar is taken away—including chattering teeth, tremoring forepaws and the shakes."[9] Rats plied with a fatty processed diet of Ho Hos, cheesecake, bacon, and sausage at the Scripps Institute didn't do too well either; the rats

quickly started overeating, and wouldn't stop gorging themselves even when the scientists began zapping them with electri-
cal shocks. The study's authors concluded that "junk food elicits
addictive behavior in rats similar to the behaviors of rats addicted
to heroin."[10]

Call it addiction or craving or compulsion, it does seem certain that having a little candy causes many people to want to eat
more. What makes junk food so irresistible, according to former
FDA commissioner David Kessler, is its "hyperpalatability." In
his book *The End of Overeating*, Kessler shows how the food industry manipulates its products to make us want to keep eating
them. The addition of large quantities of fat, sugar, and salt is what
makes processed foods taste good. But these additives do more
than just make bland ingredients taste better. Sweetness, salti-
ness, and fattiness, alone or in combination, may actually stimulate our appetites, and the more we eat, the more we crave. Thus,
this food isn't just palatable, it's "hyperpalatable." The arts of the
food chemist and the food technologist bring us this experience
in ever more perfect and irresistible forms. Witness the food-
engineering marvel that is the Snickers bar as Kessler describes it:
"as we chew, the sugar dissolves, the fat melts, and the caramel picks
up the peanut pieces so the entire candy is carried out of the mouth
at the same time."[11] It's a sensory symphony of fat, sugar, and salt:
perfectly delicious and completely impossible to re-create at home.

Hyperpalatability (i.e., extreme yumminess) plus aggressive
marketing by corporate parent Mars, Inc. explains Snickers's
permanent perch at the top of the best-selling candy bar lists. The
caramel, nougat, and peanut confection has been an American
favorite since its introduction in 1930; now it dominates the international markets too, with annual global sales projected to exceed
$3.5 billion.[12] And Snickers is but one star in a globalized candy
universe; in 2012, total worldwide retail candy sales were estimated at $118 billion.[13] Hershey vies with Mars for top spot in
the United States, while global conglomerates Ferrero, Mars,

Kraft, and Nestlé rule the traditional candy markets of Europe and North America. New markets in far-flung locales previously innocent of American-style snack foods are getting bigger every day. Russian sales of Snickers have doubled in the last five years, and in 2011 the emerging middle classes in Russia, Brazil, India, and China accounted for over half the growth in retail candy sales.[14] In more and more places, people are eating candy in the American style: as a snack, on the go, any day, or every day.

And candy in the United States is still going strong. It is true, as Steve Almond so morosely recounted in *Candyfreak*, that its prominence in American life today is much diminished from its heyday in the 1930s and 1940s. But though the parlor candy dish may have passed out of fashion, plenty of candy is still finding its way into American mouths. Despite the loss of variety (in American manufacture, at least) and the disappearance of many old-time favorites, the quantity of candy sold on a per capita basis in the United States is higher today than it has ever been. Retail sales amount to some $32 billion per year and are growing, in good times and in bad, even through the most recent recession. Susan Whiteside, vice president of communications for the National Confectioners Association, suggests a simple reason for candy's success: "When economic times are tough, the things that bring you a lot of happiness that don't cost a lot of money tend to stay in your budget."[15]

Candy is one of those simple pleasures that make people feel good, and it's a pleasure that's never hard to find. Candy is conveniently located right next to the cash register in just about every retail establishment, from suburban megastores to urban bodegas and every store in between, and sold from vending machines in schools, libraries, athletic parks, and wherever else people gather. It's so plentiful and so ubiquitous that most of the time we don't even notice it. As to how we define candy, I suspect that most of us operate on a pornography principal—we know it when we see it—but as I'll explain later, the definition of candy is never quite so simple as one might think. For the time being, however, when I say "candy," I mean (somewhat tautologically) those things that people commonly call candy, made by manufacturers who describe their business as the manufacture of candy. People who think about these things every day, like indefatigable candy reviewer Cybele May, who posts at candyblog .net, sort candy from not-candy with a few specific qualities in mind: a sweet substance with a base of sugar, not liable to spoilage, ready to eat without preparation or utensils, and consumed primarily for pleasure.[16] This is pretty good, so far as commonsense definitions go, but, as I hope to show, it is getting a lot more difficult to say with confidence what sorts of foods ought to be included in the broad category of candy.

Usually, if we think about candy at all, it's as the stuff of happy memories: cotton candy at the state fair, the birthday party piñata, the overflowing Easter baskets and Halloween bags, the glittering Hanukkah gelt, the comfort of the lollipop at the doctor's office, the reward of M&M's for potty training, the chocolates from a loved one on Valentine's Day, or the prettily wrapped favors at weddings. But even when candy is freely given to children, and intended to heighten the pleasure of special events, it's almost always accompanied by a warning: don't let all that candy spoil your dinner, and remember to brush your teeth right afterward.

It seems paradoxical that the candy that gives us some of our happiest experiences is the same candy that rots our teeth, ruins our appetite, and sucks tender innocents into a desperate life of sugar addiction. Candy joins the ideas of pleasure and poison, innocence and vice, in a way that's unique and a bit puzzling. The older name for a candy maker is *confectioner*, which comes from Latin roots that mean, roughly, "making together" or "putting together." According to the *Oxford English Dictionary*, a confectioner is "one who makes confections, sweetmeats, candies, cakes, light pastry." But there is another meaning for confectioner: a "compounder of medicines, poisons." It is a troubling thought: sweetmeats and poison originating from the same source.

Killer Candy

Once a year, when the leaves start to fall from the trees, the contradictions between candy as treat and candy as poison become impossible to avoid: Halloween—the high holy day of candy. When we get swept up in the spirit of the season, all the good intentions to cut back on junky sweets and avoid the candy dish come crashing down like a tower of Necco Wafers.

Halloween wasn't always a candy bacchanal. Up until around 1960, trick-or-treaters might receive just about any small desirable thing: candy to be sure, but also small toys, coins, nuts, homemade cookies, or popcorn balls. Today, however, the sole treat that every trick-or-treater demands is candy, in vast quantities. There's always a neighborhood curmudgeon who insists on handing out apples, a "virtuous" treat. They usually end up in the garbage can. Halloween is not a time for healthy snacks.

But some see the giant sack of Halloween candy not only as unhealthy but also as potentially deadly. When I was growing up, parents everywhere were always on high alert for the evil machinations of the "Halloween sadist," the local psychopath who was out to get the neighborhood kiddies with strychnine-laced Pixy Stix and razor blade–studded caramels. We couldn't touch our candy until Mom or Dad had inspected every piece for signs of tampering. Local hospitals even volunteered their radiology labs for post–trick-or-treat candy X-rays.

It turns out that the Halloween sadist is about 0.01 percent fact and 99.99 percent myth (I'll get to the full Halloween story later, in chapter 12). Nevertheless, many parents are very, very nervous about leaving all that candy in the custody of their children. Some go so far as to seize the haul and confiscate it. Most kids in my neighborhood get to keep a few morsels and then are cajoled or forced into relinquishing the rest. The irony, of course, is that these parents who worry at the prospect of little Jayden eating all that candy are the very same ones who likely sat at their own front doors dispensing mountains of Skittles packs and Dum Dum pops to other people's kids earlier that evening. It has become a uniquely American overparenting ritual: we give our kids candy, then we take it away. Even though people don't worry as much anymore about the hazards of needles or arsenic lurking in the Halloween haul, there is still a nebulous feeling that candy may be dangerous, perhaps even deadly.

These days, the menace of candy feared by parents looks less like a child-hating sadist and more like a simple sugar cube. In one of the most prominent recent attacks, *The New York Times Magazine* ran an April 2011 cover story titled "Sweet and Vicious: The Case Against Sugar." The article, by nutrition journalist Gary Taubes, publicized the work of biochemists who believe that sugar is not just "empty calories" but something far more dangerous. As Taubes put it, "Sugar has unique characteristics, specifically in the way the human body metabolizes the fructose in it, that may make it singularly harmful, at least if consumed in sufficient quantities."[17]

Dr. Robert Lustig, a pediatric endocrinologist at the University of California at San Francisco, has become the most prominent and credible spokesman for this view. He was featured in April 2012 on *60 Minutes* in a segment titled "Is Sugar Toxic?" and nearly three million viewers on YouTube have watched his ninety-minute lecture called "Sugar: The Bitter Truth," which explains the underlying science. The biochemistry may be complex, but his message is simple: sugar is a killer.

The attention given to Lustig and others who are investigating the potential dangers of sugar heralds an epochal swing in the dietary pendulum. Up until recently, the orthodoxy shared by most experts in health and nutrition was what Taubes has called the "fat hypothesis." From the 1960s up through the 1990s, the irrefutable rise in chronic diet-related diseases after the Second World War was blamed on dietary fat. But these days, it's carbohydrates in general, and sugar in particular, that are starting to draw attention. In variations on what Taubes calls the "carbohydrate hypothesis," researchers are increasingly turning their attention to the dangers of and damages caused by what used to be called comfort foods: refined flour (goodbye, pasta and bread), refined sugar (farewell, cakes and candies), and, most reviled of them all, high-fructose corn syrup (so long, sodas and sweet teas).[18]

The latest figures from the USDA for total sweetener consumption are about 130 pounds per capita per year, a significant improvement compared to the 150 or so pounds ingested by each American in the late 1990s but still a substantial increase over the approximate 110-pound consumption in the 1960s. Candy accounts for only about 6 percent of the total sugar in the overly sweetened American diet—most comes from processed foods and soft drinks—but it has the misfortune of lacking a foodish alibi behind which to hide its saccharine ways.[19] If added sugar is our main dietary villain, then candy is among the most obvious culprits; unlike high-fructose-corn-syrup-laced hot dog buns or ketchup, candy shows its sugar on the outside.

Candy as Food

If you've read Michael Pollan's excellent book *The Omnivore's Dilemma*, then you already know that when you eat conventional beef, you're mostly eating corn. But do you know you are eating candy too? There is an entire underworld of food salvage that sells "secondhand" food to livestock owners: things like bakery scraps and restaurant scrapings, along with expired and disfigured but still edible candy (wrappers and all—the expense of separating the wrappers would raise the price too much).

The feedlot operators are quite sanguine about it: "It has been a practice going on for decades," livestock nutritionist Ki Fanning told a CNN reporter in October 2012, "and is a very good way for producers to reduce feed cost, and to provide less expensive food for consumers." Since the price of corn started rising in 2009, even more of the relatively cheaper salvage candy is ending up in cattle feed mixes, a development that prompted CNN's investigation, which was headlined "Kentucky Cows Chow Down on Candy." The story features feedlot owner Joseph Watson, who praises the virtues of his candy blend. He says it fattens his cattle up nicely, with "a higher ratio of fat than actually feeding straight corn." Farmer Mike Yoder claims that feeding ice cream sprinkles to his dairy cows has increased milk production. Chuck Hurst, a livestock nutritionist in Idaho, explains that the sugar in candy provides "the same kind of energy as corn," but he is silent on the possible effects of the candy wrappers.[20]

There's something deeply unsettling about this story. Despite the reassurances that candy is really the same as corn, common sense rebels. Cows shouldn't be eating candy (much less candy wrappers). Candy is just . . . not food. As for humans, well, maybe a little candy is okay, but with all the warnings about sugar and worries about obesity, we know we probably shouldn't eat too much. We, like cows, should eat food. Sounds simple enough.

The problem for us humans is that unlike the captive cows in the feedlot, we have to choose what to eat. And in the grocery store, we are surrounded by an array of choices our grandmothers would never have dreamed of. There are convenience foods promising to eliminate kitchen drudgery and "functional" foods promising health-enhancing benefits, low-fat and low-carb foods that will put our diets back on track, frozen foods and shelf-stable foods to hoard against the Apocalypse—a cornucopia of modern food engineering and packaging. Michael Pollan calls them "edible food-like substances": we can eat them, but their relation to foods like fresh spinach and grandma's meatballs is a little sketchy. It is practically impossible to escape these ubiquitous foodlike substances, even at the fancy natural grocery store. Labels that say *organic*, *all-natural*, and *whole grain* all sound very reassuring, but even the supervirtuous specialty foods like Annie's Homegrown Organic Berry Fruit Snack or Earth's Best Organic Crunchin' Grahams Apple Cinnamon Stick are versions of Pollan's "edible food-like substances." They do, however, look a lot more like real food when compared with something that is clearly not food at all. Something like candy.

The idea that there is a hard line separating candy from food might be reassuring, but reality is never so simple. I've already suggested that it might be difficult even to define candy. So what about food? For millions of years, our hominid ancestors had no problem figuring out that anything they ate that didn't kill them or make them sick must be food. Today, however, it's impossible to talk about food without talking about nutrition, about how different foods may be more or less beneficial, about which foods are better and which worse for healthful living. We know all about calories; we study nutrition labels to see how much fat, protein, and carbs are in our food; and we worry about increasingly arcane food elements like trans fats and soluble fibers. Nutritional experts caution us to avoid the "empty calories" found in junk food like soda, chips, and candy, calories that add nothing but inches to our waistlines. Instead, we are taught to seek out "nutritious" food that will provide our bodies with the optimal materials for health and vitality.

This idea of food as a delivery device for nutrients is a result of the way of thinking that Pollan and others have called "nutritionism."[21] Nutritionism reduces every edible substance to its components (those we know about, at any rate) and then compares and measures and evaluates those components in isolation. So we don't have meat or apples or bread; we have fats and carbs and proteins and vitamins and minerals and fiber. The fats and carbs and protein in meat or apples or bread are the same as the fats and carbs and protein in a bottle of Ensure, or in a package of PowerBars, or in a Swanson's TV dinner. In the modern nutritional framework, food isn't food so much as a modular accretion of chemical building blocks.

Nutritionism is what makes it so easy to blur the lines between food and candy. Looking at food in terms of calories and carbo-hydrates puts gumdrops in the same category as both apples and dinner rolls: they may have more or less of this or that nutrient, but they're not fundamentally different.

Spelling out the consequences of nutritionism this way seems an affront to contemporary common sense, but there was a time when this logic would have appeared quite sound and candy was widely accepted as a very good kind of food. As I'll show, the idea that candy could be good food laid the groundwork for the idea that all sorts of other manufactured, artificial, highly pro-cessed stuff could also be good food. And from the resultant confusion about what food actually ought to be originates much of our current dietary woe.

A Hidden History

Although candy was first mass-produced in England in the 1850s, the great candy industry of the early twentieth century was an American phenomenon. Candy as we know it today is a result of the fantastic powers unleashed by the Industrial Revolution, and it was one of the first factory-produced foods in the late nine-teenth century. Subsequent developments led to the spread of American-style candy throughout the world, beginning with the empires built by Mars and Hershey in the 1920s and 1930s, and aided by the American military troops who traveled the globe during World War II, their rations packed full of candy, making new "friends" by passing out Baby Ruth bars and Tootsie Rolls.

By the second half of the twentieth century, America was exporting not only its candy bars but also its eating habits. Candy paved the way for a panoply of other highly processed foods that, like candy, were convenient, portable, palatable, and cheap. Some nutritionists and reformers now believe that the fundamental problem of the current food system is the excessive consumption of highly processed foods. This is a global issue, and the question of how to improve the accessibility of less-processed and more nutritious food is a complex one. I don't pretend to have a solution. But I do believe that understanding how we got here is a good way to start.

When I first began researching the history of American candy, I read every book I could find about the great candy companies, along with books about the history of candy making (you'll find a list of essential books in the bibliography). These books were interesting, but I wanted to understand how candy fit into the broader picture of food in general. I knew that manufacturing—and consumption—had grown quickly in the early 1900s, and I assumed that food historians would have something to say about the growing place of candy in the American diet. I was very wrong.

One of the first books I read was the classic work by Waverley Root and Richard de Rochemont, *Eating in America: A History*. This 1976 study aims to cover it all, from the Pilgrims to the present. I turned eagerly to chapter 29, "The Great American Sweet Tooth," and found . . . two pages on chewing gum. That's it. The rest is soda, ice cream, and sugar as a condiment. Do Americans eat candy? You wouldn't know it from this history. My cravings were not much more satisfied by the next "big book" on the shelf, Richard J. Hooker's 1981 history titled *Food and Drink in America*. Hooker does manage to amass material for a full two pages on candies, but it is his contention that "most candies were made in the home."[22] Focusing on fudge parties and taffy pulls, domestic entertainments popular at the turn of the century, he leaves the reader to conclude that America's interest in candy has been confined to tittering girls in the drawing room.

More recent food histories do nothing to fill in the gaps. Carole Counihan's 2002 anthology *Food in the U.S.A.* is pretty comprehensive, a good textbook for a food studies course. Alas, as for candy, not a peep. Andrew Smith describes thirty "turning points" in American food history in his book *Eating History*; the rise of industrial candy is not one of them, though the chapter on Cracker Jack comes tantalizingly close, and to be fair, Smith does pause for two pages to talk about chocolate. You won't find candy in Harvey Levenstein's *Revolution at the Table* or *Paradox of Plenty*, or in Laura Shapiro's *Perfection Salad* or *Something from the Oven*. These are essential works for understanding how our food got to be the way it is today. But somehow they leave out the part about the candy. It can't be that these experts are unaware of the millions of pounds of candy consumed each year, yet the way they define their subject matter makes candy irrelevant—they don't consider candy a food.

I think they're wrong. When you start looking at its history, candy isn't separate from food at all. The story of food in America looks to me like one of those jacquard-woven beach towels. A colorful pattern shows on one side, and when you flip it over, the colors reverse. This is candy's relationship to food history: on the top side, intended to be displayed to the world, candy doesn't show. But when you peek underneath, you see the candy thread is an essential part of the whole story.

Sweet

Tim Richardson, the author of a comprehensive history of sweets from a British perspective, believes that the deafening silence surrounding candy is because it exists in a "culinary limbo."[23] Candy isn't a staple or a necessity, it isn't part of ordinary meals or food rituals, and most of the time it isn't even considered food. When it's eaten with a meal, it's given its own separate category—dessert—and when eaten at other times of day, it becomes a snack, as if calling it something else means it doesn't really count. (But why should *when* we eat something have any effect on what it actually is?) Nutritionists make quick work of candy as "empty calories," while anthropologists and food historians tend to consign such trivial morsels to scholarly oblivion.

But there are perhaps also more subtle reasons for candy's relegation to the sidelines. Think about the meaning of the word *sweet*: it isn't just a flavor, it's a personality trait. Sweet people are nice, pleasant, kind, and helpful. They put others' needs before their own. But calling someone sweet isn't always a compliment. Men are almost never referred to as sweet. Sweetness implies smallness and unimportance, like candy. And who are the people we refer to as "sweet"? Women and children.

How did the taste of candy come to be connected to stereotypes about the character of women and children? Wendy Woloson, author of *Refined Tastes: Sugar, Confectionery and Consumers in Nineteenth-Century America*, argues that the association of femininity and weakness with sweet-tasting foods has to do with the changing value of sugar. In the seventeenth and eighteenth centuries, sugar plantations were sources of immense wealth, and whoever controlled the sugar trade also wielded substantial political and economic power. Sugar was dear, and sweet foods costly. Powerful hosts would display their wealth at banquets with sumptuous sugar-spun centerpieces, a form of conspicuous consumption made all the more excessive by the fact that the sugar would go to waste. As production became more mechanized in the nineteenth century, the price of sugar fell. By the second half of the nineteenth century, sugar was both cheap and widely available. As a result, Woloson suggests, sugar "became linked with femininity: its economic devaluation coincided with its cultural demotion."[24] Sweets were banished to the margins of the table, just as women and children were banished to drawing rooms and nurseries.

It is a common belief that women and children are the ones who crave candy—the masculinity of a man who likes candy too much is often seen as somewhat suspect. This turns out not to be the whole story; historically men have also eaten their share and have even, at some points during the last century, been the primary market for it. But perhaps food historians have paid so little attention to candy because of this cultural connection between sweet, trivial people, i.e., women and children, and sweet, trivial candy.

Yet despite the fact that it seems so unimportant, candy provokes strong feelings in many people, feelings that seem much larger and more complex than the simple substance itself. Sweetness is just the beginning of these intense cultural associations. As I discovered with the jelly bean incident, many people fear the effects of candy on their children, and sometimes those fears can seem all out of proportion to the actual potential for harm. Adults also often act ambivalent about the pleasure they take in candy. Despite the fact that the actual physical substance of candy is fairly simple and, when broken down into individual ingredients, not that different from many other foods, somehow the meanings associated with it are extremely complicated and contradictory.

The language of candy spoken by many adults is the language of sin: guilty pleasure, temptation, indulgence. People apologize for eating candy, hide their stash in drawers and closets, eat it alone where no one will see, confess their cravings as though seeking absolution. It seems ironic; our culture aspires to be resolutely post-shame, as the frankness surrounding sexuality and sexual pleasure reminds us every day. Sometimes it seems like the guilt formerly reserved for sex has returned in our attitude toward confectionery. For some—perhaps women in particular— even previously unspeakable forms of sexual pleasure are less shameful than a midnight raid on the chocolate box.

Chocolate has long been associated with seduction, its exotic origins and sensual pleasures making it an easy metaphor for courtship, and when given as a gift, it's an obvious token of desire. It is a long-standing tradition: men give women chocolates, with the implication that they will be given reciprocal pleasures in turn. But increasingly in the postfeminist era, chocolate is being marketed directly to women, as an easy indulgence and escape from everyday pressures and worries. As the luxury chocolate market has expanded, eating chocolates has been depicted as a form of female "self-love," a private enjoyment that women choose and control. The "My moment. My Dove" ad campaign, which ran from 2005 to 2010, depicted women in private settings writhing in pleasure as they savored a morsel of Dove chocolate. And this is how Pepperidge Farm described the delights of a 2012 European-style chocolate biscuit called Signatures Chocolate Medallion Cookies Milk Chocolate Caramel: "Savor richness . . . followed by lightness . . . and a hidden silky caramel filling. Taste waves of pleasure, building to the Signatures sensation. Then revel in the afterglow of . . . Chocolateness." After that experience, you'll probably want a cigarette.

In the wake of the sexual revolution, women supposedly have the full right to their bodies and their desires. And yet, where candy eating is concerned, the pleasure seems all too often to bring with it a dose of guilt. Perhaps chocolate pleasure is not a sin against God, but it is certainly a sin against Diet. The indulgence demands penance. Maybe it wasn't such a good idea to eat that Snickers bar for lunch, but we promise ourselves we'll make up for it later with salad for dinner, no dressing. It's the familiar binge-and-purge, sin-and-self-flagellation rhythm of perpetual dieting: chocolate pleasure today, mortification of the flesh tomorrow. No one would deny that candy has a lot of calories. But the language of candy eating goes far beyond the rational realms of science and nutrition. Candy is the apple in the garden, and we, particularly women, are the fallen who were too weak to resist temptation.

Innocent

Women, fallen from dietary grace, may experience shame and regret in connection with their confectionery longings. But what about those true innocents, the children? Increasingly, there are more and more people like Gary, who would say that giving candy to a toddler amounts to some kind of alimentary child abuse. Food reformers have been making arguments about the damaging effects of candy on children since the beginning of commercial candy. But the current language of child abuse, and the association of feeding the wrong foods with physical assault, is gaining popularity. When food activist and chef Jamie Oliver appeared on *Oprah* in early 2010, she asked him point-blank: "Do you feel that parents who consistently feed their children junk food are practicing child abuse?" Jamie didn't flinch. "Absolutely," he replied.

As adults, we make our own choices about when and what and how to eat, and we acknowledge that our own bodies bear the consequences of those choices. But we view the bodies—and choices—of children differently. As adults, and especially as parents, we bear the responsibility for the health and well-being of our children's bodies. We are responsible for nourishing them, providing rest and physical comfort, offering opportunities for play and exercise to make their bodies strong. So candy poses a serious complication to the issues of adult responsibility for children and also adult control of children. We are told that we should never give candy to children because it's bad for them, but also that we shouldn't deny our children what they want (whoever came up with the expression that something easy is "like taking candy from a baby" never tried to pry some from the bone-cracking grip of a toddler's hand). It is incredibly difficult to navigate through this thicket of contradiction and fear.

The worries don't stop with the effects of candy consumption. As ambivalent as we might be about when or how much candy to give our children, there is one thing everybody can agree on: children should never, ever, take candy from strangers. Candy is known as the secret weapon of the child snatcher, the pedophile, the local psychopath who tries to lure little girls and boys with lollipops. We're always on the lookout for predatory men in white panel vans roving the neighborhood with sacks of sweets. But, as with the urban legends of Halloween candy poisoners, this fear turns out to be only tangentially related to reality. As FBI agent April Brooks of the Crimes Against Children Unit explains, "Most children are taken by people they know. Out of the many thousands of cases we see each year, only a few hundred are stranger abductions."[25] Despite this fact, the potent image of the candy-wielding child snatcher says a lot about how our society views children: they are innocent and therefore unable to tell the difference between generosity and malevolence, and they also are foolish and therefore easily lured by the simple pleasure of a candy treat into doing something their parents have warned them not to do. Children have not always been seen this way, and we might pause to wonder whether our own children are necessarily as naïve and gullible as we think they are.

But perhaps our fears about the sinister stranger luring innocents with candy also reflect something of our own vulnerability. Can we trust our senses? Like the child who can't tell the difference between malevolent stranger and benevolent neighbor, we are often unsure if the enticing things that surround us are really good for us, whether we're talking about candy or other foods. "Candy from strangers" might be a good metaphor for everything we eat. We don't really know what most food we buy is, where it came from, or who made it. Is it as good as it looks? Or does the alluring surface hide something harmful? As adults, we're supposed to know enough to tell the difference, but perhaps we are more like children faced with a proffered lollipop, so distracted by the sticky promise of pleasure that we ignore the warning signs.

Do You Eat Enough Candy?

It was over a century ago that America came to be known, in the immortal words of one 1907 visitor, as "a great candy eating nation."[26] In the next several chapters, I'll show how candy grabbed hold of the American imagination and stomach in the early decades of the twentieth century, after developments in manufacturing technology and food science made it possible to create mass quantities of increasingly complex confections. Candy stories from the first part of the century are full of a sense of adventure and possibility: athletes who swore on the performance-boosting powers of candy, aviators surviving record-breaking flights on chocolate bars, sober scientists insisting that candy could fuel the nation to greatness. During the first two decades of the century, the popularity of manufactured candy encouraged many women to take up home candy making and then to start cooking with candy. Soon home cooks were adding marshmallows to omelets and stuffing chopped-up candy bars into tomatoes. (These intrepid pioneers inspired me to attempt some practical experiments; in chapter 6, you'll learn what happened when I went to candy school to try my hand at boiling sugar, and why lima beans might be the next big thing in confectionery.)

The frivolous fun of candy might seem to have little to do with the serious stuff of international conflict; yet as I'll explain, war has had a tremendous impact on the growth of candy's importance in American life. The First World War inspired new methods of manufacturing which, when the war was over, unleashed a frenzy of candy bar innovation. The candy bar craze of the 1920s and 1930s brought into existence thousands of brands of bars: from the jazzy delights of Black Bottom and Gypsy bar (in honor of stripper Gypsy Rose Lee) to the delicious-sounding Chicken Dinner and Denver Sandwich—named for a meal, with a size and heft to match. The golden age of the candy bar ushered in a whole new style of eating. This was the era that gave us Admiral Byrd loading up his ship with ten thousand candy bars for vital food energy on his polar expedition, Shirley Temple warbling about the "Good Ship Lollipop" in the movie *Bright Eyes*, and magazine ads that queried anxiously, "Do you eat enough candy?" (plate 1).

And yet, as I'll show, there was a dark side to all that candy fun. From the mid-nineteenth century onward, many Americans voiced worries about the potentially sinister effects of indulgence. In the late 1800s, confectioners were repeatedly accused of selling to children candies that were "adulterated" with fillers and toxins, including nasty things like "white earth" and floor scrapings. Candy—with its deliberately unnatural forms and surprising colors—was also exhibit number one for food reformers who railed against the dangers of artificial foods. When a child got sick in the early 1900s, newspapers were quick to post headlines blaring "Poisoned by Candy"—much to the outrage of candy makers, who went to great lengths to defend their product.

Many of the social and moral ills blamed on candy in the early twentieth century are surprising today. The temperance movement, for example, railed against alcohol and warned the nation of the dangers of drunkenness. But many Americans also believed there were significant similarities between alcohol and sugar (an impression perhaps enhanced by the vibrant trade in rum)—candy seemed perilously close to booze. As the nation moved toward national prohibition of alcohol, a controversy ensued: Would eating more candy distract from drinking, or would it actually stimulate the body to a state of drunkenness? Children's indulgence in candy was of special concern to reformers sometimes derided as "Sunday school" moralists, who saw chocolate cigars as but the first step on a slippery slope toward the worst kinds of vices. Smoking, drinking, gambling, even masturbation might be the soul-crushing results of an early candy habit. Writers painted in vivid hues the horrors that would befall the child who ate too much. As for overindulging adults, the consequences were all too visible. Diet popularizer Lulu Hunt Peters went so far as to declare chocolate creams a mortal sin against the waistline.

Candy inflamed passions on every side, yet despite all the panic and controversy, it has never been as harmful as the worst critics have charged. From our enlightened perch, it's easy to laugh at the seemingly irrational belief that the stimulating powers of candy would provoke paroxysms of sexual desire or induce intoxication in a manner akin to liquor. But to this day, many of the other suspicions about candy's damaging effects persist more or less unquestioned. For example, when I started researching this book I believed that there really was such a thing as "poison candy" back in the early days. But when I looked carefully, I was surprised to discover that the charges leveled against early American candy makers were mostly the result of prejudice and fabulation. In fact, the most disturbing stories that I'll share in this book aren't about bad candy, but about people who have used candy to do bad things: parents who hid poison in their children's treats, spurned lovers who took revenge with a tainted box of chocolates, scientists who subjected mentally disabled hospital patients to gruesome experiments to test the effects of excessive candy consumption.

American candy soared to new heights during the Second World War, when Uncle Sam bought up one-quarter of the factories' production to send to the troops, for everything from daily rations to emergency survival kits. A new advertising slogan captured the mood perfectly: "Candy Is Delicious Food—Enjoy Some Every Day!" But in the period of peace and prosperity that followed, the perception and the importance of candy shifted dramatically, as ideas about it became tangled up in broad-ranging social controversies about safety, nutrition, and health. Candy was part of the story of how we got fluoride in our water, and of how the artificial sweetener cyclamate came to be seen first as diet salvation and then as cancer-causing menace. Changing views of food pushed people away from eating as much candy in the 1960s and 1970s as they had before the war. Artificial sweeteners made candy seem that much more fattening, "sugarphobes" warned that the sweet white powder might be just another drug, dentists gained new ammunition in their charge that candy was the primary culprit in tooth decay, and the growing popularity of "health foods" made "junk foods" like candy look that much unhealthier in comparison.

Candy didn't go away under this pressure, it just changed its face. In the second part of the twentieth century, candy ended up everywhere, from the breakfast table to outer space. And in our own day, we are surrounded by all sorts of never before imagined versions of candy, even if words like *fruit* and *vitamins* have the effect of making candy seem to magically disappear.

In these pages, I'll argue that candy was at the leading edge of a broader transformation in food processing that, over the course of the twentieth century, would completely upend traditional assumptions of what to eat, when to eat, and how to eat it. Candy was the first ready-to-eat processed food, the original ancestor of all our fast, convenient, fun, imperishable, tasty, highly advertised brand-name snacks and meals. Candy bars were the first packaged snacks, the first kind of food that was made to be eaten on the go and that could serve as a meal in a pinch. The idea that candy was a food that could be eaten anytime and anywhere planted the seeds of what we now call the "culture of snacking." And the goals of candy makers—variety, novelty, deliciousness, with nutrition as a low priority—have become the universal guiding principles of processed-food innovators.

While candy shares much with its processed-food kin, candy is the one kind of processed food that proclaims its allegiance to the artificial, the processed, the unhealthy. This is something I really like about candy: it's honest. It says what it is. But this honesty also makes candy an easy target. By blaming candy for bad nutrition, cavities, and obesity, we can keep buying without worry the foods that stock the rest of the grocery store aisles.

The ease with which all the other foodish stuff gets let off the hook is what makes candy scapegoating especially troubling to me. Beyond a few cosmetic "fresh food" trappings, the foods that line the grocery shelves and are served up in fast-food and convenience outlets today are what Brazilian nutrition researcher Carlos Montiero has called "ultra-processed foods," foods processed so far beyond their original form as to be better described as fabricated rather than grown.[27] These hyperpalatable products get the bulk of their calories from a few cheap commodities (corn, soy, wheat) flavored with cheap fats and cheap sweeteners. The ancestral relation between candy and today's ultraprocessed foods is a compelling reason to look a little more closely at the rise of the candy industry and the controversies and worries that accompanied it. The story of candy in America is a story of how the processed, the artificial, and the fake came to be embraced as real food. And it's also the story of how it happened that so much of what we call food today is really candy.

So what about that handful of jelly beans? Are they evil or just misunderstood?[28] The tale of how we came to be asking this question is a strange and fascinating one. For the answer, read on.

2 ⊙ The Machine Candy Revolution

In the early years of the twentieth century, Manhattan, Boston, Chicago, Philadelphia, and Brooklyn vied for top ranking among confectionery-manufacturing cities. Brooklyn alone boasted a production of 130 million pounds of confectionery and chocolate in 1908, at a value of some $10 million. A visitor to Brooklyn in that year could have wandered along the waterfront past hulking sugar refineries, to arrive at the docks where bustling workers loaded ships with tons of lemon drops for American soldiers stationed overseas in territories won in the 1898 Spanish-American War. This visitor would have smelled burnt caramel wafting over the factories and marveled at the size of the biggest candy factory in the world, Greenfield's, at 107 Lorimer Street, which churned out 36 million pounds of confectionery a year for the candy-starved masses.

There were plenty of places for the visitor to buy that candy too. Brooklyn boasted some 560 shops dedicated to the sale of candy, and many of those were also making their own candies onsite. Candy could be purchased at drugstores, newsstands, stationers, department stores, train stations . . . nearly everywhere.

Factories weren't producing just for the local market, either. As a 1908 *Brooklyn Daily Eagle* headline boasted, "Brooklyn Leads Country in Candy Export." Brooklyn shipped more candy than any other city, to every state of the union.[1]

To the visitor wandering the streets of Brooklyn in those days, watching the wagons loaded with crates of lemon drops trundling toward the docks, or stepping out of the way as another barrel of candy corn arrived for delivery at the corner shop, it might seem as if things had ever been so. But in fact, there had been a time not so long before when it would not have been unusual for an American to go her whole life never having sucked on a lemon drop, much less tasted candy corn. Candy corn, and most of the other hundreds of varieties of candy pouring out of those turn-of-the-century factories, didn't exist before 1880. In fact, even fifty years earlier, simple sweets like candy sticks and lozenges were something special, especially outside the major cities. And a hundred years earlier, around 1800, most Americans lived and died never having eaten any manufactured candy at all. The generations of colonists, settlers, and revolutionaries who shaped early American history could not have dreamed of the candy future that was just over the horizon.

The colonists would have known but a few confections, expensive to acquire and reserved for very special occasions. Massachusetts Puritan Samuel Sewall, not so fondly remembered for his role in condemning twenty people to death in the Salem witch trials, is on record as enjoying sugared almonds.[2] The Dutch bakers of New Amsterdam offered such morsels as "sugar wafers, marchpanes [marzipan], macaroons, pasteys, roundels and sugar plums," on special order, to grace the table at weddings and holiday feasts. In Boston, New York, and Philadelphia in the years leading up to the American Revolution, there were a handful of confectioners; one advertisement from 1774 boasts "preserved fruits, all sorts of sugar plums, dragees [sugar-coated nuts], barley sugar, white and brown sugar candy, ice cream and fruits, sugar ornaments which are now ready for sale or to lend out."[3] Almost all imported from Europe, these confections were expensive and luxurious, out of reach for anyone outside the wealthy elite.

Until around 1845, domestic candy manufacture was, as one observer put it plainly, "in a somewhat crude state."[4] In the early decades of the nineteenth century, some enterprising individuals began making more simple sorts of candies for sale to a wider market, mostly stick candies and taffies. Druggists were not in the candy business, but since they made sugar lozenges for medicinal uses, they often sold them as candy as well. Chocolate could be had, but its coarse texture and bitter taste were better suited to cooking and drinking than to candy. Outside cities and larger towns, most Americans were content with homemade sweets. Molasses was plentiful and cheap, and just about everybody knew how to boil molasses or maple sugar to make it into candy. In households that could afford to splurge on real cane sugar, fruit preserves and candied roots and flowers were popular homemade treats. There's a reason those little tykes in Clement Clarke Moore's 1823 poem "A Visit from St. Nicholas" fall asleep on the night before Christmas with "visions of sugar plums" dancing in their heads: back in the early 1800s, it would have been at Christmastime, and only at Christmastime, that most children would have anticipated such a treat.

And then suddenly, over a few short years, there was an explosion in both volume and variety. The numbers tell the story. The value of manufactured candy leapt from $3 million in 1850 to over $60 million in 1900. By 1948, the equivalent figure topped $1 billion for the first time.[5] The per capita story is even more telling: from two pounds per capita in 1900, to fifteen pounds in 1923, to more than twenty pounds in candy's banner year, 1944 (although fully one-quarter of this production was sequestered for military use, leaving many civilians frustrated in a nation awash in product).[6] Once candy eating was established in

American life, the yearly pound-per-person figure never dropped below sixteen, and in recent years has been hovering in the mid-twenties. Is that a lot or a little? In 2009, Americans' twenty-four pounds per capita candy consumption was similar to the amount of fresh citrus fruit (twenty pounds) or rice (twenty-one pounds), less than cheese (thirty pounds), but more than fresh and frozen fish and shellfish (sixteen pounds).[7] From an occasional luxury to a staple of the American diet, candy has come a long way.

The Candy Big Bang: Sugar and Steam

To make a lot of candy, you need many things, but number one is a lot of sugar. We think of sugar as that clean, white, evenly granulated stuff that pours so nicely from the shaker. But sugarcane passes through a tortuous path before it emerges table ready. Until the advent of steam-powered machinery in the 1830s, sugar refining was a laborious and slow process that severely limited availability. Juice extracted from sugarcane was boiled in open pots, skimmed, filtered, and boiled again, over and over. The end product would have appeared only sugarish to our contemporary eye: a hard baked loaf that was most likely brown and full of impurities, strongly flavored with the dregs of the processing and generally unrecognizable by today's standards. Before manufacturing could begin, the confectioner starting with this raw material had to further refine and clarify the sugar, repeating the process of boiling and skimming begun at the refinery.[8]

Not only was the sugar available in the early 1800s unsuitable for good candy making, there wasn't much of it. In 1800, there were seven refineries in the United States. By the 1830s, that number had expanded to thirty-eight, a significant increase but still small for a growing nation.[9] The scarcity and expense of refined sugar meant that most Americans sweetened their bread with molasses, the cheaper "dregs" of sugar processing. Maple sugar and honey were also used for eating or cooking, but for candy making there was no substitute for sugar.

Sugarcane is a difficult crop, temperamental and finicky about its growing conditions. Planting, tilling, and harvesting were all done by hand, work so horrible that it was only by using enslaved Africans for the labor that it got done at all. The cane was highly perishable, and refining the juice to a usable state was difficult and labor intensive. If candy was to be made affordable, and in large quantity, sugar production was going to have to change dramatically.

The power of steam, unleashed by the rapid technological developments of the Industrial Revolution, transformed the sugar-refining process. Two steam-powered innovations were especially significant: the vacuum steam pan (1855), which made sugar crystallize at lower temperatures, and the centrifuge (circa 1860), which mechanized the separation of sucrose from impurities. Now sugar could be made faster and more cheaply, but it was also much better for candy making: whiter, purer, cleaner, more uniform, and more purely sweet.[10] With better quality and more kinds of sugar, innovators quickly began developing new ways to cook and combine ingredients to create new candy sensations.

Even with plenty of raw material, makers were still hampered by the slow and tedious work of boiling sugar and shaping confections by hand. For example, to make comfits (sugar-covered seeds or nuts) in 1800, a skilled sugar worker would have to spend days "panning," shaking a carefully heated pan over coals while slowly adding layers of sugar syrup to build up a hard sugar shell. Success depended on slow and regular heat, constant motion, and close attention. Only the most dedicated and skilled would bother going to the trouble. Depending on the size of the finished product, a batch could take several days to complete.[11]

The limitations of handwork inspired innovation. Consider,

for example, Oliver Chase, an inventor whose simple device would launch one of the biggest candy success stories in America. Chase was working in a pharmacy in 1840, where one of his jobs was to prepare medicinal lozenges to treat his customers' various ailments. Lozenges were made from a paste of uncooked sugar and gum, pressed flat and then cut by hand. One of the difficulties of medicated lozenges was getting them all exactly the same size, so the dose of medication would be consistent each time. Not every customer needed medication, so Chase made some lozenges that were just sugar. They proved to be so popular that Chase couldn't keep up with the demand. In 1847, he hit on an idea that would solve both his problems at once, a machine that would make his lozenges faster and make each one identical.

Necco Wafers
Glazed Paper Wrapper

Hub Wafers
Transparent Paper Wrapper

are perfect accompaniments to the afternoon tea, the children's party or the more formal occasions.

For an after-dinner tidbit or a between-meal nibble, these dainty wafers are indescribably delicious. Nine old-fashioned flavors in each package.

At leading candy shops

NEW
ENGLAND
CONFECTIONERY CO.
BOSTON, MASS.

identical. His machine resembled a hand-cranked laundry wringer, with cutters on the rolling plates. He could feed lozenge dough through the plates, crank the handle, and turn out lozenges quickly and easily. This was the first candy machine to be made in America, and Chase's lozenges became famous as the candy that would become Necco Wafers.[12]

American inventors were also inspired by innovations happening on the other side of the Atlantic. Confectioners who traveled to London for the Great Exposition of 1851 were dazzled by the array of candies on display, as well as by the marvelous new inventions for mechanizing production. England was some three decades ahead of America in candy innovations because the Industrial Revolution was well advanced in England by the 1850s, and because sugar had been available in quantity earlier in the century due to England's dominance of the sugar trade. Visitors to the Crystal Palace were charmed by the variety and ingenuity of molded "boiled sweets," what Americans call hard candy. English makers were using drop machines similar to Chase's lozenge cutter to mold candy into any shape that could be imagined. Imprinted interchangeable rollers allowed a single candy maker to turn out buckets full of candy in multiple shapes. By the 1860s, American manufacturers were offering drop machines that could be powered by either hand crank or a belt attached to a steam engine, as well as a range of other machines for making confectionery, including mixers, cutters, and rollers.[13]

Today we take the machines for granted, but in the beginning, there was wonder and amazement at what even a simple device like the drop machine could do. An 1864 book describes the "art of sugar boiling": "Twenty years since [circa 1840] it was considered rather a clever thing (with a pair of scissors, the principal tool a sugar boiler used) to cut a seven pound boil of acid drops to size, and, with the help of a practised boy, make them round and press them flat, with the hands, in half-an-hour. The same quantity may now, with the machine, be made into drops, by the boy alone, in five minutes."[14] The machine enabled that same boy to be six times as productive. And the skill required to work the machine was far less specialized than the craft of working hot sugar.

Increasingly, candy making ran on steam. By the 1880s, large candy factories were using steam engines to power the machines. The same vacuum steam pans that revolutionized sugar refining were quickly adopted by confectioners to boil sugar, the essential first step in any candy-making operation. The most potent mid-century transformation was the combination of steam power and steam heat in the revolving steam pan, which regulated the temperature while also freeing the worker from all but the occasional task of adding ingredients. Not only was the process simplified, but the potential for enormous volume was unleashed. New techniques for shaping soft candy centers in cornstarch molds also made it possible to produce candy faster, easier, and in greater volume. But the real leap happened sometime around 1899, with the invention of what would come to be known as the starch mogul.[15]

With a system of belts and gears and funnels, the mogul mechanically emptied the starch boards, refilled and leveled them, printed the starch with the candy shape, and then filled the molds with candy syrup or cream. All these operations, which had previously been done at different stations in the factory, were now enclosed in what looked like a long and lumpy box. The first versions were made of wood, but by 1915, moguls made of steel were in common use in candy factories. The labor savings of the mogul were substantial: three men attending a machine could do the work that previously took twelve or fifteen men, hard at labor.[16]

The mogul also made the candy factory a substantially safer workplace. Before the mogul, workers in the "starch room" would be covered in a sticky film and suffered from respiratory ailments caused by breathing in the dust all day long. The fine airborne particles were also at constant risk for explosion, and many a factory suffered the dire consequences. Explosions caused by the ignition of airborne cocoa powder, sugar, or cornstarch would remain a danger in the candy industry (and in other industries with similarly dusty conditions, especially grain mills), but the starch mogul improved conditions immensely.[17]

Once delicious cream centers rolled out of the starch mogul, they were treated by other new machines. The first chocolate-dipping machine appeared around 1892. Called a "basket machine," this device submerged a basket of candy in a vat of chocolate in an attempt to replicate the effects of the more tedious hand- and fork-dipping techniques. The results were less than satisfactory, however, and machine-dipped chocolates were derided for poor quality and appearance. Matters improved substantially around 1900 with the invention of the chocolate enrober. Candy moving on a wire belt passed under a stream of melted chocolate, while at the same time the bottom was coated by a system of rollers underneath. The resulting coating was even and attractive, although it was much thinner and less decorative than the results that could be achieved by a skilled hand dipper.[18] (These are just a few examples of new candy production technologies; see plate 2 for a look at the multitude of machines from the early 1900s.)

Although the results might not be comparable to the products of handwork, the new machines did save labor and make manufacturing much less arduous. The Confectioners' Machinery & Manufacturing Company of Springfield, Massachusetts, offered an enrober that promised to achieve an emancipation equivalent to that achieved by President Lincoln. "Human slavery to-day is no more inexcusable, or more out of date than hand labor in the process of chocolate dipping," a 1909 advertisement proudly proclaimed. "THE ENROBER has struck off forever the shackles of hand dipping. If you still wear them, it is of your own volition—and to your own hurt."[19]

As it happened, hand dippers, shackled to their labor, had all been women, and thanks to the emancipating enrober they were out of a job. Highly skilled hand dippers working on fancy chocolates could earn up to $9 a week in the 1910s. An unskilled "floor girl" feeding cream centers into the enrober earned less than half that.[20] Although concerns about labor practices and lowered wages seldom filtered into the awareness of the candy consumers benefiting from the lower-priced goods, the "emancipations" of the machine revolution did come at a significant human cost.

Labor expenses go down, productivity goes up, cheap candy zooms out of the factory and into the belly of the nation. Productivity is the theme of the machine revolution, for candy and for everything else, from doorknobs and bedsheets to safety razors and toothpaste. Less labor and less time add up, in the miraculous arithmetic of capitalism, to more: more to sell, more to buy, more to profit. Call it the candy big bang: an explosive transformation that abruptly launched a whole new universe of possibilities.

All Sorts

So what did the candy universe look like in the moments just after the big bang of the 1850s? Americans of this era were experiencing a dramatic transition from the time when sweets were occasional and limited to a new era when any sort of candy could be had at any time at a price to suit any pocket. But what exactly were these first postbang candies? How did they look? How did they taste? Like the physicists who puzzle over the traces left by the explosion that created our own universe, candy historians have only fragmentary knowledge of the earliest machine-made American candies. Later in the century there would be company catalogs and advertisements and all manner of print ephemera, but to reconstruct candy in the 1850s we have fewer sources.

A bit of archival good luck brought me an item in a teachers' journal from 1857, which included a list of candies that fifth-grade pupils in Cincinnati had named when they were invited to list "things to be eaten": "cream candy, pop-corn, peppermint, molasses, rose, clove, nut, Butterscotch, sugar plums, lemon drops, lemon candy, peppermint drops, French kisses, cinnamon, Ice-cream, wintergreen, sour drops, hoarhound, lavender, gum drops, vanilla, Rock, birch, cats-eyes, orange, cough, kisses."[21] Of course they must have known many others as well, but these were the candies their teacher wrote down as they shouted them out, the candies that were the most well known and popular among the kids of Ohio in the 1850s. These are not exotic imported bonbons but the sweets that would soon come to be known as "penny candies": mass produced, inexpensive, easy to get, fun to eat.

The young connoisseurs who generated this catalog of favorites are poised on the cusp of two distinct candy eras. Already, they expect variety, novelty, a certain beguiling sparkle in the candy jar. They are sophisticated in their desires: they know their French kisses from their cats-eyes. And they expect plenitude. Candy is a common part of their lives, something to take for granted alongside the twenty-seven kinds of cake and fifteen varieties of apple they also listed for their teacher. Candy, by this point, is finally easy to get and cheap enough that it can be bought by and for children.

From crude beginnings a mere decade before, this cornucopia of variety in flavor and texture is stunning. But it's also instructive to notice what is missing: just about every candy we eat today, including many we consider "old-fashioned." The Ohio youth of 1857 were living in a universe with no jelly beans, caramels, chocolate bars, candy corn, or gummy bears. Not even licorice or toffee, candies that were well established in Britain by that time. Marshmallows were made in France and Britain, and probably available in Ohio, but evidently were not too familiar. Chocolate in the form of sweetened dark cakes would have been obtainable but primarily used for making drinking chocolate rather than eating as a confection.

The lack of these candies is obvious only from our modern-day perch. Americans in 1857 would have been thrilled and amazed at the multitude of variously colored, textured, and flavored candies being sold from jars and bins at grocers and specialty candy shops. Perhaps these Ohio schoolchildren, in their sugar-fueled exuberance, already sensed the future: the candy revolution was just getting started.

Leap ahead a few decades, into the early years of the next century, and the candy variety would spin anyone's head. Caramel had come into its own in the 1880s and 1890s, but it was quickly being surpassed by chocolate as Americans' candy of choice. Marshmallow was being sold in four-ounce boxes and five-pound tins. Jelly beans and candy corn were top picks with the penny crowd. And what about licorice? Today, you have your pick: sticks, laces, or rolls. But back in 1908, there were scores of specialties with attention-grabbing names like Big Lorimers, Monster Tubes, Eagle Twists, Teddy Bear Cigars, Electric Light Wires, Blow Pipes, and Skidoo Bars. And there were many kinds of candy we can't even imagine. Candy company inventories from this era list tens, sometimes hundreds of items with names that often don't even hint at what the confection might be: Kokokrisp, Neapolitan Bricks, Sphinx Package, Keep Kool, Scorcher, Chocolate Krumble, Mayflower Corn Cake . . . Our contemporary candy selection seems quite meager in comparison to the effusive bounty of the early machine pioneers.

Coconut, nougat, caramel, and chocolate are still among our favorite candy flavors. But the candy craze of the early 1900s inspired some experiments with less conventional ingredients. For Mrs. Ellen Gillon, of Honesdale, Pennsylvania, candy making was a way to support herself after her husband died. But coming to candy fresh, she had some fresh ideas. "One day," she told a Philadelphia reporter in 1911, "when I was thinking of schemes to make money, the idea of vegetable candy occurred to me. I experimented for several weeks before I hit upon the process, and as far as I know, I am the only one in the world who knows it." She wouldn't say how she made the candy, only what it was made of: the finest vegetables she could gather from the garden. She herself claimed to live "almost entirely on vegetables" and to eat little candy, but she was happy to cater to the neighborhood sweet tooth. At her shop, you could sample potato caramels, parsnip nougat, turnip fudge, beet marshmallows, and bean taffy.[22]

Despite her insistence on her originality, Mrs. Gillon wasn't the only one thinking about the candy potential of common vegetables. In 1912, Mary Elizabeth Hall put out an entire cookbook featuring vegetable candy recipes. *Candy-Making Revolutionized: Confectionery from Vegetables* included recipes for such novelties as potato-sugar modeling dough (an economical alternative to marzipan), candied carrot rings, candied parsnips, sweet potato patties, and tomato marshmallow. For early twentieth-century Americans, the idea of turning garden produce into candy wasn't as odd as it sounds today. English confectionery manuals that traveled to the colonies in the eighteenth century were replete with recipes for candying fruits, aromatic roots, and flowers. In Gillon and Hall's era, the inspiration for using vegetables in confectionery was less dietary than a mix of economy and creative context: vegetables were cheaper than sugar, and so many new kinds of candy were appearing every day that candy made from vegetables wasn't so outlandish. Whatever their appeal, none of these vegetable formulas resulted in commercially successful candy products.

Ingenuity wasn't restricted to ordinary garden-variety produce. In the frenzy of creativity during the 1910s, it seemed anything could be candy. In 1915, a man in Montana claimed he could make seventy-five varieties of candy from alfalfa. *Confectioners Journal* published a recipe for boiling horseradish in sugar syrup and using this as a base for a chewy candy. And when the Saint Louis Cotton Oil Company found itself with a lot of extra cottonseed on its hands in 1915, it thought, *Why not cottonseed candy?* The company produced caramels and a chewy taffy. The project never took off, as the market value of the oil was too high to make the candy a practical proposition, but tasters found it agreeable and said if they didn't know what it was, they would have taken it for a good brand of molasses candy.[23] In Louisiana in 1918, someone came up with an idea for cactus candy, "a palatable confection, with only a reasonable amount of sugar used, the cactus being peeled, dipped in hot sirup or molasses, and coated with granulated or powdered sugar." The recipe was recommended for Southern housewives who found themselves with time and some cactus on hand.[24]

Inventors were tinkering at the edge of the edible, and manufacturers were expanding into hundreds of different varieties—they couldn't help themselves. With the machines and the ingredients and the know-how at the ready, why not just see what might be possible? Buyers were thrilled with the continual stream of surprising delights and rewarded the most original novelties with their pennies. "We must confess that the nature of the candy business is such that we must have a certain amount of variety," averred accounting expert Don White in the pages of *Confectioners Journal.* "There is a demand for temporary originality. And it is such items that pay us the better profits. Why? No competition, a higher price—why not?"[25] White estimated that the average confectioner of 1915 was making something like fifty to six hundred varieties of goods. A few were making even more, going into the neighborhood of fifteen hundred. Multiply that variety across some two thousand manufacturers in the country, and the multitude of candy possibilities available dazzles the mind.

Attempting to sate consumers' craving for novelty was a perilous venture for the candy maker hoping to turn a profit, and many an enterprising manufacturer was lured into the bankrupting folly of excessive variety. Confectioners tended to be more interested in candy making than in bookkeeping, and modern accounting methods and efficiencies in production were not widely known or practiced until well into the 1920s. The trade journals in the 1910s continually reminded their readers of the need to understand and track the costs of each of their products; the more different products, the more complex and inefficient the costs. Staying profitable while maintaining hundreds of varieties of candy was nearly impossible, and business failures were common. White counseled overly ambitious confectioners to "weed out the superfluous and useless products and condense

the list to a reasonable number . . . and instruct our buying public to a like way of thinking." But despite the sober warnings of
the number crunchers, the demand for novelty and variety continued to inspire amazing flights of fancy.

Factories and Laboratories

It wasn't just a shop full of machines that differentiated the professional candy factory from the home candy kitchen. While the
home cook was limited by the ingredients that could be found at
the grocer, professional confectioners had access to a growing
array of industrial food products.

First appearing in the 1890s and quickly becoming a staple
for commercial candy makers, Nucoa was an economical cocoa
butter substitute derived from coconuts; its primary use was
in chocolate, but it could also be used for caramels and creams.
Eflorose, a new kind of sugar syrup, promised confectioners less
sticky and longer-lasting candies. The Eflorose Sugar Company
developed recipes using this new sugar product and claimed in
one advertisement to "have on our own shelves candy as much as
eighteen months old that has not yet shown any deterioration."[26]
Glucose derived from corn or wheat starches was an important
candy ingredient from the 1860s onward; by the 1910s, several
grades of corn syrup were available, as well as novel grain syrups
such as Acarose, a derivative of barley and corn. No one had ever
before made candy with Acarose, but no matter. Manufacturers
wouldn't just get a case of Acarose; they'd get a case of Acarose
and a booklet, *Twenty Tested Formulae for Better Candy*.[27]

Acarose at least had the advantage of being similar to the
better-known corn syrup. In contrast, some of the new industrial
food products being advertised in the early 1900s were so far from
familiar foods that they defied description. One of the strangest
of these was Numoline, a "soft spongy substance" made of dextrose crystal. Candy companies could host a Numoline adviser,

who would come and explain how to use the product to make what the product's inventor called "an entirely new type of candy, which can roughly be placed in the marshmallow-nougat group, with almost unlimited keeping powers."[28] This was candy so strange, so perplexing, that no one was even sure what to call it.

Sugar science exploded in the 1920s, as researchers discovered more ways of converting starches into sugars and developed practical processes for producing such sugars for commercial uses. One of the main sponsors of sugar research was the U.S. Bureau of Chemistry, and candy was the principal beneficiary. As a division of the USDA, the bureau's mission was to assist in the promotion and support of the nation's agriculture. Since many agricultural products—sugar included—had industrial uses, industrial partnerships were not uncommon. USDA chemist Howard S. Paine headed up the bureau's Carbohydrate Lab, which specialized in research relating to grains, starches, and sugars.

Inside a small candy factory around 1908. (National Archives)

Paine had a special interest in candy and became a leading advocate of what he described as the "application of chemistry and physics to the constructive improvement" of candy manufacture.[29] Under Paine's leadership, Carbohydrate Lab chemists—including an official candy maker—made significant advances in developing new forms of sugar and improving the quality of commercial candy.

In the following decades, the collaboration of sugar chemist and professional confectioner would become more and more important in large-scale candy manufacture. Edwin Blomquist, a vice president at the venerable Chicago candy company Brach & Sons, summed up the state of the industry in 1952: "Candymaking today combines both engineering and chemistry. The hit-and-miss methods are of the past. The laboratory is staffed with scientists whose time is devoted entirely to the maintenance of the purity of our products, to the perfection of their taste and to the rigid maintenance of their uniformity."[30] Blomquist's rosy confidence in the purity and perfection of factory candy reflected a widespread midcentury confidence in the superiority of technology and machine products. But back in the early years of the machine revolution, Americans weren't so sure how to feel about candy or any of the other novel sorts of foods that were emerging from the hulking, noisy, dirty factories. The excitement over novelty and variety was offset by serious worries about what sort of dangers might be lurking underneath candy's alluring manufactured surface.

3 ⊙ Fake Sweets and Fake Food

In 1911, Dr. Edwin Rosenthal of Mt. Sinai Hospital in Philadelphia described for *Pearson's Magazine* a gruesome scene of daily carnage: "The adulteration of candy and soda-water sold to children is one of the worst outrages we have to contend with. Every day we have a clinic of about twenty children suffering from candy and soda-water poisoning. Of these about six daily are new cases. In addition several are brought to my office in the evenings by their parents."[1]

For readers in the early 1900s, this account would not have come as any surprise. Since the 1890s, hundreds of cases had been reported, in newspapers across the country, of innocents sickened or killed by poisons in candy. The disturbing image of toxins festering in children's stomachs and seeping through their organs inspired some of history's most impassioned calls for food regulation and reform. Many other foodstuffs were viewed with suspicion and alarm in this era—reformers warned of diluted and spoiled milk, diseased meat, and grocers' goods laced with noxious fillers and chemicals. The prospect of tainted food was distressing in itself. But for sentimental and conscientious

Americans at the dawn of the twentieth century, who recollected fondly the innocent molasses pulls and simple candy sticks of their youth, the corruption of children's candy was especially alarming. Children were sympathetic victims, the very embodiment of innocence and inexperience. More than any other consumers, they needed protection from the hazards of the marketplace. The youthful victims of poison candy represented a horrifying manifestation of the damage being wrought by greedy merchants and unscrupulous manufacturers, who were increasingly suspected of cheapening and contaminating factory-made foods to increase their profits.

The rapid developments in candy technology and chemistry that took Americans from expensive comfits to cheap jelly beans were just one small corner of a bigger food revolution. Steam power, machines, railroads, chemistry—things were changing fast. In the nineteenth century, the processing of more and more kinds of foods moved from home to factory. For the first time in history, humans were confronted with edible substances that were so far removed from plants and animals as to appear mysterious, even unnatural. The fears surrounding poison candy weren't just about candy, but about a much broader, more diffuse sense of the dangers that might be unleashed when familiar local and small-scale food producers began to be pushed aside in favor of distant, anonymous manufacturers and their factory-made wonders.

Bad Food

In order to understand why worries about poison candy were so closely connected to the rise of new food products, we need to take a brief detour through the early history of commercial food processing and the subsequent debates about food adulteration and food fraud that dogged both food and candy makers around the turn of the twentieth century.

For most of human history, everybody was a locavore. In pre-industrial America, as elsewhere, people either grew and made their own foods, or purchased them from some nearby and known source. There weren't any easy ways to move fresh food around. Rutted dirt roads kept horse-drawn wagons to a leisurely pace. And slow-moving food was quick to spoil. Eggs and milk could be got fresh from chicken and cows, your own or your neighbor's—even in cities, where the entire farmyard menagerie often shared close (and smelly) living quarters with their owners. Preserving fresh foods for later use was an important part of the rhythm of household life. Meats could be dried or salted or smoked, fruits preserved in honey or maple sugar, and vegetables pickled. Roots and grains could be kept in cold cellars or icehouses. So it was that well into the 1800s, American food was a home-based affair: food sourced from nearby, processed by hand, prepared and cooked by home cooks for family consumption.

Rapid innovations in the nineteenth century—including such disparate inventions as the steam locomotive, the icebox, and the tin can—radically transformed food from a local to a national commodity. Great networks of rail lines began snaking across the country in the midnineteenth century, opening up the Great Plains, linking inland markets with port cities, bringing oranges from Florida and apples from the Northwest. Railroads made available more kinds of food, and cheaper food as well. In the case of meat, that meant tastier, more tender roasts and chops, since cows could take the train instead of walking to the slaughterhouse and toughening up on the way.[2]

In the cold months, meatpackers could centralize the slaughter and dressing of meat, and send it out by rail without worrying that it would spoil. But what about fresh meat in summertime? Gustavus Swift, who would become one of the great meat barons of the era, was the visionary who invented what he called an "integrated system for operating and reicing refrigerated rail cars," which made long-distance refrigerated transportation a reality for the first time in 1878.[3] Soon, the refrigerator cars were adapted for fresh fruit and vegetables as well, and the nation's produce vendors suddenly had much more enticing and varied displays of goods (though mechanical refrigeration would not arrive in American homes until the twentieth century).

Meatpacking was the earliest and simplest form of commercial food processing: the animal was killed and butchered in one central location, then shipped out to different markets. The next step in commercial food processing came in the form of the tin can—or rather, in the form of thousands of tin cans. Until the 1850s, cans were made laboriously by hand: a skilled tinsmith with metal shears and solder could make fifty a day. With mechanization, two unskilled laborers could churn out fifteen hundred cans a day.[4] The Civil War created a huge demand for imperishable foods that would be easy to transport, and canned food fit the bill perfectly. When the war was over, the soldiers who had developed a taste for canned food on the front lines started asking for the same kind of food at home. By 1870, Americans were opening thirty million cans of food per year—not just basics like corn and tomatoes, but also peaches and grapefruit, oysters and pineapple, all manner of foods that previously, for people living outside major cities, would have been exotic and unknown.[5]

The benefit of all these innovations in food processing, transportation, and storage was a new sort of bounty on the American table: more kinds of food in more places during more months of the year. But the variety and longevity of food came at a price. Before tin cans and refrigerated railcars, food processing—all that "putting up," salting, preserving, and drying that filled the family's pantry and cellar for winter—had happened at home. Commercial food processing, on the other hand, happened somewhere else, out of sight. When food appeared on the grocer's shelves in a box or can whose contents could not be opened or inspected before purchase, the customer was left to trust . . . or to wonder.

One of the things customers would have to wonder about

canned food in particular was whether this particular can was safe. Early nineteenth-century canning was an imprecise art, especially in the days before canners understood the importance of sterile conditions. Spoilage, exploding cans and jars, and food poisoning from either metals or bad foods were frequent hazards. French scientist Louis Pasteur had discovered in the 1850s that a living organism was responsible for food going rotten; he called it a "ferment." Around the same time, a revolution in chemistry began in Germany, unleashing whole new classes of chemicals, many derived from the by-products of coal. Although the properties and uses of these new organic chemicals were not immediately evident, some intrepid scientists wondered whether some of them might counteract the effects of rot and putrefaction in food.

Sir Joseph Lister (whom we remember with each swill of Listerine) was the first to publish his not-so-successful findings on "Food Preservation" in 1882: evidently, dropping a leg of chicken in a vat of carbolic acid—which was used in surgery—was not a good idea. Soon after, researchers searching for a solution to rot hit on boracic acid, which maintained meat's freshness quite nicely. Very quickly, food processors began to add preservatives to their canned goods. This probably did protect many people from bacterial illness. The motivation, however, was a bit less altruistic: chemical preservatives that hindered fermentation proved a cheap means of preventing cans and bottles from exploding from the pressure of gas buildup.[6]

Preservatives made it easier to pass off bad food to the customer. Chemicals could be used for such nefarious purposes as deodorizing rotten eggs and disguising rancid butter. Not to mention the potential dangers of dumping a bunch of newly discovered and untested chemicals into the nation's food supply. Did anyone really want to eat salicylic acid, or benzoic acid, or formaldehyde? Since producers did not have to declare what was in the food they sold, consumers had no way of knowing whether or what invisible and tasteless chemical preservatives might have

been added. And even the manufacturers often didn't know what they were putting in the food; many chemical preservatives were sold to processors under trade names like Perservaline or Freezine or Freezem, with no hint as to what the exact chemical might be.[7]

It was easy for distant factory bosses and wholesalers to care more about their balance sheets than whether the customer would be pleased to discover her "potted chicken" was something quite other. Food processing in the 1880s and 1890s was capitalism, Wild West–style: the point of business was to profit, and if profits could be enhanced, it was a fool who didn't leap at the opportunity. The conditions were ripe for an epidemic of adulteration and fraud. Padding flour with ground rice; extending butter with lard; selling sugar water spiked with artificial flavors and colors as "grape juice"; concocting "apple jelly" out of peelings, glucose syrup, and coloring; putting six ounces in an eight-ounce can: here was the genius of American business run amok.[8] It wasn't right, but it wasn't illegal, either. There were no uniform national laws governing food labels or food standards until the Pure Food and Drug Act of 1906. Individual states had their own laws regulating the quality and sale of food, but they were uneven and poorly enforced. So even when processed food came in a labeled package, there was no sure way of knowing where it came from, who made it, or how it got there.

How bad was the food, really? State food inspectors began studying various goods for adulteration as early as the 1870s, and in 1886 the federal government began funding studies of food quality at the Bureau of Chemistry under the leadership of Harvey Wiley, who would go on to an illustrious career in defense of "pure food." Wiley commissioned journalist Alexander Wedderburn to write a book summarizing the findings of Wiley's team; *A Popular Treatise on the Extent and Character of Food Adulterations* appeared in 1890 and began with this alarming observation: "Every article of food is to a greater or less extent the subject of adulteration. The people have no idea of the extent to which this damaging imposition is practiced; from the cheapest and most simple article of diet to the most expensive the art of the manipulator has been applied."[9] Based on Wiley's work and the reports of other state inspectors, Wedderburn hazarded that 15 percent of the nation's food was adulterated. The good news was that most of the adulterants were harmless, intended to increase weight or bulk and thereby cheat the buyer. But there was harm as well. Milk and other foods that were typically consumed in their whole form might be diluted or bulked with water or other nonnutritive matter; this would deplete nutrition over time. Tainted or decayed meats could sicken. Drugs that were adulterated or mislabeled would not cure, or worse, might themselves cause harm.

Before this time, it wasn't so hard to tell good food from bad. Sniff the meat, squeeze the tomato, taste a drop of milk: spoil and rot were easy to detect in fresh food, and the difference between the edible and the inedible was obvious. As for fraud, a vegetable garden doesn't lie, and the farmer or baker who cheated his neighbors wouldn't last long. But in the new, anonymous commercial landscape, processed foods—products of the "art of the manipulator"—presented much more mystifying appearances. Whether something was good, wholesome, or safe was more and more difficult to tell.

It wasn't just that food was skillfully disguised or hidden behind packaging. There were more profound questions raised by new food products. Was Butterine butter? What substance was implied as the basis for the beverage mix sold as Postum? How could any ordinary citizen explain the miracle of Bromangelon, a pink powder that, with the careful administration of boiling water, would transform into a glistening ruby gel? In the early days, no one was quite sure whether the novelties of food manufacture were food or fraud. As with candy, innovations of chemistry and technology were making possible new kinds of food products, entirely different from what had gone before. Were these by definition fake even if they weren't imitating anything? Food processing was making it more and more difficult to know the difference between "fake" and "real."

A Greasy Counterfeit

Most of the food frauds that caught the public's attention involved pretty primitive sorts of fakery. Adding other sorts of leaves to tea or puffing up mustard powder with flour may have been ingenious ways of padding the shelves and the bottom line, but they involved little beyond the creative manipulation of ordinary stuff. But commercial food processing was moving far beyond the techniques and materials of the home kitchen. Experiments with coal tar derivatives and esters derived from alcohol had created a virtual pantry in the chemistry lab. Food could appear in never before imaginable colors and flavors and forms. And conversely, chemists manipulating basic substances could fabricate familiar forms of food in entirely novel ways. Such was the case with oleomargarine, a butter substitute that took the possibilities of fake food to a whole new level.

Oleomargarine, invented in the 1860s, was a lot like butter in texture and in taste. In fact, the inventor of oleomargarine claimed that it actually was butter, created by other means. But anyone could take a pint of cream, shake it up, and plop a pat of butter onto the table. Oleomargarine, or oleo, or margarine as we call it today, was way beyond the simple churn and shake. Butter was from the farm and kitchen; oleomargarine was a patented invention, born in the lab and raised in the factory.[10]

Hippolyte Mège-Mouriès, who patented the first form of oleomargarine in 1869, possessed immense confidence in man's ability to improve on nature. His boss, Emperor Napoleon III, wanted to feed his armies with a cheaper, longer-lasting bread spread. Could Mège deliver? *Mais, bien sûr!* Back in the lab, Mège asked himself a question: Where did the cream in milk come from? After all, cows eat grass, no butterfat there. But cows' flesh was fatty; Mège concluded that some internal process must be converting some of that body fat into the butterfat of creamy milk. If the cow could do it inside the body, Mège figured the scientist could do it in the lab. All he had to do was to synthesize a sort of artificial cow body out of cow body parts. So he took some fatty beef trimmings, extracted the liquid oils, and churned them with chopped-up cow udders, on the theory that something in the udder was making the fat into butterfat. It actually worked: with a little salt and color, the result was so much like butter that experts had trouble telling the difference.[11]

Soon, others were leaping into the greasy fray. By 1886, the U.S. Patent Office had received 180 applications for patents to make butter substitutes. The Chicago meatpackers were especially eager to take advantage of this new and potentially lucrative use of beef and pork fat. They figured out their own formulas for something they called "Butterine." It seemed a fair name, since they were actually adding some butter to improve the taste. One formula called for 40 percent lard, 20 percent oleo oil from beef fat, 25 percent butter, and 15 percent milk.[12]

There were certainly advantages to this new synthetic butter. It was cheaper, it didn't spoil as quickly, and it could be made from various fats so it could be supplied more consistently. Also, in a day when rancid butter was a serious problem, and some merchants doctored spoiled butter to sell as fresh, it was often the case that at point of sale the oleo could be more wholesome than the butter it resembled.

Was this oleo a real food in its own right? Or was it a pale and fraudulent imitation of the real thing, butter? In 1886, Congressman Robert La Follette branded oleo counterfeit and deceit: "To counterfeit an article of food [means that the food] is made to look like something it is not; to taste and smell like something it is not; to sell for something it is not, and so deceive the purchaser."[13] For La Follette and other like-minded critics, butter was

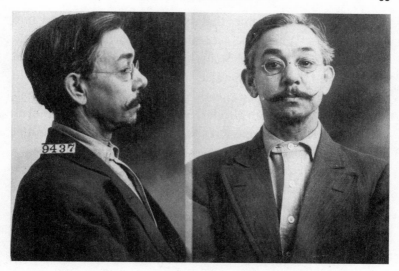

Charles Wille, sent to prison in 1915 for unlawful trafficking in margarine.
(National Archives)

the original, the real thing. Oleo, measured against real butter, was obviously a fake and a fraud.

Congress intervened with the Margarine Act of 1886, which decreed that oleo could be sold, but only if it were clearly labeled as oleo. Shoppers who wanted butter and paid for butter should get butter. Oleo would be taxed: two cents a pound. The tax did little to appease dairy farmers, who feared the loss of market share, but it did launch an entirely new class of bootleggers. "Crimes against butter" entered into the annals of American prison lore.[14]

Oleo makers didn't think what they were producing was fraudulent. True, oleo had begun as an attempt to copy butter. But once oleo was produced, there was no reason to see it only as imitation butter. Even the president of the New York State Dairymen's Association was forced to concede that "oleomargarine is a perfectly legitimate product when sold as oleomargarine."[15] Oleo defenders emphasized the superiority of their product on its own merits: cleaner, longer keeping, and unadulterated by the beets, carrots, and potatoes that sometimes made their way into butter churns. With all its advantages and virtues, why should oleo be tarred as "fake"? Sometimes the relationship between real and imitation even spiraled into reverse. Natural butter in winter might be very pale, nearly white. Oleo producers, imitating butter, colored their product yellow. To compete with oleo, then, some creamery operators were dying their winter butter yellow to imitate the oleo that was imitating the butter.[16]

Oleomargarine seems a long way from candy. But the same ideas about fake and real that spurred the debates about oleo were dogging candy makers, especially those who replaced some or all of the sugar in their candy with glucose, a cheap sweetener derived from starch.

Filth and Poison

Was glucose candy a fraudulent version of real candy? And more troubling, was the glucose in candy not just a cheat but also a dangerous and potentially poisonous adulterant? The answer to these questions required not only investigating the safety of glucose but also figuring out what might be the difference—if any—between "real" candy and "fake" candy.

Glucose was singled out for special abuse in the early 1880s by anti-adulteration crusader George T. Angell. In speeches calculated to raise alarm, Angell claimed glucose was not food at all but a revolting and lethal stew concocted by pouring sulfuric acid over rags and sawdust. Deadly acid residues could be expected in the product of such a vile procedure, but there was more: Angell brandished the name of a Chicago chemist who supposedly had found poisonous residues of tin, iron, calcium, and magnesia in glucose.[17] These were not foods, but metals and chemicals, the stuff of heavy machines and dark greasy factories. Glucose oozed from the underbelly of industrial food, the antithesis of the sweet grass and bright sunlight of the farm and field.

It turned out that glucose was quite fine as a food. Government inspectors examined the factories, chemists analyzed the product, and all agreed: the glucose manufactured and sold for food use in the United States was "of exceptional purity and . . . contains no injurious substances," according to the official 1884 report published by the National Academy of Sciences.[18] This report was quickly embraced by the candy manufacturers. Glucose had been declared by the highest authorities to be "in no way inferior to cane-sugar in healthfulness" and to have no ill effects.[19] How could there be any objection at all to the use of glucose, a pure and wholesome food, in the manufacture of candy?[20]

Yet neither the protests of the confectioners nor the sober and scientific assurances of chemists and food officials did much to defuse the popular sway of the muckraking alarmists following in Angell's crazed wake. Glucose was "poison" and "adulteration": these words reverberated in the popular imagination, fed by the thrilling accounts published in popular magazines that repeated rumor more often than they investigated to discover truth. Having heard for three decades about glucose's evils, what reader would pause to doubt this sober scientific explanation, offered in a 1911 magazine article: "Glucose is the cheap sirup produced by treating corn, corncobs, cornstalks or saw dust with sulfuric acid."[21] The logic that starts with corn and ends with garbage is irresistible: if corn, then why not corncob? And if corncob, then why not cornstalk? And so on, all the way to sawdust.

The Supreme Court of the state of Michigan turned its attention to the matter of glucose in 1903, and the picture it portrayed of glucose's public image wasn't pretty: "Glucose is obnoxious to many, if not a majority, of the public, and is misunderstood by them." And what was it that common folk assumed when they heard there was glucose in their food? The court explained: "The public generally supposes glucose to be an inferior product made from animal fat, or a product of the glue factory."[22] So from the attacks on glucose as taking the place of real sugar, now an even worse idea emerged: glucose in candy was nothing other than glue.

What we call sugar is sucrose, a disaccharide consisting of one molecule glucose and one molecule fructose. Sucrose is what you get when you process sugarcane. But as our tongues well know, sweetness is not only in sugarcane. As early as the 1790s, chemists started working to unleash the sugar from other kinds of plants. Grapes were the first fruit to yield a usable sugar substance, a form of glucose commonly called "grape sugar." But what really made glucose a viable commodity was the discovery that it could be derived from cheap, plentiful starches: think potato, the source of glucose in Europe, or think corn, as in corn syrup: in the United States, corn quickly grew to become the number one source of glucose production.*

Sugar has always been a difficult commodity. Sugarcane thrives in only a few tropical regions. It is extremely difficult to grow, brutal to harvest, and expensive to transport to the major markets. In contrast, glucose from corn is a sugar product that can be produced domestically and relatively cheaply. As a result, by the 1880s there were twenty-nine factories in the United States annually producing some ten pounds of glucose per capita.[23] The total consumption of sugar in the 1880s was about fifty pounds per person per year.[24] This means glucose was adding another 20 percent to the quantity of sweeteners people were consuming, all of which was in the form of processed foods.

It's easy to see why glucose was popular with food manufacturers. Substituting glucose for sugar saved money in canned

---

*In the early years of corn refining, the terms *glucose* and *corn syrup* were used interchangeably. This can create confusion, because glucose also is the technical name for a particular sugar molecule. However, corn syrup is not pure glucose—there are some other sugars and minerals present in small quantities. To add to the confusion, after the 1920s, the predominant sugar in corn syrup was frequently called dextrose. Dextrose, either in corn syrup or in a more pure form derived from corn, is chemically the same as glucose.

fruits, jams, jellies, bakery goods, and confectionery. In its crystalline form, it could be used to extend cane sugar, and in its liquid form, it could "enhance" honey, jams and jellies, and cane and maple syrups. It's pretty safe to assume that most of the time, Americans were oblivious of the fact that a great deal of the syrup, honey, and jelly in the stores was "adulterated" with cheaper glucose.

As for glucose in candy, the confectioners never denied using it. People wanted cheap candy, and using glucose instead of sucrose made candy cheaper. Glucose has other useful properties. It is only about two-thirds as sweet as sucrose—a benefit for candy making, as too much concentrated sweetness is not pleasant. Another advantage of the glucose syrup used in confectionery (typically corn syrup) has to do with its molecular structure. Glucose syrup contains certain long and stringy molecules; when added to a sucrose solution, these molecules get tangled with the sucrose and get in the way when the sucrose molecules start trying to organize themselves into crystals. This is the reason that today you'll find corn syrup on the label of everything from clear hard candies to softer creams and fudges; corn syrup is also important for making chewy candies like caramels and gummy bears.*

Despite its evident usefulness, glucose was not universally embraced outside the candy industry. There were some stern experts who insisted they knew exactly what candy ought to be, and glucose wasn't in it. Mr. G. A. Kirchmaier, state chemist of Ohio, was one such naysayer. In 1895 he took to the pages of a Toledo newspaper to launch an attack on "cheap, adulterated"

---

*Corn syrup—one kind of glucose syrup—is not the same thing as the high-fructose corn syrup we've been hearing so much about. HFCS is corn syrup that has been further processed to convert some of the glucose into fructose. The balance of fructose and glucose in HFCS is roughly the same as the balance in sugar (although HFCS can be manipulated to be higher in one or the other). HFCS is not normally used in candy making.

penny candies. When a representative of the candy manufacturers wrote him a letter demanding to know which specific candies
he considered to be adulterated, he sputtered that he didn't mean
that the candies actually had anything harmful in them. What
he meant was, evidently, that the candies were not made the way
he thought candy should be made. "All sorts of things are being
used nowadays in the manufacture of sweets," he complained.
According to Kirchmaier, candy should be candy, not some
strange brew of newfangled industrial ingredients. The substitution of glucose for sugar was a particularly disturbing source of
confectionery abomination. "I take it that 'candy' is a preparation
of sugar," said Kirchmaier, "and when I do not find sugar in confections that are sold for candy I claim that they are adulterated."[26]

Fake sweets! That's what food reformer Mary Theiss called
those morsels confected from the unfamiliar products and processes of industrial candy. In 1911, she and her husband, Lewis,
published an alarming account in *Pearson's Magazine* to warn
mothers of the dangers lurking in the corner candy shop.[27] They
painted a picture of the "unscrupulous" and "crafty" candy manufacturer who employs chemists to "tell him how much of those
[poisonous] ingredients he can use without fatal results." For a few
extra pennies, these villains "bulk their candies large with cheap
materials that often have no real food value or are positively injurious, flavor them with harmful ethereal extracts, and color them
with dyes that corrode and destroy the tissues of the body."

And in the pages of *McClure's Magazine*, a periodical famous
for its muckraking exposés, writer Burton Hendrick warned
readers in 1915 of the dangers of "counterfeit jams, jellies, candy,
ice cream and soda waters" teeming on the shelves of grocers
and sweet shops.[28] According to Hendrick, these deceitful delec-
tables were made "poisonous" by the use of substitutes and syn-
thetics, fillers and fakes, including "glue, soapstone, talc, paraffin,
shellac, radiator lacquer, and other materials." What was bad
about these fake sweets wasn't just that they might swindle the

customer by passing off imitation goods at real prices, or even that they might cause physical harm (although actual cases of harm were difficult to come by). It was more the very deceptiveness of the foods themselves, that the goods passing themselves off as candy and ice cream were not what they seemed to be.

Moral outrage fueled the fires of reformers like Theiss and Hendrick, who warned of the pernicious effects of fake sweets and of the food adulterers who dared to copy and imitate real food and to pass off the degraded copy as the real thing. In Hendrick's account, the food adulterator was a skilled and deliberate artist of fakery: "Many concoctions contain practically nothing that is genuine. Their substance, color, and taste are all fabrications," while penny-candy manufacturers "are perhaps the most active conspirators against the well-being of childhood." Wholesome sugar ought to furnish children with good energy; instead, "millions of American children are daily consuming enormous quantities of 'near candy.'" Neck and neck for wickedness with the "near candy" confectioner was the fake ice cream maker, "a modern magician [who] can make quite convincing ice cream without any cream at all."[29] When such nefarious characters were plying their devious trade, no normal consumer—much less a child—could be expected to tell the wholesome from the dangerous, or to distinguish the real from the fake.

Candy—the pinnacle of food artifice—was especially liable to accusations of adulteration, poison, or worse. A convenient summary of the frightening state of American confectionery in the early era of industrial manufacture, as viewed by its critics, can be found in an 1877 New York Times exposé titled "Adulterated Confectionery: The Poisonous Compounds That Are Sold in Cheap Shops for Candy." Readers of this little catalog of confectionery horrors learned that cheap candy was made of "some of the most deadly poisons known."[30] Exhibit number one: color. Unsuspecting candy eaters could end up with a dose of "red lead, gamboge, vermillion, chromate of lead, Prussian blue, verditer or carbonate of copper, arsenite of copper, Brunswick green, the various oxides of iron, white lead, &c." Whatever the exact chemical nature of these substances, the mention of lead, copper, and arsenic made one thing quite clear: candy colors were a veritable cocktail of poisons.

And if the color didn't get you, the dirt surely would. According to the author, candies were being made and eaten in which terra alba—powdered gypsum or white clay—formed "50 to 60 per cent. of the manufactured article." The examples are repulsive: fruit candies filled with a "thick, tasteless paste without sweetness or flavor" and chocolate creams filled with moistened chalk dust and coated with chocolate tallow. Glucose is next on the list, another "dangerous article" used to adulterate candies reputed to "produce paralysis of various portions of the system." The litany of abuses continues with the most disgusting additive, scrapings: "When a sugar ship comes into port and is emptied of her cargo, a good deal of syrup has adhered to the sides of the vessel and run down into the bilge water. The first is scraped off and the second pumped out, mixed together, and boiled, and of this compound candy is made." If the ship scrapings didn't end up in candy, the floor scrapings most likely would, especially in that lowest of confectionery forms, taffy: "The whole sweepings and scrapings of the [candy] shop are put into it, and what is too dirty for anything else is clean enough for taffy." This was candy: filth and poison, poison and filth. Candy eaters, beware.

Vincent L. Price, executive secretary and later president of the National Confectioners Association (also the father of actor Vincent Price), took a glum pleasure in collecting the worst and most imaginative candy adulterations described in newspaper accounts, which he listed for his fellow confectioners in 1911:

Fudge made of Glucose and Iron Rust
Marshmallows made of Glue

Banana flavored Candies Flavored with Lacquer in which
   are dissolved Bronze and Silver Paints
Scrapings from Soles of Workmen's Shoes used to color
   Chocolate
Grease Drippings from Machinery Used to Soften Chocolate
Spitting on Candy to Make it Stick
Wash Water used by workmen to Give Candy Polish[31]

What these distorted views of candy have in common is a shared idea of the relation between candy and the new industrialized food production. Imagining factory-made candy as grease drippings and floor scrapings made it seem like an edible version of the filth and danger of the factory itself. It's difficult to understand how anyone actually believed that such candies could and did exist. But perhaps for ordinary people struggling to keep up with the rapidly changing times, the possibility that candy makers were spinning glue and paint into food didn't seem so implausible. Critics saw bad candy as the product of unprincipled and corrupt manufacturers working in filthy industrial conditions. Bad candy was what resulted when you mixed the dirt and grime and greed of industry with food. Bad candy was proof of the worst excesses and dangers of the Industrial Revolution.

In the years around the turn of the twentieth century, the idea that candy was so bad that it could kill needed no supportable evidence or explanation. Alarming newspaper headlines announcing yet another casualty appeared with disturbing regularity between about 1890 and 1910: "Candy Kills a Little Boy," "Poison in Christmas Candy," "Children Poisoned by Candy Rabbits," "Candy Caused Death," "Two Dead, One Dying, Two Ill from Poison Candy." The stories were sensational. The fact that they were based on rumor, innuendo, supposition, or error seldom prevented their publication.

A vast compendium of these and other newspaper accounts

of candy poisoning began to be assembled in the late 1880s by a group of confectioners who had organized in 1884 to defend candy. They called themselves the National Confectioners Association (NCA). The collection was published in 1907 as *Facts: A Compilation of Various Newspaper Reports on the Subject of Supposed Poisoning by Candy and Investigations of the Circumstances by Our Association.* This 479-page volume includes both original accounts and the ensuing investigations undertaken at the confectioners' request; after publication, the NCA continued until 1911 to investigate newspaper accounts and report the findings in the monthly *Confectioners Journal.*

Occasionally poison candy was all too real, but it had little to do with the conditions of manufacture. In 1925, Mrs. Jane Hartman was charged with sending her estranged husband a box of candies laced with mercury; her lover was said to have bought the stamp. Mr. Hartman ate some; luckily, he got to the hospital in time to have his stomach pumped. In 1920, Mrs. Helen Reid Marshall, a high-society type from Richmond, Virginia, was accused of sending her daughter-in-law a box of arsenic-laced chocolates; fortunately, her daughter-in-law didn't bite. These were hardly isolated incidents; candy poisoning appears to have been a very popular method for revenge or eliminating rivals in the early twentieth century. One of the saddest such stories was the tale of Miss Rena Nelson, of Pierre, South Dakota, who died in 1904 as a result of eating poison candy she received in the mail. Police initially suspected Mrs. Sherman Dye, the wife of Miss Nelson's lover. But soon they discovered that Miss Nelson had staged the poison candy so it looked like Mrs. Dye's doing; her death was ruled a suicide.[32]

As prospective poisoners knew, the sweet taste of candy could cover up many a crime. But criminal intent aside, one wonders in retrospect how so many could have found the charges of candy manufactured as poison to be so credible. When Easter eggs or lollipops were blamed for a child's sudden demise, no account gave any theory as to how one child could have been stricken dead by the very same candy eaten without harm by hundreds of other children. Investigations revealed much more plausible explanations: gas leaks, tuberculosis, meningitis, tainted meat— such mundane stories were evidently not as headlineworthy as the always shocking charge of "poison candy." There were no cases in which there was actual evidence that anyone had been harmed or killed by ordinary candy. For decades, the NCA offered a $100 reward for physical proof of poison candy. No one ever claimed the money.

Despite the best efforts of the NCA to cleanse candy's reputation, a popular view persisted: poison candy was expanding and metastasizing, an industrial serial killer on the loose. No child was immune to its virulent effects. The newspaper stories warned of candy bought on the way to school, eaten at a friend's house, received as a gift, purchased by parents, won at Sunday school. Mothers in particular were held accountable for the candy consumption of their youngsters and the inevitable effects. "You [mothers] don't poison your own children. You let the children do it themselves," Mary and Lewis Theiss warned ominously. "You are very careful as to how you handle poisons. You label them with a red label so that you cannot mistake them, and you put them up in a high closet where little fingers cannot reach them. And then, with mammoth inconsistency and sublime faith in crooked human nature, you give your child money—to go out and buy poison for himself. Every time you give your child a penny to buy a stick of candy you do it."[33]

The poisons presumably hidden in candy were varied and devious. Arsenic was a common culprit, alone or as an assumed ingredient in the dyes used to color candy. "Ptomaine poisoning" (a popular but scientifically meaningless diagnosis) was another frequent verdict. But often no specific toxic agent was named: "poison candy" was enough explanation for the general public, to whom the words *poison* and *candy* had become virtually synonymous. If candy had been eaten, and the victim had fallen ill, that was evidence enough that candy must have been the offender.

In the fertile imaginings of muckraking journalists and a sensation-seeking public, candy was the edible inedible: it might look like food, and it might taste good, but it was made of a mix of poisons and, in reformer Burton Hendrick's words, "materials . . . which perform no function in the body's economy." And so industrialization showed its dark side. What came out of the machine and the factory looked okay to eat, but its tantalizing appearance and taste were a false promise. When control of food was given over to the factories and machines and chemists, what came out was candy: fake food, deceitful and deadly.

Poison or Indigestion?

Candy was but one of the many foods examined for adulteration and fraud by Dr. Harvey Wiley at the Bureau of Chemistry. Wiley published his report on the state of candy in 1887. His team put 250 different kinds of candy through a gamut of rigorous chemical and physical trials. The candies had been chosen to represent the average sort of sweets eaten by your typical American young-ster: "cheap kinds bought at the small groceries."[34] In hopes of snaring some dangerous mineral colors, they chose candies of bright and unnatural hues. What did they find? Nothing. The only serious mineral contaminant was traces of copper, likely introduced through the use of uncoated copper kettles. Many of the candies contained starch, glucose, and gum, but none con-tained mineral or nonfood fillers like terra alba. The investiga-tions were thorough and the conclusion confident: candy was good, and getting better.*[35]

---

*This was not the message that Alexander Wedderburn chose to emphasize in his recounting of the same investigations. His *Popular Treatise* began with the

Wiley was not alone in his sunny assessment of the sf candy. In the early 1900s, food commissioners and health bὺ. across the country were doing everything they could to track down poisoned or adulterated candy, and they just didn't find any. This put public health officials in an embarrassing position: they were supposed to be cracking down on the malfeasants, and if they weren't coming up with the goods they didn't seem to be doing their jobs. Investigators for the Dairy and Food Department of the state of Michigan sounded quite defensive: "The Department has been asked why we do not prosecute dealers who sell cheap and 'adulterated' candies . . . Analyses made at the Department laboratory of 220 samples . . . fail to show any on which prosecution could be successfully brought."[36]

Like Wiley, the Michigan investigators had chosen the most suspicious-looking candies being sold in the least reputable outlets. They were determined to root out the poison candy scourge but met with the same lack of evidence. In Illinois, the story was pretty much the same. The state food commissioner reported in 1904 on the analysis of 113 samples of candy, noting "no serious adulteration of the better class of candies as sampled in this investigation": meaning no terra alba, no barytes, no talc, no mineral compounds, no arsenic or lead.[37] In Minnesota too, officials were finding that candy was pure. "We have found that glucose is very largely used, but we do not understand that this can be classed as deleterious," Dairy and Food Commissioner W.W.P. McConnell explained in 1902. "We also think that coal tar or aniline colors are used but are not prepared to state that these

predictable but still disturbing claim that "the most poisonous adulterants in use are those used to color and cheapen confectionery and liquors." Wedderburn may have been attuned to the prejudices of the day, but there was little in Wiley's actual report—or in the independent investigations being carried out elsewhere that Wedderburn included in his volume—that actually substantiated this allegation.

are deleterious."[38] Glucose and coal tar colors were, according to the pure food laws of the state, neither adulterants nor deleterious. Although there were critics who continued to protest both these ingredients, there were no government officials or chemists who viewed either of them as inherently harmful.

By 1908, Wiley was giving press interviews in defense of candy. "This talk of poisoned candy is for the most part exaggerated," he said. "In the first place 'poisoned candy' is a misnomer. I have never yet eaten any candy that was deadly poison. I will go further than that and say that I have never seen any candy that was deadly poison or even poisonous to a degree that might be feared. There is such a thing as overeating, and this human frailty sometimes extends to candy eating with the same dire effects that follow a gourmandizing of plain bread and butter."[39] Wiley, the nation's foremost food safety advocate, the man who deserved the lion's share of credit for the passage of the first national law governing food safety (the 1906 Pure Food and Drug Act), was comparing candy to bread and butter: not poisonous at all.

What Is Real?

Commercial confections of the early 1900s went far beyond the simple and familiar candy made of sugar, nuts, chocolate, and molasses that people of the previous generation had probably grown up with, maybe even made in their own homes. The fact that glucose and cornstarch were themselves foods, or that many artificial colors and flavors had been studied and approved for food use, hardly mattered to the reformers. When they lobbed accusations of "fake" at glucose caramels and chemically flavored marshmallows, they were attempting to freeze candy in the past. The idea that there was a true kind of candy that was more real than these, and against which these new manufactured candies would be judged fakes and frauds, was the last gasp of an old way of thinking about food. The candy juggernaut that had been unleashed by the revolutions in machine technology could not be stopped.

Harvey Wiley's 1887 report for the Bureau of Chemistry proposed a more modern definition of candy, one that embraced the new possibilities of technology. Wiley defined a pure confection as "one that contains saccharine flavoring and coloring matters, so mixed and adjusted as to be attractive both to taste and sight."[40] Saccharine in that era did not mean the chemical sweetener we know by that name, but rather *saccharine matter*, whatever the sweet substance in the candy might be. This could be sugar, but it also could be other sweet ingredients like honey, syrup, molasses, or even the reviled glucose. Wiley's pure candy was sweet, but beyond that the possibilities were wide open; the flavoring and coloring matters could be just about anything. The only limitation was that they not be harmful.

Wiley's definition might have been happily aligned with the candy makers' interests, but he was hardly an industry dupe. In another context that was also important for confectionery, he argued vociferously against the corn refiners' request to deflect consumer suspicions by changing the name of glucose to the more friendly and natural-sounding "corn syrup." Wiley was outgunned, but he persisted in arguing that the word *syrup* meant a syrup commonly used at the table, and specifically a sweet liquid directly extracted from the plant. Wiley argued that corn glucose was neither, however syrupy it might be.[41] His position was consistent with his general approach to food regulation: each food should be defined and the name used only when the definition was met. In the politicking around the food law, Wiley was often alone in his insistence on creating food standards that would clarify and specify the real food against which adulteration would be measured. Candy, however, was a different story. As Wiley saw it, the standard of candy was not to be found in ingredients or recipes. The standard for candy was only "to be attractive both to taste and sight."

In 1902, NCA president Robert Moses testified before the congressional Committee on Interstate and Foreign Commerce during hearings leading up to the eventual passage of the 1906 Pure Food and Drug Act. The committee was interested in how adulteration should be defined in candy, and how a federal law should be crafted to best protect the public against adulteration. The committee members agreed with the NCA's position that harmful adulterants should be outlawed. But they also wanted to know which of the harmless adulterants should be covered by a pure candy law. Moses replied, "There cannot be any harmless adulterant in candy."

The NCA's view was that where candy making was concerned, *harmless adulterant* was an oxymoron: if it was in candy, and it was harmless, it was not an adulterant. Moses elaborated, echoing Wiley's definition: "Confectionery must of necessity be pleasant to the eye and palatable to the taste. If there is any ingredient that can go in confectionery that is palatable to the taste and agreeable to the eye, and is harmless, then we claim it is not an adulterant."[42] The point of candy was to please. There could be no limit on what the candy multitude might contain. Wherever pleasure could be found or invented, there candy would fearlessly go.

Candy, in its infinite possibilities of edibility, presaged the brave new world of food engineering. Most Americans didn't see it that way in the early days; in its complete detachment from the natural realm, candy seemed unique and strange. So in recognition of this unique and strange substance, Congress included a special "confectionery clause" in the final version of the Pure Food and Drug Act prohibiting the addition of minerals, poisonous colors and flavors, and any "other ingredient deleterious or detrimental to health." In the law, the definition of adulteration for food and beverage was actually more restrictive than the definition of adulteration that applied to candy. Harmful ingredients were banned from food and candy alike. But food would also be considered adulterated if it had something mixed in to "reduce or lower or injuriously affect" its quality, or if any other substance were substituted for the food that the food purported to be. With this definition of adulteration, the law created a clear, nationally consistent, legal standard for the difference between real food and adulterated food. Pure coffee, real honey, genuine maple syrup could now all be legally set apart from the adulterated imitations that substituted ingredients like chicory for coffee or glucose for honey or syrup. Adulterated food, by this definition, was fake food. Unadulterated food, in contrast, was real.

In the confectionery clause, candy was assigned a special position. Unlike real food, which could be compromised by "harmless adulterations," candy was just candy. There could be nothing that would "reduce or lower or injuriously affect" its quality because it had no essential, original quality that could be diminished. Anything candy could be was true candy. So no matter what was in it—no matter how strange or novel or surprising or seemingly uncandylike—if it was harmless and good, it was fine. Inexpensive glucose taffy had just as much right to be called candy as expensive French nougat; marshmallow bananas made with chemical flavorings were no less worthy than hand-dipped chocolate creams flavored with dried banana. Whatever was pleasing and delicious, whatever the confectioner could craft or concoct with the materials available, whatever people wanted to buy—all of that was true and good candy. As Harvey Wiley had recognized back in 1887, there was no absolute standard or form from which candy could deviate. Bread had to be bread. Coffee had to be coffee. But candy could be anything.

There was of course much profit to be made in fake foods, and there was a major loophole in the law: so long as a manufacturer didn't actually say what product was being imitated, and used a proprietary brand name, the FDA could not intervene. So there were imitation foods that avoided direct reference to the original, often via clever brand names that evoked but did not name a type of food. There was Salad Bouquet, which was not vinegar; Peanut Spred, which didn't have much by way of peanuts; and Bred-Spred, which did spread and probably led some people to believe that it was jam, which it was only by way of the most creative interpretations of what you should call a mixture of pectin and coloring.

It wasn't until the 1940s and 1950s that the FDA belatedly responded to the multiplying variations of foods and fakes by regulating many common foods with recipe-based standards, drawn mostly from cookbooks.[43] This was food regulation as common sense: if you were selling jam, it had to have the appropriate jam ingredients. Likewise raisin bread, chocolate, peanut butter. These recipe-based standards preserved the idea of real food: stray too far from the authorized recipe, and it wasn't jam anymore, it was "imitation jam" or something else entirely.[44]

By the 1960s, the system was coming under increasing strain. Quaint recipes for jam or pot pie could not accommodate the multitude of additives, enzymes, enhancers, emulsifiers, and the like that took up more and more space in the list of ingredients. Meanwhile, the number of new processed and fabricated foods was growing, and the FDA staff was scrambling to figure out what an appropriate recipe standard might be for instant coffee or frozen TV dinners.

The food that finally pushed the FDA to adopt an entirely new approach was the humble frozen breaded shrimp.[45] In 1961, the FDA issued a standard for this delicacy. What exactly should frozen breaded shrimp contain in order that it could legally be called frozen breaded shrimp? By the old recipe-based standards, this might include shrimp along with a recipe for the coating including things like bread crumbs, egg, and seasoning. Recipewise, this would certainly make breaded shrimp at my house. Over at the FDA, though, a new idea emerged. Rather than specify the contents of breading, the new standard called for "safe and suitable" ingredients to be used. As for what was "safe and suitable" to include in shrimp breading, the FDA left it to the breaded shrimp folks to decide. While there was no official ruling or court case, the new breaded shrimp standard heralded a dramatic change in the very definition of food.

The shift from the recipe standard for food to "safe and suitable" was the candy clause writ large: there can be no harmless adulteration. As it was for candy, so it became for processed foods of every sort. Anything you put in the food that is not harmful is not adulteration. A law had been passed in 1958 requiring new food additives to be proved safe before they would be approved for food use. But all additives that were already in use at the time of the Food Additives Amendment were deemed to be "generally recognized as safe," or GRAS. Others were soon added to the list. The number of GRAS additives ballooned quickly from 182 on the original list to 718 by 1961. Any food could include any GRAS additive. So for food engineers hoping to concoct the latest breaded shrimp sensation, there were more than 700 possible candidates to make that breading crispier, crunchier, tastier, more irresistible. The breading on breaded shrimp could be made of bread, or cornmeal, or puffed rice, or more likely a mess of corn and soy extracts stewed in some complex chemical process to yield synthetic bread crumbs. Any of these would still be allowed in "breaded frozen shrimp."

By the new rules, innovative foods would not be marked as fake, fraudulent, or adulterated. If it was tasty and pleasing, if it was something people wanted, well, then it was food. This meant that henceforth, processed food would be, in its essence, no more real or fake than candy. Because once you've gotten rid of the idea that there is a single, true, real standard, anything goes. There is no such thing as imitation candy, and there never has been—because there is no "real" candy to imitate. And once the FDA got finished with its work on food standards, all food fell to the same logic.

Even as early as the 1890s, innovations in food processing

were creating foodstuffs that had no resemblance to any food that had gone before. Bromangelon was a dessert, but not like any dessert anyone grew up with (Bromangelon was the first commercially successful gelatine dessert mix, developed around 1895 by Leo Hirschfeld, better known today as the inventor of the Tootsie Roll). Grape-Nuts had neither grapes nor nuts, but what else they might contain was anybody's guess. From those tender beginnings, the pace of innovation and food invention since the twentieth century has been truly dazzling, bringing us Twinkies, Cheetos, Pop-Tarts, and PowerBars. What original food would these be measured against? McNuggets hint at fried chicken, but as anyone who has eaten actual fried chicken would realize upon biting into one, the resemblance is not convincing. As the judge in a 2003 case against McDonald's opined, McNuggets are "a McFrankensteinian creation of various elements not utilized by the home cook."[46]

The new "McFrankensteinian" cuisine that surrounds us today is food unleashed from any tether to agriculture or dairy or meat, food as a pure fantasy of pleasure and sensation. And while most of the processed foods that line today's grocery shelves neither look nor taste much like candy, they spring from the same rootstock. Candy never had a use for "real" food. Perhaps it should not surprise us that our freezers and pantries and cup holders are filled with tasty, convenient morsels that have come more and more to resemble candy.

4 ◎ Demon Candy, Demon Rum

The horrific imaginings of candy as factory scrapings and glue in the years leading up to the passage of the 1906 Pure Food and Drug Act might not have been literally true, but for many alarmists they perfectly captured a deeper truth about candy. No matter how pure the ingredients, how sanitary the factory, how hygienic the wrapper, candy could still be very, very dangerous. For those who looked at candy through the lens of moral righteousness, candy risked harm that was not simply physical, but spiritual as well.

A vivid condemnation of candy's sinister effects is portrayed in "The King of Candy Land," a poem by Ella Wheeler Wilcox published and reproduced through the 1890s in the *Christian Advocate* and elsewhere. Wilcox was best known for her inspirational and sentimental popular poetry: "Laugh, and the world laughs with you; weep, and you weep alone." But when it came to candy, she had no time for such levities. From the promise of candy pleasures, Wilcox spun a vision of dire suffering and decay:

Have you heard of the King of Candy Land?
Well, listen while I sing;
He has pages on every hand,
For he is a mighty king,
And thousands of children bend the knee,
And bow to this ruler of high degree.

He has a smile, O! like the sun,
And his face is crowned and bland;
His bright eyes twinkle and glow with fun,
As the children kiss his hand,
And every thing toothsome, melting sweet,
He scatters freely before their feet.

But woe! for the children who follow him,
With loving praise and laughter,
For he is a monster, ugly and grim,
That they go running after:
And when they get well into the chase,
He lifts his mask and shows his face.

And O! that is a grewsome sight,
For the followers of the king:
The cheeks grow pale that once were bright,
And they sob instead of sing;
And their teeth drop out and their eyes grow red,
And they cannot sleep when they go to bed.

And often they see the monster's face,—
They have no peaceful hour;
And they have aches in every place,
And what was sweet seems sour.
O, woe! for that foolish sorrowful band
Who follow the King of Candy Land.

The victims of the King of Candy Land experienced the most commonly depicted physical consequences of candy indulgence: the twin evils of rotten teeth and rotten stomach. But beyond the bodily ills of tummy aches and fading appetite, Wilcox made it clear that candy imposed worse burdens, and plenty of her contemporaries agreed with her assessment.

In a slightly less sinister tone, a Pennsylvania teacher blamed candy for his pupils' laziness and distractibility. Of the all-day sucker, he lamented in an educators' magazine in 1900, "I have never yet had a child who was persistently devoted to this candy who was of any account."[1] The potentially damaging effects of candy on moral character were not limited to children. Dr. James Redfield, writing in 1852, cautioned his readers against the dangers of sugar intemperance. He warned that once a man had indulged his appetite for sugar, he risked a downward spiral into depravity. The candy eater "requires larger and still larger portions of sugar to satisfy him," Redfield admonished, and "rushes from candy-shop to candy-shop as the toper goes from one coffeehouse to another to satisfy himself with the drams."[2] Redfield likened this candy obsession to the craving for alcohol, a behavioral metaphor that demonized candy quite effectively. Yet other temperance-minded reformers posited an even more direct link between the evils of candy and the evils of liquor. A writer in *Ladies' Home Journal* in 1906 described a short and slippery slope from candy nibbling to alcohol tippling: "The first craving from ill feeding calls for sugar; later for salt; then tea, coffee; then tobacco; then such fermented beverages as wine and beer; and lastly alcohol."[3]

If the simple joys of the candy stick could lead so easily to the depravities of alcohol, then here was real cause for concern. Was candy an innocent pleasure, or the first step on a path that would culminate in drunken degeneracy?

A Drinking Nation

On a pleasant spring Sunday in 1893, parishioners of Jersey City's Grace Methodist Episcopal Church were regaled by the crusading words of Rev. M. L. Gates. How alarmed must the parents in the congregation have been to learn that "thousands of children die annually of *confectionery diseases*"![4] If Gates meant that ordinary afflictions like cholera or typhoid might be made worse by eating candy, he did not say so. What he seemed to be saying was that disease—generic, horrible, deadly disease— was a consequence of candy itself. He exhorted his listeners to teach their children to avoid the dread candy lure and pro- fessed the (perhaps naïve) faith that "when the little children once learn the gigantic evils contained in confectionery and the incurable harm it entails and the many little graves dug by it and the multitude of children it renders weak and puny, they will quickly enlist in the ranks against the candy shop." As for those places where candy was sold, they were no less dangerous, Gates warned his flock, than the saloons and bars where liquor was dispensed. The candy shop was "responsible for more deaths than any place of dissipation save the rum-shop."

The evangelical moralism of preachers like Gates built on the nineteenth century's growing prohibition movement and lik- ened the evils of candy to the evils of liquor: each one an alluring pleasure leading to dissipation and decay. Liquor had a signifi- cant head start on candy in the colonial era. The first colonists filled their ships' holds with wine and beer, with a bit of water as an afterthought. The earliest apple orchards in America were planted to slake the thirst for hard cider. By the early nineteenth century, more than fourteen thousand distilleries were provid- ing Americans with some seven gallons of pure alcohol per person per year; that's the equivalent of ninety bottles of liquor per adult, an average that includes the teetotalers and abstainers.[5]

With all that drinking going on, it was inevitable that there would be quite a lot of drunkenness. And then as now, drunkenness was not all fun and games. By the 1840s, privately held anti-alcohol sentiments were beginning to coalesce into larger anti-alcohol movements. With a zeal drawing heavily on the searing language of Christian evangelists, anti-alcohol crusaders like John Bartholomew Gough exhorted the habitual drinker to "snap your burning chains, ye denizens of the pit, and come up sheeted in fire, dripping with the flames of hell, and with your trumpet-tongues testify against the deep damnation of the drink!"[6] Satan, hellfire, and alcohol were, in this powerful imagery, one and the same. To succumb to the temptation of drink was to fall into the clutches of evil. Abstinence was the only sure path to Christian perfection and salvation.

The sinfulness of drinking, the moral pathology of laziness, the abuse or neglect of family, the tendency to licentiousness and crime—these were bad enough. But in the minds of temperance crusaders, these sins were compounded by a sin to the body, God's corporeal temple. Alcohol caused physical injury, weakening the constitution and undermining its resistance to disease. Delirium tremens was but one sign of alcohol's ravaging effects on the nervous system, a vicious stimulation that would lead inexorably to insanity. Death by alcohol could take many forms; in some fantastical accounts, alcohol caused dehydration of such an extreme degree that the inveterate drinker risked death by spontaneous combustion.[7] The moral and physical effects were twinned faces of the same evil, for anything that so damaged the body must also take its toll on the soul.

The fiery rhetoric of the temperance movement was echoed by another strand of dietary reform that began stirring in Christian evangelical circles around the same time. Most critics of the American diet in the first half of the nineteenth century were not interested in the food itself; instead, they worried about Americans' tendency to eat too much, too fast, with little regard for taste or conviviality. Americans were, in a word, gluttons.

But on America's religious fringes, ideas were simmering about the morality of various kinds of diet. A growing vegetarian movement that first took hold in the early 1800s drew on Christian scriptural traditions to prove the "wickedness of flesh food."[8] These Christian vegetarians believed that eating meat caused animals to suffer. Carnivorousness, in this view, could not be part of God's plan. Forswearing meat was a path to righteousness, to living in harmony with nature as God had created it. Therefore, some concluded that the vegetarian diet was the most healthful and natural.

These strands of temperance and vegetarianism, both suffused with Christian zeal and righteousness, met and flowered in a man named Sylvester Graham. While Graham is best known today for the brown cracker that bears his name, he is better known to history for launching a peculiarly American gospel of salvation through dietary temperance and vegetarianism.[9] Before Graham, in the early 1800s, the vegetarians and the anti-alcohol crusaders were making a lot of noise, but no one was really listening. To anyone who didn't share their extreme religious views, they sounded like a bunch of crackpots. What Graham added in the 1830s was a way to translate the moralism of Christian vegetarianism and temperance into a scientific language suited for the modern age.

Graham got his first big professional break as a lecturer for the Pennsylvania Temperance Society, but after only six months of preaching the abolitionist gospel, he grabbed hold of a new theme: diet. As a cholera epidemic menaced New York in 1832, Graham began lecturing on the prevention of disease through proper eating. Graham's claim that fresh fruit and vegetables could stave off infection came as a surprise to an audience accustomed to hearing warnings about uncooked produce.[10] That wasn't the only unusual idea Graham espoused. In packed lecture halls and in numerous publications through the 1830s, he advocated what is sometimes referred to as an "Edenic diet": eating foods in their natural state, uncooked if possible, and avoiding flesh as well as all manner of "stimulating" foods, including alcohol, coffee, tea, salt, and spices.[11] For Graham, nature was the purest expression of God's will and wisdom. Therefore, food in its natural state must be the most perfect and wholesome food for the human organism.[12]

Graham was suspicious of all the products of food processing that took foodstuffs farther and farther away from their origins. Commercially baked bread was especially alarming. Wheat flour might be contaminated with ground peas, beans, or potatoes. To make the bread whiter and softer, commercial bakers were known to add chemical leaveners or whiteners. Even yeast was suspect, since it created gas through a process akin to alcoholic fermentation. Graham devoted much of his efforts to advocating for home bread making using unrefined whole-grain flours. This coarse dark bread came to be called Graham bread.[13] Today's version of the cracker, a lifeless factory artifact concocted from refined flour, sugar, hydrogenated oils, and a grab bag of chemical enhancers, is Graham in name only.

In Graham's view, food was composed of two sorts of stuff: the nutritive and the nonnutritive. The nutritive stuff stimulated the digestive organs to spring into action, while the nonnutritive diluted and delayed digestion. Trouble came when you stripped away the nonnutritive and left only the stimulating nutritive matter. Without the nonnutritive buffer, the digestive organs would be lashed into a frenzy of activity. The system would be irritated, exhausted, unable to cope with the assault. Hence the importance of whole-grain flour in bread. The bran and the fiber were what Graham regarded as the nonnutritive portion of wheat. Bran and fiber prevented the bread from overstimulating the system and also, as a delightful bonus, kept the plumbing in good working order. Grahamites could enjoy their coarse Graham bread in total digestive serenity. Not so those who indulged in a diet heavy in refined products like white flour and sugar.

Without the nonnutritive matter, these were too concentrated, too much stimulation without any dilution.[14] Candy, as we have seen, was sufficiently uncommon in Graham's day that he did not prohibit it directly, but he did have this to say on the matter of confectionery generally: "All those mixtures and compounds of flour and butter or lard, and the sugar or molasses or honey, and eggs and spices, etc., comprehended by the terms 'pastry,' 'cakes,' 'confectionery,' etc., are among the most pernicious articles of human aliment in civilized life."[15]

Many today would surely agree with this pronouncement on the dangers of pastry. Graham's vegetarian whole-foods diet seems, to the contemporary mind, a promising approach to good health. But Graham's views of the importance of dietary rectitude went well beyond the basic aim of bodily wellness. Meat and white flour, pastries and cakes, sugar and alcohol, mustard and salt would stimulate the nerves and organs. *All* the organs. So much stimulation could only lead to trouble.

For Graham and his fellow reformers, the good and Godly life was free of passions and excess, free of sensualism and fleshly temptation. The moral decay brought on by drunkenness needed no explanation. And the decay of dietary sin was easy to grasp by an audience accustomed to evangelical Christian doctrine. The stimulating effects of meat, sugar, alcohol, and the rest would inflame the flesh and drive the passions; it was but a small step from mustard to masturbation. Dr. John Harvey Kellogg, who put many of Graham's principles into practice at the Battle Creek Sanitarium in the 1880s, put the matter succinctly: "Candies, spices, cinnamon, cloves, peppermint, and all strong essences powerfully excite the genital organs and lead to the same result."[16]

Graham's unstimulating and unexciting diet promised to free the body not only of disease but also from lust and licentiousness. So celebrated was this aspect of his prescription that the Shakers adopted the diet for a time in the hopes that it would promote celibacy.[17] Suppressing sexual desire, forswearing masturbation, avoiding all but the most procreative of marital touching—these were paths to moral and physical purity. In the morally upright home, purity in the dining room and purity in the bedroom were mutually defining and mutually reinforcing.

By 1837, Graham had more or less retired from the lecture circuit. Legions of followers filled the void, continuing to extol the virtues of their vegetarian transformations, and his basic message of the dangers of "stimulating" foods passed down virtually unchanged to the next generation of reformers. The intertwining strands of temperance, vegetarianism, and Christian evangelical moralism created a unique lens for looking at food that continues in some form to this day. Food is not just good or bad nutrition. Food has a moral weight: good or evil.

Same as Alcohol

In January 1898, the young pupils at New York City Grammar School 78 were acting strangely. Bright eyes had gone dull. Heads were nodding. Simple questions like, "Who is the president of the United States?" were met with perplexing responses such as "Li Hung Chang." Parents and teachers were mystified, until a mysterious informant showed up at the police station and coughed up the truth: the kids were doped on "brandy drops." They had purchased those boozy bonbons from Mr. Abraham Goldman, the proprietor of a cigar and candy story at 316 Pleasant Avenue. Police sent in a fourteen-year-old patsy to set up a sting. Pennies changed hands, and the cops swooped in, dragging Mr. Goldman out in handcuffs. Selling liquor without a license was the charge, a violation of the excise law, which levied a tax on all liquor sold.

Mrs. E. Frances Lord, of the Woman's Christian Temperance Union, took note. If local candy makers were doping the kids, she wanted to know about it. She headed over to the school to get the full story and soon discovered that there was no story at all.

The original report had been ginned up in the *New York Journal*, "a sensational sheet." The school principal knew nothing about it. When Mr. Goldman came up for trial, the judge took one look at the evidence and threw out the case.[18]

The potency of those brandy drops—perhaps even their very existence—was the figment of somebody's overactive imagination. Yet newspaper readers found it all too easy to believe that schoolkids were coming to class loopy from alcoholic candies. By the 1890s, prohibitionists were gaining ground against "demon rum," and more and more Americans were coming to accept the view that drinking had become a little excessive. F. N. Moore of the Pennsylvania Pure Food Commission estimated in 1897 that a single pound of some candies might contain a "large whiskey-glass of rum or brandy." Moore blamed childhood treats for inspiring in the youngest palates a taste for something stronger: "With alcohol in infant food and rum and brandy in candy, no wonder we, as a nation, are acquiring abnormal appetites for alcohol as a stimulant."[19]

By the early 1900s, the easy slide between candy and booze was gaining more rigorous scientific rationales. Dr. A. C. Abbott, chief of the Philadelphia Bureau of Health, set off a minor flurry in 1907 when he opined that the appetite for candy and the appetite for alcohol were one and the same. He backed up his conjecture with a plausible scientific theory: "Both sugar and alcohol are carbohydrates, with the same organic molecules, differing only in arrangement, and I believe both administer to the same organic craving." Never mind that the same could be said for cake, or bread, or even carrots for that matter. The press leapt on the headline: "Candy Same as Alcohol."[20]

If candy and alcohol were the same in the body, there were nevertheless important differences. Alcohol was considered more stimulating, more harsh, more harmful than dainty sweet candy. Thus, according to Abbott, men preferred liquor, and women, bonbons. Alcohol was more masculine, more virile, even if prohibitionists claimed its effects might lead to weakening and dissipation. This would explain why Dr. John Chalmers Da Costa of the Jefferson Medical College in Philadelphia thought that blondes craved candy while "more vital" brunettes were more drawn to alcohol.[21] Meanwhile, Dr. Abbott had brought his insights from his epiphany into his own home. He reported that he had begun feeding his three children a daily allowance of sweets. It was only by building up their preference for candy, he explained, that they would be fortified against an eventual craving for rum.

Those who were willing to take the carbohydrate idea a little further began to view candy as a dietary prophylactic against alcoholic harm. In this light, confectioners could claim to be on the front lines in the battle against demon rum. One version promoted in the pages of *The International Confectioner* in 1916 went like this: carbohydrates metabolize into alcohol in the body. Therefore, there is a certain amount of alcohol just naturally running through the veins of every man, woman, and child. Nothing wrong with that. But if a person is really active, and burns through all his natural alcohol, he'll need more to replenish his body's stores. He can get it from booze—or he can get it from candy. And here's the good news: "The candy gives him the alcohol without injury, while whiskey and other stimulants are not gentle in their after effects." From this, a commonsense approach to detox emerges, one that is as inexpensive as it is enjoyable: "If you are unfortunate enough to have some dear one addicted to the drink habit, get him (or, we regret to add, her) to EAT MORE CANDY. It may not cure, but it will help."[22] Just think of the millions of dollars in rehab bills that could be saved with such a sweet treatment.

On the other hand, if candy was turning into alcohol inside the body, what was the difference between eating a box of candy and tossing back a shot of whiskey? For the more extreme anti-alcohol advocates, there was no difference at all. The metabolism of sugar as described by modern science sounded suspiciously akin to an internal distillery. The stomach was believed to convert candy into alcohol; therefore, eating candy seemed the first step toward intoxication. In this view, prohibition of alcohol itself was insufficient. "Candy eating is a form of alcohol dissipation," declared Dr. Charles Mutthart, a Philadelphia physician speaking at the 1916 convention of the Pennsylvania Osteopathic Association. "There is such a thing as becoming overstimulated or intoxicated on candy."[23] The implication was disturbing. Candy was available anywhere, and any child old enough to grip a penny was old enough to buy some. Just a year earlier, an esteemed Savannah physician had warned his local board of education that "the candy shop is as much of a menace to the juvenile community as the barroom is to adults."[24]

Luckily for the juvenile community, candy prohibition was a distinctly minority view. Quite the contrary, in fact. If candy could cure the craving for alcohol, then it was good news for temperance that candy was gaining ground with the primary consumers of alcohol: men. Ads in the early 1900s started featuring active, virile, heroic men who fortified their potent lives with candy. By the 1920s, even candy packaging was changing to reflect the new role of candy in men's lives. Traditionally, men had purchased fancy candy boxes to give to women, but the Ah-Ha! Four Queens candy box designed by the Milwaukee Paper Box Company in 1926 was obviously not for romancing the ladies. It featured a complex system of windows: pull a cord and enjoy an alternating view of four voluptuous nudes. One could easily imagine this naughty peekaboo candy box getting pulled out in some executive suite, where the good old boys could gape and guffaw, away from the disapproving glares of their wives.

As early as 1908, candy had become a common accessory in the masculine-dominated world of business, as described by one reporter: "Today you will find a box containing candy in a drawer of the office desk of the 'old man' who directs things in two-thirds of the business places in the larger cities."[25] A 1914 writer from a confectionery trade journal suggested candy was displacing cigars and whiskey in the rituals of male sociability: "It is no uncommon thing to go into the office of a business man, the leader of law or finance who is constantly dealing with problems involving the outlay of a big sum of money, and find on his desk a box of bonbons or chocolates. These he will offer to a visitor much in the same way that he used to think it proper courtesy to offer a cigar or invite his guest out to have a drink with him."[26]

Was there any truth to the candy trade's claims that candy could take the place of alcohol? There were some signs that pointed to yes. Sales were going up and up. And as various states passed their own dry laws, it looked on the surface at least that alcoholic consumption was falling. Bars and saloons were closing their doors, while soda fountains and candy counters were booming.

The beginnings of the huge expansion in the candy industry of the 1920s and 1930s did coincide with Prohibition, so it's tempting to conclude, as many insisted at the time, that candy was taking the place of alcohol. In the legal sense, liquor was outlawed, and the laws had some success. Experts estimate that the quantity of alcohol consumed fell 70 percent in the years immediately after the national amendment, although consumption then began to rise as Americans adjusted to the new regime.[27] But quite a lot of liquor just went underground. Bootleggers and speakeasies, mobsters and rumrunners—these were the new players in dry America.

Daniel Okrent's history of Prohibition, *Last Call*, paints a portrait of a nation mobilizing its powers of invention and creativity to exploit loopholes and squeeze through the gaps of Prohibition law. There was whiskey pouring across the Canadian border, rabbis and priests welcoming their swelling flocks to enjoy sacramental wines, home brewing and winemaking, and plenty of bribes and corruption to ensure that when bootleg or legitimate alcohol appeared, authorities looked the other way. Soda shops did sprout like mushrooms after the rain, but that didn't mean soda was just soda. Okrent's survey of Sheboygan, Wisconsin, hints at what was actually going on. There were 113 establishments in the town licensed to sell soda during Prohibition. Of those, Okrent notes that the two that failed were the two "that actually confined themselves to nonalcoholic beverages."[28]

The candy/liquor substitution theory in fact rested on some shaky sociological data. Experts like Dr. Abbott who recounted scientific-sounding reasons why candy would take the physiological place for alcohol "proved" their point by citing the widely held belief that men were big drinkers and women were big candy eaters. According to the substitution theory, the reason women didn't drink like men was that they were eating so much candy. The problem with this theory, though, was that women too enjoyed the pleasures of liquor. They just found other, more private or circumscribed ways. Like, for example, that nostrum for every female complaint, Lydia E. Pinkham's Vegetable Compound.

Female Complaints

Lydia Estes Pinkham cooked up her first batch of tonic in 1875, and although she died in 1883, her famous Vegetable Compound went on to become one of the great commercial successes of the late nineteenth and early twentieth centuries. An early pioneer of cross-platform marketing, Pinkham advertised extensively in newspapers and women's magazines across the country, and affixed her brand name to sewing kits, manicure sets, a *Private Text-Book upon Ailments Peculiar to Women*, and instructional booklets. Pinkham's tonic was marketed specifically to women, promising "a positive cure for all those painful complaints and weaknesses so common to our best female population."[29] The fact that the bitter herbal concoction was 20 percent pure alcohol certainly addressed one female complaint of the era: middle-class women were excluded from public drinking establishments, and even social drinking at home was considered unseemly. Pinkham herself had been a temperance worker and claimed the alcohol in the tonic was necessary to keep the many herbs and essences in solution. As preservative or otherwise, "a single 14.5 ounce bottle of Pinkham's contained the equivalent of 7.5 ounces of 80 proof whiskey."[30] Where whiskey drinking would have been unthinkable for most women, a little bit of Lydia Pinkham's to smooth out the day was quite respectable. It was an irresistible package for many women, and Pinkham's company was incredibly successful, grossing $300,000 annually after less than a decade and peaking at $3.8 million in 1925.[31]

Perhaps some of the women who found solace in Vegetable Compound were not aware of the alcoholic content. After the Pure Food and Drug Act began requiring labeling, many women who'd planted themselves firmly in the dry camp evinced shock and dismay when they discovered what was actually in the bottle. But the alcoholic content wasn't exactly a secret. Pinkham's was notorious enough to inspire drinking songs, like this one from the 1890s:

We'll drink a, drink a, drink
To Lydia Pink a, Pink a, Pink
The savior of the human ra-hay-hayce
She invented a medicinal compound
Whose effects God can only replace.[32]

Lydia Pinkham's target market was women with sufficient leisure to realize that they had "female complaints": middle-class women whose domain in the home was increasingly marginal to the bustle and business of trade, commerce, and manufacturing. These were women with time on their hands, women searching for something to do. Some spent their days in rounds of socializing or in charity work. And many began to cultivate as hobbies household activities that formerly had been necessities.

One of the new hobbies popular with elegant women in this era was home candy making, which was an ideal expression of middle-class femininity at the turn of the century. Women were supposed to be sweet and dainty, and the sweet stuff of candy was closely associated with feminine ways. Everybody knew women were insatiable candy eaters. An 1899 *New York Times* reporter summed up the common wisdom of the day: "Three-fourths of the candy made is consumed by women, and half the other fourth by children, leaving men a pitiable fraction of the total amount."[33] Creating dainty confectionery was a way women could demonstrate their skill without challenging the status quo. Popular cookbooks at the turn of the century began devoting more and more pages to confectionery. The folks at Lydia Pinkham took note of the rising popularity of candy making among the women they served and hit on a brilliant new marketing device: a recipe booklet devoted to candy, which would also promote the Vegetable Compound. They called it *Fruits and Candies*.

Fruits and Candies was first published sometime around 1900. It is not unlike hundreds of other recipe booklets published as commercial promotions in this period. Producers of products like baking soda and marshmallows were eager to teach their customers how to use new ingredients in cooking and baking. But Pinkham's Vegetable Compound was not something you could use in cookery. Unlike, say, the pamphlet *Jell-O: The Dainty Dessert*, the promotional and the informational aspects of Lydia Pinkham's candy booklet are quite distinct. The result is a very peculiar juxtaposition of recipes for candies and sweet fruit desserts alternating with testimonials from ladies whose "female complaints" had been cured by a regular dosing with the Vegetable Compound. One page offers a recipe for Maple Fondant, followed on the next by a testimonial on how the correspondent's sorrows of childlessness were alleviated with Lydia

Pinkham's. Another page gives instructions for Buttercups and Molasses Candy, and then a treatise on Painful Monthly Periods and the use of Vegetable Compound to relieve them.

Lydia Pinkham may have looked at "female complaints" and seen a business opportunity, but contemporary health reformers like Ella Kellogg noted women's increasing reliance on tonics and compounds and elixirs at the end of the nineteenth century and felt a wave of despair.[34] Ella Kellogg began her career in health reform as a leader in the Woman's Christian Temperance Union. As the temperance movement gained momentum in the 1880s, the WCTU began developing the notion that temperance could not be separated from other aspects of health and hygiene. This meshed well with Kellogg's own interests. Ella Kellogg was the wife of Dr. John Harvey Kellogg. At his famous sanitarium, the weakened wealthy could recuperate through a regime of diet and rest. Ella worked with John to put out the magazine *Good Health: A Journal of Hygiene*, which promoted vegetarianism as well as abstinence from all alcohol and narcotics, and she became especially interested in the health of American women beyond the walls of the sanitarium. In particular, she worried that tonics, nostrums, and patent medicines were turning American women into an army of addicts.

Lydia Pinkham's was the best-known brand of tonic in the 1880s and 1890s, but the problem of alcohol and other artificial stimulants disguised as medicinal preparations wasn't confined to her Vegetable Compound. Americans were avid consumers of a range of tonics and proprietary medicines, peddled in carts and storefronts and by mail, that promised all manner of vivifying effects. The ingredients of these tinctures were closely guarded secrets cloaked in mystery, typically described as herbal or natural remedies. But what some of these tonics actually contained were potent and potently addictive narcotics, starting with alcohol and moving through the full range of opiates and stimulants including morphine, laudanum, and cocaine.

The abuse of what Kellogg and her followers called "habit-forming poisons" was not the intentional and direct narcotic abuse of opium dens or seamy city streets. Many people believed the medicinal claims of the "snake oil salesmen" and took tonics in the sincere hope for better health. Temperance men and women, avowedly sober, were found by researchers for the WCTU to be consuming "vast quantities of alcohol and narcotics in patent medicines."[35] Female customers for the patent formulas weren't bums or addicts—they were fancy ladies looking for a boost after a night on the town, exhausted mothers just trying to cope, and women considered "nervous" or "weak," who saw in the tonics a cure for the mysterious ailments of femininity. Yet in Kellogg's view, mother's little helper or a seemingly innocuous "pick-me-up" was but the first step along the merry path of addiction and ruin.

The injurious effects of these tonics were clear. But what was the cause of so many women's reaching for their little bottle of Lydia E. Pinkham's Vegetable Compound or Mrs. Winslow's Soothing Syrup or any of the other myriad curatives that promised to take the edge off? Why were women so nervous and exhausted and racked by their female complaints? According to popular ideas about the fairer sex current in those days, this was just how women's bodies were: weak, frail, overcome by their ovaries and uterus. But women on the front lines of social activism were quite positive that this was not true. The problem, in the view of Ella Kellogg and her generation of feminist reformers, was not the intrinsic weakness of the female body. The problem was poor nutrition.

In classes and lectures designed to educate American women about the principles of good health, Ella Kellogg drew the connection between female enervation, alcohol, and a depleted and unnatural diet.[36] Kellogg argued that a diet overly rich in meat, fat, refined sugar, white flour, and contaminated or adulterated foods would deprive the body of nutrients and push vulnerable women toward artificial sources of stimulation. Tonics containing alcohol and opiates might seem to help, but their true effect was to overstimulate the nervous and digestive systems and to destroy the health of the organism. Making matters worse was the addictive nature of such tonics. Once women came to rely on the false sense of well-being they provided, they would be ever more tightly bound in their clutches. What nervous, sickly women needed was fresh air, good food, and exercise, not 20 percent alcohol tonics.

For reformers like Ella Kellogg, the juxtaposition of Lydia E. Pinkham's Vegetable Compound and candy recipes would have made perfect sense. All that candy eating was making women sick, and sick women were turning to the Vegetable Compound: a stiff drink in virtuous dress. To the innocent eye, *Fruits and Candies* is just a clever advertising gimmick which appealed to women's interest in home confectionery. To Ella Kellogg and her sisters-in-arms, *Fruits and Candies* was nothing more than a veiled enticement to overindulgence, licentiousness, and sickliness.

The Seed of an Evil Habit

The good citizens of Montclair, New Jersey, were pretty sure of candy's evil nature when they organized in 1924 to ban the display of candy in shop windows. Hundreds of signatures were appended to the petition calling the displays a "constant temptation to the morals of the young." The mere sight of candy risked drawing impressionable youngsters down a path of turpitude and dissipation. As one petitioner insisted, "The greatest vice among school children is that of loitering in front of candy and cigar stores."[37]

Where the vice actually lay was somewhat murky. Was it the loitering? The candy eating? Or did it have something to do with the proximity of candy and yet another morally suspect substance, tobacco? By the late 1880s, candy cigars and cigarettes were extremely popular. Cigars made of chocolate were simple affairs—just dark brown cylinders. Cigarettes brought out more fanciful packaging. One writer described "a cylinder of chocolate wrapped up in a paper resembling cigarette paper. It is packed in boxes precisely like those used for the genuine article, and until closely examined the candy cigarettes are very deceptive."[38] Licorice could serve double duty as a tobacco surrogate, either drooping from the lips like a cigar or chewed and spit like chewing tobacco.[39] Licorice makers caught on quickly; pipes and sticks were popular shapes for the soft chewy candy. And in many shops, candy and tobacco were sold side by side. The diminutive customer who first came in for candy cigars might one day grow into the devoted client for real tobacco products.

Although tobacco did not in 1900 have the toxic reputation it has today, its stimulating properties were widely recognized. Hygienists who followed the tradition of Sylvester Graham viewed tobacco as akin to alcohol, coffee, spices, and the like: stimulating and therefore physiologically harmful. Even for those mainstream Americans who saw tobacco as neither physically nor morally noxious, smoking was still considered somewhat outside the bounds of propriety. Tobacco was acceptable for men, perhaps, in certain situations, but not for ladies, and certainly not for children.

Candy cigars seemed perfectly designed to lure impressionable youngsters into dangerous habits. A 1900 lesson for Sunday school students featured a lisping toddler handing over his pennies at the grocery counter and happily chomping on his prize: "That was only a candy cigar, in itself, perhaps harmless, but it was a stepping stone to his ideal of a man. The seed of an evil habit had already been sown in his infant heart."[40] Civic reformers shared the view that, in the words of Chicago schools superintendent William Bodine, "The candy cigar is the first step toward ruin in the lamentable careers of schoolboy smokers."[41]

But did candy really deserve the blame for luring children into a life of tobacco vice? In the nineteenth century no less than today, tobacco clearly had its own attractions, especially for boys who bolstered their tentative masculinity by copying the cigar-chomping ways of their fathers and other adult men. Children had access to tobacco as well; not until the late 1880s did municipalities begin passing laws prohibiting the sale of tobacco to youth under sixteen. And "stimulation" aside, it must be noted that from a strictly empirical perspective, the immediate sensations of candy are quite different from the feeling of inhaling one's first lungful of fragrant smoke. If the kiddies were sneaking out behind the shed to light one up, it was hardly due to candy. At least, that's what the defenders of good clean candy-smoking fun insisted. As one sarcastic commentator queried in 1923, "Might we ask if the consumption of candy doll babies leads to cannibalism . . . ? Or does the purchase of a licorice 'pistol' indicate that the juvenile purchaser is headed towards a life of crime?"[42]

Candy smokes were marketed not only to children. Chocolate cigars and cigarettes were packaged to appeal to adults as well. The chocolate was tasty, of course. But there was another attraction: chocolate cigars and cigarettes promised to slake the appetite for tobacco smoke. We think of the Hershey bar as an icon of wholesome candy goodness, but before Milton Hershey hit on the milk chocolate formula that would make his fortune, his chocolate company was a premier supplier of tobacco surrogates marketed to adults. Hershey's Little Puck Cigars offered "A delicious and harmless smoke," and Petit Bouquets Chocolate Segars were advertised as "pure and delicious." Men might take special pleasure in Hero of Manila Chocolate Segars, which commemorated Admiral Dewey's victory in the Spanish-American War of 1898. Esquisitos or Cuban Chocolate Cigars evoked the exotic origins of the finest cigars, promising the best in ersatz-tobacco enjoyment. Women too would enjoy a candy smoke: Smart Set Chocolate Cigarettes featured a very finely dressed lady-about-town on the cigarette-pack-like box of ten. Milady might also like to try Le Chat Noir Chocolate Cigarettes for a Frenchy sophistication, or perhaps Opera brand to feel luxurious and refined.[43]

From Evil Candy to Good Food

The chocolate cigars and cigarettes were good fun, but they were toys, not intended to compete with food or anything nutritious. In 1900, however, Hershey released his first milk chocolate bar. Here was the serious business—something more than a treat. It was, as the label announced, "a nutritious confection." By 1903, Hershey was including on his labels the phrase "More sustaining than meat." This was the new face of candy: nutritious, sustaining, even meaty. This was a new direction for candy as well. The candy industry would grow in the twentieth century not by selling toys and novelties, but by selling something everybody needed every day: good food.

5 ◎ Becoming Food

Eat less, move more: we hear it every day, our first line of defense in the ongoing battle against obesity. Behind this prescription is a basic concept of caloric balance. Food is calories in; activity is calories out. When calories in are greater than calories out, the extra is stored in the body as added weight.[1] But as familiar as it may be, seeing food as "calories in" is in fact a pretty recent way of thinking about what we eat. The idea of the calorie as a measure of food value wasn't even around before the late 1800s.

During the nineteenth century, scientists developed a new understanding of food based in chemistry and physiology that came to be known as the "new nutrition."[2] Scientists in the 1850s and 1860s built on the pioneering work of German chemist Justus von Liebig to separate foodstuffs into three basic components: protein, fat, and carbon (carbohydrate). In this early stage of nutritional understanding, there didn't seem to be any practical difference between fats and carbohydrates: both were used by the body as fuel. Proteins, on the other hand, were associated with tissue building. However, once the tissue-building needs of the body were satisfied, protein also could be used as fuel. All food seemed to come back to this simple function: fuel. How much fuel did the body need? And how much fuel did different foods provide? To answer these questions, there needed to be some quantitative measure common to all foods. That common measure we still use today: the calorie.

For twenty-first-century weight watchers, food is measured as calories, and activity is measured in calories burned. The calorie is our basic unit of food accounting, a notion so deeply ingrained in our thinking about food that it is difficult to imagine accounting for food in any other way. People concerned about food can find out the calorie content of everything they eat. For most foods, it's right on the label: Hershey bar, 210 calories. We say the chocolate bar "has 210 calories," which sounds like those calories are something you'll find inside the bar. But when you put that Hershey bar under the microscope, you won't find any calories at all. The technical meaning of calorie, as you may remember from high school physics, is the energy needed to increase the temperature of one gram of water by one degree Celsius. So this is the calorie: not a unit of food but a unit of heat energy.

Lab experiments carried out in the late 1800s gave the calorie values for one gram of protein, fat, and carbon—scientists would burn the substance in a closed box called a bomb calorimeter that would allow them to measure the heat given off. It's a little trickier to measure calories used by the body, but in the 1890s a fantastic contraption solved the problem: the respiration calorimeter. This is a closed chamber in which a human subject can do what humans do: sit, sleep, jump rope, play the violin. The device precisely measures changes in temperature and gas caused by the subject's activity. These measurements in turn provide an index of energy expenditure that can be expressed in calories. Calories thus became the common measure of eating and living, a way of associating food intake with the work of the body. The bomb calorimeter would measure the calorie values of foods, and the respiration calorimeter would measure the calories expended in activity. This model of the relationship between food and activity became the foundation for mainstream nutritional science in the twentieth century.

The study of metabolism and caloric values was the chief obsession of Wilbur O. Atwater, the first director of research activities at the USDA. Atwater had seen a respiration calorimeter in use in Germany, and he was so smitten with the idea of tabulating human activity by the calorie that he persuaded the U.S. government to pay for him to build one in his own laboratory. Based on his work with the bomb calorimeter measuring food, and the respiration calorimeter measuring humans, Atwater began publishing detailed tables of the caloric and chemical breakdown of thousands of foodstuffs, which in turn became the basis for

Dr. Wilbur O. Atwater. (National Archives)

USDA dietary recommendations, the first of which was published in 1917. And what did the body need? Atwater and his
colleagues who studied American eating habits came to the conclusion that energetic American laborers needed about thirty-
five hundred calories a day, and that they should be distributed
as 15 percent protein, 33 percent fat, and 52 percent carbohydrate. Expressed this way, as numeric abstractions, it did not
seem to matter where these calories came from.[3]

In the beginning of the twentieth century, experts began
spelling out the inevitable conclusion of the new nutrition:
"Candy is a nourishing and sustaining food." This was the thesis
argued by Professor John C. Olsen of the Brooklyn Polytechnic
Institute at the American Museum of Natural History in New
York City in 1910. Professor Olsen explained to his audience the
modern view of nutritional science. The usual candy ingredients—
sugar, glucose, chocolate, nuts, gelatine—"contain all the four
chief food elements, fats, carbo-hydrates, proteids, and mineral
salts, and have a higher calorific value than fish, meats, vegetables, and fruits." In a demonstration that became legendary,
Professor Olsen held up a jar containing two-thirds of a pound
of chocolate creams and a similar jar of peanuts and declared the
virtues of a cheap and wholesome candy diet: "Any vigorous
adult could make a good breakfast on those chocolate creams
and peanuts. Moreover, there would be enough left over for luncheon and dinner besides . . . A person living on candy could
feed himself on 50 cents a day easily."[4] Better candy than eggs,
even, according to the professor. For while the most expensive
chocolate creams might total $1.00 for the day's ration, an equiv-
alent "calorific value" in eggs would cost $1.84.

The Calory Restaurant

Today we worry obsessively about eating too much. But a century ago, experts were far more concerned with the problem of

eating too little. Food scientists and reformers in the early decades of the twentieth century worried about the dangers of
undernutrition, especially when working and poor Americans
couldn't afford to eat more or better food. Wages were hit hard
by the industrial depressions of 1907 and 1914–1915; at the same
time, food prices began rising sharply after decades of relative sta-
bility, as a result of crop shortfalls in 1916 and the disruptions and
shortages in Europe caused by the outbreak of war. In 1917, food
riots broke out in New York City, Boston, and Philadelphia. With
chants of "We must have food" and "We want potatoes," hundreds
of marchers took to the streets and accosted food merchants. Pro-
testers stormed grocery stores and burned pushcarts.[5] With food
costs rising and war looming, the poor were especially vulnerable.

For reformers concerned with providing working-class Americans with adequate nutrition, "value" was paramount: with limited money, it was urgent that every penny be made to count. At
the same time, a new method of estimating the cost of a nutritionally adequate diet using Atwater's caloric standards seemed
to show that an alarming number of the poorer classes were un-
derfed and malnourished even when they could afford to buy
food.[6] The problem was not only lack of money but also lack of
modern knowledge: people were wasting their precious dollars
on the wrong sorts of foods. What was needed was a nutritionally adequate diet, as measured in calories, at the lowest possible
cost. Thus, food value could be reduced to a simple metric: price
per calorie.

And so the Calory Restaurant, imagined in the July 28, 1917,
issue of *Scientific American*, where patrons chose their portions
based not on taste or preference but on food value. The cover depicted a tantalizing spread of foodstuffs, each marked not with a
price but with a calorie value. Today many restaurants are beginning to post calorie values to discourage overeating; in 1917, the
aim was precisely opposite. The purpose of this special feature
was to encourage readers to adopt a new, scientific view of food

as fuel measured in calories. Rational meal planning and economical food shopping required that "exact knowledge of the food
values be substituted for appeal to the eye as a marketing test."
Although it was cutting-edge science in the day, the conclusions
as to the relative merits of various foodstuffs are surprising:

The well-thought of, but humble banana, is far above the
    aristocratic orange and tomato

Catsup shows a large increase over the tomato

Fish is an excellent food, but the lobster is disappointing
    when compared with the shad

Celery is almost worthless as a fuel-producer and so is
    asparagus

Crullers deserve their popularity owing to their large
    absorption of grease

Chocolate is true to its reputation as a hunger chaser, candy
    and sugar in almost any shape are good[7]

As the Calory Restaurant demonstrated so vividly, the calorie was the best thing that ever happened to candy, or to candy lovers. All calories being the same energy, the calories in candy were just as good as the calories in carrots or pickles. Better, in fact, because when you needed energy to fuel your body, there were a lot more energy calories in a little piece of candy than you would get working your way through a vat of pickles. And viewed from the point of view of economy and price, the calories in candy were much better, because you could get more food value for your dime or nickel spent on chocolate creams. Tables of food values expressed as calories per pound were an especially effective tool for making this point. Confronted with calories-per-pound values like sugar-coated almonds (2,410) or chocolate-dipped caramels (2,155), and comparing them with eggs (765), potatoes (370), or even sirloin steak (1,130), anyone could see that, as the secretary of the National Confectioners Association Walter Hughes put it, "The average food value of candy is higher than most of our common daily foods."[8]

There were a few naysayers. Under the title "Candy as Food," *The Literary Digest* pointed out in 1919 that it was absurd to draw the conclusion that since candy has a lot of calories, candy could serve as a primary source of food.[9] Dr. Ruth Wheeler, writing on children's diet for a 1919 U.S. government publication, cautioned against overly relying on sweets in the diet: "[Sweets] are entirely unbalanced foods, supply only fuel and no building materials in any permanent sense of the word. They must, therefore, supplement and not replace other food."[10] In that same year, the editors of *The Journal of the American Medical Association* worried about the overly narrow focus on calories as the expression of a food's value: "A properly selected diet represents the inclusion of many items, some of which are not to be evaluated primarily in terms of calories . . . [Milk] represents nutrient virtues that put it into the cheap-at-any-price class. The green vegetables contribute factors to our diet that candy can scarcely imitate."[11]

Yet those other "food factors" that might make milk, green vegetables, or meat important in the diet were less known and less easy to understand than the raw numbers of calories per pound and per dollar. Vitamin science was still in its infancy in 1919; it had been only a year since the publication of Elmer McCollum's *The Newer Knowledge of Nutrition*, which summarized for the first time recent advances in the discovery of vitamins and their role in diseases of deficiency. As a result, vitamins did not figure very prominently in the debate. Instead, against the charge that candy was unbalanced or too concentrated, defenders had a ready response in the form of nuts, eggs, milk, and chocolate. Even later, in 1926, NCA secretary Walter Hughes would confidently assert in a promotional booklet called *The Story of Candy* that "candy is a combination of various kinds of foods, all rich in energy and fuel value and containing all the important food elements, carbohydrates, fats, protein and minerals."[12] No one was advocating a diet of chocolate creams alone. But the idea that eating candy was as good as eating other kinds of food certainly was attractive. And those with an interest in selling candy were adept at turning the scientific view to their advantage. Viedt's Confectionery of Chicago advertised with a pitch that turned the worries about undernutrition that had inspired the caloric investigations into a demand for candy: "Are you eating Candy Enough? The hunger for sweets is natural. The normal man or woman who is not eating a reasonable amount of candy daily is not being properly fed. Recognizing the wholesomeness of the candy DEMAND, we have equipped our store to meet it with a wholesome SUPPLY."[13]

Sugar on the March

The carbohydrates in sugar translated into energy for the body. And in an era of industrial expansion and business growth at home, and a rising ambition for military, economic, and diplomatic influence abroad, nothing was more important than energy. A 1906 USDA publication, *Sugar as Food*, introduced the new idea of sugar as energy food to a broader audience.

Sugar as Food was the work of Mary Hinman Abel, who prior to her work as a nutritional expert in the United States had lived for many years in Germany with her husband, a pharmacologist.[14] During her time in Germany, she was exposed to the groundbreaking nutritional research of European scientists as well as numerous innovations in providing nutritional food to the poor. On her return to the United States, she brought with her ideas about food that were modern and scientific. During the 1890s, she applied her expertise to the experimental programs at the New England Kitchen, a philanthropic institution organized to elevate the poor through the knowledge of good food. Through the New England Kitchen, she came to know Wilbur Atwater and other researchers at the Department of Agriculture.

Although Abel lacked official academic credentials, her deep knowledge of nutritional science coupled with her access to scientists and dietary experts made her the ideal choice to write the Farmers' Bulletin on sugar, one in a series of educational publications undertaken by the USDA to promote agricultural products and educate Americans about food and nutrition (the series would eventually number more than twenty-two hundred titles). The new nutrition science had identified sugar and starch in foods as two forms of carbohydrate. The digestion of both sugar and starch would produce sugar in the blood. The main function of sugar in the blood was understood to be "the production of heat and energy." But scientists believed there was an important difference in these two forms of carbohydrate: because the body must convert vegetable starch to sugar in order to use it as fuel, dietary sugar was a more efficient way of getting energy. As Abel explained, "The fact that we have in this manufactured article [sugar] practically the same substance as that which results from the digestion of starch as found in vegetable foods at once suggests its substitution for starch to the advantage of the system, since it does not burden the digestive tract and less force is required for its digestion."[15]

Scientists in America and Europe had begun testing the implications of the new nutritional theories in the early 1890s. The first studies of the effects of dietary sugar on strength and fatigue were carried out in 1893 by an Italian investigator, Professor Angelo Mosso. Using a special instrument that measured hand strength, Mosso compared the work his subjects could do eating their regular food with the work they could do with a sugar supplement. Mosso's conclusions were definitive: "Sugar in the food," Abel summarized, "in not too great quantities and not too concentrated, lessens or delays fatigue and increases working power."[16] Professor Vaughan Harley followed up with experiments comparing the work he could do while fasting with the work he could do while taking nothing but about a pound of sugar dissolved in water. On the sugar day, he found he was much more productive, nearly as much as if he were on his full ordinary diet. The demonstrated energy boost from sugar first investigated in these laboratories would have a profound effect on ideas about food for many decades.

By the late 1890s, the reputation of sugar as a fatigue fighter and energy booster was beginning to percolate beyond scientific circles. The Prussian war office got wind of Professor Mosso's work and commissioned studies of its own. The results, published in 1898, showed that "sugar in small doses is well adapted to help men to perform extraordinary muscular labor."[17] This was what the war office was looking for: sugar, if it did indeed fuel "extraordinary muscular labor," might be the ideal ration for soldiers in the battlefield. The German army put the idea to the test over a thirty-eight-day period during their autumn training maneuvers. All soldiers marched and drilled, but some received an added ration of ten lumps of sugar per day. "The results were in every way to the advantage of the men using sugar," Abel wrote. "On long marches it appeased hunger and mitigated thirst; a feeling of refreshment followed, which helped the tired man on his way, and none of the soldiers allowed sugar were at any time overcome by exhaustion."[18] The Berlin researchers had recommended chocolate as the best medium for taking sugar in solid form; soon, chocolate cakes were added to the German army ration, along with other sugar stuffs.

The German army's discovery of a new battlefield advantage did not remain secret for long. In 1900, *Scientific American* announced that "candy has been added to the regular ration of the American soldier."[19] A New York manufacturer was preparing sealed tins of chocolate creams, lemon drops, and fruit drops to government specifications and shipping the candies to troops stationed in the Philippines, Cuba, and Puerto Rico. And not just a few cases: fifty tons a year. At the Brooklyn Navy Yard, every ship that left the port carried a load of candy for the men. A candy manufacturer, who did admittedly have an interest in the matter, explained to *The Brooklyn Daily Eagle* in 1908: "It is a good food for them; men can fight better on chocolate than on meat—that has been proved in the German army."[20]

Very soon, the question of who could fight better would become even more important. War broke out in Europe in 1914, and in 1917 the United States was drawn into the conflict. As the European casualties mounted, the lifesaving virtues of chocolate made the headlines. On June 1, 1917, two British aviators who had been shot down over the North Sea were finally rescued. They had been floating on wreckage for five days, sustained by only a small piece of chocolate, which they shared. The U.S. navy took note. In July, it announced "a new emergency ration, for issuance to the marines and sailors who may be ordered into action under circumstances which may result in their being separated for more than a day from their base of supplies. The ration will consist of biscuit and either a highly nutritious form of chocolate or peanut butter."[21] In the end, peanut butter did not make the cut. After deliberation, the War Department arrived at a slightly different requirement for emergency rations: three one-ounce chocolate bars, and three three-ounce portions of the far less delicious-sounding "ground meat and wheat pressed into a cake."[22] The ground meat cake was practical, but the chocolate was what every soldier craved. There was only one serious complaint about this emergency ration, as Colonel Roland Isker of the Quartermaster Corps recalled: "It was so tasty that the men would eat it shortly after issue instead of holding it for an emergency!"[23]

Emergency chocolate was just the beginning. With an eye on potential sales to the military, confectioners began to believe, with a certain perverse optimism, that the possibility that the United States might be drawn into the European conflict represented a significant business opportunity. "We know that a country at war does not lose its desire for confectionery," explained an article on "Preparedness" in *The International Confectioner*. "The European war has taught us however that huge standing armies consume huge quantities of candy, and it is a fact that thousands upon thousands of men who seldom if ever [ate] candy before, begin to crave for sweetmeats after they feel the rigors of active army life."[24]

The American army lived up to that prediction. From September 1917 to March 1919, the army consumed some 225 million pounds of sugar, or almost a quarter of a pound per man per day. On top of that was a substantial candy ration. Lemon drops were especially popular, with peppermints a close second. The army was a demanding customer; its regulation lemon drop recipe had been developed after testing every lemon drop in the country. A number of candy manufacturers were given the formula and supplied the army with two hundred thousand pounds of especially sour lemon drops each month: a lot of candy but only 15 percent of the total monthly amount furnished to the army in the war years.[25]

Shortly before the United States formally declared its intentions, a press photo of a Marine holding a tin box of candy was sent out to newspapers with the caption: "The American soldier has a weakness for candy. Like the matinee girl he craves it at frequent intervals. In recognition of which fact, the commissary department of the army annually buys, under contract, great quantities of candy for our boys in khaki."[26] It was probably the last time a soldier eating candy would be compared to a matinee girl. By the time the war was over, candy was universally embraced as real food, fit for men, women, and children alike.

Vital Fuel

Sugar as Food was not a wholesale endorsement of a sugar diet. Abel was careful to caution readers about the dangers of excessive sugar, particularly if consumed in concentrated form. She warned that too much sugar taken at one time might "overload the system, bringing on indigestion or overloading the excretory organs" and that concentrated sugar could irritate the stomach and other organs and have "ill effects on the system." But the sugar allowance for your average adult would still be quite generous; Abel observed that "about one-fourth of a pound daily, taken as it is in connection with other foods, is well utilized by the system."[27]

For Coke guzzlers in the 2010s, four ounces of sugar is easy to gulp down without even noticing—three twelve-ounce cans will do the job. But a century ago, in a day innocent of soft drinks and high-fructose corn syrup, a quarter of a pound of sugar translated into quite a few sugar lumps, and even more jam, cakes, candies, and sweet coffee or tea (any of which Abel would have found preferable to lump sugar, since they dilute or extend the sugar and therefore avoid the danger of irritating the system with too much concentrated sugar). Since about two pounds a week of sugar per person was the current estimate of sugar consumption among the "well-to-do," Abel's caution was in fact permission to keep eating sugar the way more and more people were becoming accustomed to, that is to say, in enormous quantities.*

In 1920, Americans were eating about the same number of

---

*To put this in perspective: nutritionists today are deeply alarmed at the high rates of added sugar consumption—something between four and five ounces per day—primarily because nutritionally empty added sugar displaces other more nutritious sources of calories in the diet and contributes to weight gain. There are many theories about why high sugar consumption might be a factor in chronic disease, as summarized in Taubes, *Good Calories, Bad Calories*. (The consumption numbers are estimates based on production and assumptions about "loss," so different researchers end up with slightly different numbers. For USDA estimates of sugar consumption see USDA *Agriculture Fact Book 2001–2002*, Table 2-6, p. 20, and USDA Economic Research Service, "Sugar and Sweeteners Outlook," February 2011, www.ers.usda.gov/publications/sss/2011/02Feb/SSSM270.pdf.)

calories as they had been eating in 1900.[28] But a lot more of those calories in 1920 were coming from sugar, which meant that sugar calories were displacing calories from other sources. The general diet was sweetening up. American sugar consumption had been increasing dramatically over the past few decades: from 30 pounds annually per capita around 1860, to 50 pounds in the 1880s, up to a previously unimaginable 68 pounds per person in 1901.[29] In 1921, sugar consumption was an astonishing (for that time) 97.8 pounds per capita—one-third of the total world supply was going to feed the American sweet tooth.[30] Researchers in the early 1900s had not established an upper limit for sugar digestibility, although Abel reported that Professor Harley had experienced digestive irritation after a month on a regime of about a pound of sugar a day taken in a water solution.[31] Abel supposed two pounds per person per week to be a sensible sugar portion; that also just happened to be about what the average person was consuming from the 1920s well into the 1950s, when sugar consumption again began to climb.

Today, more and more mainstream nutritional researchers are warning of the dangers of sugar consumption. But in the early decades of the twentieth century, sugar was exonerated by the most advanced scientific minds of the day. The new nutrition had shown that refined sugars, naturally occurring sugars (in fruits, for example), and vegetable starches, seemingly so different in foods, were all converted to sugar in the body. In laboratories and medical schools throughout North America and Europe, this modern view of carbohydrates swept away old dusty suspicions about sugar's unwholesome effects. Some fringe figures continued to blame refined sugar for a variety of ills, but mainstream experts in nutrition and physiology increasingly agreed with Abel's assessment that so long as one did not overindulge, sugar in any form was fine energy food, "rapidly available for muscle force."[32]

This is why, Abel explained, "sugar is so relished by people who are doing muscular work and by those of very active habits," like children, athletes, and lumberjacks.[33] Rowing clubs in Holland encouraged their boatmen to eat sugar, Abel reported: "The rowers who used sugar always won because of superior endurance."[34] And by the same reasoning, children should be eating more sugar, since they would burn it up so fast. Many experts echoed this opinion; in the place of the previous generation's warnings about poisoning and moral decay, mothers in the early 1900s might find advice like that of domestic expert Marion Harris Neil, who wrote in 1913, "Parents do their children a great injury by denying them good, pure candies. The child requires a large amount of sugar, for sugar assists in the processes of growth as no other food element can possibly do.[35]

Sugar wasn't just for children and champion rowers. After all, everybody has muscles, and every muscle demands fuel. "Sugar is comparable to gasoline," wrote Dr. Leonard Keene Hirshberg of Johns Hopkins University in a summary of the "New Discoveries About Sugar" in 1914: "As the latter is the fuel of the internal combustion engine, so sugar is the fuel of the human machine."[36]

Sugar was gasoline for the human engine, and as Americans in the early 1900s were quickly coming to learn, an engine without gasoline was in serious trouble. These were the years when gas-powered automobiles were suddenly appearing on city streets and country roads, portending a dramatic new age of transportation. Automobiles were powered by a new, cutting-edge technology: the internal combustion engine fueled with petrol or gasoline. In popular explanations of how sugar works in the body, the mechanical action of the internal combustion engine was a common metaphor for the invisible and mysterious workings of human metabolism. Dr. Woods Hutchinson, a well-known writer and lecturer on public health in the 1910s and 1920s, explained in a 1909 magazine article: "[Sugar in the muscle cell] serves as the fuel for the muscle engine. Each of those tiny explosions, which we call a contraction, of muscle, burns up and destroys a certain amount of sugar, and as soon as the free sugar in the muscle has been used up, then that muscle is as incapable of further contraction as an automobile is of speed when its gasoline tank is empty."[37] If sugar was the essential fuel of muscles, then the role of dietary sugar must be essential in providing that vital fuel. Dr. Hirshberg put it succinctly: "Sugar is the staff of life, and man can produce more energy from sugar than from any other food."[38]

The Strenuous Life

Sugar was food for energy, and candy was a simple, delicious, and convenient way to eat it. This new knowledge quickly passed from specialized publications about food and nutrition like Abel's *Sugar as Food* into the popular imagination. It wasn't just soldiers on the front lines who needed their candy rations. Through the early decades of the century, wherever there was action, adventure, or danger, there was candy.

"We ate sandwiches and chocolate," said aviator Captain John Alcock, who together with Lieutenant Arthur Brown achieved the first nonstop flight across the Atlantic Ocean in July 1919. On their way into the record books, the duo endured a sixteen-hour journey through dense fog and mist in temperatures so cold that ice caked on the instruments. The wireless radio was destroyed in the first minutes of flight. The story of their journey was harrowing: climbs to eleven thousand feet, dives to sea level, instruments jamming, the craft free-falling into loops and spirals. The fliers relied on their wits and their luck to bring them safely to land in an Irish bog. Anxious observers on both sides of the Atlantic cheered the news of their safe arrival. It was another triumph for flight. But it was also a triumph for chocolate, trumpeted in headlines as "a food for endurance."[39]

"Candy Diet Helped Mountain Climbers," announced *The*

New York Times in a 1923 report on George Mallory's successful ascent to the heights of Mount Everest. The great explorer was said to have abandoned all other foods for the final stage of the climb, subsisting for three days on lemon drops, peppermints, and chocolates. Soon after his return, Mallory embarked on a lecture tour to promote and raise funds for his upcoming 1924 attempt. To rapt audiences hearing of his high-altitude adventures, Mallory explained the utility of candy for the extreme explorer: "Eating candy was one of the ways of conserving energy. At great elevations, no one has any strength to waste on unnecessary processes of digestion . . . [Sugar] can be digested quickly and easily and converted into muscular energy."[40]

Mountaineer and adventurer Annie Peck preached her faith in chocolate on the slopes and at home. In popular lectures recounting her mountain conquests, she never omitted mention of the particular brand of milk chocolate that sustained her in her adventures. Born in 1850, Peck was a restless and ambitious woman from a wealthy family. She gained fame in 1895 when she became the third woman to scale the Matterhorn—and the second to do so in trousers, at a time when women could be arrested for wearing them in public. When she wasn't climbing mountains, she boasted of her economical food budget: at breakfast, coffee with bread and peanut butter; at dinner, two eggs and spinach; and "for lunch I ate a cake of milk chocolate."[41]

Athletes had a special fondness for the powers of candy. Boxing champion Willie Ritchie boasted in 1914, "I have a regular sugar habit . . . In the middle of the night [I get up to eat] a box of candy . . . When I go to the theater I like to take a pound box of candy along . . . I believe that sugar is partly to thank for my speed and strength." Distance runner Hannes Kolehmainen described in 1916 a scientific approach to calibrating sugar and performance: "Early in my youth I found that I was a fair runner, but I seemed to lack the necessary endurance. One of my friends advised me to eat sugar. He suggested that I eat five or six lumps in the morning and the same number at night. I tried the experiment, and in less than a month I found that I could run double the distance . . . I never let a day go by without eating 12 or 15 sugar lumps or a large quantity of milk chocolate or other kinds of candy." Dr. William Brady, an authority on health and dietetics, advised marathon runners "to eat candy during the race to replenish the blood sugar reserve which is heavily drawn down on in any severe prolonged muscular effort." Six-day bicycle riders reported eating a half pound of sugar candy or milk chocolate daily. Tennis stars ate sugar regularly. How could any ordinary soul expect to have enough energy to make it through the day without a little boost from candy?[42]

Heroes in the arena, on the slopes, and in the air were getting their lift from sugar. In these early versions of celebrity endorsements, sugar and candy as energy food were sources not just of physical strength and endurance but also of moral courage and triumph over adversity. It wasn't much of a leap to connect the energy force of sugar with the destiny of the nation. In a 1921 booklet titled *The Strength We Get from Sweets*, C. Houston Goudiss writes, "Without sugar, there never could have been such a thing as the strenuous life! With sugar . . . it has been possible to maintain the pace of civilization and keep up physically with the rapid development of the human mind."[43]

The athletes and lumberjacks and aviators who extolled the virtues of candy were obviously leading the "strenuous life." But the appeal of a strenuous life extended to ordinary Americans in their daily routines as well. It was Teddy Roosevelt who first promoted the idea, in his famous speech by the same name delivered in Chicago in 1899. Roosevelt sought to inspire his compatriots to heights of accomplishment: "Our country calls not for the life of ease, but the life of strenuous endeavor." Roosevelt had in mind not only the energetic pursuit of sport and commerce at home but also a grander vision of America's role as a leader in the "great affairs of the world." Only defeat and humiliation would await the one who embraced what Roosevelt derided as "a life of slothful ease, a life of that peace which springs merely from lack either of desire or of power to strive after great things." Work, strife, toil, vigor, strength—these were the virtues that Roosevelt demanded of his fellow citizens. Sugar lumps, lemon drops, chocolate bars, and peppermints would fuel both individual and nation in their struggle to achieve their glorious destiny.

The Truth About Candy

The triumphant march of candy into the pockets and pantries of the nation faced its first serious obstacle in the fall of 1917. The United States was being pulled into the European conflict, and food shortages abroad were beginning to have an effect on the country's food supply. Enormous quantities of meat, wheat, and sugar were being sent overseas to support the army and bolster the Allies. In August, President Wilson appointed Herbert Hoover to act as U.S. food administrator and establish wartime food controls. Sugar, a major commodity, was vulnerable to rapid price inflation and profiteering. The Food Administration's efforts to stabilize the sugar market were directed toward persuading sugar producers to accept price controls and distribution agreements. Along with controlling production, the Food Administration sought to reduce consumption.[44] America's growing sweet tooth faced its first major challenge.

At the beginning of the crisis, Hoover believed that manufacturing, and candy in particular, was the most significant user of the sugar supply. Hoover hinted that he might order the rationing of candy if Americans would not voluntarily reduce their sugar consumption.[45] On October 20, 1917, the Food Administration issued instructions to sugar refiners and processors to stop selling any sugar to candy manufacturers. This was a catastrophe in the making: cutting off all sugar supplies would have

Sugar conservation poster, circa 1917–1919. (National Archives)

effectively shut down candy production and driven most candy manufacturers out of business.

Candy manufacturers were fortunate to have a strong and well-organized trade association to represent their interests: the National Confectioners Association, based at that time in Chicago. Walter Hughes got on a train to Washington as soon as he heard the news. In a series of heated meetings with Hoover and George Rolph, chief of the Sugar Division of the Food Administration, Hughes insisted that squeezing candy manufacturing would not have a significant effect on the total sugar supply because candy used only a small portion of the nation's sugar. Hoover was convinced, and Hughes was probably not exaggerating when he recollected years later how that conversation had "saved the day for the candy manufacturers."[46]

In recognition of Hughes's special expertise in the sugar markets, Rolph invited him to join the Sugar Division and help the Food Administration formulate sugar policy. Although Hughes had persuaded Hoover that candy was using less of the total sugar than Hoover supposed, this was merely informed conjecture. Little was known of the actual sugar usages of various industries. With Hughes on board, the Sugar Division undertook a survey to better understand where the sugar was going. The results, which were compiled in early December 1917, were surprising, both in terms of the various industries using sugar and the amounts. The candy industry was the largest single industrial user of sugar, but candy's portion of the total use for all industries was only 8 percent.[47]

The survey also revealed some surprising facts about household sugar usage. Americans were putting 440,000 tons of sugar into coffee and 220,000 tons into tea every year. Household beverage sugar use accounted for nearly twice the 350,000 tons of sugar used each year to make candy. Beyond beverages, households were also using huge quantities of sugar for baking, canning, preserving, sprinkling, and general sweetening. The survey showed that households—not factories—were the biggest sugar users by far, accounting for 70 percent of the total sugar supply. To bring down sugar consumption, it was households that would have to bear the brunt of the economizing measures.

To reduce sugar consumption, the Food Administration announced that the American housewife would be "put on her honor not to use more than three pounds of sugar each month for each member of her household." It was not rationing in the strict sense, but it was quite a cut from Abel's estimate of two pounds per person per week as an ideal amount.[48] By the summer of 1918, the Food Administration had put in place more wide-reaching restrictions on consumers' use of sugar. In addition to deep cuts at home, all public eating places would have sugar rationed based on the number of meals served. Worse, the administration announced that "sugar bowls must not be placed upon the tables in public eating houses" and "the supply of sugar at each meal must be limited to two half-lumps or to one teaspoonful of granulated sugar to each person."[49] The new rules pinched hard on the daily life of Americans (plate 3). Citizens cried foul.

Candy was an obvious scapegoat for the feeling that the whole sugar business was rigged against ordinary folk. Hoover received hundreds of letters from citizens complaining that their use was restricted while the candy makers continued running their factories. One letter captured the sense of unfairness: "I live in East Orange, New Jersey. All the sugar that I can buy is a half pound a day for my whole family. I have no kick on that if it is necessary. I am absolutely loyal in thought and practice to the Food Control scheme. But listen, I can go to any candy store in New York and carry away all the candy that I can stagger under, what is the answer? . . . In the name of Democracy and Humanity stop the manufacture of candy."[50]

In a similar vein, a Nebraska citizen complained of the disparity between his own meatless and wheatless days and the overflowing shelves of the candy shops. "I read just a day or two ago that there was not more than fifty sacks of sugar to be had in the city of Lincoln," wrote Henry Allen Brainerd to the *Lincoln Star*. "I also read about the same date that in New York City alone in one day there was $1,500,000 worth of sugar made up into candy . . . We are asked to observe a meatless day a week and a wheatless day a week, and we presume that soon . . . we expect to be obliged to drink black coffee, and eat butterless bread, and crustless pie, but never a word have we heard about a candyless day."[51] J. W. Vogan, the president of a Portland, Oregon, candy company, reported that "people in our territory began to openly criticize the candy industry . . . So far as could be determined by general evidences and newspaper comment [the public] was willing to do without candy and seemed to prefer the elimination of the use of sugar in candy, to making any sacrifices in their homes."[52]

Here was an alarming thought for the candy industry: people would rather go without candy than without sugar in their homes. Sugar was a necessity, but candy still seemed to be a luxury, something that could be dispensed with in difficult times. And worse: the public seemed to have come to the conclusion that, as Walter Hughes put it, "Candy is the thief that has robbed the sugar barrel."[53]

In 1918, candy manufacturers went on the offensive. To show that candy was in step with sugar conservation, they started promoting "war candies" made with less sugar. "If you are going to turn out 'war candies,'" suggested the editor of the *Confectioners Journal* in January 1918, "give them snappy war names and watch the result. You are going to save sugar for other purposes and in doing so disarm the current assertion that 'candy is a luxury.'"[54] Many traditional candies could easily be reformulated as war candies: less-sweet chocolate with nuts or fruit, hard candies, gumdrops and jellies using more glucose and a small percentage of sugar, marshmallows made primarily with corn syrup and gelatine.[55]

Some confectioners took advantage of the climate of conservation and patriotism to promote entirely new lines of candy. George Close Company, a major Massachusetts manufacturer, came up with a new line of children's novelties. Hooverites were chocolate-covered "corn products" at two for a penny. Chocolate-covered animal crackers yielded Amalkaka (baby talk for animal cracker, I presume), while the same treatment applied to oyster crackers produced the more easily pronounced Chocolate Niblets. "By pushing these specialties," Close told retailers, "you are not only performing a patriotic duty in conserving sugar but, at the same time, are helping yourself and customers to maintain a normal volume of business."[56] Manufacturers of prepared candy bases and coatings like White-Stokes's Karmel Kreme and Mazetta took advantage of the sugar shortage to align their products with patriotic support of the war effort. (Some of these prepared bases and coatings did use less sugar, but some products conserved sugar only insofar as they saved the manufacturer from having to add its own sugar to make the candy.) In a bit of sloganeering that seemed to apply equally to the industry as a whole, White-Stokes boasted that it was "A Business Closely Allied with the Food Administration."[57]

By consuming these war candies, Americans could have their candy and conserve sugar at the same time—all the reason to eat more candy. In fact, wartime candy eating could be justified as the ultimate in food conservation. The argument went something like this: by eating more candy, Americans were conserving on other foods, which could be sent to support the war effort. Every candy bar lunch at home was another loaf of bread for a starving soldier in France. The Touraine Confectionery Co. of Boston made this a theme in its trade advertisements promoting the Touraine five-cent fruit-and-nut-filled chocolate bar:

> We All Must Help the Government in its commendable efforts toward Food Conservation. The use of highly concentrated, nutritive food preparations helps to conserve wheat, meat, potatoes and all the necessary bulk foods much needed for our own and our Allies' soldiers. The 'YELLOW LABEL' 5¢ bar contains over 190 calories food value—more than the food value of two boiled eggs. Three TOURAINE BARS are more sustaining than the average meal.[58]

By this line of thinking, refusing to eat candy was downright treasonous.

Candy Is a Food!

Although Walter Hughes was doing everything he could at the Food Administration to protect the candy industry, he was worried. If the public was blaming candy for taking away their sugar, cutting sugar to the candy manufacturers would be an easy way for Hoover to shore up support for other food controls. The problem, as Hughes saw it, was that "the public has not yet learned the food value of candy—the confectioners have been asleep at the switch—they have neglected their greatest opportunity."[59] To address this deficit, Hughes arranged for the NCA to distribute hundreds of thousands of copies of a special educational booklet titled *The Food Value of Candy* for the use of candy manufacturers and retailers.

The Food Value of Candy was printed on thin paper and designed to fold into a small size: a perfect insert for every box of chocolates, candy bar, and sack of gumdrops. It explained the modern scientific view of calories and food value, a view that gave candy a more respectable place in the diet. The booklet also directly addressed the public accusations that candy was stealing sugar from other uses. With figures drawn from the work of the Food Administration, *The Food Value of Candy* demonstrated that candy was but a small portion of the total sugar output, and that overall candy was only about 50 percent sugar, the rest being other wholesome food products like milk, nuts, and fruits. In the face of the serious crisis confronting the industry, Hughes encouraged all in the trade to distribute the booklet as a "constructive educational work that will correct the unsympathetic attitude of the public."[60]

The pressure to justify candy as a legitimate and valuable food created a new form of promotion. "We advocate that the slogan 'Candy is a Food!' be sent broadcast all over the country," read a plan of attack outlined in a 1919 *Confectioners Journal* editorial. "It should be included in all newspaper and magazine advertising; all circulars and window cars. It should be printed on letterheads, billheads and envelopes, 'Candy is a Food!' Make the people read it! Keep it going! Slowly but none the less surely the idea will prevail."[61]

This style of advertising was new. Up until the war, most candy was sold on its merits: as attractive, as novel, as delicious, as convenient, as pure or high quality. But now candy would be promoted as a kind of food and implicitly or explicitly compared to other kinds of food. Manufacturers quickly developed new advertising in line with the "candy is a food" theme. Mason, Au and Magenheimer, for example, promised retailers an easy sale for Mason's Peaks candy bar. "Why? Because it is a Candy with tremendous food value." The ad included a comparative chart of calories per pound: Mason's Peaks, 2,000; whole milk, 315; beef-steak, 1,090; corn, 1,685; white bread, 1,180; whole eggs, 695.[62]

The comparative calorie chart was a tool for convincing the consumer to see candy in a fresh light, as interchangeable with milk or eggs. And if the consumer could be persuaded to see candy in this way, then she could also be persuaded to spend her nickel on a candy bar instead of eggs or milk or bread. In the years leading up to the Great Depression, the NCA would carry out ever more ambitious cooperative advertising campaigns that would saturate the national media with the good candy news. But even as early as 1920, *Printers' Ink*, the premier advertising magazine of the day, praised the industry for its success in using modern advertising techniques to remake candy in the image of food: "Not so very long ago candy was regarded as a mere luxury and not a very healthful one at that . . . Up-to-date advertising, though, has asserted itself to a point where now candy is regarded as what it actually is, namely: nourishing and altogether desirable food."[63]

At least for this twenty-first-century reader, some of the "candy is a food" educational literature that first appeared during the war years comes up against the limits of credibility and common

sense. My favorite bit of apparent sophistry comes from the
Candy Manufacturers of Oregon, who in 1918 produced a series
of informative leaflets under the title *The Truth About Candy* in
an attempt to win over an increasingly hostile public (the series
was reproduced in other states as well). One called "The Story of
a Chocolate Cream" promises to answer the burning question of
whether candy is a food or a "non-essential luxury":

> In the first place, what is a chocolate cream made of? The prin-
> cipal ingredients are: Cocoa, milk and sugar, which, mixed,
> make the chocolate. Milk, sugar and some corn syrup make up
> the filling. Every one of these ingredients is a food product of
> highest worth. No one questions their separate food values. We
> all know that milk, cocoa and sugar, making chocolate, forms a
> wonderful food. No one questions the food value of milk. We
> all know that sugar is an essential food. And when nuts are
> added to the chocolate creams, as is often done, another splen-
> did food product is added. Taken separately, each is high in
> food value. Naturally, combined into a delicious confection,
> they are equally high in food value. All these ingredients are
> food products which the human system craves and demands.
> That is why the active man, woman and child like this combi-
> nation of these food products which we call "candy."[64]

This combinatorial logic, whereby candy is dissected into its
constituent parts and then reassembled as the sum total of those
parts, would become a favorite theme of promotions for years to
come. And yet, wasn't there some truth to candy's claim to be
food? Certainly the manufacturers and sellers believed it; there
may have been some hyperbole in their self-promotion, but they
were not being cynical when they insisted that their product be
defined as food. According to the most up-to-date research and
the most scientific and modern views of the day, candy *was* food.
It may seem preposterous from our more enlightened perch.

And yet, the fact that nutritional science defined food in a way that benefited the candy industry is hardly candy's fault. The trouble was not with the sellers; the trouble really was with the science of nutrition and its tendency to lose sight of the whole in favor of the (always poorly and partially understood) parts. "Candy is a Food" was the truth of the new nutrition.

6 ⊚ In the Kitchen

Home candy making was a fashionable women's pastime in the early twentieth century, and for many also a potential source of profit. The arts of modern confectionery had been developed by professionals, but enthusiastic amateurs could learn the craft from a burgeoning list of candy-making manuals and candy cookbooks. The publication of these volumes increased dramatically between 1880 and 1930, the same period that witnessed the explosive growth of machine-made candy. Whether the ubiquity of these cookbooks reflected the amount of candy actually being made in the home is difficult to say. But whatever the practice, clearly the idea was enormously appealing, particularly to women. When George V. Frye published *Frye's Practical Candy Maker* in 1885 for the instruction of professional confectioners, he received letters from women begging him to create recipes suitable for home use. He did publish a second book of recipes "especially adapted for manufacture in the American kitchen."[1]

In most cases, the authors of candy recipes and cookbooks intended for home use were not professional confectioners. They were more often professional cookbook authors and domestic experts. Christine Terhune Herrick, who in her 1914 book *Candy Making in the Home* urged women to take up the activity as a regular part of their household routine, was a successful and prolific author of housekeeping manuals, guides to health and hygiene, and cookbooks from the 1880s into the 1920s. Her career was no doubt helped by a family connection: she was the daughter of one of the best-known domestic experts of the day, Marion Harland, with whom she also collaborated in publication. Herrick and her mother, along with many other professional writers of cookbooks and domestic manuals, advocated preparing food with a scientific understanding.

Domestic scientists, as these experts frequently called themselves, approached cooking as formula rather than instinct or tradition. Ellen Richards was one of the movement's founders; historian Laura Shapiro describes her as "the first woman to cross into man's scientific world and return with good news for housekeepers."[2] Richards was admitted to the men-only Massachusetts Institute of Technology as a "special student" in 1870. There she studied chemistry and then paved the way for more women to be admitted by organizing a Women's Laboratory where women were incorporated as regular students.

Women at the time had little opportunity for the professional practice of chemistry, but Richards was not deterred. She conceived of a new specialized knowledge that would elevate the traditional role of women, a branch of applied chemistry that she dubbed "household chemistry." Women would learn the chemical actions of such common household products as baking soda and vinegar, and also learn to use chemical analysis to detect adulteration in food and other products. Richards gradually expanded the idea of household chemistry to a more all-encompassing vision of "domestic science," referring to the application of expert knowledge to the traditional chores of housekeeping.[3]

As Shapiro explains in *Perfection Salad: Women and Cooking at the Turn of the Century*, Richards and other leaders in the domestic science movement were feminist reformers who saw the professionalization of housekeeping as a way to create more opportunities for women to teach and study in universities. Domestic science, as a rigorous and expert field of knowledge, also was meant to enhance the status of housework and thereby improve the social status of women more generally. Beyond these explicitly feminist aims, though, the idea that housekeeping could, and should, be taught by professional experts inspired new ways to meet the needs of a changing population.

In the late nineteenth century, fewer and fewer women were learning to cook from their mothers, either because they had moved from rural areas into the city or because they had emigrated from another country. Domestic science filled the breach, offering to teach women a systematic approach to nutrition and modern cooking. Much of the work of domestic science happened in cooking schools. Schools, however, couldn't possibly reach every woman who floundered in front of a stove. Cookbooks were an economical and convenient alternative to professional instruction and took on an ever-increasing importance.

The old cookbooks of the nineteenth century and earlier were vague and imprecise, suggesting a little of this and a pinch of that. This style would not do for scientific cooking. Modern cookbooks, beginning with Fannie Farmer's *Boston Cooking-School Cook Book* (1896), included exact measurements and step-by-step instructions.[4] In the spirit of domestic science, Farmer insisted that cooking should be informed by the latest scientific knowledge of nutrition and chemistry. Her cookbook reflected the broader spirit of the machine age: that precision, efficiency, and rigor of method would assure superior results. Farmer's influential and beloved cookbook included a substantial section on candy and confections in each of its many editions.

For women attracted to the ideals of domestic science, home candy making was perhaps the apotheosis of science in the kitchen. It required precision in measurement, temperature, and timing. Special equipment might be needed, especially the candy thermometer, which looked more like something to be found in a laboratory than in a kitchen. Encyclopedic cookbooks from the 1880s onward included sections on candy making, but candy making was also the primary topic of hundreds of specialized cookbooks. This helped create a sense that skilled home candy making went beyond ordinary or traditional forms of home cooking, and encouraged practitioners to feel that it was a very modern thing to do.

Virtually every candy cookbook from the period begins with at least an allusion to the perils of cheap candies coupled with an assertion of the food value and energy provided by wholesome, homemade candies. Mrs. Snyder's 1915 book, *The Art of Candy Making Fully Explained,* informed readers that "children have a natural craving for sugar, which should be satisfied to a normal degree, but all factory candies containing deleterious ingredients should be guarded against."[5] Another book published in the same year begins with the reminder that "wholesome candy in a limited quantity at proper times has an acknowledged food value. It is only in the eating of cheap sweets that the great harm lies."[6] For women with an eye on their household budgets, home candy making was also an attractive way to provide their families with the best foods, as Mary Wright pointed out in the introduction to her 1915 *Candy-Making at Home*: "By making our own candies in the home we have the assurance that they are at least pure and clean, and that they will cost us no more than the cheaper grades of candy."[7] Authors who described home candy making as a way of practicing economy and protecting family health elevated it from the fun and the frivolous to a more respectable and serious pursuit.

The irony was that at the same time some domestic experts were cautioning women to protect their families from the dangers of manufactured product, other experts associated with the same magazines and cooking schools were promoting new manufactured food products as the pinnacle of purity, quality, and convenience. Crisco, touted as an entirely "synthetic fat," was embraced as clean, white, pure goodness. Marion Harris Neil, an editor at *Ladies' Home Journal* and a teacher at the Philadelphia Practical School of Cookery, straddled both sides of the processed food divide in 1913 with her simultaneous publication of *The Story of Crisco: 250 Tested Recipes* (the first of many Crisco cookbooks created under the sponsorship of Procter & Gamble) and *Candies and Bonbons and How to Make Them*, an instruction manual that did not advocate the incorporation of Crisco or any other "synthetic" food. The Corn Products Refining Company promoted Karo Corn Syrup with a booklet of recipes in 1908, including a candy section provided by Janet McKenzie Hill, editor of *The Boston Cooking-School Magazine*. Cooking teacher and author Helen Armstrong, who contributed recipes for cakes and other sweets, lent her endorsement to Karo, which she called "a wholesome, desirable article with real food value."[8] Hill's recipes for caramels, fudge, nougats, creams, and more feature large quantities of said ingredient, also known as glucose. She did not comment on the fact that in that same year any sort of commercial candy known to contain glucose would have been branded "adulterated."

Culinary historian Laura Shapiro has shown how domestic scientists were closely aligned with food product manufacturers in the 1890s and 1900s; both embraced the idea that "technology was transforming food, and for the better."[9] This was certainly true for the new products like Crisco and Karo that were elbowing their way into American pantries and pots. But it was absolutely not true for that most technological of foodstuffs, candy. No teacher or expert aligned with the domestic science movement ever extolled the virtues of factory-made candy, despite the fact that it shared the same qualities that gave Crisco and Karo their allure.

Perhaps the difference was that Knox Gelatine, Crisco, and Karo Syrup were still ingredients. They were raw materials for the cook in the kitchen and required some transformation before they emerged as food. In contrast, candy came ready to eat, an artificial food that did nothing to disguise its origins. In the early 1900s, domestic scientists were eagerly embracing processed food as the product of modern advances that would improve America's ways of cooking and eating. At the same time, the demonization of factory candy and the elevation of homemade candy seemed to reflect the continued ambivalence about the consequences of the technological transformation of food.

Wholesome Candies

Pure, clean, and *wholesome* were the watchwords of homemade candy—in deliberate juxtaposition to the impure, dirty, and dangerous candy made in the factory. Usually just the fact that candy was made at home was sufficient to declare it "wholesome." But some recipe writers advanced the notion of wholesomeness to incorporate unusual ingredients and inspire some innovative recipes.

A 1923 cookbook called *The Candy Calendar,* published by *Woman's World Magazine,* encouraged mothers to make candy for schoolchildren to enjoy with their lunches that would fortify them for their "afternoon tasks." For this purpose, the authors proposed the usual molasses, butterscotch, and nut varieties along with several recipes making use of cereals, including puffed rice fudge, puffed rice brittle, and corn flake kisses. Mary Elizabeth Evans's recipes for simple children's candies in *My Candy Secrets* (1919) were mostly confined to conventional taffies like pistachio, peppermint, and vanilla, with one dramatic exception: bran taffy, which she explained as "a very palatable way to take bran, nowadays so often recommended as part of the daily diet."[10]

An especially intriguing use of alternative ingredients was proposed in a book I have already mentioned in conjunction with candy innovation: Mary Elizabeth Hall's *Candy-Making Revolutionized* (1912). Hall advocated an entirely new species of candy to sate children's saccharine longings: vegetable candies. Recipes utilizing vegetables were not entirely novel; as I discussed in chapter 2, the first two decades of the twentieth century were a time of wild experimentation with candy ingredients. But Hall explicitly connected the idea of making candy from vegetables with the broader concerns about offering more wholesome candies to meet children's appetites. Where mothers might be torn between their children's craving for candy and their own worries that the candy might not be good for them to eat, vegetable candy "offered an ideal solution of this difficulty. It contains sugar, of course, but the vegetable base supplies no small part of the bulk; consequently children may eat their fill of it and satisfy their natural longing for candy without having gorged themselves with sugar."[11] It is an appealing thought: eat candy to your heart's content, without all the bad effects of overindulgence.

The idea seems to presage some of the dietary innovations of our own day that are designed to get more leafy greens into recalcitrant stomachs: Jessica Seinfeld's cookbook *Deceptively Delicious* encourages feeding the family food "stealthily packed with unseen veggies," and Missy Chase Lapine, the Sneaky Chef, advocates "hiding healthy foods in kids' favorite meals."[12] But unlike these contemporary disguisers of vegetables, Hall wasn't really interested in using subterfuge to force children to eat more kale and spinach. In her view, vegetable candy was worthy in its own right. She emphasized the particular colors, flavors, and textures that vegetables might impart to confectionery. Tomato marshmallow, for example, is interesting less as a tomato-delivery device than for its delicate flavor. The portions of vegetable matter in most of the confections were quite small—one would have to eat the entire batch of such candies to consume a "serving" of vegetables, which doesn't sound at all like healthy eating.

Vegetables back in the early 1900s did not seem as nutritious a food as they do today. Many people were suspicious of fresh vegetables, which were often thought to transmit disease.[13] Even nutritional experts did not emphasize vegetables as something you should eat in preference to other kinds of food. Prior to the discovery of vitamins, the scientific understanding of vegetables was that they provided dietary carbohydrate and water, and mostly water at that.[14] This was the reason Hall emphasized the role of vegetable as providing bulk in the place of sugar, rather than a more positive valuation of the vegetable itself.

Mary Elizabeth Hall's "vegetable revolution" did not catch on, despite her hopes that both home and professional confectioners would soon be making candies the vegetable way. It may have been as much the idea as the actual candy that put people off; "Bean Taffy" does sound preposterous and repulsive. To see if it really was that bad, I decided to try Hall's recipe. It turns out that the candy is not such a crazy idea. Hall suggests using lima beans, which have little flavor or toughness once the skins are removed. And the taffy isn't actually all that "beany," since her recipe calls for only ½ cup of bean puree for 2 cups of sugar. I admit my attempt was not entirely successful texturewise, turning out more soft goo than toothsome chew, which solidified on the second day into an inedible crystalline mass. Nevertheless, before that happened the flavor was excellent: buttery and mysterious. One of my young friends pronounced it the best candy she'd ever tasted.

Hall was ahead of her time, but her vegetable revolution seems perfect for our modern-day sensibilities. Candied carrot rings, candied parsnips, and sweet potato patties with coconut and nuts would find, I suspect, an eager market in the artisanal food stalls popping up in every major city these days. Tomato nougatine would be delicious, especially if you didn't know it contained tomato. And maybe I shouldn't discount the nutritive benefits of the vegetables in Hall's candies, even in such tiny amounts. In the strange landscape of contemporary food politics, where ketchup and pizza have been contending for the status of vegetable, Hall's candies are certainly an improvement over your average Twizzler. It remains to be seen, however, whether, as Hall predicted, "the candy of the future will be purer, more wholesome, more nourishing than that of the past has been."[15]

When Mother Lets Us . . .

Mothers weren't just making wholesome candy for their children; they were teaching their children how to make candy too. One of the most charming of the candy cookbooks produced in this era is *A Little Candy Book for a Little Girl*. The little girl is Betsey Bobbitt, who begins the book with a serious dilemma. She loves candy, but her mother won't let her buy it because "'penny candies' were unsafe for little children to eat, on account of the cheap, impure materials used in the making, as well as the bright, dangerous colors used upon the outside, to make them look attractive." Full of regret and longing, Betsey continues to crave the candy so tantalizingly displayed in the shop she passes every day. One day, as she lingers in front of the penny candy on her way home from school, she decides that when she grows up she will go to college "to learn how to become a teacher of 'Domestic Science,' which included knowing how to cook just everything, the best of all being the most, *oh! most* delicious candies."

"Why wait until you are old enough to go to college?" her mother replies. "Wouldn't you like to begin to learn now?" Betsey Bobbitt nearly falls off her chair, and when she really understands that her mother is to teach her to make candy, she bobs about the room, exclaiming: "Oh! mother, may I really and truly?" and, again: "Oh! mother, I don't think I'll even want to look at penny candy again!"[16] Much candy making ensues, with recipes and tips given along the way, as Betsey spends all winter and spring happily boiling and pouring.

When Mother Lets Us Make Candy by Elizabeth DuBois Bache and Louise Franklin Bache (1915) was one of several titles in a series of When Mother Lets Us . . . books published by Moffat, Yard & Co. instructing children (and their mothers) in various leisure activities including acting, sewing, gardening, and cutting out pictures. When Mother Lets Us Make Candy is replete with cute illustrations of "candy land" and silly poems about fudge making and caramel that are meant to appeal to the juvenile reader. When Mother Lets Us Make Candy promises that candy making will lead to "a knowledge of the principles underlying cookery" as well as a way to share some "wonderfully good times."[17] The fact that it was written by a school "domestic science" teacher collaborating with a school librarian can only seem ironic from the vantage point of the classroom cupcake wars of the 2000s, which have resulted in the banishment of most sweet treats from many schools.[18] Today, When Mother Lets Us Make Candy would probably be called When Mother Lets Us Get Third-Degree Burns or When Mother Lets Us Get Diabetes.

Fudge, taffy, basic hard candy—these are the candies of the molasses stews and fudge parties of the nineteenth century, and mothers and children were making such goodies at home well into the twentieth century. I myself have fond memories of fudge and taffy pulls with my mother and little sister. But many of the cookbooks encouraged their readers to attempt more aspirational, complicated, and likely-to-fail sorts of candy. French creams, nougats, chocolate-dipped centers, and fruit jewels were candies that would impress a critical eye or stand up to comparison with a professional product.

Much Profit

In the 1910s candy cookbooks began to encourage amateurs to aspire to professional results. Mary Elizabeth Evans's *My Candy Secrets*, for example, boasted in the subtitle that it was "a book of simple and accurate information which, if faithfully followed, will enable the novice to make candies that need not fear comparison with the professional product." Another writer cautioned would-be candy makers on the importance of hewing to professional standards if her product was to meet with approval: "The amateur candy maker who wishes to bestow sweetmeats upon her friends at the holiday season will do well to study the designs of the best confectioners. Before beginning her work she may find it wise to purchase a box of the best styles and use them as models for tint and shape."[19]

Some women aspired to professional results in their candy making for pleasure. But others hoped that their skills might lead to something more. *"Dame Curtsey's" Book of Candy Making* (1920) was overt in its promise: "There is much profit in candy making."[20] The authors of *The Candy Calendar* (1923) suggested that "by reading the articles contained in this book on the making and packing of candy for sale, anyone may easily establish a reputation for good candy which will prove a source of profit at holiday times or the basis of a permanent year-round business." According to Ellye Glover, the author of *"Dame Curtsey's,"* "many a woman is making her living, and a generous one, too, by manufacturing bonbons that are known to be pure."[21]

In an era when there were few business opportunities open to women, candy making was a way for a woman to put her domestic skills to profitable work, although it seldom became a full-time profession. For most women who sold their candies, the income was small and supplementary. In her survey of major city directories from the late nineteenth century, confectionery historian Wendy Woloson found few women listed as professional confectioners and substantial turnover from year to year. Some women helped run their husbands' businesses, and a few did set up their own shops or make money selling home-produced goods to local drugstores or candy shops. But according to Woloson, "Very few women actually did rely on candy-making businesses for their sole support . . . Those who tried to rival the fine confectioners could not escape the stereotype of being mere amateurs or hobbyists."[22]

One well-known female success story in the candy business was Mrs. Ora Snyder, who presided over a Chicago candy empire. She got her start in 1909, when a devastating illness prevented her husband from working to support the family. Snyder started making candy to sell to the neighborhood children, and the next year she found a little peanut and coffee store that would sell her product in paper bags. Her candy was a hit, and soon she had her own shops all over the city. She was known far and wide for both her delicious confections and her savvy business sense. In 1931, Snyder was the first woman to be elected president of the Associated Retail Confectioners of the United States. At the time of her death in 1948, she owned sixteen confectionery shops.[23]

Ora Snyder's business success would have been remarkable on its own; it is even more extraordinary given how rare such success was for a female confectioner. Many Americans may have thought that candy chains with names like *Fanny Farmer*, *Fanny May*, *Laura Secord*, and *See's* (named for Mary See) were founded by women. But the reality was that these candy empires were built by men who used the image of motherly homemade candy (and sometimes even the image of their own mothers, as in the case of See's) to sell their mass-manufactured product. For the most part, men and women had very different roles to play in the business.

While the cookbooks extolled home candy making as the ideal expression of daintiness and maternal care, professional candy manufacturers excluded women from candy making

Mrs. Snyder's Candy Shop, Chicago, 1927.
(National Archives)

almost entirely. Male workers did all the cooking and shaping of
candy and ran all the machines. Female workers, who made up
about 60 percent of the total confectionery workforce in the
1910s, did the chocolate dipping, wrapping, and packing. A 1913
study found that 53 percent of the women employed in candy
manufacture worked as packers and wrappers, 25 percent as
helpers, 10 percent as supervisors, and 13 percent as hand dippers, the most skilled and highly paid of the jobs open to women.
The pay was decidedly unequal: 90 percent of male machine operators made more than $11 per week, while 96 percent of female
hand dippers made less than $11 per week.[24] Although a few cou-
rageous and savvy women succeeded in building up a candy
shop or a small chain, the big business of confectionery was ruled
by men. Group photos from the annual National Confectioners

Association conventions in the 1910s show a sea of coats and pants unsullied by any feminine flounces. I'm aware of only one major candy manufacturer owned and run by a woman in the first half of the twentieth century: the Nuss Confectionery Company.

Isabel Nuss took over the company in 1920, when her father, George H. Nuss, died and left her in charge. Nuss was a leading manufacturer of buttercream candies, most especially candy corn. George had gotten his start with Goelitz Confectionery, then and now (as Jelly Belly Company) a major force in buttercreams. In 1909, George left Goelitz to start his own company in Cincinnati. By the time of his death, the company had grown to seventy-five employees and a market capitalization of $100,000, a good-sized company in the day. Once Isabel took over the business, she took advantage of her unique position as a female proprietor by promoting her own image alongside the candy brand. The editor of *Confectioners Journal* asserted in 1923 that "the success she attained for the Nuss Company is an evidence that there are women fully as capable as men to perform the various duties called for in the affairs of the world." Even so, a biographer writing in 1920 took pains to note that although her business abilities might be valuable, she "still retains her interest in the lighter affairs of existence, and is greatly popular with a wide circle of friends."[25]

For a woman in the 1910s and 1920s, one of the obstacles to business success was an idea of femininity that excluded weighty and serious affairs that many in the day believed were the sole province of men. If a woman was going to be making candy, most people thought it would be better that she do it in the feminine and domestic context of friends and family rather than venture into the terrain of pants and mustaches. Selling homemade candy was an acceptable way for women to earn money because the commercial side could be made to seem almost accidental. Women were supposedly naturals at cooking. And women at the time were also idealized as having a nature much like candy: sweet and frivolous. Thus, if women could put their natural attributes to work by making candy, and they happened to turn a profit, they were still perceived as enacting a conventional feminine role.

Women's homemade candy was often endowed with symbolic and emotional value, given as gifts to friends and social circles to simultaneously express affection and display skill. As the authors of *The Candy Calendar* suggested, "For holidays, birthdays or for any other occasion where a gift remembrance is desired, nothing could be more acceptable or more appropriate than an attractive box of home-made sweets. Inexpensive in itself, it is nevertheless highly prized for the thought and care that the donor expended in its making."[26] One writer observed that "home-made candies are quite a fad now-a-days. The young ladies all over the country are becoming quite expert confectioners, and no money-making function, for the church or any charity, is considered complete without its home-made candy table."[27]

While no one would expect a professional confectioner to give away his product, women home candy makers routinely did just that. The high emotional value of candy given as a gift papered over the truth: making candy at home wouldn't earn most women a real living. In this way, sentimental and charitable candy making was similar to many of the other kinds of unpaid tasks that women undertook, from keeping house and cooking to caring for children and family. Women were working. They just weren't getting paid.

Home Candy Failures

Mary Elizabeth Evans was one of the handful of successful female candy makers of the early twentieth century, known for her glamorous eponymous confectionery shops located on the most fashionable avenues in New York and Boston. As a prosperous businesswoman she was the subject of admiring magazine profiles that described her rise from tragic beginnings to rule over a chain of luxury candy shops and tea salons favored by the finest families on the Eastern seaboard.[28] Today, however, there is no trace of her business empire or any mention of her in culinary histories or American biographies. Even her identity is difficult to track down, since she published and did business as "Mary Elizabeth."

Mary Elizabeth Evans got her start in Syracuse, New York. When she was thirteen, her father died, leaving the family in desperate financial straits, and her mother struggled to support them with a small grocery business. The oldest of four children, Mary Elizabeth pitched in by helping in the shop and then by making a few candies to sell at local bazaars and fairs. The candy was so popular that she decided to set up a little candy cupboard in the student center at Syracuse University. She didn't have the money for a shop, so she called it the Help-Yourself-Booth and explained that customers should choose their candy and put their money in the till.

Mary Elizabeth's reputation as a fine candy maker grew, and by the age of twenty she was the proprietor of a three-story factory with some two dozen employees. Her candy was known for its superior quality (and commensurate high price), which appealed to Syracuse society types. Her elite clientele persuaded her to decamp with them to Newport, and from there to ever grander candy and teashops in the major cities.

In the years before and after the First World War, Mary Elizabeth was one of the most revered names in fine candies. Her professional ambition was matched by a strong sense of civic responsibility. During the wartime sugar shortages, Mary Elizabeth completely abandoned her normal candy recipes to promote alternative confections that used fruits and other sweeteners to create patriotic treats. She also developed meatless and wheatless recipes for soups, salads, and savory plates, which she served to her tearoom patrons to great acclaim. In 1918, she compiled her recipes and published them as *Mary Elizabeth's War Time Recipes*, to "help some folks who have the same earnest desire as myself to aid the Food Administration in every way but lack the facilities and time to work out their own recipes."[29]

After the war, Mary Elizabeth published *My Candy Secrets*, a more comprehensive introduction to home candy making. In her preface, she explains the necessity for such a guide, even as she gives a vague hint of the struggles she overcame to become such a successful businesswoman: "As much as I had inherited and learned as a child of candy making, it was not enough to save me many trials and sad mistakes when at sixteen I really began to make candies to sell. There was no book to teach me the things I needed to know. I had to learn almost entirely from experience— bitter experience. For a mistake meant loss of materials and time—a loss indeed in those days."

The loss of materials and time was, of course, also a loss of money, and although Mary Elizabeth was too polite to come out and say it, the impoverished conditions she labored under in her early days must have made such mishaps seem catastrophic. In a magazine profile published in 1915, she described one of the many calamities of her early candy-making days. One Christmas season, when money was still tight and the candy was cooked up at home, Mary Elizabeth stayed up all night with her sisters boiling and pouring treats for the holiday trade. When the work was finally done, they staggered off to bed, but not before turning off the furnace to conserve fuel. It seemed a clever way to economize, until they woke up the next morning to find all their candies ruined by the sudden change in temperature. Christmas, the biggest candy holiday of the year, found them with no supply to sell and no way to recoup their loss. It was a harsh lesson in the finicky ways of candy.[30]

Mary Elizabeth learned the hard way, by trial and much error. She hoped that *My Candy Secrets* would save others the mistakes and losses of her own initiation into the art. I'm not so sure such salvation is possible. Hoping to re-create some of the delicacies I'd been reading so much about, I signed up for a two-day candy-making class with a group of about twelve students at a serious culinary academy. With the instruction and guidance of the teacher, a professional confectioner, we attempted some fifteen varieties of candy. Virtually every candy of any complexity failed. The marshmallows were tough. The fudge was grainy. The coconut fondant shattered when we tried to cut it into pieces. The caramel was too sticky. The nougat oozed. The *pâté de fruit* was crunchy in a most unpleasant way. Despite what Evans claimed, our results most certainly did fear comparison with the professional product. By the end of the course, I could say only that I had learned a lot about how *not* to make candy.

The problem was, and is, that candy making goes against nature. It is the nature of sugar to crystallize; all the tricks and secrets of candy making are about how to delay, divert, or otherwise interfere with this natural tendency. Despite this inconvenient fact, the candy cookbooks published in the early twentieth century invariably assured their reader success if she assiduously followed the instructions. This is the optimistic spirit of domestic science: food preparation should be uniform and rational, with predictable and repeatable results. For some cooking tasks, this approach works beautifully. Your average fourth grader with just a bit of experience in the kitchen can follow the instructions for a basic banana bread or chicken soup and achieve acceptable results. Soup will be soup, almost impossible to ruin. Baking is a little more complicated to be sure, but something like banana bread leaves a lot of room for variation: more or less airy, more or less crumbly, more or less moist, it's still recognizable and edible. Candy, on the other hand, works only when everything is precisely right. Even with something as simple as fudge, disaster is imminent at every moment: a wrong move or misjudgment anywhere along the way means that instead of creamy fudge, the unhappy cook will end up with a grainy, runny, crumbly, greasy mess.

Even the cookbook authors most fervently committed to the ideals of domestic science occasionally admitted the futility of their instruction. Sarah Tyson Rorer taught women the new scientific ways at the Philadelphia Cooking School and was the editor of influential women's magazines *Table Talk* and *Household News,* which spread new ideas about cooking and housekeeping. Her *Home Candy Making,* published in 1889, encouraged her readers to start with a simple "French cream," an uncooked candy made from egg whites and confectioners' sugar. Unfortunately, this candy, although easy to make, wasn't actually very good. Witness Rorer's lukewarm endorsement: such candies "*may* be pleasant for home manufacture or for church fairs" (Rorer's italics).[31] And what of the good candies, the ones that required mastering the tricky stages of sugar boiling? Even the most hopeful home cook might put aside a book that continued with the disheartening observation that "the mere following of recipes in candy making will not always insure success, as much judgment must be used."[32]

Despite the evident challenges, Rorer exhorted her reader to press on in the spirit of feminine mastery. "The confectioner's art is ranked among the first of the graceful accomplishments that belong to domestic economy," she wrote. "The tempting dainties manufactured by our first-class confectioners may be as daintily made by an amateur, but it requires time, patience, and much practicing."[33] To describe candy as "tempting dainties" was, for Rorer and her peers, the highest compliment one could bestow on an item of food. The word *dainty* at the turn of the twentieth century connoted a more complex array of meanings and associations than it does today. A twenty-first-century reader is likely to take it to mean "delicate" or "petite." But for a culinary enthusiast circa 1910, fare such as ketchup, casserole, and canned meat could also be "dainty." The idea was to prepare (and often disguise) food attractively and artfully, and to allow for a certain delicacy when transporting the food from plate to mouth.[34]

Candy itself, as a food entirely constructed by artifice, might seem the ideal substance for the achievement of daintiness. Professionally made candy was, almost by definition, dainty; the magazines of the era are populated by images of elegantly dressed women offering and receiving chocolate candy that promised to be the most dainty imaginable. Homemade candy did not often achieve the same aesthetic results. As one writer put it, rather gently, "Home-made candies are often too large, especially those which are dipped in another mixture, and are thus less attractive than those made by experienced hands."[35] For aspiring home confectioners, the cruel reality was that most homemade candy would be misshapen, crude, gloppy, and unattractive, the veritable antithesis of dainty.

Of course, the publishers of home candy cookbooks were unlikely to emphasize the improbability of success. Much more common was an appeal to the spirit of quick and easy, as in the case of the $3 Home Candy Making Outfit offered for sale by the proprietor of Goldberg's Fancy Candies in Canton, Ohio. Ironic that the outfit is sold under the name of a fancy candy shop, since the pitch for home candy making is the excessive expense of store-bought candy: "Why pay 50¢ to $1.00 a pound for candy?" With the help of this home candy kit, anyone can produce the "best candy" for far less. "It's easy . . . No experience needed." And again the tantalizing promise of profit: "Many ladies have started in business with [this] outfit."[36]

Professional candy makers who were not selling home candy-making kits or cookbooks, and who knew something about the difficulties of candy cookery, had nothing but disdain for this popular view of home confectionery. One remarked in 1915 in the pages of *Confectioners Journal*, "Those who are such fools as to suppose they can turn out kitchen stove candy as good as the cheapest sold by any respectable confectioner are soon undeceived. Candy making calls for skill and experience."[37] The author continued to try to refute the popular belief that inexpensive factory-made candy was cheap because it was poor in quality.

The truth, from the candy manufacturer's point of view, was that "it is cheap because it is made in large quantities and by the use of machinery." This was the ultimate difference between home and factory: the home kitchen could never replicate the economies of scale possible in the modern factory, nor could the kitchen stove and stew pot achieve the level of control and predictability of professional candy machinery.

The popularity of home candy cookbooks fell off precipitously in the years after the First World War. The few books that were published during the Depression emphasized (rightly) the technical difficulties of successful candy making. Women's magazines might suggest simple recipes for homemade candies at Christmastime, but otherwise the idea of making candy at home went into decline. Most women who believed the promise of "no experience necessary" probably labored over their kitchen stoves once or twice and soon gave up. And why not, when what could be purchased was so plentiful and tasty? Furthermore, the improving reputation of commercial candy made home creations seem less necessary.

By the 1920s, more and more candy was being sold under brand names. Brands allowed candy to be advertised and promoted more easily and held manufacturers to a reliable standard of taste and quality. No longer were the evening papers peppered with stories of adulteration and poisoning. With candy, as with other new consumer goods, advertised brand names were becoming familiar, and with familiarity came trust. The brand name gave a personal face to the distant, anonymous factory. And in many cases, the brand name was an actual face: the label on a Hershey's chocolate bar, for example, referred not just to a brand but also to Milton Hershey, a larger-than-life figure who was well known both for business success and philanthropic goodwill. For everyday eating, making candy at home hardly seemed worth the trouble. An anonymous poet in *Confectioners Journal* put the contemporary feelings toward store-bought candy to rhyme in a poem called "'Lasses Candy":

> *How ways have changed since dearest grandma's time,*
> *"In lots and lots of things," she says, "it's so."*
> *When she was young and in her girlhood prime*
> *Store candy was a luxury, you know.*
>
> *"But," she says, "when farmhouse work was done*
> *And company'd come—just country girls and boys—*
> *They'd have a candy pull." I'll bet 'twas fun,*
> *In those old times of simple, homely joys . . .*
>
> *What fun 'twould be, if mother'd only leave*
> *Me have a "candy pull," like grandma did.*
> *With boys and girls to come and make believe*
> *That each was just a jolly country kid!*
>
> *But mother'd say: "Who put such notions in your mind?*
> *Don't let me hear such nonsense anymore.*
> *I guess, when grandma comes to town, she'll find*
> *Much better 'lasses candy at the store."*[38]

Candy in the Pantry

Although home candy making was fading from the scene, candy did not disappear from the kitchen. Candy had a new role to play there: not as something to cook but as something to cook with. The transformation of marshmallow from candy to cooking ingredient, which began in the 1890s and was fully embraced by 1920, heralded a new place for candy in the national diet.

The city of Rochester, New York, claims to be the home of the first marshmallow factory in America. According to local legend,

Rochester native Joseph B. Demerath was the first confectioner to dedicate himself to churning out marshmallows on a commercial scale. Traditional marshmallows sold by fine confectioners were made by hand with expensive gums. New formulas allowed inexpensive gelatine to be substituted for the gum, while the recently invented steam marshmallow machine (which mechanized the beating of sugar and gelatine into the requisite fluffiness) made it possible to produce marshmallow in hitherto unimaginable quantities. Demerath began his ambitious enterprise in 1895, and his factory became known as the Rochester Marshmallow Works. With his distribution network, suddenly marshmallows could be acquired in all sorts of candy-selling outlets. Other large commercial marshmallow makers soon followed, and by 1900 marshmallows were available everywhere.

Marshmallows similar to the ones we eat today were sold as candy simple. The typical shape was a sort of puffy domed square with a flat bottom. But because marshmallows were made in starch molds, they could just as easily be made in all sorts of shapes and variations. Marshmallow babies, fish, sandwiches, cones, fruit, rabbits, and the exceedingly popular marshmallow bananas were all mentioned in a 1911 analysis of cheap confectionery carried out by the Pennsylvania Department of Agriculture.[39] Marshmallows were dipped in chocolate or coconut, or combined with crackers or sweet biscuits to make still more kinds of marshmallow confections.

Marshmallows everywhere inspired a new entertaining sensation that tickled the fancy of everyone from Middle America to the high-society set: the marshmallow roast. Beginning around 1904, the city newspapers in Boston and Philadelphia and New York frequently featured stories of fashionable marshmallow-roasting parties. One such party in August 1908 brought a group of young revelers to the beach in Sea Girt, New Jersey. "A marshmallow party took a lot of young people from the Parker House down on the beach Wednesday evening," *The New York Times* reported, "and there, making a fire, they gathered around the pile of burning driftwood and spun yarns, roasting just enough marshmallows to give an excuse for the gathering."[40]

Marshmallow roasts weren't restricted to the seaside. At mountain and lakeside resorts in the summer months, roasting marshmallows around the campfire was a highlight of the holiday season. Summer society pages described the marshmallow-roasting revels at popular destinations including Schroon Lake, Groton, Lake Placid, Belmar, and Pinehurst. Another *New York Times* story, describing a 1911 party in Allenhurst, New Jersey, imparts the flavor of these evenings: "A marshmallow roast was given on Wednesday night by a number of young women and men from the cottage colony. They built a bonfire in front of the Casino and there toasted the sweets. When all the candy had been eaten they strolled along the beach in the moonlight."[41]

It wasn't just society types who were roasting marshmallows at the turn of the century. Across the nation, camping was becoming more and more popular, fueled by the creation of the National Park system and stories about President Theodore Roosevelt's rugged fortitude and fresh-air adventures. And anytime there were beach bonfires or mountain campfires, there were marshmallows—a perfect, highly portable treat for city dwellers looking for a brief respite from urban life, or for the growing number of children wanting to rough it outdoors. The Boy Scouts of America would be founded in 1910.

The Scouts quickly developed a reputation for being inveterate marshmallow eaters. In 1924, a *Boys' Life* magazine editor, seeking to distinguish the useful magazine article from the obvious, zeroed in on the matter of marshmallow eating as an example of common Scout knowledge:

Eating marshmallows is an exercise that every scout knows perfectly well how to perform, and reading a hundred paragraphs about scouts who burned their tongues and smeared their faces with marshmallow powder would not increase their capacity for marshmallows. But, if the Podunk Scouts discovered some new, novel and brilliant stunt for acquiring those marshmallows, or developed some method by which they could be placed in the mouth blazing without taking the skin off their tongues, or invented some automatic gauge that would stop a scout just before he absorbed enough marshmallows to make serious trouble in the department of the interior, that would be big news.[42]

The first printed evidence for s'mores is in a 1927 Girl Scouts of America handbook, but even without the chocolate and the crackers, marshmallow roasts promised delicious outdoor fun.

The years of the marshmallow's transition from specialty confection to national craze were also years of rapid innovation in American kitchens. At the pinnacle of the new "scientific cooking," according to Laura Shapiro, stood white sauce, the ultimate in making food appear dainty.[43] There was no dish that could not be improved by the addition of a coating of white sauce, a bland mixture of milk, butter, and flour. Recalcitrant meats and bulbous vegetables would lose their disturbing contours under an oozing blanket of blanche. And while marshmallow was perhaps slightly less versatile, to a generation of scientific cooks trained at the knee of white sauce, its white, bland appeal must have been irresistible. The versatile marshmallow presented the inventive cook with sweetness, volume, and texture, but no particular flavor or color to intrude on other ingredients. Just as white sauce improved every meat and vegetable, so would marshmallow improve every cake, pudding, and ice cream.

At first, the marshmallow incursion was limited to the sweetening of already sweet desserts. Fannie Farmer's *Boston Cooking-School Cook Book* included a recipe for Marshmallow Cake in the 1896 edition, yellow cake with a marshmallow crème in between the layers. Recipes for marshmallow cakes and marshmallow frostings were published several times in *The Boston Daily Globe*'s "Housekeeper" column in the early 1900s, suggesting that homemade cakes featuring marshmallows were a popular dessert item. The recipes added sweet to sweet: marshmallow's pure sugar hit would intensify the sensation offered by tender cakes and succulent sugar frostings. Shapiro shows how by the 1910s, the layering of sweet on sweet led to dessert innovations like gingerbread with melted marshmallow, ice cream refrozen with melted marshmallow, then topped with marshmallow, and cakes with names like Ecstasy or Heavenly Pudding, which she describes as a combination of "marshmallows, candied fruit, macaroons, white cake, gelatine, and whipped cream in one fashion or another."[44]

Nothing was immune from improvement by marshmallow. The line between dessert and salad quickly blurred. Fannie Farmer's famous Los Angeles Fruit Salad consisted of canned pineapple, grapes, walnuts, and marshmallows. Shapiro calls it "an innovation in sweetening that was remarkable even by [Farmer's] own standards."[45] And many marshmallow concoctions defied categorization entirely. Culinary innovations like cream-cheese-and-marshmallow sandwiches to be served for tea, or toasted marshmallows stuffed with raisins as a luncheon buffet specialty, fell entirely outside traditional categories of salad, dessert, or even candy.

Marshmallow eventually graduated to the main course. Sweet potato with marshmallow topping still makes its annual appearance on Thanksgiving tables across the land. In a 1930s variant, the clever hostess would surround a marshmallow center with a mashed sweet potato patty, roll it in crushed cereal flakes, and bake.[46] Other marshmallow savories did not survive the test of time. In 1927, the California Lima Bean Council ran ads featuring a dish of baked lima beans topped with bacon and marshmallow, with the promise that "you'll like them even better served these tempting ways" (plate 4). Even meat dishes could benefit from marshmallow, as suggested, for example, by Mary Chambers's recipe for Shepherd's Pie with Marshmallow Crust.[47]

As early as 1913, the grocery magazine *Table Talk*, which promoted new food products in concert with manufacturers and retailers, was pushing marshmallows as a regular pantry staple. In an article titled "Marshmallow Mixtures," Eva Alice Miller scolds the cooks of America for their narrow prejudices: "Many housekeepers consider marshmallows simply a confection, and make no use of them in their cooking. They are very useful, however, in many ways, and make a pleasing variety in the bill of fare."[48] Alongside the pudding and pie recipes, Miller included instructions for Marshmallow Omelet, Marshmallow Toast, and Marshmallow Fruit Salad, all of which would seem at home on a breakfast or lunch plate.

Marshmallow manufacturers also found more direct ways to encourage home cooks to stock up on their product. In 1917, the company that made Angelus Marshmallows hired an expert to develop a recipe booklet to include with each package of marshmallows. Alongside fudge and cocoa, the booklet included what a recent researcher has discovered to be "the first documented appearance of mashed sweet potatoes baked with a marshmallow topping."[49]

In 1919, competitor Campfire Marshmallows responded with its own multipronged marketing assault on the country's kitchens and pantries. Campfire began by changing the shape of the marshmallow to round, the better to cook with. It put the marshmallows in larger packages. It launched a new advertising campaign that promoted marshmallow desserts like jellies, cakes, and parfaits, and pushed it all with a new slogan, "The Household Candy, on Every Pantry Shelf." Their own cookbook demonstrated "the many uses of Campfire in preparing dainty desserts, puddings, cakes, etc."[50] (plate 5).

There was much to be gained in this push into the kitchen. As an admiring 1921 article in *Printers' Ink* explained the logic: "It is easy to see why Campfire keeps entirely away from the confectionery idea and bases its whole appeal on cooking and baking . . . Regarded as candy, marshmallows would be purchased only semi-occasionally. Looked upon as a cookery staple most valuable in the preparation of new and dainty dishes it can have a steady demand."[51]

The example of marshmallows inspired forward-thinking candy makers to ponder: "If marshmallow could be moved from the luxury table to the dinner table and transplanted there to stay, surely some other confection could be treated likewise. Then it could be extensively advertised and pushed as a food; its consumption would be multiplied many times, and much business and large profits would ensue."[52] Unfortunately, it wasn't immediately obvious how to go about transplanting other candies into the pantry and from there onto the dinner table. But by the 1920s, candy makers had a new plan for transforming their product into an everyday dietary staple, with no cooking necessary. Enter the candy bar.

7 ⊙ A Nourishing Lunch

Chicago, New York, Boston, Philadelphia—the major Midwest-ern and Northeastern cities usually get all the credit and all the fame in the story of American candy. But to visit the birthplace of the first "combination candy bar," the primal ancestor of Milky Way, Snickers, and all the rest, we need to travel south to Nash-ville, Tennessee, where Howell Campbell founded the Standard Candy Co. at the beginning of the twentieth century. Campbell was known for high-quality confections and chocolates, but the name that would put him on the map was hardly sophisticated. Together with his plant supervisor Peter Moore, Campbell came up with the idea around 1912: a mound of peanuts, caramel, and marshmallow covered in milk chocolate. They called it the Goo Goo Cluster.[1]

Like most other candies at the time, the first Goo Goos were bare naked. Campbell sold them out of glass display jars, and customers learned to ask for them by name. But there was noth-ing on that lumpy mound of candy to tell you that it was, in fact, a genuine Goo Goo Cluster. And to get one, you had to wait for Mr. Campbell or one of his clerks to pick a cluster out of the jar and wrap it up in a scrap of paper or maybe a little paper sack, along with whatever other candies you might have chosen from the enticing selection at the counter.

Around the time of the Goo Goo Cluster, few candies had their own wrappers. There were certain kinds of candy that required individual wrapping—caramels, for example, which would stick into a massive blob if they weren't each twisted into a bit of waxed paper. The problem was that adding a wrapper made the candy more expensive to manufacture. Somebody would have to be paid to sit all day twisting and folding each morsel into its own little bundle, which was slow and tedious work. Up until the early 1910s, no one really had a good reason to want to wrap candies anyway. If it wasn't necessary for practical reasons, candy went unwrapped. Penny candies were sold in bulk to retailers, who portioned them out of glass jars or barrels. More expensive dipped chocolates were also displayed without wrappers and placed by the piece or by the pound into larger bags or boxes when the customer made her selection.

All those unwrapped candies didn't mean the stores were squeaky clean. Not by a long shot. If a twenty-first-century shopper were to step out of a time machine into a grocery or candy shop circa 1900, she would surely be revolted by the filthy conditions. The customers of 1900 didn't feel that way at all. Flies were everywhere, but that was normal. As for dust, well, it was just dust. They didn't have window screens, they didn't have vacuum cleaners, and for the most part they didn't really care. Didn't care, that is, until there was a reason to care: germs.

The nineteenth-century discovery that microscopic creatures were the cause of many kinds of illness and disease filtered into popular consciousness around the turn of the century, creating a new mania about cleanliness and sanitation. All of a sudden dust wasn't just dust, it was visible particles that might be carrying germs. And the flies weren't just friendly visitors or mild nuisances, they were carriers of death. Public hygienists and antipoverty reformers sounded the alarm to warn the public about the dangers of flies and dust. Customers started seeing open displays as exposed and dirty, and therefore potentially dangerous.

In the 1910s, candy makers and candy sellers began responding to the new demand for hygienic candies by wrapping and covering as much as they could. Clean candy was the theme emphasized by the New England Confectionery Company in 1916 in consumer ads in *The Saturday Evening Post*:

> Who Touches the Candy Your Children Eat? Most of the candy you buy for the children is dished up into a bag while you wait. You don't know how many hands, possibly unclean hands, have touched it. Yet it is for some curly-headed little youngster to eat. Necco Seal-packed Confections are made in the cleanest of factories. They cannot be touched by human hands on their way to you. And they are guaranteed always pure, fresh and tasty.[2]

The Necco "seal pack" was very reassuring: no dirty shopkeeper would paw these candies before an innocent child popped them in his eager mouth. But part of the reassurance also was the name brand Necco. The New England Confectionery Company was one of the first candy manufacturers to advertise heavily in popular magazines for a national market. Putting its candy in a wrapped package, and putting its name on the package, were important steps in building those relationships we so much take for granted today: brand awareness, brand reputation, and brand loyalty. Wrappers transformed cheap generic candies into brand-name commodities. And brand names meant growth, in the form of bigger distribution, wider markets, and more sales. Wrapping, branding, and advertising were what transformed the generic 1850s catalog of candy sticks and gumdrops into the twentieth-century candy lexicon of Necco Wafers and Hershey bars.

Snirkles? Damfino.

Milton Hershey was far ahead of the crowd when it came to wrappers and branding. Maybe it was because he'd gotten his start in caramels, a candy that couldn't be sold unwrapped. When he decided to sell the first ever American-made milk chocolate bar, he knew from the start that the bar would be wrapped, and that it would have the Hershey name on it. This was in 1900, well before the 1913 advent of wrapping machines, so all the early Hershey bars were wrapped by hand. But Milton Hershey knew that quality wasn't enough. He wasn't just selling chocolate; he was selling the Hershey name. And he was good at it; the Hershey Chocolate Company would ring out the twentieth century as one of the biggest candy manufacturers in the world.

Hershey first started working with chocolate in the early 1890s, after he saw German-made machinery in action at the 1893 Columbian Exposition in Chicago. His first idea was just to make chocolate to coat his caramels, but the popularity of "sweet chocolate" novelties convinced him to put more and more of his workers on the chocolate line. Soon he was selling chocolate cigars, fans, cigarettes, and other specialties, all in very attractive packaging that imitated European styles. These chocolate candies were all what we would call "dark chocolate," sweetened with sugar and flavored with some spice or essence, usually vanilla. Good, but not as good as milk chocolate.

To the American palate of the 1890s, milk chocolate was much tastier and more desirable than dark. Nevertheless, most Americans of that era didn't eat it. The technique for making milk chocolate was a closely guarded European secret, and all milk chocolate was imported and expensive. Although it seems like an obvious pairing, the chemistry of combining milk with chocolate turns out to be pretty tricky, since chocolate is mostly fat and milk is mostly water (to get an idea of the problem facing aspiring milk chocolate makers, drop a spoonful of butter into a glass of water and shake it up). Many had struggled with how to get the milk into the chocolate in solid form, but it wasn't until 1876 that a Swiss chemist hit on a formula using condensed milk instead of fresh. Unfortunately for the chocolate-loving masses, the Swiss weren't telling their trade secret, and nobody else could figure it out.

Until Milton Hershey, that is. Hershey had been making caramels with milk for years. He took his know-how into the workshop, and after years of trial and more than a few rancid batches of chocolate sludge, he discovered his own technique for manufacturing milk chocolate on a commercial scale. His first milk chocolate bars hit the market in 1899; in 1900, he sold his caramel business and committed himself to the chocolate future.[3]

In addition to his chocolate-making talents, Hershey had an extraordinary instinct for mass marketing. He set his price at five cents—solid, quality chocolate would be affordable for everyone—and decided that Hershey bars should be available everywhere, not just in the drugstores and candy shops that were the typical outlets but also in luncheonettes and newsstands, groceries and bus terminals, and anywhere else people might hanker for a bite of chocolate. Every Hershey chocolate bar bore the same style label, instantly recognizable, emblazoned with HERSHEY'S in big, bold letters. Legend had it that whenever Milton Hershey spied one of his wrappers littered on the ground, he would make sure it was flipped right side up so that the Hershey name would show. Hershey's chocolate bars were an instant success; by 1907, annual sales were approaching a mind-boggling $2 million.[4]

Through the 1910s, hand-wrapped chocolate bars and chocolate almond bars were sold by Hershey and other companies. But candy shops were still just as likely to have a slab of chocolate behind the counter. Clerks used a little hammer to break it into rough chunks for the customer's order. There wasn't much else in stores that approximated the modern candy bar. The unwrapped Goo Goo Cluster was sold locally; its national fame came much later, in the 1920s, when it gained a wrapper and wider marketing and distribution. The Goo Goo was a sign of things to come, though. Candy was getting bigger, heftier. There were other similar bar-type candies being sold at baseball parks, too—almond nougats and chocolate-coated marshmallows that were sturdy enough to pass along the bleachers.[5] But it wasn't until the soldiers came home at the conclusion of the First World War that candy bars—full portions, individually wrapped— would really take off as a popular and ubiquitous everyday food.

During the war, every soldier had been issued at least one of the one-ounce wrapped bars, known as "emergency rations," and just as likely, every soldier had eaten his almost immediately. On top of the official chocolate bar rations were the tons and tons of chocolate bars sold through canteens and commissaries. In training camps and overseas bases, the canteens were selling candy as fast as the factories could provide it. There was no time to weigh out bulk candy or count out morsels of penny candy. The preportioned, prewrapped chocolate bar solved the problem of selling candy quickly. To a soldier who might be called to battle or stranded behind the lines, the size and wrapper of a candy bar made it ideal for stashing away in a pack or pocket or under a bunk, ready for any contingency. When the troops came home, they were primed to demand the same kind of convenience and taste they had become accustomed to while in service.[6]

The end of the war ushered in the golden era of the candy bar. Thousands of variations were introduced in the years between the world wars. No one knows how many exactly, but in 1927, a Milwaukee printer who was churning out wrappers estimated that there were fifteen thousand new bars coming out every year. That did not mean there were fifteen thousand different new kinds of candy being invented every year. These bars were made by different companies, and they had different names, but there were popular formulas that were copied: nut bars, marshmallow bars, nougat bars—combine and repeat. Some were national products, but many more were local or regional with limited distribution. Estimates of the total number of candy bars introduced in this period are completely unreliable and range from forty thousand to one hundred thousand and up. The actual number doesn't matter very much. Whatever the figure, it was a crazy time in the candy business.

Although both American and British soldiers had eaten huge quantities of candies during the war, they didn't eat candy in the same ways once they got back home. The explosion of candy bars in the 1920s was a uniquely American phenomenon. The American trade commissioner in London wrote home in 1929 to warn U.S. candy makers that their candy bars would not meet such an eager market in Britain. He explained, "There is a popular prejudice in the UK against eating in public and, consequently, since most of the confectionery is consumed in the home, it is usually bought in larger sized containers."[7] In the United States, however, bar goods sold in individual portions totaled nearly half the market, and Americans were more than happy to eat in public. And what better food to eat in public than the candy bar. But which one?

Most of the challenges of producing candy in huge quantities had been surmounted by the 1920s. Machines could mix and cook and beat and cut and wrap at dizzying speeds. The new challenge was not in the factory so much as in the marketplace. Advertising was in its infancy, but already consumers were becoming fairly sophisticated about discerning products on the basis of brand names and packaging. For candy bars, even the simple matter of giving a name to the candy could prove daunting. Prior to 1920, most wrapped candy bars were just named after what they were. Mason's Candy Company sold Mason's Walnut Bar, Mason's Marshmallow Bar, Mason's Fruit and Nut Bar, and on and on. But by 1920, there were too many bars using variations on old standbys like *nut* and *roll* and *good* and *tasty*. Marketers started reaching farther and farther afield for a snappy, memorable, catchy name.

Most of the names were just silly: Snirkles, Cold Turkey, Nut Pattikins, Wild Oats, Toasted Waffel, Sunny Jim, Old Nick, Old King Tut, Sphinx, Kid Boots. Some teetered on the brink of respectability, like the punning Damfino. And then there were the jazzy names that were a little more suggestive, or a little more louche: Red Hot Liza, Big Dick, Jazz Hound, Fat Susie, Sloppy Sally, Fat Emma, Black Bottom. These slang names seemed to ooze from the dance halls and speakeasies. "This style of name perhaps will meet popular favor amongst the flappers and the cake-eaters," sniffed one upright citizen to the *Confectioners Journal*. "On the other hand it sounds repulsive to a modest and refined customer."[8]

The modest and refined customer wouldn't be caught dead with Red Hot Liza, not to mention Liza's pal Big Dick. The jazzy names aligned this new form of candy with a new style of living and approach toward fun that thumbed its nose at manners and etiquette and matronly dos and don'ts. Candy bars were designed to be eaten on the go, standing up, walking around. They didn't require forks or plates or napkins. Candy bars were an invitation to forgo the meal and the dining room and to gobble hand to mouth. The new candy bars pointed to important, far-reaching, and perhaps unwelcome changes in American eating ways. No wonder they were knotting the knickers of the "modest and refined" customers.

Meals, and Between

Today, it appears that our traditional meal patterns are collapsing under the assault of perpetual snacking. Eating between meals bleeds into eating instead of meals, with more and more foods packaged to eat hand to mouth instead of with plates and utensils at a table. Whether by choice or by necessity, perpetual snacking appears seamlessly woven into the hyperaccelerated rhythms of contemporary life: we're on the go, we're moving fast, we're in cars or subways or buses half the day, we work eighteen-hour shifts, we never sleep.

While the magnitude today is unprecedented, snacking is not in fact a recent invention. The word *snack*, defined as "a mere bite or morsel of food, as contrasted with a full meal," was in common usage by the eighteenth century in England and Scotland. The word didn't have such a broad popularity in 1800s America, but the idea certainly did. Andrew Smith, an American food historian who has written books on both peanuts and popcorn, says that "snacking—eating foods between meals—has always been a part of America's diet."[9]

Snacks in the 1800s might have included fruits, nuts, baked goods, or cheeses at home. Crowds at the fair, the circus, or the amusement park would have found vendors selling peanuts, popcorn, ice cream, and candy. Domestic manuals and medical practitioners might warn about the dangers of eating outside mealtimes, but for the most part snacking in the nineteenth century wasn't controversial, and few considered it to be something worth worrying about. Despite the availability of a limited number of snacking foods, and the acceptability of enjoying food outside mealtime on occasion, the snack did not displace any traditional meal. The real challenge to proper eating and proper meals in the late 1800s wasn't the snack. It was lunch.

The earliest American colonists organized their days around breakfast, dinner, and supper. For farm families, the meals were necessary fuel for hard work in the fields and pens. The rhythm of eating matched the rhythm of labor: big breakfasts before dawn, hearty dinners at midday, lighter suppers before an early bedtime. Midday dinners were hot, cooked meals eaten at a table, and required that both cooks and diners be at home to prepare and to enjoy the food. But with industrialization and the rise of cities, people began moving away from farms and going to work farther from home. Big midday meals made less sense and became more difficult. A new pattern of three meals began to emerge, a pattern much like our own. Breakfast got smaller, and the most important and substantial meal, dinner, moved to the end of the day when the family returned home and there was more time for leisurely dining. People were hungry at midday, but they were far from home, busy at the factory or the office or the school. There wasn't time to go home for a hot meal. There was barely time to eat at all.

Lunch was the shortened form of luncheon, both in name and in spirit. A few leisurely ladies still had their luncheons, with linen napkins and dainty sandwiches, and a few business types still settled into restaurant banquettes for afternoon-long "three-martini lunches." But for schoolchildren and most workingmen and -women, the point of lunch was entirely utilitarian: to stave off hunger as quickly as possible, in order to get back to whatever you were supposed to be doing. For those lucky enough to have a cafeteria at their workplace or a kitchen at their school, lunch might be soup or a simple hot dish. Most of the time, lunch was something that wouldn't squash or spoil, something that could be taken along in a tin pail or a brown bag and could be eaten standing up or walking down the street in a few bites.[10]

For those looking for lunch alternatives, the ideal food would be portable, sturdy, compact, filling, and easy to eat. And here was the candy bar, a substantial, hefty unit that was packaged and formed to be eaten in one go, the perfect innovative product for a new consumer demand. Hershey's had promoted its milk chocolate bar as early as 1903 with the slogan "more sustaining than meat." So why not pass on the meat and skip right to the chocolate? That was the plan suggested by the Knickerbocker Chocolate Company of New York around 1916. Its nickel bar, called Sportsman's Chocolate Bracer, was advertised as "two flat cakes of delicious eating chocolate, which can be eaten straight or between two slices of buttered bread in the form of a sandwich." What made this proposition feasible was the new food gospel: "Consumers eat it for a food as well as for a confection," Knickerbocker explained in an industry ad, "for it really has more food value than any solid chocolate [bar] for sale today."[11]

If candy bars like the Sportman's Bracer lent themselves to the sandwich treatment, it was only a small leap from the candy bar to the lunch bar. One company went so far as to give its chocolate-and-peanut-bar the very name. Klein's Lunch Bar was introduced in 1914 and sold for three cents, a pretty good price for lunch. One of its slogans was "Lots of Milk, Smooth as Silk, Eat One Every Day."[12] For lunch, one presumes. (Evidently Klein was on to a good thing; today Cadbury makes a peanut-caramel-wafer-chocolate bar under the name Lunch Bar. Perhaps in deference to contemporary American attitudes about lunch, which tend to be less tolerant of bald-faced candy consumption, the bar is not distributed in the United States.)

Klein's got into a bit of trouble over the Lunch Bar in 1917. The U.S. attorney charged the Klein Chocolate Company with violation of the Pure Food and Drug Act of 1906. The problem had nothing to do with the name Lunch Bar. Quite the contrary; if you were going to be eating chocolate for lunch, Uncle Sam wanted to be sure that you got the genuine article. It seems that the milk chocolate Lunch Bar was not in fact "a combination of Pure, Sweet Milk, Chocolate and High Grade Peanuts," as the candy bar label claimed. According to court documents, the candy contained undeclared sugar (!), as well as "a fat or fats foreign to milk chocolate." The U.S. attorney charged that this was imitation milk chocolate passing itself off as real. Klein did not contest the charges and agreed to pay the court-imposed fine. Evidently, the court did not find the inclusion of sugar in a chocolate bar to be a terribly serious transgression: the fine was $10.[13]

Klein got a lock on the trade name Lunch Bar, but other candy bars were not shy about associating their product with a midday repast. Goo Goo Cluster was marketed in the 1920s and 1930s as "A Nourishing Lunch for a Nickel." The Graham Lunch was a peanut-butter-and-graham-cracker sandwich, dipped in chocolate. The Sweets Company of America even marketed their popular Tootsie Rolls in a special pocket-size tube emblazoned with the word *Lunch*.[14]

And what else could you have for lunch? The ready-to-eat sandwich was an obvious midday choice. It followed that "sandwich" would resurface in the 1920s as a popular candy bar theme: there was the Denver Sandwich, the Manhattan Sandwich, several versions of Club Sandwich, and the Waleco Sandwich Bar "made from fresh opened cocoanuts between layers of chocolate."[15]

As delicious as a lunchtime sandwich might be, some people were still yearning for the pleasures of a hot meal, even as the midday hot meal was going the way of the crinoline. Many candy bars of the 1920s and 1930s made direct reference to the meat and potatoes of yesteryear. In 1923, Sperry Candy Company of Milwaukee introduced the Chicken Dinner bar with the slogan "Candy Made Good." "[It is a] name which suggests the best of something good to eat," an ad to the trade explained.[16] While the chocolate-covered nut roll did not contain poultry products or taste like a chicken dinner, it did supposedly evoke the essential idea of deliciousness and satisfaction. In the early days, neither in the ads nor on the package did they say much about what was actually in the candy bar. The innovation and excitement of Chicken Dinner wasn't nuts or nougat, it was the name.

Chicken Dinner was a huge success and spawned a whole family of succulent candies from the same company, including Chicken Dinner Junior, Chicken Spanish, Club Sandwich, and Denver Sandwich. As enticing as these candies sound, they survive in memory more for their lip-smacking names than for their taste, which—save the nut roll Chicken Dinner, which continued to be manufactured into the 1960s—have, alas, been lost to history.[17]

If you had a big appetite, the Idaho Candy Company was there for you with Big Eats. Hoffman's Chicken Bone bar might have seemed a little less promising than the full Chicken Dinner. The Idaho Candy Company also made Toasted Taters and the better-known Idaho Spud, which can still be purchased today by those who like chocolate-flavored marshmallow covered in chocolate and coconut. The Spud met competition in the Idaho Russet made by Dainty Maid, while Utah had its own Spud Bar from Ostler Candy.

The size of candy bars varied considerably. It was almost impossible to charge anything other than a nickel or a dime, so when the price of sugar or chocolate fluctuated, it was reflected in the size of the bar instead of the price. On the other hand, every buyer wanted more, so makers had an incentive to swell up their product in order to boost sales. This is one of the reasons so many candy bar makers went out of business; it was very difficult to master the delicate balance between value and profit, especially with sugar prices swinging all over the place, as they did in the 1920s. Five-cent candy bars could be one and a quarter, one and a half, even two ounces. As for the upper limit, there was no consensus on the appropriate heft of a candy bar portion. Several ten-cent bars topped out at a full quarter pound.

This was also the reason fluffy nougat and marshmallow were popular candy bar cores: more air, more volume, bigger bar. The Pendergast Candy Company was planning to sell its nougat bar as the Emma, but when the nougat puffed up more than they expected, the famous Fat Emma was born.[18] One version of the Milky Way bar origin story begins with the rivalry between Mars and chocolate competitor Hershey. Forrest Mars bragged about his creation: "People walked up to the candy counter and they'd see this flat little Hershey bar for a nickel and right next to it, a giant Milky Way. Guess which one they'd pick?"[19] Mars got it right; the Milky Way was one of the most popular candy bars of the day and would go on to a long and happy life on the best-seller lists up to the present day.

Most of these candy bars were introduced in the 1920s, a time of economic growth and optimism. When times got very bad in the darkest days of the Depression, though, candy bars made a real difference for some, regardless of whether they resembled a home-cooked chicken dinner. Don Gussow, the founder and executive editor of *Candy Industry*, recalled the 1930s as "the days when Baby Ruth and other candy bars, weighing a quarter pound, retailed at 3 for 10 cents. Baby Ruth and other candy bars soon became a basic food (if not the only meal of the day) for many people. As a matter of fact a quarter pound of Baby Ruth and a glass of milk was considered a very substantial, nourishing meal."[20]

Through the 1920s and 1930s, candy bars weren't just for working stiffs on the shop floor or down-on-their-luck folks making do until their next real meal. Candy bars were making their way all the way up to the executive suite. "In the U.S. it is often impossible for an executive to go to lunch," Joseph Nathan Kane, a journalist who also worked for a time as the export manager for New York confectionery manufacturer D. Auerbach and Sons, noted in 1928. "Either his lunch is brought to him or some make-shift is devised. Because of its nutritive value often a bar of chocolate is either the whole or a part of the lunch." This practice, according to Kane, was unheard of in Europe. It was only in America, fast-paced and forward-leaning, where "the tendency to dispense entirely with a mid-day meal or to eat only a light one" was leading to the new custom: "to eat a bar of chocolate in the late afternoon."[21]

Sixty Ways to Eat Oh Henry!

With so many candy bars clamoring for customers' nickels, dimes, and attention, there was fierce competition for market share. Looking back, it's obvious what made the difference between the winners, candy bars that still survive today—Milky Way, Baby Ruth, and Oh Henry!—and the losers—the thousands of short-lived and forgotten bars of yesteryear: advertising.

Curtiss Candy Company is best known today as the name behind Baby Ruth, but behind Curtiss is the less-known figure of Otto Schnering, a true candy visionary. Baby Ruth was so successful that by the time of Schnering's death in 1953, more than twenty-three billion bars had been sold. Schnering didn't come from a candy-making family. In fact, when he graduated from the University of Chicago in 1913, he thought he would make his way in the world selling pianos. But luckily for candy history, his piano venture didn't last long, and in 1916, he began a bakery and candy business and named it for his mother, Helen Curtiss Schnering. He quickly found success; within three years he had moved to a three-story factory and was employing four hundred people.[22]

He had a big factory and impressive sales, but no single standout product to make candy buyers keep coming back. A 1919 trade ad in *Confectioners Journal* featured a collage of wrappers for generically named bars like the Maple Nut Bar, Vanilla Nut Bar, Vanilla Fruit Bar, and Chocolate Fruit Bar, which, brandwise, seemed all over the place. And then, in 1920, Schnering found his footing with a new sensation: Kandy Kake. Kandy Kake was not cake at all but rather "chocolate pudding" and nut topping coated in chocolate. It wasn't really pudding, but Schnering didn't know what else to call it. It was "a candy with a new consistency, richer than marshmallow, fluffier than nougat, better than either of them."

The 1920 Kandy Kake launch was an audacious experiment in market saturation: "Here's how it took hold in Chicago," explained a breathless trade ad in 1920. "In the heart of the business district in a few square blocks, Kandy Kake was placed on 249 candy counters in less than three weeks. Repeat orders started the second day, and are now 100%—every one of the 249 stands repeating from one to eight times and still ordering. Kandy Kake will do it in your town too!"[23] From Kandy Kake it was a small step to Baby Ruth, a bar that was one part good candy, one part marketing genius. Schnering wasn't content just to advertise the normal ways. In 1923, he dropped his first load of Baby Ruth candy bars over the city of Pittsburgh. Curiously, the candy bars pelting down from the sky on parachutes did not lead to mayhem and destruction. In fact, the spectacle of candy rain was so successful that Schnering did it again, expanding his airplane candy-drop program to forty states.[24]

And of course, there was the name: Baby Ruth. Obviously, the name was meant to evoke the glamour and cachet of celebrity. But which one? In one of the most enduring and contentious candy controversies of the century, historians and aficionados have debated: Is Baby Ruth named for President Grover Cleveland's daughter, known affectionately as "baby Ruth" Cleveland? Or is it named for baseball legend George Herman Ruth, the "Babe"? The Curtiss Candy Company continues to this day to maintain that Ruth Cleveland was the inspiration for the candy's name and to point out that "Babe" Ruth did not achieve his legendary home-run record until well after Curtiss claimed to have introduced the candy bar (these days it's Nestlé that owns Curtiss, but the story is still on the company website). On the other side, baseball fans and those parties inclined toward suspicion of official stories suggest that no one around 1920 could have possibly cared about a baby who left the White House in 1897 and died of diphtheria in 1904. If Curtiss claimed the bar was not named for Babe Ruth, it could only have been to avoid having to make any compensation or acknowledgment to the Babe, even as the candy bar gained fame by association.[25]

To the relief of historical nitpickers and trivia nuts, recent archival discoveries appear to have finally settled the matter. The answer is: both. Otto Schnering was savvy from the start about the potential confusion and the ways he could benefit from that confusion. In a recently unearthed deposition taken in 1931, Schnering's attorney asks Schnering: "When you adopted the trade mark Baby Ruth in 1919, did you at that time taken [sic] into consideration any value that the nickname Babe Ruth for George Herman Babe Ruth might have?"

Speaking under oath, Schnering replies: "The bar was named for Baby Ruth, the first baby of the White House, Cleveland, dating back to the Cleveland administration . . . There was a suggestion, at the time, that Babe Ruth, however not a big figure at the time as he later developed to be, might have possibilities of developing in such a way as to help our merchandising of our bar Baby Ruth."[26]

Schnering wasn't content to just borrow Babe Ruth's celebrity for his own purposes. In 1926, baseball hero George "Babe" Herman Ruth set up his own candy company to capitalize on his name, and Schnering went to court to stop him. Schnering charged that candy bars called Ruth's Home Run Bar and Babe Ruth's Own Candy would infringe on his own Baby Ruth. The lawsuit was resolved in 1931, when the court agreed with Schnering's contention that G. H. Ruth was attempting to weasel in on the success of Baby Ruth, a brand pulling in approximately $1 million every month by 1930.

George Williamson, the man behind the Oh Henry! bar, is nearly forgotten today, but his success in promoting his product made it another of the top sellers in the 1920s. Williamson got his start as a salesman for a small candy broker. In 1917, he decided to try making his own candies and opened a candy shop in Chicago. By 1919, he had developed the formula for the Oh Henry! candy bar and went into full-scale manufacturing. His experience as a salesman undoubtedly influenced his business plan. He understood the power of advertising and the importance of making a brand name big and ubiquitous and memorable, and in the early 1920s, he moved aggressively to establish a national market. Twenty-five salesmen blanketed Los Angeles with Oh Henry! promotions. A huge electrified sign, forty feet high, reminded Chicago to eat Oh Henry! bars. Manhattan was studded with street signs and billboards for the candy. And ads for Oh Henry! regularly appeared in local newspapers across the country. By 1922, Williamson was operating factories in his native Chicago and in Brooklyn producing nothing but Oh Henry! full time, some five million bars per month.[27]

Copying was a huge problem in the 1920s. The most delicious combinations of ingredients were pretty well established. And if there was already a good version of, say, a peanut marshmallow chocolate bar, then there was an obvious temptation to try to sell your own very similar bar. Innovation could take you only so far. Names, colors, and packaging—the stuff of trademark and trade dress—were increasingly important, perhaps even more than the candy itself.

Once Oh Henry! started knocking it out of the park, the candy bar field got crowded with copycats. The worst offender was Oh Johnnie, sold by the Ucanco Candy Company of Delaware. It wasn't just that the names sounded strikingly similar. The wrapper had the same orange and blue colors, and the bar was essentially the same candy, if a little lower in quality and a little poorer in taste. But Oh Henry! cost ten cents. Oh Johnnie, on the other hand, was half the price. Williamson was not happy. So he did what any good businessman would do: he called his lawyer and sued for trademark infringement, claiming Ucanco was deliberately attempting to fool people into thinking its bar had something to do with the more successful Oh Henry!

Delaware District Court Judge Morris agreed: "Thus far the 'Oh Johnnie' bar had the appearance of being the same as the 'Oh Henry!' bar, save in size, price, and possible quality," his 1925 ruling read. "They were alike as two brothers of different years . . . It would be a strain upon human credulity to believe that such and so many points of similarity as here found could innocently exist . . . The only plausible purpose for the similarity was to enable the smaller bar to be passed off as the product of the plaintiff."[28]

The lawsuit stopped Oh Johnnie. But lawsuits were an expensive, time-consuming, and clumsy way to swat at the flies of competition in the Roaring Twenties. Here comes Oh! Jiggs. And watch out, over there is Hey Eddie. As quickly as the lawyer could fire off a cease-and-desist letter, another pesky copycat was springing up somewhere else. So Williamson changed tactics. In 1926 he announced a new candy bar called "The Latest COPY of Oh Henry!" priced at five cents against ten cents for big brother Oh Henry! "This new 5 cent bar is a radical departure for us," proclaimed an ad in *Confectioners Journal.* "Heretofore other manufacturers have made the imitations of our product. But, in line with our endeavor to be 'first with the latest,' we have decided upon the policy new, even radical in the candy industry—of making our own imitations."[29]

Williamson conceded that it wasn't "as good as" Oh Henry! At half the price, it couldn't be. But on the other hand, he claimed it was better than the cheap Oh Henry! knockoffs everybody else was selling for a nickel. In tandem with the announcement of the new bar, Williamson launched the Confectioners' "Copy" Club. The club's founding document was published in the November 1926 issue of *Confectioners Journal*, together with a space for a roster listing the members. Here I offer the text in full, as no summary could do justice to this witty attack on the trade:

Sometime ago when Oh Henry! came into prominence, there was such a rush of imitators that the candy trade, both wholesale and retail, was seriously embarrassed. Few were able to keep up with the daily growing list of imitations.

To forestall this difficulty when "COPY" begins to be copied, and also to engender a clubbier feeling among the manufacturers who copy "COPY," we are organizing the "CONFECTIONERS' 'COPY' CLUB."

The only requisite for membership in the COPY CLUB is the manufacture of a bar similar to "COPY" ... From month to month the names of the duly self-elected members will be published in the roster of the COPY CLUB in these pages.

By this means we hope to keep the candy trade posted as to who is copying "COPY" so that there will be no difficulty in identifying the clever manufacturers who have had the originality to make a bar like "COPY."

Candy bar business was, as this snarky ad suggests, cutthroat. Margins were slim. Williamson was committed to a quality product, but that meant selling Oh Henry! at ten cents, even as more and more bars were coming out for five cents. COPY let Williamson have it both ways, defending Oh Henry! while also competing for the lower segment of the market. COPY didn't last long and seems to have been advertised primarily as a footnote to Oh Henry! But COPY wasn't really so much candy as a weapon in the ongoing skirmishes over territory.

However entertaining, such squabbles among competing candy makers over trademarks—and there were many—were a distraction from the real issue: how to expand the overall market for candy bars. Although children bought and ate candy bars, the real money was in capturing adult buyers more likely to spare a nickel or a dime. Selling candy bars to men newly discharged from the army was an easy proposition. Selling candy bars to women, on the other hand, was a little more of a challenge.

Candy bars were rough and ready, quite a contrast to the fine chocolates in fancy boxes designed to appeal to a more feminine aesthetic. Fancy chocolates were sold as a luxury good, with an emphasis on quality and appearance. In the "quality" candy stores, the customer could first choose a decorative box, and many were extremely elaborate and far more expensive than the candy that would go inside. The lace, bows, flowers, and cupids that surrounded fancy chocolates on trade cards and candy boxes suggested that women would be the ones most likely to purchase or receive these confections. Such candies were meant to be exchanged and eaten for pleasure, not for sustenance and certainly not for "lunch."

When mass-scale manufacturers started selling preboxed fine chocolates, they promoted them as another version of more expensive fancy boxed goods. Early 1900s candy ads for boxed chocolates from companies like Lowney's and Schrafft's were single-minded in their repetition of a stock set of tableaux to illustrate candy eating: a woman in a soft gown holding a morsel of chocolate to her mouth, or a dapper man holding out a morsel of chocolate to a comely woman.[30] Companies like Lowney's promoted a very specific relationship between women and chocolate: women's candy eating might be pleasurable, sensual even, but it should also be dainty and private. No proper lady would dare open a box of chocolates out on the street; "fine" candies were for the drawing room and the boudoir.

So: How to get lumpy, ungainly, awkward candy bars into the hands and mouths of women, fully one-half of the adult candy market? It was here that Williamson's genius for innovative selling shone. A 1926 Oh Henry! ad describes the problem and offers Oh Henry! as the solution: "Oh Henry! has broken that old, old tradition . . . the belief that fine candies come only in fine boxes. For America's women have discovered that under Oh Henry!'s simple, homely garb lies a truly fine candy . . . a 'personal portion' that brings a new convenience into the eating of fine candy."

A lady's gloved hands holds a wrapped Oh Henry! candy bar. The gloves, the coat sleeve, and the dangling purse tell us that

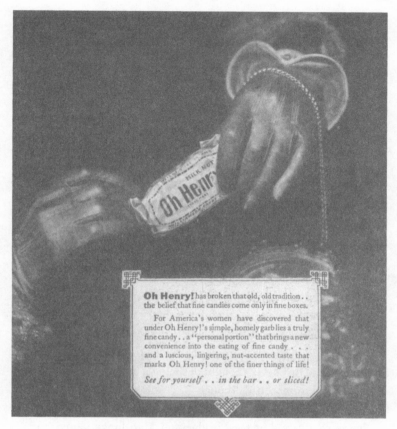

Oh Henry! has broken that old, old tradition . .
the belief that fine candies come only in fine boxes.

For America's women have discovered that
under Oh Henry!'s simple, homely garb lies a truly
fine candy . . a "personal portion" that brings a new
convenience into the eating of fine candy . . .
and a luscious, lingering, nut-accented taste that
marks Oh Henry! one of the finer things of life!

See for yourself . . in the bar . . or sliced!

Oh Henry! candy bar ad, 1926. (Courtesy of Leslie Goddard)

this lady is outside of the home, out in public. I think the image
is meant to be a bit scandalous: the woman's clothing is so refined, and the candy bar is, well, a little more rugged looking. But
if eating out of a candy box in public would be a breach of deco-
rum for this prim woman, Williamson is proposing that the
candy bar is an entirely proper alternative. The Oh Henry! bar is
a version of the candy she enjoys in private but packaged for
public consumption.

At the same time that Williamson was persuading women to

experiment with eating candy bars in public, he and other marketers were advancing the idea that modern women and men would need candy bars for their new modern lifestyles. Candy bar ads from the early 1920s are full of active, sporty bodies in light, modern clothing. Billboards and magazine ads would set the scene of golf, tennis, picnics, and auto touring as popular venues for a candy bar break.

But Williamson wasn't satisfied with getting more women to eat his candy bar outdoors or away from home. He took out ads in major national magazines promoting a new idea: slice the bar into pieces and serve them on a dainty platter to your guests. In 1924, Williamson introduced Oh Henry! to the women's home market with this ad, published in *Ladies' Home Journal* and other women's magazines:

> "Oh," cried Laura, surprised, "it's Oh Henry!, isn't it? Sliced! Well, I wonder who ever thought of that!"
>
> Oh Henry! was no stranger to Laura. Many a time, motoring, golfing, at the seashore, she had eaten this famous candy... but she had just never thought of slicing it at home.
>
> Other women had, though . . . women in Chicago. Two years ago, we found them slicing and serving Oh Henry! as a home candy, and at teas, bridge and Mah-Jongg games and other informal affairs. And so, in many, many homes, you will find sliced Oh Henry! as often as chocolates.

It was a brilliant reversal of the candy bar's past. Before candy bars came along, chocolate-dipped centers came from a box bought by the pound, little bites displayed proudly on the sideboard or coffee table. The ten-cent Oh Henry!, weighing in at three ounces, would have dwarfed these nibbles and looked decidedly undainty. Slicing the Oh Henry! to eat at home shrunk the bar back down to feminine proportions. Ladies in gloves and hats might not feel comfortable walking down the street gnaw-

Sliced Oh Henry! bar, from *60 New Ways to Serve a Famous Candy*, 1926

ing on a candy bar, but they could certainly enjoy the taste of good candy sliced into dainty morsels and served on china with silver.

In the story of Laura and the Oh Henry! bar, slicing Oh Henry! is described as a female innovation: women make this candy their own by transforming its shape and use. The ad suggests surprise at the discovery of what women are doing with the candy in the privacy of their own homes: "We found them slicing and serving Oh Henry! as a home candy." Is this what really happened? Or did Williamson invent this story to promote his candy-slicing idea? Whether the brain wave of a marketing executive or the native idea of a Chicago housewife, slicing Oh Henry! bars served the interests of both: more sales for retailers and a unique and economical way to express hospitality and modern domesticity for women. Williamson was not going to leave the adoption of this new presentation to chance. The wrappers on three-ounce Oh Henry! bars in 1924 included this information: "For Parties: Cut slices one quarter inch thick and serve on plates."

From the parlor, it was just a small step to the kitchen. In 1926, Williamson announced a major confectionery breakthrough: "And now, Oh Henry! goes into the kitchen!—opening a THIRD National Market in the 22,000,000 Kitchens of the U.S.A.!"[31] Once again, women led the way. "Possibly this may startle you as much as it did us, a few months ago, to find that women were using Oh Henry! in recipes," one ad reads. "We knew they were slicing and serving Oh Henry! as a home candy, but in recipes . . . that was new."[32] Williamson claimed that more than four thousand women had sent some seventy-five hundred recipes to the company incorporating Oh Henry! candy.

Williamson (or more likely his anonymous writers) selected the best and put together a little booklet: *60 New Ways to Serve a Famous Candy* (plate 6). Here, women aspiring to the most modern creative cookery would find recipes for cakes, cookies, pies, puddings, and ice creams enhanced with the flavors and goodness of Oh Henry! Dessert inspired many innovative recipes, like fried bananas with Oh Henry! dressing and baked apples à la Oh Henry! Breakfast would be sweeter if you loaded down the table with Oh Henry! Surprise Muffins and Oh Henry! Filled Doughnuts.

Alongside the typical sweet fare were some recipes of a more startling sort. Miss Daisy P. Rudd of Bennington, Vermont, proposed adding shaved Oh Henry! to a mix of pineapple, orange, grapes, mayonnaise, and whipped cream for a delightful and surprising fruit salad. Mrs. Strickland's Oh Henry! Candy Salad cut right to the chase, featuring the candy bar chopped with a bit of apple and celery, all slathered in a cup of salad dressing. Why stop there? From Miss Gracia Shull of Muskegon, Michigan, came the idea of slicing Oh Henry! over grated cheese on a soda

FRUIT SALAD WITH OH HENRY!

Originated by Miss Daisy P. Rudd, Bennington, Vt.

1 cup skinned seeded Malaga grapes or white cherries
1 cup diced orange, freed from pith and seeds
1 cup diced fresh or canned pineapple
1 bar Oh Henry! (shaved)
½ cup whipped cream
½ cup mayonnaise
Lettuce

Prepare and blend the fruits. Place in a cloth or strainer and drain, then chill. Just before serving add the blended whipped cream and mayonnaise and two-thirds of the Oh Henry! Serve on lettuce, and sprinkle the remaining shaved Oh Henry! over the top.

OH HENRY! CANDY SALAD

Originated by Mrs. H. Strickland, Watertown, N. Y.

1 cup diced apples
1 tablespoon lemon juice
1 cup diced celery
2 bars diced Oh Henry!
½ teaspoon salt
1 cup salad dressing

Pour the lemon juice over the apples and toss them about with it. Add the celery, Oh Henry!, salt, and half the salad dressing. Blend all thoroughly together, pile on lettuce and garnish with the remaining dressing and with a few dice of Oh Henry! reserved for the purpose.

In place of chocolates, serve Oh Henry! sliced

[34]

cracker and browning in the oven for a teatime snack. The Oh Henry! Sweet Potato recipe probably seemed quite obvious to a generation of women who were already topping their sweet potatoes with marshmallow. Pushing the envelope of the "deliciously good and novel" a little farther were recipes like Oh Henry!

Stuffed Tomatoes, tomato shells filled with a delectable mixture of diced tomato, mayonnaise, and chopped Oh Henry! bars.

No meal, it would appear, need arrive at the table without the benefit of Oh Henry! Whatever this might have meant for American cuisine, the significance for the candy trade was immediately obvious: "It means FOR YOU a THIRD market for Oh Henry!," Williamson crowed in *Confectioners Journal*, "a THIRD way to sell Oh Henry! in bigger quantities than ever . . . 3 to 6 bars instead of one!"[33] How many housewives actually cooked with Oh Henry! recipes, we can't know. But like the marshmallow before, Oh Henry! was making a fair bid to be stocked as a pantry staple. *60 New Ways to Serve a Famous Candy* staked a claim that not only the Oh Henry! bar but all kinds of candy could be served all kinds of ways. Candy bars for lunch was the least of it. Candy was food—for everyone, everywhere.

But there were a few people refusing to jump on the bandwagon. Not everybody was getting the message about the food value of candy. In fact, according to a 1929 study commissioned by the Sugar Institute, while men were happily chomping on their Oh Henry! and Baby Ruth bars, many women continued to cling to what seemed to be old-fashioned, ill-informed ideas about the bad effects of candy and sugar. The Sugar Institute and the National Confectioners Association were equally dismayed to learn that mothers continued to believe that "sugar and candy were bad for children" and that "candy decayed the teeth." Despite two decades of "modern" nutritional and medical experts insisting the contrary, and a growing sophistication in candy advertising, somehow those stubborn mothers still weren't convinced. Worse news: the familiar maternal complaints against candy were now being joined by a new worry, one specific to the fast-paced lifestyles and trim-fitting fashions of the 1920s. Women were convinced that "sugar was the principal, if not the sole producer of fat, and that to eat sweets in any form meant to hazard a slim, boyish figure."[34] Or to put it bluntly: candy makes you fat.

8 ⊚ Fattening

It's just something you know as a fact: the sky is blue, grass is green, and candy makes you fat. Even philosophers know it to be true, or at least that is the conclusion I've reached after discovering that the proposition "candy is fattening" appears with surprising frequency in mathematical and philosophical textbooks. For example, to illustrate the form of deductive reasoning known as syllogism, we have from a 2012 mathematics textbook: "All candy is fattening. All candy is delicious. Therefore, all fattening food is delicious."[1]

Who could argue with logic like that? It seems obvious today, but it wasn't always so. One hundred years ago, there was a range of opinion on whether or not candy was fattening. And even for those who thought candy was fattening, that didn't automatically lead to the conclusion that candy was such a bad thing.

In the years before the First World War, an era innocent of the idea of obesity as a potential national crisis, medical authorities tended to be neutral or even positive about the fattening qualities of candy. One expert in 1912 urged his patients to eat candy in the winter months to stay warm. In a prescription that would be utterly incomprehensible today, this doctor reminded his audience that "candy is fattening and is healthful, used in moderation."[2]

From Germany came stories of a medical spa that offered chocolate as curative: "The patients eat and drink cocoa and chocolate all the time, while they rest, admire the scenery, gossip and grow fatter every day." The tale of this delightful retreat was published without attribution in a 1914 issue of *Confectioners Journal*. It may have been all a fantasy: the account included neither the name of the village nor the name of the spa. But there was an undeniable appeal to the idea that those made unhappy by their gaunt figures and bony frames could enjoy a chocolate fattening in "just the right places, settling in the hands, the neck and shoulders, making the fair patient prettier and plumper all the time."[3]

Sadly for chocolate lovers, the chocolate cure and the condition it meant to remedy reflected a view of beauty and the body that was already waning. In the nineteenth century, soft curves and rounded figures were desirable feminine attributes, while masculine girth was a sign of power and wealth. To be at "the desired weight" in an era of poor public health and unreliable food supplies announced that one had staved off the thinness caused by disease or lack of food. But times were changing. Worries about being underweight were fading, and fears of becoming overweight were creeping in. Between about 1917 and 1920, diet advice books gave equal attention to underweight and overweight.[4] But in the 1920s and 1930s, the balance shifted decidedly. One observer noted in 1935 that "since the World War one of the major concerns of the women of America—as well as some of the men—has been how to get thin and stay thin, and usually no sacrifice has been considered too great that would accomplish this end."[5]

For both men and women, appearance mattered like never before. It was the era of the image: new technologies of photography and then motion pictures brought heightened attention to the look and shape of bodies. The personal scale, first patented in the United States in 1916 and in widespread use by the 1920s, made it possible to "watch your weight" just as you could watch your reflection in the mirror. Even before the war, Americans were paying more attention to the shapes of their bodies. A 1914 *Delineator* magazine article counseled its readers: "This is the age of the figure. The face alone, no matter how pretty, counts for nothing unless the body is straight and yielding as every young girl's."[6]

Women after the First World War were beginning to enjoy a range of freedoms unimagined by their mothers: freedom to vote, to go to college, to work in an office or launch a profession, to experiment with sex and alcohol, to smoke. The new freedoms were matched by a new kind of female body ideal, one that was more boyish and androgynous. By the 1920s, the corseted hourglass figures and the long petticoated skirts that were the last inheritance from the Victorian era were out of style. The new look was modern and simple, with less decoration and less yardage. Hair was bobbed short, and so was the skirt. Legs and arms were uncovered to degrees previously unimaginable. The beauties depicted in Hollywood films and Madison Avenue ads were wispy and slender. The youthful flappers defined a new style: flat chested, straight hipped, the very antithesis of feminine curvaceousness. Men's ideal body shape was becoming more slender as well, but the dramatic changes in women's fashions, coupled with a traditional emphasis on the importance of appearance for women, put much more pressure on them to conform to slimmer, flatter fashions.[7]

The new style put women on a collision course with their bodies. Pressure to attain the slender, boyish body came from every side: advertising, movies, magazines, friends, even doctors, who had begun to warn of the dangers of being overweight. Women who were worried about their figures and confused about how to battle the curvy tendencies of their bodies were an easy target for a booming weight-loss industry. Women's magazines in the 1920s were bursting with ads that promised surefire results if the reader would only bathe with Every Woman's Flesh Reducer or Lesser Slim Figure Bath; vibrate the tummy with the Battle Creek Health Builder or pummel the muscles with Hemp Bodi-Massager or Rollette; scrub with the Slenmar Reducing Brush and wash with La-Mar Reducing soap; or chew Slends Fat Reducing Chewing Gum or Elfin Fat Reducing Gum Drops. The schemes were varied, although the effectiveness (or lack thereof) was not.[8] There were other more extreme and dangerous remedies as well: dinitrophenol (a deadly metabolism accelerant), tapeworms, vomiting, even, as a last resort, the surgeon's knife (the adipectomy or surgical removal of body fat became a medically acceptable and popular plastic surgery procedure for fat removal in the 1920s).[9] But the most widespread and popular remedy for being overweight was the reducing diet.

Popular diets in the 1920s and 1930s ranged from the faddish to the frightening. This is the era that brought us such culinary catastrophes as the Hollywood 18-Day Diet (grapefruit and melba toast), the bananas and skim milk diet, the raw tomatoes and hard-boiled egg diet, the baked potato and buttermilk diet, the pineapple and lamb chop diet, and many more bizarre attempts to conquer fat. If seeing a smaller number on the scale one morning was the goal, such restrictive diets did work. Of course, as soon as the resolve to starve weakened, the pounds would come right back. For those desperate souls who persisted, near-starvation diets had some potentially terrifying side effects; by the 1930s, reports of death by crash diet were providing a sobering counterpoint to the breathless editorials and testimonials promising easy and painless results from food restriction. But despite the discomfort and possible danger, many persisted in drastic attempts at weight reduction. "Reducing has become a national pastime," a journalist wrote in 1925, "a craze, a national

Do you eat enough candy?

See what the modern authorities say about candy in the diet — why and how you should eat it

CANDY IS A FOOD! that's the first thing to know about it. Candy supplies definite needs of the body, just like milk, fruit, vegetables, cereals. Candy, in fact, furnishes several vital elements of the diet, without which you couldn't keep well!

So this is the word of modern dietary science—eat candy sensibly, eat it as a food—if you do this you will get the greatest possible enjoyment and benefit from it.

How candy fills important bodily needs

Candy is sometimes considered as an energy food only, because it is so remarkable in that respect. But candy is much more than that. In the candy shown on this page, for example, you will find: Proteins, carbohydrates, fats, mineral salts, and vitamins—all vital to health.

You doubtless recall having read that Gertrude Ederle ate candy for "body fuel" when she swam the channel, that soldiers, athletes and explorers use it for the same purpose.

Considered as a source of quick energy for the body—an extremely necessary food-function—candy is a near perfect food. Considered as a complex food, the source of regulative and building elements (proteins, vitamins and mineral salts) candy also has a place in the properly balanced diet.

Caroline Hunt,* noted specialist in Home Economics, has therefore recommended that candy be made a part of the "sweets" ration, which consists of about five pounds a week for the family of five. Candy may constitute whatever part of this is desired.

*Specialist in Home Economics, U. S. Dept. of Agriculture, Farmer's Bulletin Number 1313.

SWEETEN THE DAY WITH CANDY

Hallowe'en comes on October 31, the eve of All Saints' Day, an occasion for happy parties. Candy is always part of the picture.

A hint to women (and men, too) who want to be thinner

Contrary to the old superstition, candy has no unique fat-producing qualities. Such authorities as Gordon and von Stanley** even suggest the use of candy in a slenderizing diet.

Here is a suggestion: eat candy as a dessert, as often as you find it agreeable. Let it take the place of the heavy, rich desserts, which are difficult to "burn" as fuel, and which tend more to be converted into tissue-fat.

**American Journal of the Medical Sciences—Jan., 1928

Candy thus supplies the need of a sweet after meals in the most wholesome way. Serve it alone or with fruits and nuts.

How to use candy as a food

Treat candy exactly like other foods! The best diet is a *varied* diet and a *balanced* diet. Don't try to live on any one or half-dozen foods. Even milk alone, the most nearly perfect of all foods, is not enough in itself to keep you in good health. Don't make a meal of milk, or potatoes, or fruits alone—or candy! See that *all* the necessary elements are there in proper proportion.

Divide your food-budget like this, for example:

> "*About one fifth for vegetables and fruits*
> *About one fifth for milk and cheese*
> *About one fifth for meats, fish and eggs*
> *About one fifth for breads and cereals*
> *About one fifth for fats and sugar (candy)*"
>
> (Cited by Dr. Henry C. Sherman, "Chemistry of Food and Nutrition," MacMillan.)

A book for you

Dr. Herman N. Bundesen has written a scientific, modern booklet in everyday language for you—called "The New Knowledge of Candy." Beautifully printed and illustrated in colors. Use the coupon below, and send ten cents.

> Please send me Dr. Bundesen's Book on Candy. Ten cents enclosed.
>
> Name
> Address

ABOVE STATEMENTS APPROVED BY DR. HERMAN N. BUNDESEN

Mail Coupon to RESEARCH DEPARTMENT, NATIONAL CONFECTIONERS' ASSOCIATION, 180 *West Washington Street, Chicago*

1. A 1928 industry promotion asks, "Do you eat enough candy?"

2. Machines for every task: melting, refining, boiling, tempering, spinning, dipping, depositing, cutting, wrapping, and more. J. Friedman ad to the trade, 1923.

3. World War I sugar shortages forced households to cut down drastically on their sugar use, even as candy kept pouring out of the factories. Sugar conservation poster, United States Food Administration, 1917–1919. (National Archives)

4. Marshmallows make every dish more delicious, according to this 1927 recipe for Baked Limas with Marshmallows, devised by the California Lima Bean Growers Association: "Place several strips of bacon on top of beans and bake . . . Dot top with whole marshmallows, place under broiler flame until toasted a golden brown."

5. Campfire Marshmallow was one of the first brands to reposition marshmallow candy as a cooking ingredient, as in this promotion featuring "The Household Candy on Every Pantry Shelf." Redel's Campfire Marshmallow ad, 1920. (Courtesy of the Science, Industry and Business Library, The New York Public Library, Astor, Lenox, and Tilden Foundations)

6. *60 New Ways to Serve a Famous Candy* included recipes using Oh Henry! candy bars as an ingredient in baked goods, salads, sandwiches, and more. The recipes were reportedly submitted by ordinary homemakers, but they were "tested and approved by Mrs. Lily Hayworth Wallace, Food Specialist and Consultant in Home Economics." Williamson Candy Company, 1926.

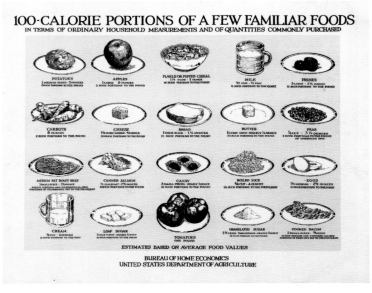

7. Advocates of the new nutrition in the early 1900s encouraged consumers to maximize food value by counting calories and comparing foods on a calorie-per-dollar basis. By this form of nutritional accounting, with food broken up into convenient one-hundred-calorie portions, a block of cheese, a plate of carrots, and three pieces of candy appear interchangeable. (National Archives)

Juicy ripe Apples are rich in Dextrose sugar

—and so is delicious Baby Ruth

The satisfying goodness of Baby Ruth is as natural as the pure foods combined to make this big delicious candy bar. Milk, butter, eggs, fine chocolate, plump crisp peanuts—and Dextrose, the sugar your body uses directly for energy—these are among the choice ingredients which give Baby Ruth its fine flavor, fresh fragrance and its real food value. How about a bar today?

CURTISS CANDY COMPANY...CHICAGO

By actual energy tests, a 150-lb. athlete (pedaling at moderate speed) can ride more than 15 miles on the **FOOD-ENERGY** contained in one 5¢ bar of delicious Baby Ruth Candy.

AT CANDY COUNTERS
EVERYWHERE

8. Advertising for Baby Ruth and other candies in the 1940s exploited the "natural" associations of dextrose sugar (derived from corn for commercial use but found naturally in other plants) to emphasize similarities between fruit grown on trees and confections fabricated in factories. Baby Ruth ad, 1940.

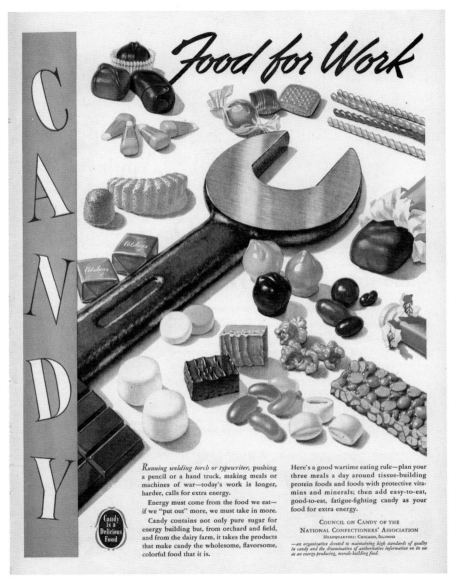

9. Demand for candy increased dramatically during World War II, as the U.S. military requisitioned huge quantities for troop rations, and as workers in war supply plants turned to candy for quick fuel. Advertisements produced in 1944 encouraged consumers to turn to candy as "Food for Work."

10. Every kind of work demanded quick energy from candy—even housework, as depicted in this 1947 ad.

11. Shotwell's Hi-Mac was one of the earliest experiments with fortified candy. The caramel-and-nougat bar claimed to have "better nutritional balance than an average meal." It included vitamins B_1, B_2, and D, calcium, phosphate, niacin, and iron—"nutrients you need to eat candy and still eat right." Shotwell's Hi-Mac ad, 1947.

152 calories in cake
with chocolate sauce
when you sweeten with sugar

70 calories in cake
and sauce combined
when you sweeten with Sucaryl

You can save a lot of calories by sweetening with Sucaryl

and you can't taste the difference

Sucaryl makes it easier for you to watch your weight ... by giving you wholly natural sweetness in your diet ... without one single calorie.

Sucaryl is the first calorie-free sweetener that tastes just like sugar in ordinary use. You'll find it sweetens drinks, fruits, and cereal to perfection. Cook with it, bake with it; use it practically anywhere you would sugar. Any Sucaryl-sweetened dish tastes just like its sugar-sweetened twin. Sucaryl, of course, is for anyone sensibly counting his or her calories, and for those who cannot eat sugar. You get Sucaryl in tablets or solution; low-salt diets call for Sucaryl Calcium. Abbott Laboratories, North Chicago, Illinois and Montreal, Canada. *Abbott*

JUST OFF THE PRESS!
Our brand-new cookbook, "Calorie-saving Recipes with Sucaryl", includes the recipes for the sugarless Sponge Cake and Low-Calorie Chocolate Sauce shown above. Also dozens of new, kitchen-tested ideas for desserts, sweet breads, sauces, dressings...50 wonderful recipes in all! Get your free copy at your drug store.

Sucaryl®
Non-Caloric Sweetener—No Bitter Aftertaste

12. The marketing of the artificial sweetener Sucaryl (cyclamate) played directly into America's postwar obsession with calorie counting. This 1957 ad was one in a series of similar side-by-side comparisons of treats like ice cream, pudding, and tropical cocktails that made it clear that with Sucaryl, "eat less" didn't have to mean deprivation.

13. This 1955 promotion was one in a series of Domino Sugar ads that favorably compared the calories in sugar with the calories in typical "diet" food like grapefruit, apples, and boiled eggs. The ad includes an offer for the recipe booklet *Keep Slim and Trim with Domino Sugar Menus*, promising a "safe, sure way to lose weight without losing pep, or giving up sugar."

Shirley Simkin's lost her sleek appeal
She never stops eating from meal to meal

Slim Sally Hayes stays light on her feet
She makes Life Savers her 'tween meal treat

The candy with the hole ... still only 5¢

14. According to this 1957 Life Savers ad, a dedicated candy habit was the secret to feminine fashion sense and sex appeal. Shirley Simkin in dowdy saddle shoes "never stops eating from meal to meal," while Slim Sally Hayes "makes Life Savers her 'tween meal treat."

15. A Post's Sugar Crisp cereal ad from 1951 presents the sugar-coated puffed wheat as a cereal, for snacks, or to be eaten "like candy!" Manufacturer General Foods had no qualms about suggesting its addictive properties: "It's so sweet and crisp you'll keep on nibbling and nibbling."

Now you can satisfy your sweet tooth. And still keep your sweet shape.

Figurines® let you give in to your sweet tooth without giving up your diet. Figurines Bars are a sweet, rich, and creamy diet treat. Yet they're only 138 calories a bar. And now for chocolate lovers there's new Double Chocolate Figurines—extra chocolate taste with no extra calories. It's another delicious way to a delicious figure.

Pillsbury

© The Pillsbury Company, 1979.

Try new Double Chocolate.

16. Figurines Bars solve the problem of guilty pleasure in this 1979 ad by offering a way to satisfy the sweet tooth without the caloric consequences. The woman's alluring pose suggests a realm of sensuous, private delights that will accompany this chocolate indulgence.

17. One of the earliest fruit snacks, Sunkist Fun Fruits boasts in this 1985 ad that they are made with "real grapes, oranges, cherries, strawberries, and other wholesome ingredients." What does it take to turn "real fruit into real fun"? Nothing but sugar, corn syrup, cornstarch, and a sprinkling of chemicals.

fanaticism, a frenzy. People now converse in pounds, ounces, and calories."[10]

The reducing craze of the 1920s turned food on its head. The desirable calories of the previous two decades were now seen as a menace to an attractive figure. Before the war, nutrition experts had encouraged people to understand calories so they could get more value from their food dollar; now, diet experts were exhorting the overweight to do the opposite, to understand calories so that they could avoid them. This put candy in a difficult position. It had been the calorie, after all, that had justified candy's importance as good food. Now all of those calories in candy meant something else: candy makes you fat.

Counting Calories

Lulu Hunt Peters was the first popular author to introduce the idea of calorie counting as a basis for weight loss. If you have ever endeavored to lose weight by calculating the calories of everything you eat, and restricting your consumption to some specific (low) number per day, you have Peters to thank. For today's Americans, the calculations are not so difficult (although the restricting is difficult indeed). We're practically born knowing about calories, and every package of food conveniently displays the calories per serving right on the label. But Peters's audience was far more innocent of that knowledge.

By the time Peters published her inspirational and educational book *Diet and Health with Key to the Calories* in 1918, the Department of Agriculture had been circulating calorie tables for several years. But those publications were for the most part directed toward professional audiences of health experts and domestic scientists. Moreover, the emphasis in the USDA calorie tables was primarily on economy and nutrition; the tables were meant to quantify the food value of different foods so that meal planners could make economically rational decisions about how to maximize the food budget. Peters wasn't worried about economy. She was worried about getting fat.

Lulu Hunt Peters knew the heartbreak of being overweight. Born in Milford, Maine, in 1873, Peters had taken an unconventional path for a woman of her day, completing medical training at the University of California at Berkeley in 1909.[11] But despite, or perhaps because of, her success in a field dominated by men, she was acutely self-conscious of her own feminine body and particularly her failure to achieve the slender ideal.

"It is not in vain that all my life I have had to fight the too, too solid," Peters confessed to her readers in *Diet and Health*. "Why, I can remember when I was a child I was always being consoled by being told that I would outgrow it, and that when I matured I would have some shape. Never can I tell pathetically 'when I was married I weighed only one hundred eighteen, and look at me now.' No, I was a delicate slip of one hundred and sixty-five when I was taken."[12] Although she was coy about the details, she suggested that her weight had gone as high as 220. Peters put her normal weight at 150 pounds, but in her weekly newspaper columns she wrote frequently of finding herself yet again striving to reduce by twenty or thirty pounds. This was one of the charms of Peters as weight-loss guru: not only had she struggled against her own fatty demons, but she also confessed over and over her continuing weakness and ever-renewed efforts. (Oprah Winfrey became one of America's most beloved public figures in more recent years with the same formula.)

Diet and Health was a huge success. It was "the first weight-reducing manual to become a best-seller," notes Hillel Schwartz, author of *Never Satisfied*, a cultural history of dieting in America.[13] Peters's book was lighthearted and humorous, enlivened by stick-figure drawings that she attributed to her precocious nephew Dawson Hunt Perkins, "the little rascal." In a voice that was part drill sergeant, part smart alec, part mother confessor,

Peters encouraged her readers to stop making excuses and start counting calories. The book was just what a weight-worried nation had been waiting for. By the time Peters began writing a regular column for the *Los Angeles Times* in 1922, *Diet and Health* was in its sixteenth edition and would stay in the top ten nonfiction best sellers from 1922 to 1926. Her column, also called "Diet and Health," was syndicated nationally through the 1920s and was a popular feature on the "women's pages" of papers across the country; she was in that decade, according to Schwartz, "undoubtedly the best known and best loved woman physician in America."[14]

Peters described eating as an economic exercise in prudent planning. Each of her readers should plan a restricted-calorie budget, to be expended over the course of the day and the week: "You may eat just what you like—candy, pie, cake, fat meat, butter, cream—but—*count your calories!*"[15] Learning to eat properly, to reduce or to avoid becoming overweight, would require a new lens, one that saw through the alluring surface of roast beef or pudding to the calories beneath: "Hereafter you are going to eat calories of food. Instead of saying one slice of bread, or a piece of pie, you will say 100 Calories of bread, 350 Calories of pie."[16] (Peters's admonishment to eat through the lens of one-hundred-calorie units was an echo of a similar campaign waged by the Department of Agriculture for the purpose of encouraging more economically advantageous food choices; see plate 7 for an example. Our modern-day one-hundred-calorie snack packs descend from this novel perspective on food.)

Basing a reducing plan on the supremacy of the calorie heralded a new kind of diet that treated all foods equally. Popular manuals like Vance Thompson's *Eat and Grow Thin* (1914) eliminated foods of which many were avidly fond: sugar, bread, beer, butter, fatty meats, and others. The resulting menus that Thompson included in his book ranged from the dull to the depressing; Peters described this option as "a little meat, fish, and sloshy vegetables."[17] If this was reducing, the option of remaining fat did not seem so bad. *Diet and Health* was the anti-Thompson: by converting all food into calories and working with a calorie budget, the dieter could enjoy any of her favorite foods, so long as she continued to count—and limit—the total calories consumed. As Peters phrased the attractive proposition, "eat *what you like* and grow thin" (emphasis added).[18]

Peters's book made much of the new nutrition, with its explanation of calories alongside fats, proteins, and carbohydrates. But although the science-based rationalism of the calorie made all foods equal, Peters did not actually think this was so—or maybe better to say, she believed it and she didn't believe it. On the one hand, she asserted that particular foods were fattening only when they were eaten in excess of the body's needs. In this light, any food could be permitted, even candy. On the other hand she insisted that "the caloric value, and therefore the fattening value, depends upon the amount of fat and the degree of concentration."[19] This meant that some foods were in fact worse than others. Along with the calorie, Peters introduced another dietary feature that would shape reducing practices through the century: the forbidden foods.

Although forbidden foods did have more calories than most other foods, this was not the only reason they were forbidden. What was important was that the forbidden foods were temptations to stray from the diet. These foods were so desirable that no one could stop at just a taste. They would derail any attempt at calorie counting by leading the hapless dieter from one bite to the next, until the entire week's calorie budget had been blown in one glorious debauch. One could imagine a wide range of candidates for "forbidden" proscription, but Peters actually mentioned very few. Nuts were one forbidden food; pastry was another. But the worst, the most dangerous, the most insidious of all, was candy.

By the time Peters's column was appearing in national syndication in 1922, convenient candy bars and other wrapped, ready-to-go confections were within easy reach, no matter where one might happen to be. And for more refined customers, there were plenty of candy shops and candy counters to be found, with their attractive displays designed to tantalize the senses. One could hardly walk down the street without being assaulted by the sights and smells of delicious candies. "I know everything you have to contend with," Peters commiserated, "how you no sooner congratulate yourself on your will power, after you have dragged yourself by the window with an exposure of luscious fat chocolates with curlicues on their tummies, than another comes into view, and you have it all to go through with again, and how you finally succumb."[20] Peters sympathized with this weakness for the "fat chocolates," as she herself was also sorely tempted. But she continually reminded her readers that it was this succumbing to temptation that would thwart every effort to reduce.

In her weekly newspaper columns, Peters suggested some mental tricks for dealing with the constant candy temptation. To a correspondent who moaned that she could not withstand her daily candy cravings, Peters suggested that she "buy one of those little five-cent packages of hard candies. Take three or four out and throw the balance away—throw it away before you taste the first!" But even this small indulgence was too dangerous in Peters's calculation: "The best way to do [it] is to 'lay off' candy completely. One indulgence seems to start the habit again."[21]

Is candy habit-forming? In her column of August 25, 1926, Peters answered with an emphatic "I'll say it is!" Whether this was necessarily true for everyone, it was certainly true for Peters: "If an alcoholic longs for his dram any more than I have longed for my candy (and do yet, occasionally) I can appreciate his temptation." Peters's example of an alcoholic's longings was not at all coincidental. Despite her firm grounding in the most rigorous nutritional science of the day, she also was willing to embrace more tenuous theories about the alcoholic fermentations of candy, which could affect the body in the same way as alcoholic beverages. Thus, she cautions her readers, "Maybe some of us do carry around private stills in our tummies and it is quite possible that this may account for the craving candy engenders."[22]

Clearly, when it came to candy, Peters did not believe that you could "eat what you like and grow thin." Candy was the anti-diet, the powerful pull toward loss of control that would lead from one piece of chocolate to the entire box, and from there inevitably and lamentably to more miserable fat. As she put it, "When you see a pound of candy you would like, don't think of it as candy, but as a lump of fat annexed to your fattest spot." Much as she craved it—because she craved it—there was no place for candy in Peters's diet universe, not as a treat, not as a dessert, not in moderation. The only safe place for candy was in the trash bin: "If you have any candy around, and can't give it away, throw it away."[23]

Peters's view of candy as uniquely pernicious wed the new nutrition, with its deconstruction of all foods into a handful of nutrients, to an older idea of dietary moralism that we encountered earlier. Under the new nutrition, all foods were created equal: protein was protein, fat was fat, no matter the source. In contrast, nineteenth-century reformers like Sylvester Graham and John Kellogg distinguished different foods as having different qualities, both physiological and moral. Christian reformers in particular associated wrong eating with sin against God's creation, but for them, redemption could be gained only in the hereafter. Peters crafted a modern and secular revision of this Christian account, using the language of religious revival to exhort the overweight to work toward their own salvation in the here and now, in the form of thinness: "You are in despair about being anything but fat, and—! how you hate it. But cheer up. I will save you; yea, even as I have saved myself and many, many others, so will I save you."[24]

For Peters, wrong eating was tantamount to sin—not against God but against the waistline. Peters reflected a broader emerging consensus about women's beauty and fashion. Beauty experts of the day "preached a credo of self-denial: to be beautiful, most women must suffer," writes Joan Jacobs Brumberg in *Fasting Girls: The History of Anorexia Nervoxa*.[25] Peters herself was liable to fall, as she confessed in her description of her "chocolate cream debauch"—ten luscious chocolates downed at once. As penance after this indulgence, her dinner would be limited to fifty calories: bouillon and a cracker. This formed the basis for a new dietary catechism of sin, penance, and redemption: "Every supposed pleasure in sin (eating) will furnish more than its equivalent of pain (dieting) until belief in material life (chocolate creams) is destroyed,"[26] Peters wrote, with little irony. If eating for pleasure was sinful because it was fattening, then the pleasure of the chocolate creams was a cardinal sin. Redemption could come only through the pain of bouillon and fasting: banish the chocolate creams, sanctify the soul.

Reach for a Lucky Instead of a Sweet

With the roaring success of the candy bar and the general growth of the industry, candy manufacturers were slow to wake up to the threat that worries about being overweight might pose to their business. It wasn't until 1928 that the NCA organized an advertising committee to "meet the widespread prejudice against candy without putting the candy industry on the defensive."[27] And just in time. Lulu Hunt Peters could be easily dismissed by deprecating her credentials and denying her allegations. But while candy makers were busy blustering over the contents of syndicated newspaper columns, a much bigger challenge was brewing. The American Tobacco Company, one of the biggest and richest companies in the country, had a new plan for selling cigarettes. Their strategy was to attack candy.

At the end of 1928, a new slogan for Lucky Strike cigarettes was plastered on billboards, announced on sponsored radio programs, proclaimed from the pages of newspapers and magazines: "Reach for a Lucky instead of a sweet." Why? It hardly needed saying: because candy makes you fat.

A diverse and eclectic array of public figures, both male and female, including actresses, businessmen, athletes, opera stars, and dancers, were employed as celebrity spokespeople to offer personal testimony in support of the campaign. In 1929 ads, stars like Rosalie Adele Nelson, famous as the "Lucky Poster Girl," confided, "I'm a 'Lucky Girl' because I've found a new way to keep my figure trim. Whenever the desire for a sweet tempts me, I light up a Lucky Strike." Grace Hay Drummond-Hay, in 1928 the first woman to travel around the world by air, appeared in another, saying, "I smoke a Lucky instead of eating sweets." Johnny Farrell, golf champion, declared, "Pass me a Lucky—I pass up the sweets." The advertising copy was hardly subtle in its pitch for smoking as an optimal approach to reducing; accompanying these celebrity endorsements was the explanation: "When fattening sweets tempt and you dread extra weight, light a Lucky instead. The sensible and sane way of reducing—no discomfort, no trouble, just a common sense method of retaining a slender figure."

It was, as NCA president Philip Gott recollected, "war," a "bombshell dropped on the confectionery industry."[28] It was hardly an even match; American Tobacco was pouring millions of dollars into the Lucky Strike campaign, placing ads in newspapers and magazines, and on radio across the country. The NCA had a budget in the neighborhood of half a million dollars, raised by contributions from member manufacturers—enough to put monthly ads in *The Saturday Evening Post* but not nearly enough to take on the deep pockets of American Tobacco. So rather than counterattack and be drawn into a retaliatory war of candy vs. cigarettes that candy was bound to lose, the NCA took the high road, declaring outrage at the unethical tactics of Lucky Strike and undertaking a flurry of letter writing and podium pounding aimed at shaming tobacco into playing fair. George Washington

Lucky Strike cigarette ad, 1929

Hill, the president of American Tobacco, agreed to some minor concessions, for example changing "instead of a sweet" to a slightly more nuanced "instead of a fattening sweet" in some of the later ads, but it seemed an equivocal concession.

The candy company presidents leading the defense were not mollified, especially when Hill sent each of them a box of Luckies at the close of 1928 with the message "Best Wishes for a Happy and Prosperous New Year."[29] In a meeting with representatives of the candy industry, Hill was reported to claim not only that the campaign was selling more Lucky Strikes, but also that the confectioners ought to be grateful for the extra publicity for their own product. According to Hill, "The calling of attention to the sweets industries, by means of [American Tobacco's] pocketbook, has, paradoxically, resulted in an enormously increased consumption of sweets."[30] While it was true that candy consumption was showing a modest rise over the previous year, attributing this to the Lucky Strike campaign seemed preposterous from the candy industry's point of view.

In any event, the manufacturers were already sensitive to the damage being done by the popular sentiment that "candy is fattening." To some, it seemed terribly unfair and one-sided. "The belief [that candy makes you fat] has grown up because certain fat persons have been observed to like candy," complained a writer in *Confectioners Journal.* "It has taken no account of the contrary fact that a great many thin persons like candy and also eat a great deal of it."[31] Another writer in the same issue pointed out the lack of "painstaking and expensive research needed to make answer one way or the other." In the absence of scientific proof, confectioners ought to "state in their advertising that candy is no more fattening than other foods, and may indeed be less fattening, and no one can prove they are wrong."[32] Logical as these arguments refuting the "candy is fattening" proposition might have been, they were faint solace in light of the alarming spectacle of millions of dollars of tobacco money underlining the prejudice against candy.

In addition to the implicit attack on candy, the campaign pitted cigarettes against candy as direct competitors in the marketplace. As one observer noted, "Since cigarettes and candies compete for the spending money of the flapper and the young woman of fashion," the tobacco companies appear to have reached the conclusion that "it is good business to discourage the customer from spending her money on candy, and to try to get her to spend it, instead, upon cigarettes."[33] The spending money that might buy either cigarettes or candy was obviously not the same money that went to paying rent or putting food on the table. Purchases of things like cigarettes and candy are what economists call optional or "discretionary" spending. The idea that consumers might be choosing between cigarettes and candy was a tacit recognition of a fact manufacturers of both didn't want people to think about: nobody really needed either one.

The cigarette segment of the tobacco market was expanding dramatically in the early 1900s. Thirteen billion cigarettes were produced in 1912; by 1930, the total topped 119 billion.[34] Unlike more costly hand-rolled cigars, cigarettes could be rolled by machine. The machine revolution in tobacco had the same effect as the machine revolution in candy: more product, faster, and at lower cost. Even if the manufacturers didn't realize it, candy and cigarettes were in the same boat: mechanization and industry expansion had created a glut. Solving the problem of overproduction (or, from the industry's perspective, underconsumption) required creative marketing to stimulate new demand. Most people enjoyed candy; the expansion of the market for it was less about finding new consumers than about encouraging consumers to eat more candy on more occasions. This had been the objective of slogans like "candy is good food" and "sweeten the day with candy." To the extent that this worked, it was because candy was food, at least within some definitions. Candy as food could seem to be a necessity. The same couldn't be said for cigarettes.

If tobacco companies were going to flourish and grow, they needed to get people to smoke despite the fact that there was no obvious reason to take up smoking at all. Candy sold itself; in fact, Milton Hershey was so confident in his superior product that Hershey chocolate was not advertised in national media until 1970.[35] Even in the 1920s, there was only a handful of candy companies—Mars, Curtiss, Williamson, Life Savers—that attempted ambitious advertising campaigns. In contrast, tobacco companies invested heavily in advertising from the beginning of the twentieth century. In 1910, industry expenditure for advertising was around $13 million. Between 1916 and 1926, American Tobacco spent more than $100 million promoting just one brand of cigarette, Lucky Strike. With cigarette sales doubling and tripling, it was no wonder that anti-tobacco campaigners pointed the finger at "the nefarious power of advertising."[36]

In the appeal to the weight conscious, the "Reach for a Lucky" campaign was aimed right at women's lungs. Up until the late 1920s, cigarette marketing had targeted men, while "women frequently appeared in tobacco ads in rapt attendance to an attractive and powerful smoking male," as Alan Brandt observes in *The Cigarette Century*.[37] Even though tobacco wasn't advertised directly to women in the 1920s, more women were taking up smoking as part of the new liberation, and their smoking was becoming more socially acceptable. According to Brandt, the motivation for the "Reach for a Lucky" campaign was to "make Lucky Strike the cigarette of choice among this vast, largely unclaimed market."[38] The reducing craze had made many women desperate to try anything to be thin. This was the genius of the not so subtle message that candy was fattening but cigarettes weren't. And even more: cigarettes were not fattening *and* they could quash the craving for a "fattening sweet." For women struggling to attain the ideal "boyish" figure, reaching for a Lucky promised an easy solution.

Early in the campaign, representatives of several industries that felt unfairly maligned by the bad-mouthing of sweets wrote letters of protest to George Hill at American Tobacco, asking him to withdraw; when he thumbed his nose, the fight intensified. Industry leaders lodged complaints with the Better Business Bureau, and merchants sent out circulars and posted signs in their stores in defense of their wares. One chain of New York candy stores embellished its advertising with retaliatory rhetoric: "Do not let anyone tell you that a cigarette can take the place of candy. The cigarette will inflame your tonsils, poison with nicotine every organ of your body, and dry up your blood—nails in your coffin."[39]

The NCA's official position was to discourage such aggressive retaliation and instead to appeal to ethics and fairness: business could not grow when advertising stooped to this low level. And this was just the sort of thing the Federal Trade Commission, formed in 1914, was supposed to prevent. American businesses were legally obligated to compete fairly, which the NCA took to mean that companies should be promoting their own products rather than criticizing someone else's. A group of confectioners and other representatives of trade groups who felt maligned by the antisweets tone joined to file a formal FTC complaint.

The FTC was inclined to investigate the matter. The ad campaign used the glamour and popularity of celebrities to burnish the image of Lucky Strike; but were all these celebrities really reaching for a Lucky? Thirty years later, NCA president Philip Gott called it "the most far-fetched testimonial advertising ever seen."[40] It was the testimonials more than anything else that forced American Tobacco into settlement with the FTC. Government investigators tracked down the celebrities whose enthusiastic testimonials were selling cigarettes and found that these endorsements were mostly fabrications. Al Jolson could be heard on the radio boasting that "Lucky Strike was always my favorite brand of cigarette" and its toasted flavor "satisfies the craving for sweets," but the FTC discovered that "he did not prepare, see prior to its use, or sign" this statement. In a print ad that featured showgirls from the musical *Whoopee!*, the actresses are quoted saying, "We know our Luckies . . . that's how we stay slender." But the FTC learned that the girls in the ad were not smokers at all, and their likenesses had been acquired from their theatrical press representative. This seemed the very definition of "false

and misleading advertising" that the FTC was charged with
regulating.

In the November 1929 cease-and-desist ruling, the FTC prohibited any testimonial that was not "the genuine, authorized
and unbiased opinion of the author" and required that paid testimonials be clearly identified. As for the promises that "women
retain slender figures" and that being "overweight is banished
when you banish sweets and light a 'Lucky,'" the FTC cried foul.
In its ruling, it asserted that "in truth and in fact health and vigor
to men, slender figure to women and the reduction of flesh in all
cases will not necessarily result from the smoking of Lucky
Strike cigarettes and/or the elimination of sweets from the diet."[41]
Score one for candy.

Get Thin on Candy

The same month that American Tobacco took its "Reach for a
Lucky" campaign national, the NCA's *Saturday Evening Post*
advertisement addressed the fattening question head on. The
headline on the January 19, 1929, ad promised that "you can get
thin comfortably on candy":

> Are you one of those people who love candy and deny them-
> selves because they think "candy is fattening"? If so, see how
> modern dietary science uses candy as the mainstay of a reduc-
> ing regime!
>
> According to a great modern discovery, "fats burn in the
> flame of the carbohydrates." This means that a diet high in sug-
> ars (such as candy) may be very effectively used by people with
> a tendency to overweight, in helping them to "get thin."

Like others in the series, this ad was buttressed with scientific footnotes. An asterisk led from "fats burn in the flame of
the carbohydrates" to the putative source: a book by Meyer

Bodansky, Ph.D., called *Introduction to Physiological Chemistry*, published by John Wiley & Sons in 1927. Bodansky was a recognized researcher and expert in biochemistry, and his book went into four editions as a standard textbook. He was appalled to discover that his book had been appropriated in a candy promotion. *Introduction to Physiological Chemistry* did not in fact contain any explicit or implicit endorsement of any particular diet, nor did it suggest that eating any kind of carbohydrate would lead to reducing. As he wrote in a letter to the editor of *The Journal of the American Medical Association*: "Neither was the specific reference to my textbook authorized by me nor have the implications, so far as I know, adequate clinical or scientific basis. It appears to me, therefore, that such use of scientific references is objectionable."[42] Letters from disgruntled scientists in *JAMA*, however, were hardly a match for the impact of a full-page ad in *The Saturday Evening Post*.

The allusion to biochemistry in the advertisement made it sound as if eating carbohydrate-rich foods like candy would burn body fat. Bodansky certainly didn't endorse this interpretation. Yet there were other scientists whose investigations more directly supported the reducing potential of candy. At Jefferson Hospital in Philadelphia, Dr. Burgess Gordon and his assistant, E. von Stanley, put forty-four obese patients on a carefully controlled diet, limited to between fourteen hundred and sixteen hundred calories per day. Researchers had found that dieters often began with grand intentions, but after some period of calorie restriction, the constant hunger and fatigue would wear down even the steeliest resolve. Gordon and von Stanley had an idea about how to keep dieters motivated and on track: give them candy. Candy, they hypothesized, would serve as a source of quick energy to counteract the effects of reduced calories. By giving candy between meals during periods of exercise, the researchers hoped to have it both ways: increased energy *and* weight loss. Not just a little candy, either; after the sixth day of dieting, participants were given between one-quarter and one-third of a pound of candy daily before and during exercise.

It worked! According to the results published in a medical journal in 1928, the dieters lost weight and ate their candy too. Sixteen of the patients completed three months of dieting with candy and averaged 15.5 pounds of weight loss. Candy for energy, according to this study, was a winning proposition even for dieters. The diet was successful because, the authors explained, "carbohydrates supplied during exercise would not build up fat, but would be used to a considerable extent as necessary fuel for the body." Whether this was sound science, or sound dieting, mattered little. What was important from the point of view of candy defenders was the existence of a study showing that people could lose weight *and* eat candy. In fact, candy might even help the weight-challenged stick to their otherwise tortured diets.[43]

This study was described in detail in an NCA-sponsored educational publication called *The New Knowledge of Candy*. The NCA distributed over half a million copies of the forty-seven-page booklet in 1928 and 1929 through candy retailers and representatives. More than fifteen thousand copies were individually requested by *Saturday Evening Post* readers responding to the offer included in the "Candy Is Good for You" ad campaign (see plate 1 for an example).[44] The author, Dr. Herman N. Bundesen, was an unimpeachable champion of public health. He had served as Chicago's commissioner of health from 1922 to 1927, during which time he made important progress in reducing the spread of syphilis and improving infant and maternal health; in 1928, he was elected president of the American Public Health Association. He would go on to an illustrious career, returning to his former post as commissioner of health in Chicago in 1932 and gaining a national reputation as an expert in infant and child care. His syndicated newspaper columns, magazine articles, and books, including *Our Babies: Their Feeding, Care, and Training* and *The Baby Manual*, were read by millions.[45] When he lent his name to the candy defense, it was a major coup.*

For the most part, the argument of *The New Knowledge of Candy* was basically the same as the official USDA position described in 1906 by Mary Hinman Abel in *Sugar as Food*: sugar is energy for muscle work, therefore candy, as sugar, is a good energy food. Bundesen put it this way: "Sugar helps make the body move . . . A chocolate cream is not just a luscious mouthful which most of us crave; it is the fire which helps keep the engine going." Bundesen's chocolate cream as fuel was the mirror image of Lulu Hunt Peters's chocolate cream as fat. But Bundesen went even further, explaining that "sugar in the proper proportions not only burns itself up daily but aids in burning the fat of the body as well."[46] Bundesen's metaphor of sugar as kindling and fat as wood in the metabolic fires seemed to promise a sort of perpetual-motion machine of weight loss: by eating more sugar, one might actually end up with less fat. As preposterous as this idea was, its scientific aura lent credence to what the candy industry hoped would become the "new knowledge of candy": candy was not fattening at all. In fact, quite the contrary: used in the right way, candy could actually be slenderizing. (The idea is new again; the NCA has funded two recent studies that show a correlation between lower body weight and candy consumption based on national diet and health data.[47] Skeptics will reply that correlation is not causation.)

---

*In 1934, Bundesen again appeared as the medical authority for a food processor, this time the United Fruit Company. As Susan Yager recounts in *The Hundred Year Diet*, Bundesen subjected three women to a twenty-eight-day reducing diet that consisted of little more than bananas and skim milk. When they did indeed lose weight (not surprisingly), he boasted that "dieting to reduce is practical, easy and healthful." There isn't any evidence that Bundesen was actually corrupted by his affiliations with the NCA or United Fruit, but he certainly benefited from the fact that his opinions aligned so closely with the promotion of certain foodstuffs.

The NCA was not alone in its promotion of candy—and sugar carbohydrates more generally—as playing a role in the healthy diet. The sugar refiners lent their support through the work of a trade association known as the Sugar Institute. The Sugar Institute's strategy was to align sugar and candy interests with the concerns of medical and public health officials by echoing and amplifying the growing warnings of the dangers of restrictive dieting. The institute recommended that candy and allied industries (including baked goods, carbonated beverages, and ice cream) "seize every opportunity to promote sane eating habits as opposed to the doctrines of extremists who advocate a reduction in the individual's consumption of foods that are essential to a properly balanced diet."[48]

As anyone who has attempted to function on one thousand calories a day can attest, reducing food intake diminishes mood, energy, and performance. And the longer-term health consequences of a severely restricted diet are even more dangerous. Peters soberly advocated a "balanced diet," but all too many of the more faddish reducing plans omitted significant nutrients to achieve their promised dramatic results. The legitimate and well-grounded medical criticism of reducing diets provided a perfect opening for the Sugar Institute to coordinate a counterattack. Dieting leads only to suffering, fatigue, and ill health. Instead, the institute encouraged Americans to eat properly and enjoy their food. Especially sugar.

The Sugar Institute was very successful in placing "news" items in periodicals; some were attributed to the institute, but many were not. Under headlines like "The Reducing Craze" and "The 'Boyish Figure' Fad," readers would be informed of the "injurious propaganda" that was unfairly and inaccurately maligning sugar and sugar-containing foods. One piece, titled "Achieving a Boyish Figure a Peril to Health for Many," emphasized the injury and risk inherent in dieting to reduce weight, citing a "famous doctor" who was obliged to tell his young female patients "to whom motherhood has been denied" that "they have sacrificed their children for the sake of a boyish figure." In contrast to the dangers of dieting, the Sugar Institute urged "the use of a wide variety of healthful foods," first among them sugar: "The best and cheapest fuel for the body . . . nature's perfect flavor . . . makes nearly all other foods more enjoyable."[49]

Soon, the Sugar Institute would trumpet another reason to eat more sugar. A study published in 1929 showed that sugar was an ideal antidote to the "wide-spread business disease" of mid-afternoon fatigue. Twenty female office workers spent four weeks eating under the supervision of Dr. Thaddeus Bolton of Temple University. All received regular meals; in addition, some also were given cake, candies, and orangeade in the midafternoon. The others went snackless. All the workers took tests measuring their "working capacity" at 9:30, 2:30, and 4:30. The candy and cake eaters sustained "higher working gains" throughout the day, leading Bolton to conclude that afternoon fatigue "can be largely, if not wholly, prevented by the timely eating of foods that in small volume act as quick fuel for the body engine"—sugar, he meant. He recommended that "hard-working professional men and women would do well to keep in the drawer of the desk a box of good candy or candied fruit" as an "emergency ration" for the inevitable midafternoon slump. The Sugar Institute sent out press releases describing Bolton's study, and the NCA jumped on the opportunity to publicize another scientific endorsement of candy's superiority.[50]

Dr. Bolton's findings were featured in the March 1930 issue of *Scientific American*, five months after the October 1929 stock market crash. As the months went by, it was becoming clear that the effects of the crash would reverberate through the entire economy. The country slid further into depression in the early 1930s, and fatigue was just one of the many problems facing Americans struggling to get by. Many people were less likely to be worried about what was fattening and more likely to be worried about what was filling. Once again, candy would be sold as good food. And more than just good food; as Dr. Bolton had shown, candy was an emergency ration, good for battling exhaustion and restoring that pep in your step. Candy for energy, to fight fatigue and, soon, to fight the war: this would be the new candy message.

9 ◉ A Fighting Food

Once upon a time, around about 1938, there were two white rats who lived in a classroom in Somerset, New Jersey. Their names were Happy and Grumpy. Happy and Grumpy were nice little rats, and they spent their days doing the things rats do: running on their exercise wheel, eating rat chow, curling up for naps. All the children loved to watch their little friends play and explore. One day, the teacher announced that Happy and Grumpy were to live in separate cages for a while so they could try some new foods. Every day, Happy would eat what good little children should eat: cereals, milk, fruit, and vegetables. Grumpy, on the other hand, would get nothing but candy, cake, and coffee.

The children were all a little envious of Grumpy at first. But as time passed, they noticed something very unsettling. In the old days, both Grumpy and Happy were just as healthy and active and busy as any young white rat could be. Happy was still this way. But a dreadful change had come over Grumpy: he had grown thin, his coat was rough, and he was sluggish and only about two-thirds as big as Happy. Grumpy's sad fate was witnessed by Dr. Carry C. Meyers, the head of the Department of

Parent Education at Western Reserve University (now Case Western). He wrote about Happy and Grumpy in a syndicated newspaper article as a demonstration of an effective school lesson on the subject of proper eating. The divergent fortunes of Happy and Grumpy were evidence that any schoolboy or girl could understand, evidence that proved candy was most certainly not what candy makers liked to call a "good food."[1]

Grumpy and Happy played out in miniature the dramatic research of a Johns Hopkins University biochemist named Elmer McCollum. In the 1910s and 1920s, McCollum had gained fame for his research demonstrating the vital necessity of the hidden nutrients that came to be known as vitamins. McCollum and others fed various artificial diets to rats and found that the absence of these nutrients led to a dramatic deterioration in health. Having discovered a fat-soluble substance he called vitamin A, McCollum showed that rats who didn't get it in their diet lost their vision and suffered from stunted growth. He took vitamin B out of the rats' diet and proved that the deficiency caused beriberi, a disorder of the nervous system. McCollum spent years inducing rickets in rats and eventually figured out just what it was in food that prevented the softening and weakening of the bones. He called that one vitamin D. McCollum summarized the current state of vitamin research in a 1918 book called *The Newer Knowledge of Nutrition*. Others were also pursuing vitamin research, but McCollum's well-timed and well-titled book established him as America's foremost authority.

McCollum had a flair for memorable phrases and dramatic visual effects. It was his idea to start naming all the vitamins after letters of the alphabet. He coined the term "protective foods" to describe those foodstuffs—milk, eggs, leafy green vegetables— that would provide the necessary factors for full strength and vitality. And it was McCollum's deliberate publicity efforts that introduced America to the newest participant in the quest for better health through diet: the laboratory rat.[2]

Shortly after his book was reissued in 1922, McCollum invited reporters to his laboratory to inspect his hundreds of experimental rats in order to witness firsthand the effects of a vitamin-deficient diet. At this time, the use of rats in nutrition experiments was still novel, and the creatures made quite an impression on a visiting reporter for *The New York Times*. He described some of the rats as being healthy and sleek. But others—those who were being fed diets deliberately deprived of one factor or another—presented a frightful spectacle of disease and decay: "Their coats will go without the attention usually given them, and eyes will become dull. Rapidly they become thin and emaciated, and are ready to bite the hand thrust into the cage. Soon afterward they die." The effects of deficient diets on mother rats were especially dramatic and worrisome. The properly nourished mothers lavished care on their offspring, but if McCollum changed their diet, "The mother will become nervous, and will eventually attack and destroy her family."[3]

The newer nutrition explained what was wrong with bad American mothers, and also what was wrong with classroom rat Grumpy: he was suffering from a severe vitamin deficiency. While Happy was busy feasting away on a diet of vitamin-rich "protective foods," Grumpy was doomed—with his decidedly unprotective cakes and candies—to waste away. As Grumpy vividly illustrated, hunger was not the same as malnutrition. Grumpy had plenty to eat, but it was food of the wrong sort.

By the 1930s, the American diet had been turned topsy-turvy by ideas about vitamins, even if most people had only the vaguest notion of what they were or what they did. In a 1930 *New York Times Magazine* article, food writer Eunice Fuller Barnard called vitamins "mysterious elements . . . essential to health and growth" that were dooming the traditional fare of meat, potatoes, and bread to the culinary dustbin.[4] New dietary heroes like lettuce and orange juice, Barnard observed, "were taken up with the enthusiasm of a Lindbergh or a Babe Ruth" (the ball player, not the candy bar). She gave a sense of the tenor of the times: Americans were instructed to dine on "a quart of milk a day and salad twice a day," New Yorkers were eating twice as many fruits and vegetables as previously, and spinach had been "irrevocably installed in the menu as childhood's major sorrow."

But while Barnard claimed that foods in general were "gaining and losing popularity according to their vitamin scores," she noted one exception: sugar. What she called the "vitaminless viand" had not suffered at all as a result of dietary upheaval, but rather was "fairly skyrocketing in vogue." After a dip during the Depression, per capita candy consumption recovered to reach a new postwar high of sixteen pounds a year in the late 1930s. People were crazy for candy. In 1939, tens of thousands of revelers stormed candy shows staged in major U.S. cities. The Philadelphia show (the city's first in thirty years) went on for five nights and counted an attendance of one hundred thousand. In Chicago, the Exhibition Hall of the Hotel Sherman was transformed into a "fairy-like setting of gumdrop, marshmallow and licorice stick trees" where a Candy Queen was duly crowned. There were reports of women fainting in the crush at the Boston show, where "a fun-making, high-spirited crowd jammed every available space, packing aisles and stairways, and overflowed into the streets."[5]

The candy shows were joyful expressions of carefree revelry. The music was loud, the economy was back on track, and the menacing figures of Hitler and Hirohito seemed far away. Behind the scenes there were other forces at work to keep candy desirable in the minds of Americans. What did these forces look like? Picture a Baby Ruth candy bar. And then an ear of corn.

Candy Is Delicious Food—Enjoy Some Every Day

Otto Schnering, the man who had made Baby Ruth one of the biggest-selling candy bars ever, was an obvious choice to lead the candy industry in its next big advertising push. He was appointed chairman of the NCA's merchandising and advertising committee in 1937 and assigned the task of figuring out how to boost sales without incurring too much expense. This called for a more creative approach than the typical Madison Avenue buy-up of billboards and magazine pages. The inspiration came from an unlikely place: flowers. The Society of American Florists had increased sales dramatically with the use of a simple slogan: "Say It With Flowers." Why not, Schnering mused, figure out a way to make people say it with candy? A slogan could do on the cheap what would otherwise cost thousands of dollars. Schnering explained his strategy: "If we could pack a strong message into a few words and then get those words before the public on a million window transfers and on millions of mailing pieces, we would soon have more people doing more thinking about candy. And if we could do that, we knew it would mean more sales for everyone in the business."[6]

Schnering's new slogan "Candy Is Delicious Food—Enjoy Some Every Day" hit every base: the pleasure of candy, the reinforcement of candy as a food, and the utility of candy in the everyday diet. But there was only so much a low-budget campaign of window decals and store posters could accomplish—he needed something bigger.

In April 1938, Schnering announced that a dramatic expansion of the NCA's publicity campaign would be financed by the Corn Products Refining Company, "one of the leading processors of ingredients for candy."[7] He described the new windfall as "the most wonderful thing that could have happened to the [candy] industry," which would "enable us to broaden and intensify the campaign in a manner we never dreamed possible." Best of all, there were no strings attached to the money. In fact, Corn Products was said to be "quite content to remain in the background."[8] To the public, the NCA campaign would appear to be entirely the work of candy interests. It was a complete reversal from the 1890s, when candy makers and corn refiners publicly joined forces to advocate calling "glucose" by the more reassuring name of "corn syrup." This time, corn would be candy's little secret.

The Corn Products Refining Company had been formed in 1906 as a merger of leading U.S. corn refiners. The company had gone on to create Argo laundry starch, Karo corn syrup, and Mazola corn oil, and in 1929 it patented a crystalline form of glucose from corn called dextrose.[9] Corn Product's interest in candy was obvious: candy makers were a significant market for corn syrup, cornstarch, and, increasingly, dextrose.

Corn syrup was a liquid compound of glucose and salts—it had important uses in candy making, but also limitations. Dextrose significantly expanded the potential uses of corn sugar in candy making. It was a crystallizable sugar, so it could be used in some cases as a substitute for cane or beet sugar (sucrose), although it was not as sweet. Corn Products advertised dextrose under the trade name Cerelose to candy and ice cream manufacturers with the promise that it "improves texture and flavor, adds health appeal, helps increase sales, is always pure and uniform, lends character to other products, is economical."[10]

Since dextrose was cheaper than beet or cane sugar, food processors had a strong incentive to figure out ways to substitute where they could. Beet and cane sugar processors were not happy about this; in 1940 they sued to force peach canners to identify dextrose as an ingredient when they used it as a sugar substitute. In an earlier ruling, the Department of Agriculture had allowed the use of dextrose without disclosure on the grounds that it was not an injurious ingredient. But the beet and cane sugar refiners argued that dextrose had only recently begun being used for canning, and therefore people expected their canned peaches to contain sugar, not dextrose. Sugar refiners claimed that if the label didn't specify dextrose, it was a "violation of honesty and fair dealing." A labeling requirement wouldn't stop canners from using dextrose. But the lawsuit implied that sugar refiners hoped that peach canners might be less likely to substitute dextrose if they had to claim it on the label.[11]

Unlike beet and cane sugar refiners, candy makers could afford to be a little more expansive in their thinking about alternative sugars. And what Schnering figured out before anyone else was that candy makers could leverage dextrose to their own advantage. In 1936, the Baby Ruth candy bar got a makeover. The new label featured a prominent boast: "Rich in Dextrose." Full-page magazine ads like one that appeared in *Boys' Life* in December 1936 explained the value of dextrose: "Dextrose is called 'body' or 'muscle' sugar by doctors. It is 'fuel' for the body . . . Your own doctor will tell you that every moment of your life, to breathe, walk, talk, yes even to think, your body uses Dextrose. It is the most important form of food-energy known to medical science." (Baby Ruth advertising continued to promote the natural virtues of dextrose well into the 1940s, for example the ad in plate 8: "Juicy ripe Apples are rich in Dextrose sugar—and so is delicious Baby Ruth.") To back up the medical claims, Schnering had even secured the American Medical Association Council on Foods seal of approval, which was awarded to foods based on the legitimacy of their nutritional claims. The seal was stamped on every Baby Ruth wrapper from 1934 until 1937, at which point the AMA decided that the nutritional "energy" claims for candy were no different from the energy claims that could be made for any food containing calories and therefore did not merit special endorsement.[12] But with or without the AMA's help, the idea of dextrose energy proved a winner for promoting candy. Schnering had shown that cooperation between candy and corn could be mutually beneficial; the NCA campaign was the same strategy writ large.

Despite some early successes, within a year the "Candy Is Delicious Food" campaign was faltering.[13] While the Corn Products money had proved an enormous boon, it also relieved pressure on candy companies to support the campaign. In July 1940, *Confectioners Journal* editor Eugene Pharo devoted his column to berating the candy trade for its passivity. In Pharo's view, everything good that had happened to candy was someone else's doing: scientific progress pioneered by machinery and supply firms, transportation and distribution systems developed by government experts, and even the efforts at cooperative advertising. The latter he called "a sort of largesse handed to it by producers of supplies and materials who wished to sell their products to confectioners, and who therefore were willing to do all they could to help swell the confectionery markets."[14]

Pharo had a good point. Why had Corn Products paid for Schnering's campaign if not to enhance its own profits? The president of the Corn Products Refining Company emphasized the close relation between corn and candy when he spoke at the 1941 NCA convention, including the startling revelation that "the confectionery industry uses one-fifth of the output of the corn refining industry."[15] Selling more candy meant selling more corn products. From the point of view of the corn industry, candy was corn in another guise.

Enriched with Dextrose

It wasn't long before the corn industry began to look past candy in search of a wider market. They took out full-page color ads in popular publications like *Time*, *Fortune*, and *Life* magazine touting dextrose as the "radiant energy of the sun" crystallized in food form. Dextrose was portrayed as the "All-American sugar," made from American corn grown on American soil. One ad even featured a cornucopia of fruits and vegetables spilling from Uncle Sam's stars-and-stripes top hat, with an ear of corn front and center.[16] In another, a stork delivered a baby bundle with the caption "Life Begins with Dextrose Sugar."[17] While the ads varied in focus, their underlying message was constant: consumers should demand dextrose in their foods. Each ad included pictures of the various foods that could include dextrose: bread, juice, jam, ice cream, soda, and of course candy. Accompanying the illustrations of plentiful food, every ad culminated in a slogan along these lines: "Better foods are enriched with Dextrose," "Enjoy foods 'Enriched with Dextrose,'" "Demand foods 'Enriched with Dextrose.'"

The word *enrich* was especially meaningful in the context of food and nutrition in the early 1940s. Since the 1920s, nutritional experts had been aware that processing robbed white flour of important nutrients; Elmer McCollum had called white flour "notably deficient in more dietary factors than any other single food entering the marketplace."[18] Millers and bakers resisted doing anything to improve white flour, in part because sources of supplementary nutrients were expensive at that time. Instead of fixing the flour, they mounted a public relations offensive against whole-wheat bread and succeeded in gaining the endorsement of both the American Medical Association and the U.S. Department of Agriculture for the food value of white bread.[19] But the new vitamin awareness in the 1930s brought attention back to the deficiencies of white flour.

There were many vitamins and minerals destroyed in flour processing, but the one that was most worrisome was thiamine, or vitamin B_1. In 1940, researchers put ten young female inmates at a Minnesota mental hospital on a reduced-thiamine diet in an experiment described by Harvey Levenstein in *Fear of Food: A History of Why We Worry About What We Eat*. As Levenstein recounts, the consequences were dramatic: psychological and mood changes marked by fatigue, depression, weakness, and "psychotic trends." Once the thiamine was restored to their diets, the women bounced back, experiencing "a feeling of unusual well-being associated with unusual stamina and enterprise."[20] What did this mean for a nation whose population was consuming a staggering 30 percent of its total calories in the form of white bread? *The Journal of the American Medical Association* painted a stark picture: "moodiness, sluggishness, indifference, fear and mental and physical fatigue."[21] If the United States were to be invaded (say, for example, by Germany), thiamine—"the morale vitamin"—might make all the difference between energetic resistance and impotent defeat. The solution was to add back into flour the vital thiamine that processing had destroyed. The new product was called "enriched" flour, and its product "enriched" bread. Enriched flour—boasting the morale-boosting powers of thiamine, as well as several other vitamins and minerals—would provide energy, strength, and vigor.

Millers began enriching flour in February 1941, and through 1941 and 1942, local newspapers and agricultural extension services educated homemakers about the importance of enriched flour. On the food pages of the *San Jose News*, a writer reassured readers that enriched flour and bread looked and tasted the same as the old familiar staples. Most important, they cost no more than ordinary flour or bread and "contribute more nutrition to the diet." A 1942 Oregon State University Extension Service publication explained that adding vitamin B_1, niacin, and iron to flour and bread helps "to build strength, mental alertness, steady nerves, and vitality." Eating enriched bread was important not only for individual health but also for the future of American democracy. "In wartime our country needs us strong," the Extension Service reminded local citizens.[22]

As for "enriched with Dextrose," although the Corn Products ads were extremely vague about what nutrients would be provided by dextrose, they were quite adamant that "'Dextrose' among the ingredients" is "your assurance of high quality and higher food value!"[23] If dextrose could "enrich" breakfast rolls, soft drinks, strawberry jam, and candy bars, then it presumably had some of the same health- and growth-promoting virtues as the vitamins.

The dextrose promotion was so convincing that even members of the sugar industry began to believe that dextrose sugar had some superior nutritional qualities. The *International Sugar Journal* reported in late 1941 that cane sugar producers were demanding greater government control of dextrose production because it was more and more often displacing cane sugar in preserves. The writer went on to explain the reason: "Originally this use of dextrose was comparatively negligible, mainly because consumers believed that preserves prepared with corn syrup were inferior to those made with cane syrup. However, with the discovery and boosting of certain vitamins in corn syrup the production and consumption of dextrose has increased by leaps and bounds."[24]

Vitaminless Viands

That dextrose was in ascendance was beyond doubt. Its vitamins, however, existed only through suggestion and innuendo. A confused Mr. J.S.P. wrote to diet and health newspaper columnist Dr. Logan Clendening in 1939 to inquire about the "special food value" of dextrose and what benefits it might have over sucrose. Dr. Clendening explained that dextrose is chemically simpler than sucrose and might be useful for infant feeding or cases of indigestion. However, as to nutrition and the putative special food values, in a comparison of dextrose with sucrose "there is no advantage."[25]

The fact was, neither dextrose nor sugar provided any nutrients at all beyond carbohydrate calories. In the 1940s, doctors and nutritionists started referring to sugar and cooking fats as "empty calories," foods that provided energy without any protein, vitamins, or minerals. Twenty-five years earlier, in the run-up to World War I, the measure of dietary adequacy had been the calorie, full stop: the strength of the nation depended on having enough food. But by the time the United States began preparing for the next war, nutritional experts had come to distinguish between what they called the "hollow hunger" of an empty belly and the "hidden hunger" of vitamin deficiencies.[26]

While only the very poor might suffer from hollow hunger, hidden hunger seemed to afflict nearly everyone. Half the men called up in the first draft in 1940 were rejected for reasons that were believed to be related to vitamin deficiency, such as poor eyesight and bad teeth.[27] A 1943 study of upper-income diets—plentiful from a caloric perspective—revealed that some three-quarters were deficient in key nutrients.[28] In 1941, Paul McNutt, head of the Federal Security Agency, warned the young readers of *Boys' Life* that "'hidden hunger' saps initiative and alertness" and threatens the "health, strength and security of America." Americans just weren't eating the right kinds of food. "The 'he-man's diet' of the laborer who avoids vegetables and milk, and fills up on meat, potatoes and coffee," warned McNutt, "is just as wrong as an office worker lunching on soda pop, chocolate bars, and sundaes."[29]

McNutt's vitamin-deprived office worker sounded a lot like our rat friend Grumpy, whose sugary diet of candies and cakes had indeed sapped his initiative and alertness. The idea that vitamin deficiencies could cause disease had originally applied only to very specific conditions like scurvy (vitamin C), beriberi (vitamin B), and rickets (vitamin D). These were major diseases; you would know if you had one. But what about the hidden hunger of vitamin deficiencies that didn't lead to rickets or beriberi? If it was hidden, how did you know that it really existed? Even Grumpy's bad condition didn't really prove that candy and cakes were bad to eat, only that eating nothing but candy and cakes wasn't such a good idea, which every sensible person knows. Beyond experimental rat cages, the dramatic consequences of hidden hunger were nowhere to be found. As Harvey Levenstein shows in *Paradox of Plenty: A Social History of Eating in Modern America*, nutritionists equivocated on the consequences of subacute vitamin deficiencies, suggesting that people suffered from such invisible maladies as "latent malnutrition" or "a borderline . . . condition, the signs of which are not detectable by the ordinary methods."[30] But the wholesale condemnation of favorite foods and ways of eating was a hard sell, especially when the consequences of bad eating seemed to be completely undetectable.

Medical doctors of the time were adamantly opposed to artificial vitamin supplementation. The way they saw it, taking extra vitamin pills to ward off disease wasn't so different from treating disease with vitamins. And it was doctors, not vitamin salesmen, who were supposed to be the ones treating diseases.[31] The AMA took an official stance on vitamin enrichment in 1942: it was fine to add vitamins to fortify bread and milk, but nothing else.[32] Despite this, vitamin manufacturers were busy promoting vitamin supplements directly to consumers; in 1939, vitamin sales accounted for nearly 12 percent of all drug sales, at a wholesale value over $41.6 million.[33] From the consumer's perspective, there didn't seem to be any practical distinction between food that naturally contained vitamins, food that was lacking vitamins but could be enriched to restore them, and food that had no vitamins at all but could be accompanied by a vitamin pill. The result was a conflicting message about the relation among vitamins, food, and poorly understood products like dextrose that made vague promises of "enrichment." As a consequence, the alarms of government nutritionists of hidden hunger were easily distorted.

In the early 1940s, as the worries about hidden hunger sounded most loudly, candy makers were extremely alert to the possibilities of using vitamin supplementation to "improve" the nutritional value of candy. But in 1943, the FDA foreclosed that possibility with a ruling that clarified the restrictions on selling fortified foods: "Enrichment of those foods which are not a substantial part of the [diet] . . . tends to confuse and mislead consumers through giving rise to conflicting claims of nutritional values and by creating an exaggerated impression of the benefits to be derived from the consumption of such foods."[34] In other words, the FDA would likely frown on vitamin-enriched candies that might confuse consumers into thinking they could live on candies and cakes.

But it really didn't matter that candy had no vitamins. There were plenty of vitamins to be had elsewhere. And vitamins or no, candy was still "a delicious food." The value of candy in the Second World War was no different from the value of candy in the First: concentrated carbohydrates, portable and palatable calories, quick energy. War itself—with its relentless and urgent demands on body and spirit—created a compelling demonstration that candy wasn't just delicious food; candy was essential food.

Candy for Victory

At the end of each broadcast of the radio program *Washington Reports on Rationing*, sponsored by the Council on Candy of the NCA and produced by the Office of Price Administration, the host summed up the wartime candy message: "Remember, candy is a fighting food for our fighters, an energy food for our workers, a morale builder for our citizens."[35] Philip Gott, NCA president, further boasted of candy's role in the war effort: "We are making some very important 'candy bullets' for the new army rations."[36]

Gott was referring to the enormous quantities of candy that the army, navy, and air force were demanding to provision the forts, naval bases, aviation stations, and military camps being fitted out for war. As a writer for *The New York Times* in 1942 explained, "Along with guns and gasoline, candy is going to war wherever American soldiers and sailors go."[37] There was candy included in the specifications for meals prepared in camp (A and B rations), and for meals packed in cans as portable C rations. Candy for the soldiers wasn't just for dessert, either. In September 1941, the quartermaster added five pieces of hard candy to C rations (the quartermaster is the officer—and by extension, the division—responsible for supplying provisions to the troops). A *New York Times* report on the new menu explained that the hard candy would "provide tempting tid-bits so that the consumption of sugar between meals may be employed to revive the energy of marching men."[38]

When soldiers were back in camp, there was plenty of ordinary candy that they could purchase between meals, to the tune of twenty-five million pounds in 1942 alone. Candy bar manufacturers reported that they were selling 15 percent of their production to the quartermaster for military use.[39] Captain Joseph Burkhart of the Chicago Quartermaster Corps told a meeting of area candy makers that as of the end of 1943, "Uncle Sam's seven million or more soldiers are eating candy at the rate of 50 pounds per year per person," which meant that each soldier was enjoying "one candy bar a day in addition to candy contained in their rations."[40]

Meanwhile, laborers in war supply plants were clamoring for more and more candy. A *Wall Street Journal* reporter wrote in 1943 that workers in war factories were frequently choosing not to stop for a break and instead would "[patronize] rolling candy stands and munch 5-cent bars while working, to reduce fatigue and give them a quick energy pick-up."[41] A survey of war workers found that six in ten were eating candy at least once a day, while eight in ten claimed to eat candy no less than once a week. When those who had not eaten any candy in the past twenty-four hours were asked why, the top answer given by nearly half was that candy was "not available."[42] To keep morale and productivity up in the defense plants, in February 1943 the Food Distribution Administration asked candy manufacturers and distributors to give the greater portion of their production to provision war plant workers.[43] As more candy was diverted to war-related uses, candy manufacturers took advantage of the opportunity to

Milky Way candy bar ad, 1945

highlight the importance of their product to the war effort. A 1943 Mars ad promoted Milky Way as a source of "good cheer on both fronts," featuring a civilian worker and a soldier in uniform enjoying the same chocolaty treat.

Since the 1920s, the candy industry had promoted its product as a food ideally suited for every energy need. The war mobilization provided yet another opportunity to highlight its "fatigue-fighting" potential. In 1944, the NCA ran eye-catching advertisements in popular magazines featuring a gleaming wrench surrounded by gumdrops and caramels under the banner: "Candy: Food for Work" (plate 9). The juxtaposition is striking: by showing a steel tool next to confectionery, the consumer sees that candy is just as powerful, and just as essential, as the sturdy wrench. No more frilly bonbons and lacy negligees; candy is serious stuff.

The association of candy with work during the war years wasn't simply an assertion of "masculinity." The wrench implied industrial labor, but the ad copy emphasized a much wider range: "Running [a] welding torch or typewriter, pushing a pencil or a hand truck, making meals or machines of war—today's work is longer, harder, calls for extra energy." These different kinds of work might be sorted into typically male and female jobs, but with able-bodied men called into military service, women were entering the labor force in unprecedented numbers and many were learning skills and performing tasks previously considered "men's work." Rosie the Riveter became an enduring icon during this era; in 1944, even the welding torch in a munitions factory had the same chance of being wielded by a woman as by a man.

Candy ads in the mid-1940s reflected and played up these societal changes by depicting women as workers, often alongside men. At the same time, some candy ads also promoted the idea that women's traditional tasks in the home were a significant form of work. As one 1947 NCA candy ad put it: "Housework—any work—uses energy" (plate 10). The ad's language highlights the similarity between domestic skills and other forms of manual labor: "You've steered a broom. You've swung an iron. You've done your duty by the dishes." The woman depicted wears a house apron with just enough ruffle to distinguish it as feminine. On a quick break from her labor, she holds a morsel just selected from a candy box, a pose that echoes ads from the early 1900s that showed feminine beauties sampling chocolates. But in the

1947 version, the woman is not a lady of leisure but a worker replenishing her energy. Consumer advertising in the twentieth century usually reinforced gender stereotypes and contributed to the devaluing of women's activities and social roles. In the wartime candy promotions, however, there is a surprising alignment between valuing women as consumers and as workers, both in paid jobs and in the typically disregarded sphere of domestic work.

With vast amounts of candy being diverted to fueling the war effort, candy stores started having trouble keeping their shelves stocked. The candy available for civilians in 1943 was half what it had been in the previous year. Five-cent candy bars all but disappeared; they were the most popular items at army and navy canteens as well as in war plant commissaries and vending machines. Curtiss Candy ads for Baby Ruth and Butterfinger candy bars explained that "our food plants are working day and night to keep pace with the demands of the Armed Forces" and apologized to customers who couldn't find their favorite bars at the candy counter.[44] To cope with the shortages, Fanny Farmer stores started limiting their customers to half-pound purchases. Other candy shops cut their business hours from thirteen or fourteen per day to just six.[45] Children suffered the most. Candy manufacturers diverted their production to the most profitable lines, and that meant the children's market went begging. As a 1946 article in *The Washington Post* lamented, "The kid with a penny is a pauper today—there isn't any more penny candy."[46]

Candy factories struggled to keep up with all the demands on their production. Many manufacturers converted part of their factories to war work, from packaging dehydrated food to assembling small electronics and armaments.[47] A Curtiss Candy ad from early 1943 titled "Make It Snappy!" showed a frantic Uncle Sam working the phones: "I want millions of special Dextrose energy tablets . . . millions of candy fruit drops. I want you to package tons of biscuits, bouillon powder, dehydrated mincemeat, prune and apricot powders."[48] But even with factories in operation around the clock, it still was hard to keep up.

The quartermaster was an unpredictable customer, suddenly appearing with, say, an order for seven million pounds of hard candy. Toward the end of the war, the military's demand for candy grew so large that some candy factories reported "delivering their total output of certain items to the government."[49] The army and navy clamored for still more; in October 1944, the War Foods Administration took the extraordinary step of ordering every U.S. candy manufacturer to set aside 50 percent of its production of five-cent candies for sale to government agencies.[50] NCA president Philip Gott described the general attitude: "If the boys want candy, they are going to get it."[51]

As far as the fighting forces were concerned, candy was no luxury. Its convenience and concentrated carbohydrates made it ideally suited to all kinds of dangerous military situations involving parachutes, airplanes, and life rafts. In 1944, four U.S. airmen volunteered to test candy rations by stranding themselves on a life raft for five days with nothing but rock candy and water. The results were encouraging: "All the men lost weight but a short rest in a hospital and good food snapped them back to normal."[52] Downed fliers' chances of survival increased if they had an all-candy Parachute Emergency Ration or an Airborne Lifeboat Ration stashed in their pocket. The official Life Raft Ration included chewing gum and vitamin tablets along with fruit-flavored hard candy tablets. The instructions printed on the waterproof tin emphasized satisfaction along with dental hygiene: "One to two packages of candy and one vitamin pill should be eaten each day by each man—chewing the gum will help keep your mouth clean." The instructions also reminded the user that if he happened to catch a fish, he should save the candy for later.[53]

The Air Crew Lunch was credited with saving countless flyers from unnecessary crashes. As one combatant recalled, air force crews making dangerous bombing runs over Germany were nervous and tense. They would skip breakfast, and by the time they were on their way home, they were in serious trouble. Commanders were alarmed at the high rate of crash landings on return to home base, which seemed to be caused by hunger and exhaustion. The Air Crew Lunch was a specially designed red-and-blue package with two compartments covered by a sliding sleeve—push the sleeve to one side or the other and out dropped candy. Inside one compartment were loose candies like chocolate drops, gumdrops, licorice, and candy-coated peanuts; in the other, fudge bars and gum. The ingenious design meant fliers could open the package safely with one mittened hand so that they could "lunch" on candies in flight. Once the Air Crew Lunch was put into action in 1944, reports came back that "crashes on the home field were considerably reduced."[54]

Field Ration D, issued to every soldier, was the candy bar to grab in case of emergencies. World War I had convinced military planners of the lifesaving virtues of chocolate. But the experience in that war had also suggested that plain chocolate wasn't a good choice, since it seldom lasted until the time of true emergency. As military planners began gearing up in the 1930s for the inevitable next conflict, they were keen to develop a chocolate emergency ration that would stand up to both combat conditions and soldiers' cravings. The chocolate-making skills of the military were, not surprisingly, somewhat limited. Early experiments in the Subsistence Research Laboratories of the Quartermaster Corps combined bitter chocolate, sugar, and peanut butter to mixed success: the confection was palatable but didn't keep well and created a raging thirst.

In 1937, Captain Paul Logan of the Quartermaster General's Office arranged to meet with representatives of the Hershey Chocolate Corporation. Hershey was the leading manufacturer of chocolate in the United States, providing some three-quarters of the total consumption. Logan wanted to know if Hershey could develop a new kind of chocolate for military emergencies.

He explained that it had to resist melting so soldiers could carry it in their pockets. And it couldn't taste too good, maybe "just a little better than a boiled potato."[55] (It's not clear if this is what Logan actually said, but this phrase has become part of the lore of the D ration bars.)

Hershey's chief chemist, Sam Hinkle, came up with a formula that fit the bill: chocolate liquor, sugar, skim milk powder, cocoa butter, oat flour, vanillin, and vitamin B_1. A four-ounce bar fit very nicely in a soldier's pocket and contained six hundred calories. With less sugar and more chocolate liquor, not to mention the oat flour, the bar was much less appealing and also less melty than the typical Hershey bar. Logan approved the formula, and so was born the Logan Bar, eventually known as Field Ration D.

It took a while to set up the factory to produce D rations in quantity because the chocolate was thick and pasty and needed to be pressed into molds. By 1939, though, the Hershey factory could produce one hundred thousand bars per day. Field Ration D bars poured out of the factory, up to twenty-four million bars each week in 1945. Hershey was not the sole supplier of D rations; the formula was patented in Paul Logan's name, and the U.S. government retained the patent, which meant that any chocolate company could produce the ration bars. But Hershey had the capacity to produce far more than anyone else. Between 1940 and 1945, the company produced over three billion ration units for soldiers around the world. The military contract was good business for Hershey. It kept its factories going at full throttle during the war and made the company a tidy profit too: revenues soared from $44 million in 1940 to $80 million in 1944.[56]

The quartermaster didn't do so well in the deal. The war ended before the massive stockpiles of D rations could be used, and the military was left trying to figure out what to do with them. They were tasty enough if you were stranded behind enemy lines, but no one would eat a D ration if real candy was available. The Subsistence Laboratories tried to get candy

manufacturers interested in reusing them somehow. There were
no takers. Even if they wanted to use the chocolate, it would be
enormously expensive to unwrap each bar, which was sealed up
in a near-indestructible package of foil, cardboard, wax, and glue.
Colonel Roland Isker, who had worked closely with candy sup-
pliers during the war, was the only one who had any idea what to
do with the leftovers; he suggested the bars could be "unwrapped
by prisoners of war, packed in containers, and shipped to plants
for reprocessing into a chocolate confection that could be used
for emergency feeding of civilians in war areas."[57] The fate of this
proposal was not recorded.

Given the sheer quantities consumed and the evident necessity of candy to provide energy, relief, and sustenance to the men
and women working to win the war, the National Confectioners
Association seemed quite justified in boasting in 1944 that "the
dramatic proving ground of the war [is] giving us a brand new,
grand new appreciation of candy as food."[58] Candy makers had the
money in the bank to prove it: revenue from sales soared from
$325 million in 1938 to $650 million in 1944. The per capita consumption numbers told the same story: from 15.1 pounds to 20.5
pounds in seven years. Candy for victory, and candy victorious.

Meat Bars

World War II changed candy's form and taste practically not at
all. Wrigley Gum and Tootsie Rolls, ration perennials during the
war, dated to the turn of the century. Even M&M's, which were
first introduced during the war and seemed particularly well
suited to military needs, were a copy of a 1937 British candy
called Smarties.[59] As far as I can tell, Field Ration D was the only
new candy to come out of the war, and it was hardly destined for
commercial success.

But even if the postwar candy brands and products hadn't
changed much, a look behind the scenes revealed important de-

velopments in the technology of candy making. It was becoming faster, more efficient, and more sanitary. The 1950 candy factory looked nothing like the dingy workshop of 1900, where coal furnaces cooked fifty-pound kettles of candy and raw muscle power was the secret to pulling out taffies and pouring chocolate creams. The practice known as "straight line production" had been developed in wartime to meet the burgeoning needs of the military; in peacetime, the technique was adopted in candy factories to produce confections with speed and precision. Along the continuous assembly line, workers and machines cooperated in delicate harmony to transform raw materials at one end into fresh candies at the other.

On September 15, 1952, the beloved TV show *I Love Lucy* broadcast an episode that gave all of America a comic glimpse of the consequences of manufacturing efficiency. "Job Switching" is an episode fueled by gender mayhem 1950s style: to get even with their husbands, Lucy (Lucille Ball) and her friend Ethel (Vivian Vance) decide to abandon their housework and take paid jobs in a candy factory. They are stationed at the end of a machine that spits out dipped chocolates, which they are supposed to wrap and pack. At first, it seems an easy job as the chocolates languidly emerge from the machine. But soon the conveyor belt speeds up, and then it speeds up even more. The women scramble to keep the chocolates in check. They stuff them everywhere: in pockets, in their hats, down the front of their dresses, and most memorably, in their mouths. It is funny and also disgusting, as their cheeks bulge out and they begin to drool chocolate spit. Lucy and Ethel learn their lesson and resolve to go back to their more familiar domestic roles.

The candy factory episode reflected anxieties about social and economic changes. It was an obvious jab at women who had made their way into factory jobs vacated by men during the war; with the return of the soldiers, women were expected to put down their wrenches and go back to the kitchen. It was also an

implicit critique of the speed and efficiency of modern production, and the consequences for consumption that were beginning to become evident in the period of prosperity and growth
that followed the end of the war. The machine produces more and
more, faster and faster. The only way for Lucy and Ethel to keep
up is to consume more, to stuff themselves with candy they don't
want and don't need. Funny, maybe, but it also represented the
rapidly expanding consumer culture in the 1950s, which be-
stowed all sorts of new comforts and luxuries but at a cost of
which Americans were only barely becoming aware. The scene
of candy factory mayhem remains one of the favorite episodes
on fan sites, and in 2009 the image of Lucy and Ethel with their
mouths grotesquely crammed full of chocolate was memorial-
ized by the U.S. Postal Service in a commemorative stamp. Evidently, the scene still rings true today.

Candy may have boasted little novelty in the postwar years, but other kinds of food told a different story. Food in the second half of the century would grow to have more in common with the unpalatable yet indestructible D ration bar than with traditional fare like steak and potatoes. Even meat was becoming new. Witness, for example, Spam, one of hundreds of packaged and processed foods that arrived in supermarkets in the late 1940s and early 1950s. Food processors had spent the war years developing sturdy and imperishable rations that could meet the rigors of the battlefield. The technology and factory equipment for canning, freezing, dehydrating, and many other kinds of processing were put in place to meet the war needs. Once the war was over, all those war foods were repurposed for the civilian market.[60]

Not every offering was a success. Soldiers on the march had to eat what they were given. Shoppers, on the other hand, had a choice, and many buyers were perplexed by novelties like freeze-dried wine (just add water!) and deep-fried hamburgers in a can. But while food manufacturers experimented with the details, the overall change was dramatic. Postwar processed food looked like nothing that had come before.

There were a few visionaries who believed that food chemistry was about to usher in a new dawn for candy making as well. Some candy makers believed that candies of the future ought to have even more "food value," especially in the forms of vitamin and protein fortification. There had been quiet burbles of experimentation in wartime army and Agriculture Department labs, where chemists and food technologists investigated how to make high-protein candies with soy, wheat germ, or cottonseed flour.[61] The Department of Agriculture even set up a booth at the 1949 NCA convention to display its "candies improved in taste, texture and food value through the addition of new agricultural ingredients such as yeast and soy protein and dry milk products."[62] None of these appear to have caught the fancy of the gathered confectioners.

A Monsanto representative speculated in 1951 about a future when candy could be made even more foodlike:

> It requires no great stretch of the imagination to foresee that with current knowledge already in hand . . . a tailor-made bar could be achieved which would sustain life for a long period of time with essential elements. A 'meat bar' is already under investigation . . . If properly qualified scientists, chemists, and food technologists directed their attention toward developing the kind of product necessary for human sustenance, I am quite confident that a tailor-made, approximately balanced candy bar can be achieved.[63]

These revisions of candy enhanced with vitamins and protein remained experimental, seldom meriting more than a passing mention in the candy trade press. Only one candy manufacturer even attempted to sell fortified candy: in 1946, the Shotwell Candy Company briefly promoted a line of vitamin- and mineral-fortified bars and marshmallows, including a version of the popular Hi-Mac nougat and caramel bar packed with "nutrients you need to eat candy and still eat right" providing "better nutritional balance than an average meal" (plate 11). Despite heavy national advertising, the better-than-a-meal candies were a flop and disappeared soon after their introduction. The candy bar as well-balanced diet would have to wait several decades to see the light of day—and of course, by the time that happened, it wouldn't be called a candy bar, it would be called an "energy bar" or a "protein bar" or a "snack bar." Ordinary candy makers in 1950 were not interested in meat bars or their confectionery equivalent, and neither were ordinary candy eaters. For the time being, it seemed that candy was good enough just as it was.

TV viewers on the night of December 1, 1951, enjoyed a full-length musical tribute to candy, featured on the popular *Ken Murray Show*. There were specially written songs, costumes and scenery, and a unique candy dance extravaganza. The fourteen million viewers were entertained, to be sure. But they were also educated about the important part candy was playing in food and nutrition, the tireless labors of candy manufacturers to improve their products, and the "constant efforts being put forth to provide the buying public with delicious and wholesome candy."[1]

The sponsor for this televised spectacle was Anheuser-Busch, the famed American brewery. It might seem odd that a beer maker would underwrite what was deemed at the time "one of the greatest good-will promotions in the entire history of the candy industry." But in fact, beer and candy were happy bedfellows. The Anheuser-Busch Corn Products Division was a major supplier of corn syrup and cornstarch to the candy industry. What was good for candy was good for corn products. And what was good for corn products was good for Anheuser-Busch.

Yet despite the flashy advertising and corporate backing, something was wrong in Candy Land. From a wartime high of 20.5 pounds per person in 1944, candy consumption plummeted some 25 percent to hit a low of 15.5 pounds in 1955. The economy had slowed down, true, but previous economic contractions had not had such a dramatic effect on the candy market. A more likely culprit: for the first time since the Depression, America was feeling itself getting fat.

Obesity was the number-one concern when the American Public Health Association convened for its annual meeting in October 1952. Life insurance studies had suggested that as many as five million Americans were obese, and another twenty million overweight. According to these measures, weight problems afflicted nearly one in five of the total population. Dr. Louis Dublin of the Metropolitan Life Insurance Company reported that being "overweight was one of the prime factors in shortening life." Across the population, obesity was a bigger drag on life span than cancer or heart disease. Dr. Norman Jolliffe of the New York City Department of Health warned his colleagues that obesity was "America's number one health problem."[2]

It all sounds so familiar. Today, scientists are looking to high-fructose corn syrup, estrogen disruptors, carbohydrate overload, and metabolic disorders to understand why, despite half a century of diet and exercise, despite low-cal and low-fat and low-carb and high-fiber foods, Americans keep getting fatter. Increasingly, obesity is linked to broader forces like genetics, changes in the food supply, cultural norms, and environment as much as to daily behaviors of diet and exercise. But in the 1950s, as in the 1920s and 1930s when popular attention had also been riveted on the problem of excessive pounds, the cause of corpulence was firmly located in individual behavior. A 1954 feature on the problem of weight gain in *Life* magazine was blunt about who was to blame: "The uncompromising truth is that obesity is caused by gluttony."[3] All those empty candy calories that had played such an important role in winning the war were, in the quieter days of peacetime, starting to look like so much national flab.

No Cal

What *Life* called "the plague of overweight" was becoming all too familiar in America. But thanks to the wonders of modern chemistry, there were new possibilities at midcentury for thwarting the miseries of a reducing diet. Synthetic sweeteners revolutionized dieting in the 1950s and 1960s by providing the sweetness of sugar without the dreaded calories.

Saccharine, the first artificial sweetener, had been available since the late 1800s, prescribed by doctors for diabetic use. Although medical experts generally frowned on the practice, dieters sometimes also used saccharine as an aid to reducing. Saccharine was of limited appeal for dieting purposes, though, as it had a bitter and unpleasant aftertaste and was not easily adapted to cooking and canning processes. It was also tainted by its associations with adulteration and food fraud in the first part of the century; food manufacturers who had used saccharine instead of more expensive sugar were accused of defrauding consumers because saccharine was a chemical substitute with no "food value."[4] Before 1950, saccharine was sold over the counter in pharmacies for personal use. Diabetics and determined dieters might find a few saccharine-sweetened products, but they were not available in ordinary grocery stores and they were not advertised or marketed widely.

Cyclamate changed everything. Cyclamate was a chemical with surprising sweetening qualities discovered by accident in 1937. A lab researcher at the University of Illinois by the name of Michael Sveda was synthesizing some sort of chemical brew and paused to light a cigarette. When he brushed some shards of tobacco off his lip, he discovered that the chemical residue on his fingers was surprisingly sweet.[5] Many years and lab tests later, the pharmaceutical giant Abbott Laboratories won FDA approval for the use of cyclamate in foods. Sucaryl, Abbott's consumer trade name for cyclamate, hit the market in 1951. The timing was perfect: here was a calorie-free sugar substitute, an answer to the dreaded condition of being overweight.

Some food chemists expressed reservations about this untried food additive and encouraged Abbott and the FDA to continue testing the effects of cyclamate consumption, but between 1950 and 1969 there were no signs that cyclamate was anything but totally benign.[6] It was an era of technological optimism and, as the DuPont slogan went, "better living through chemistry." There was no immediate reason in the 1950s for most people to be worried or suspicious about chemical food additives, especially when, as in the case of Sucaryl, they seemed to have such obvious advantages. Cyclamate was about forty times sweeter than sugar, heat stable, and left no bitter aftertaste. It was economical too: in 1969, 64¢ worth of cyclamate could achieve the same sweetness as $6 worth of sugar.[7]

The chemical was quickly adopted by food processors who understood the market potential of food that could be sweetened without adding extra calories. Kirsch Beverages brought out the first No-Cal beverages in 1952, ginger ale and root beer. Royal Crown Cola's brand Diet Rite appeared in 1958, and Coca-Cola introduced Tab in 1963.[8] Canned foods were also among the early adopters of artificial sweeteners. Dole and Libby created special dietetic lines of canned fruit, which jostled for space in the grocery with specialty producers like Diet Delight and Tasti-Diet. Tasti-Diet quickly expanded its brand to encompass a range of "dietetic" foods, including canned fruits and vegetables, condiments, and low-cal desserts. "Dietetic" products quickly migrated from the fringes of specialty "health" stores into the aisles of mainstream grocery markets.[9]

Abbott's consumer marketing of Sucaryl played directly into

America's newly revived obsession with calorie counting. Full-page ads in publications like *Life* pointed out that "you can save a lot of calories by sweetening with Sucaryl." Even better, "You can't taste the difference."[10] Ads never missed a chance to hint that sugar was for chumps. After all, who would want to eat something fattening if there was a nonfattening substitute that was identical in every way that mattered? "If you are not counting calories," the Sucaryl ads suggested, "you don't need this new, non-fattening sweetener. If you are, you do." Of course, who wasn't counting calories? They might just as well have said, "If you want to get fat, eat sugar."

Sucaryl, and the new generation of artificially sweetened foods that appeared in the 1950s, heralded a dramatic shift in the image of dieting and weight loss. Dieting had always been a matter of eating less. The restrictive diets of the 1920s and 1930s were never meant to be pleasant; dieters would sacrifice good taste and pleasure in eating in order to achieve the more important goal of weight loss. But with the advent of a successfully marketed commercial sugar alternative, weight loss could be achieved without giving up pleasure. "You now know that dieting can be pleasant," explained Tillie Lewis, the charismatic entrepreneur behind Tasti-Diet. "You've discovered that food research has finally produced sweet desserts and rich dressings which make it possible to take calories out of a menu, without removing the pleasure of eating or the texture and taste from dietetic food."[11]

In the land of calorie-free sweeteners, eating less became painless, a dietary virtue achieved without any sacrifice at all. Ads for Sucaryl in national magazines featured side-by-side images of luscious desserts like creamy pistachio ice cream or chocolate-sauce-drizzled cake (plate 12). The two images look identical; the only difference is the calorie count: 152 calories if sweetened with sugar but only 70 calories when sweetened with "non-caloric" Sucaryl. The low-calorie dessert looks and (presumably) tastes the same as its full-calorie counterpart. Sucaryl

makes reducing seem almost magical: you can't see or even notice what is different about the Sucaryl dessert. Just make the
right choice of sweeteners, and your weight problem is solved.

But in candy making, cyclamate and saccharine couldn't
completely replace sugar. In candy, sugar is both sweetness and
substance; if you take out the sugar, you have to replace it with
something else. Sugar-free candies were technically possible,
using bulky sugar alcohols that created the substance but metabolized much more slowly. These candies may have been safer
for diabetics, but they had about the same calories as regular
candies. For calorie counters, candy was one sweet taste that still
required a heaping helping of guilt on the side.

Sugar Fights Back

Artificial sweeteners promised the triumph of chemistry over
the messy stuff of appetite and fatness. The marketing of artificial sweeteners didn't mince words: sugar is fattening, fake sugar
is not. This put actual sugar in a tricky spot. Compared to the
zero calories of cyclamate and saccharine, sugar did indeed have
calories. But then, so did every other kind of food. So marketers
for Domino Sugar, a product of the American Sugar Refining
Company, hit on the idea of countering the attack by proving
that other food was even more fattening than sugar. "Which is
Less Fattening?" challenged the Domino Sugar ad (plate 13). Below was a side-by-side comparison: three teaspoons of sugar, or
one sour-looking half grapefruit. Guess what? The sugar has
fewer calories, ergo the sugar is less fattening. Weight watchers,
eat your sugar! Domino went on to produce a series of these
side-by-side comparisons, comparing such seemingly virtuous
foods as a shiny red apple or a soft-boiled egg with so many spoonfuls of sugar. Pitting simple foods against sugar was a direct appeal to the deprivation dieter who was breakfasting on grapefruit
and little else: "Counting calories these days? You should know

that generous amounts of Domino Granulated Sugar, used in your favorite foods and beverages, contain fewer calories than usual servings of many foods regularly included in reducing diets!"[12]

By the logic of the calorie it still made a certain amount of sense. But the explicit pitting of sugar against real foods went beyond abstract measurements. Sugar wasn't just low in calories; according to the sugar ads, sugar was actually a better choice than other foods if you were trying to lose weight. These ads promoted a sort of "down the rabbit hole" logic, where real foods like apples, grapefruit, and eggs suddenly appeared as sinister, calorie-laden menaces to those trying to diet. A 1955 ad in the same series depicted an attractive couple at the breakfast table. He munches on an apple: "Sure, I love sugar. But I'm watching my weight!" She is heaping spoonfuls of Domino into her teacup and explains: "You need Sugar for energy! And even 3 teaspoons of Domino Sugar contain fewer calories than your apple!"[13] Why bother with the apple, this ad suggests, when you can have more pleasure and even lose weight by eating sugar instead.

The final piece of this marketing campaign was a recipe booklet called *Keep Slim and Trim with Domino Sugar Menus*. A lithe swimsuited blonde and her handsome nearly nude companion wave at the reader from the cover, promising sun, fun, and romance to anyone who follows the "reducing diet menus." The pages revealed "the safe, sure way to lose weight without losing pep or giving up sugar! . . . It's Domino's effort to put SUGAR—and sugar-containing foods and beverages—*back in* Reducing Diets . . . where they belong!"[14]

The sugar refiners' trade association was eager to help prop up candy against the threat of artificial sweeteners. In 1954, the association's education arm, Sugar Information, produced a little pamphlet called *Memo to Dieters*. At about three inches square, it was the perfect size to slip into a box of chocolates or a sack of sweets. The publication was designed to give prominent display to the name of the candy brand, and it featured the new message that sugar and candy were weight-loss aids: "New medical research findings now confirm that you can have your sweets and your waistline too . . . Sugar before meals raises your blood sugar level and reduces your appetite . . . And don't forget that candy is also a wonderful source of quick energy . . . So don't be misled into thinking candy is necessarily fattening. Candy can actually be effective in helping you to reduce."[15]

The pamphlet also introduced a new slogan for candy: "Candy is a delicious food, eat some every day to help your diet work." This slogan quite deliberately echoed the candy promotion of the late 1930s and early 1940s, which had built the business on the reminder that "Candy Is Delicious Food, Enjoy Some Every Day!" In the new view of dieting that Sugar Information was selling, candy wasn't just food to enjoy, it was food that would "help your diet work." Eating candy would help you eat less of all the other kinds of food that were making you fat.

A 1957 Life Savers ad dramatized this logic (plate 14). On one side is Shirley Simkin, sloppy and plump, munching a box of cookies. On the other side is Slim Sally Hayes, popping a Life Saver into her pert and pretty mouth. It is Slim Sally who gets all the attention from the boys, and no wonder; she "stays light on her feet; she makes Life Savers her 'tween meal treat." So it wasn't candy that was making people fat. *Food* was fattening, and candy was the solution.

Rat Tumors

However effective sugar and candies might have been as an aid to weight loss in theory, in practice more and more weight watchers were coming to rely on synthetic sweeteners. The usage of cyclamate-saccharine blend sweeteners expanded rapidly in the 1960s, from 5.7 million pounds in 1963 to 17.5 million pounds in 1967. Cyclamate was sweetening canned fruits, sodas, jams and jellies, cookies, even salad dressings; Abbott believed the value of the retail market for low-calorie food to be more than $1 billion. The most popular product continued to be the low-cal soft drinks, selling 440 million cases in 1967 alone.[16] Sugar refiners looked at those mounting low-cal numbers and gnashed their teeth. The way they figured it, that was 440 million cases of soda that should have been sweetened with sugar. No wonder they fought back.

Sugar Information launched a direct attack on artificial sweeteners in ads published in general-interest magazines in the 1960s. The language emphasized the artificiality and suspect connections of cyclamate and saccharine. Artificial sweeteners from "drug and chemical firms" might not have calories, but "where there are no calories there can be no nourishment, no energy." Instead of the familiar names for artificial sweeteners, sugar ads used the chemical names like sodium N-cyclohexylsulfamate and calcium cyclohexylsulfamate, "derived from benzene." Low-cal sodas were called "Syntha-Colas." Sugar Information offered this advice: "Next time you're tempted by a synthetic, say, 'Thanks, Chemistry, but I'll take Sugar.' "[17]

Sugar Information was not content to battle "chemistry" on the advertising pages of magazines. Abbott and other labs had undertaken numerous studies and continued to find no evidence that cyclamate was absorbed by the body or had any health effect. Sugar producers were not satisfied with this result. Starting around 1964, the Sugar Foundation (the research arm of the Sugar Association) began pouring money into research on cyclamate.[18] In 1967, it got the results it was hoping for with the publication of a study by two researchers affiliated with the University of Wisconsin Alumni Research Foundation. According to this study, cyclamate might be dangerous because rats that were fed a diet containing 5 percent cyclamate did not grow to full size.[19]

Not so good for cyclamate, except that no one would ever consume anything near that amount—to experience as much sweetness from sugar as to be equivalent to the sweetness contained in the rats' experimental dose of cyclamate, a person would have to eat nothing but sugar all day long, and then some.[20] Given the much more modest quantities of cyclamate that would be consumed in the course of a normal human life, this was not the slam-dunk result that sugar needed. Although this study received widespread media attention, it did little to slow the incursion of cyclamate into the sweetener market. When Abbott's industrial customers signaled concern, Abbott representatives reassured them that these were flawed studies funded and promoted by "malevolent sugar interests."[21]

Then, in a lucky break for sugar, Abbott's own scientists came up with a much more worrying result. Rats fed large quantities of cyclamate combined with saccharine for an extended period showed the beginnings of cancer of the bladder. It was a huge dose of sweetener, the equivalent of hundreds of bottles of diet soda a day. And even under that chemical barrage, only 8 of the 240 rat subjects developed bladder tumors. Skeptics suggested that any substance fed in such doses, even ordinary salt or sugar, would lead to similar results, and pointed to the ambiguity of a study that mixed two different chemicals.[22] Even the lead investigator questioned the conclusion that the study had proved that cyclamate was dangerous.[23] But the FDA determined that the study was sufficient to trigger the provisions of the so-called Delaney Clause, a 1958 amendment to the food and drug acts that required that an additive "found to induce cancer when ingested by man or animal" must be deemed unsafe and banned from food.

The FDA's actions confused many observers. The agency did not hold any hearings or seek any further scientific analysis. Although the FDA announced that cyclamate had been found to cause cancer, it allowed cyclamate-containing products to remain on grocers' shelves for several months. Some thought it all seemed a little fishy; Dr. Michael Sveda, who had first discovered the chemical, told the press that "the sugar lobby might be the moving force behind the declaration of cyclamate as unsafe."[24]

While there was no evidence of direct conspiracy, it was certainly true that sugar interests had for many years been planting seeds of opposition to cyclamate in the arenas of both scientific and public opinion. And sugar was without a doubt the most immediate beneficiary of the new policy. The ban on cyclamate removed a major obstacle to sugar's profitability. Observers estimated that prior to the ban, artificial sweeteners had been replacing something like 700,000–800,000 tons of sugar per year, approaching an annual loss of $80 million.[25] The ban also reinforced the idea that sugar itself was the safe alternative to cyclamate.

It did seem like a decisive victory for sugar. John Yudkin, who would gain notoriety for his view that sugar was far more dangerous than any artificial food additive, worried that banning cyclamate was tantamount to "inviting everybody to go on eating all the sugar they want."[26] But just as pressures were building to ban cyclamate and thereby return American sweet lovers to all the pleasures of the sugar bowl and the candy dish, new clouds were forming on sugar's horizons.

Sugar-Phobia

The ban on cyclamate heralded a deeper shift in public attitudes about the safety of the food supply. By the late 1960s, many were losing faith in the powers of chemistry and technology to cure every social and physical ill and to bring about a world of peace and plenty. Rachel Carson's *Silent Spring* had been published in 1962; her exposé of the effects of DDT on the environment raised public awareness of the darker side of "better living through chemistry" and sparked a broader debate about pesticides, additives, and the impact of chemicals on farming, food, and health.

"Natural" foods that had previously been associated with the faddish fringes, like brown bread, yogurt, and brown rice, suddenly seemed much less peculiar. One indicator of the change in attitudes about food processing was the rapid growth of the circulation of *Organic Gardening and Farming*, a magazine that had been advocating organic farming methods since 1940 to a tiny cohort of small farmers and suburban gardeners. In 1969, circulation surged 40 percent and continued rising, reaching seven hundred thousand in 1971.[27]

There were other signs that Americans were becoming increasingly worried about the safety and healthfulness of food made with chemicals and machines. One prominent voice for these emerging concerns was nutritionist and author Adelle Davis. In the late 1960s, Davis was a popular and well-known advocate for better health through nutrition. She was a regular guest on radio and television talk shows, and her book *Let's Eat Right to Keep Fit*, first published in 1954, eventually sold over ten million copies. Davis had the air of a professional, with tidy clothes and carefully styled hair, but she shared with countercultural critics a deep skepticism of the benefits of industrial processes to the nutritional value of food. She encouraged Americans to eat more whole and unprocessed foods, and spoke out about the nutritional losses caused by modern food-processing techniques. As a result, not everyone loved Davis, least of all those whose interests aligned with mainstream agriculture and the food industry; a 1969 White House panel called her "probably the most damaging single source of false nutrition information in the land.[28] But the anticorporate, antichemical, antifactory, and antiprocessed message that had originated in the counterculture was, for the moment, embraced by the broader public; in 1972, *Time* magazine crowned Davis "the high priestess of nutrition."[29]

In *Let's Eat Right to Keep Fit*, Davis took a close look at the typical American diet. What she saw was sugar. Not just the added spoonfuls of sugar in coffee cups and cereal bowls, but all the sugar in sweets, drinks, and desserts, as well as in "cheap, starchy foods" like breads, noodles, rice, and pastry that were the "major source of hidden sugar." Americans, too ignorant of the principles of good nutrition, were "innocent victims" who were "flooded by waves of sugar" in restaurants and at home, at meals and in between. Obesity and tooth decay were only the beginning of the "national problems [that] can be traced directly to our faulty eating habits." In particular, Davis warned her readers of the effects of excessive starch and sugar in overstimulating insulin, which in turn would lead to rapid and dramatic fluctuations in blood sugar levels, with ominous results: fatigue, nervousness, irritability, exhaustion, foggy thinking, even blackouts. Davis speculated that the social ills of the 1960s could be attributed to the stupefying effects of sugar and starch: the rising rate of divorce and automobile accidents; failing schools; the excessive use of stimulants like coffee, cigarettes, and alcohol; even "confused thinking in political . . . life" were perhaps the consequence of the sugar deluge.[30]

Despite her warnings of the dangers of excessive sugar, Davis followed the basic paradigm of nutrition science in classing sugar with other carbohydrates and acknowledging that an appropriate amount of sugar could be consumed as "a body requirement equal in importance to any vitamin."[31] But at the same time, more extreme forms of "sugar-phobia" were also gaining attention in the popular media.[32] William Dufty rode the bestseller lists with his sensational *Sugar Blues* (1975), a hyperbolic and frenzied recapitulation of sugar research and lore cross-cut by Dufty's own hell-and-back account of his sugar "addiction," all aiming to illustrate the "multiple physical and mental miseries caused by human consumption" of refined sucrose. The natural foods movement added fuel to sugar-phobia by rejecting every form of refined food in favor of the raw, the unprocessed, and the natural. By this light, refined and crystallized white sugar looked more like a drug than like a food. Honey, molasses, even brown sugar were closer to nature and therefore presumably more healthful.

The most credentialed of the antisugar critics in this era was London biochemist John Yudkin, who became a popular media figure due to his belief that even moderate consumption of sugar was potentially life-threatening. Yudkin had not always reviled sugar. He confessed, "I used to be about the most dedicated sugar 'addict' you have ever seen . . . How many pounds of milk chocolate and candy and cakes of all sorts I used to tuck away each week! At a rough guess, I would say that my total sugar consumption must have been not less than 10 ounces a day, probably nearer 15." But he had seen the light; once he realized just how damaging sugar was to the human body, he swore off the stuff almost completely: "I have cut down from five or six pounds a week to at most 2 or 3 oz a week—sometimes next to nothing— and if I can do it, so can you."[33]

Yudkin had begun researching the effects of sugar consumption on heart disease risk in the 1960s. At that time, medical researchers were confronted with alarming increases in heart disease and death due to heart attack. Although there was a consensus that it was likely something about modern living that was damaging the heart, there were many competing theories that emphasized various risk factors in diet as well as lifestyle. Yudkin was skeptical of data that had been published by Minnesota nutritionist Ancel Keys that purported to demonstrate a strong correlation between dietary fat and coronary disease. In his own laboratory work, Yudkin found that feeding sugar to animals and humans led to higher levels of blood cholesterol and triglycerides, as well as increasing the tendency of blood to clot, all of which were implicated in increasing risk of heart attack. He was also struck by the relationship in population studies between the rising rates of refined sugar consumption and the rising rates of heart disease, a correlation that seemed to be supported by international comparisons.[34]

Despite Yudkin's research, by 1960 Keys and supporters of what has come to be called the "fat hypothesis" had gained sufficient influence that the American Heart Association issued a report advising Americans to reduce the fat in their diets, and *Time* magazine took up the low-fat cause with a four-page cover story featuring Keys's prescription for a heart-healthy diet: 70 percent carbohydrate and only 15 percent fat.[35] Although the European research community continued to investigate both fat and sugar as possible causes of heart disease, in America, Keys's fat hypothesis came to reign supreme in medical and research circles.[36] The position was enshrined as official public policy in 1977, when the USDA released its revised *Dietary Goals for the United States*, advising all Americans to cut down on saturated fat and cholesterol. The beef, egg, and dairy industries were apoplectic, but there was little they could do to counteract the entrenched consensus that their animal-fat-laden products were the primary culprits in America's health crisis. Consumption of fats and red meats plummeted, and Americans turned to carbohydrates instead to fill their dinner plates.[37]

In 1970, Keys mounted a public attack on Yudkin and his rejection of the fat hypothesis, calling his arguments "tendentious" and "flimsy" and mocking his research.[38] Discredited and ridiculed, Yudkin retired from his university post in 1971. He gave up on the "scientists and physicians" who had flocked to the fat hypothesis, despite severe shortcomings in the data. Instead, he sought to bypass the scientific consensus by writing a book addressed directly to a popular audience of ordinary people. The British title was calculated to raise the alarm: *Pure, White and Deadly: The Problem with Sugar.*

Pure, White and Deadly (published in the United States as *Sweet and Dangerous*) went well beyond the evidence linking sugar consumption to heart disease. Yudkin blamed sugar for a host of chronic conditions afflicting modern bodies from head to toe, including the obvious candidates like tooth decay and obesity, as well as a diverse assortment of ailments like acne and dermatitis, arthritis, gout, vision loss, indigestion and ulcers, nutritional deficiencies, and more serious conditions including diabetes and even cancer. Yudkin warned ominously, "If only a small fraction of what is already known about the effects of sugar were to be revealed in relation to any other material used as a food additive, that material would promptly be banned."[39] Yudkin advocated regulating sugar in much the same way as tobacco: "People should not be left entirely to themselves to decide what they should or should not eat. Sooner or later, I feel, it will be necessary to introduce legislation that by some means or other will prevent people from consuming so much sugar, and especially prevent parents, relatives, and friends from ruining the health of babies and children."[40]

Today some are beginning to think that Keys and the "lipophobes" got it exactly wrong, and Yudkin's reputation is on the rise (*Pure, White and Deadly* was the fifth-most-requested out-of-print book in 2012, according to Bookfinder.com; Penguin Books issued a new edition at the end of that year). But in the 1960s and 1970s, mainstream nutritionists in the United States tended to think that Yudkin had gone too far. Many experts did voice concern about some negative aspects of increased sugar consumption, but the only widely recognized consequences of excess sugar were tooth decay and weight gain. Dr. Ruth Leverton, a science adviser to the USDA, worried mostly about excess calories when she looked at the data on sugar consumption: "Now that most of us are leading less active lives there is less and less reason to have something in the diet that gives only energy or calories." Dr. George Briggs, chairman of the Department of Nutritional Sciences at the University of California at Berkeley, saw it much the same way: "Most of us are pretty sedentary now and we don't need calories that produce only energy."[41] In 1973, congressional hearings were held to investigate the effect on children of advertising ready-to-eat cereals containing large quantities of sugar. A nutritionist brought in to testify had little to criticize in the cereals other than that they were "nutritionally 'hollow.'"[42] Most nutritional experts weren't concerned so much by the presence of sugar in breakfast cereals as by the absence of anything else.

There were also plenty who spoke up to "defend the case of old-fashioned sucrose" as Dr. Elizabeth Whelan and Dr. Fredrick Stare put it. Dr. Stare, chairman of the Department of Nutrition at Harvard University, had become a prominent advocate of the virtues of food processing, additives, and the wonders of food technology. He joined with Dr. Whelan to write *Panic in the Pantry: Food Facts, Fads, and Fallacies*, a book meant to persuade the public that the real dangers to health and nutrition were in "natural" additive-free foods.

Stare and Whelan dismissed "rumors" about the harm of sugar as the work of "food faddists and those with personal economic interests in undermining confidence about sugar use" as well as the dairy and tobacco industries, which "would enjoy having some of the 'blame' for heart disease put on sugar." They took pains to disabuse their readers of the notion that sugar was behind every ill: it did not cause diabetes, it was not a factor in heart disease, and as for obesity, well, that was a matter of calories, not sugar. The only concession these sugar advocates would make to the warnings of the sugar-phobes was this one: "For many people, sugar may accelerate dental decay." And not just any sugar. As Whelan and Stare explained: "Actually it is the sticky and excessive sugar consumption taken between meals which is involved in the acceleration of decay, not the sugar with meals."[43] By which they meant, of course, that candy rots your teeth.

11 ◎ Cavities

On the evening of January 25, 1966, millions of households tuned their TVs to the popular CBS program *National Health Test*. The trusted and revered anchorman Mike Wallace opened the program with some ominous news: "Americans consume nine million pounds of candy every day, much of it undoubtedly by children. Is there a connection between the amount of candy you eat and the number of cavities you develop?" Lest anyone out in TV land was still uncertain, Wallace continued: "Yes. Experiments have shown that most people who eat lots of sweets get three to four times as many cavities as those who don't."

Candy makers went ballistic. Why, they demanded, had Wallace failed to mention soft drinks, pastry, pie, cookies, or any other sweet thing or snack? Here once again was evidence of the deep-seated prejudice against sweet foods generally and candy specifically. The NCA director of public relations wrote to the network to demand some kind of retraction. He insisted that "considerable doubt exists among dentists as to the exact cause of dental cavities" and pointed out that "the role of candy in dental problems has never been scientifically ascertained."[1]

The candy defenders had a point. Despite Mike Wallace's authoritative tone, modern dentistry did not have definitive answers to the question of what exactly caused tooth decay or how to prevent it. Up until the late 1900s, there were many popular theories of what caused teeth to rot, but nobody really knew for sure. Elizabethan-era English notable Sir Walter Raleigh insisted that wine "deformeth the face, rotteth the teeth."[2] Sylvester Graham warned his 1830s acolytes that cavities were caused by hot food and drink, which "serve more directly and powerfully to destroy the teeth, than any other cause which acts immediately upon them."[3] Graham was willing to entertain alternative theories; in lectures to young men, he warned that bad teeth were one of the innumerable pathologies caused by masturbation, which would cause the teeth to "decay and become black and loose, and in some instances drop out of the jaws, while the transgressor is yet in the beginning of life."[4]

Candy was nevertheless a common culprit for dental woes. James Hart, a seventeenth-century English adviser on diet and health, warned that the immoderate use of "sweet confections and Sugar-plummes . . . rotteth the teeth, making them looke blacke, and whithall, causeth many a loathsome stinking-breath."[5] By the nineteenth century, candy's destructive powers were well known. In an 1879 magazine sketch, little Willie asked his mother whether "candy will rot folkses teeth?" She assured him that it did. When Willie's friend Mary Dawson came by with a sack of candy and refused to share, Willie managed to express his displeasure in terms his mother could not disapprove of: "I told her jist to eat it herself, an' I hoped it would Rotterdam teeth out."[6]

In the last decades of the nineteenth century, the discovery of bacteria dramatically changed the course of research into the causes of dental disease. Under the microscope, scientists could see the teeming bacteria whose waste products bathed the teeth in corrosive acids. Here was the mechanism whereby food—

carbohydrates, specifically—led to decay.[7] But as the twentieth
century got under way, not everyone fully embraced the bacterial theory. Weston Price, a dentist whose research would later
provide inspiration for the holistic health movement, attributed
dental deformity and disease to dietary deficiencies caused by
the excessive refined flour and sugar in the Western diet.[8] Eugene Talbot and fellow eugenicists viewed rotten teeth as symptoms of deeper racial degeneracy.[9] For these detractors, the
sugar-bacteria-acid connection was a partial view that separated
dental health from bodily health and left out the broader context
of race, history, or nutrition.

Theories blaming the Western diet or racial degeneracy remained on the fringes of dental research, however, and what became known as the "lactic acid theory" gained broad acceptance.
The theory paved the way for a whole industry of tooth-cleaning
products and services, which in turn had much to gain from
popularizing the belief that clean teeth were less likely to decay.
It is likely that the image of nasty bacteria feasting on carbohydrates and leaching acid was especially appealing to those who
already harbored suspicions about candy's corrosive qualities.
As Talbot put it, the lactic acid theory "played to the sociologic
reformer whose God is parsimony, by furnishing materials for
an onslaught on candy."[10] There were always counterexamples:
plenty of people who ate candy all the time had no cavities at all,
while some who ate no candy or sweets were still plagued with
cavities. In fact, the lactic acid theory was equally consistent
with a defense of candy and sugar, since it could be said that the
cause of cavities was not eating candy so much as failing to clean
the teeth afterward.

There were still more theories of dental decay batted around
in the 1930s, as nutritional experts influenced by Elmer McCollum and the newer nutrition became interested in the effects of
dietary deficiencies. One idea was that candy caused cavities indirectly, by "removing from the body the calcium essential for its

bone and tooth building," as Dr. D. C. Jarvis explained at a 1937 meeting of the Philadelphia County Dental Society.[11] McCollum, who by the 1930s had firmly established himself as the foremost authority on vitamins and deficiency, believed the cause was a lack of phosphates and vitamin D. He also praised the work of Dr. Gordon Agnew, who announced in 1932 that he had been able "to produce and prevent tooth decay in rats, to a degree approaching 100 per cent, by including and omitting these elements."[12] In 1941, Dr. C. G. King of the University of Pittsburgh proposed that the high rate of dental decay found in army inductees was due to "their diets [being] on the average deficient in Vitamin C during infancy and early childhood to an extent that their tooth development was necessarily poor."[13]

As for candy, Dr. Agnew echoed the views of many who looked to dietary deficiencies as the culprit when he concluded that "eating sugar, candy and other sweets had no effect in itself in causing tooth decay, except that by satisfying the appetite too quickly it tended to keep down the intake of the foods containing the elements which make for sound tooth structure."[14] This position was reflected in educational publications of the American Dental Association in that era as well. For example, a 1945 patient education pamphlet titled *Diet and Dental Health* emphasized the overall quality of diet and the dangers of diet deficiencies. On the role of sugar, the pamphlet equivocates: "Some believe that the possible detrimental action accompanying the use of sweet foods is due to [the] action of the sugar itself. Others believe that failure to include the protective foods in the diet when sweets are used in quantity is the chief reason."[15]

In general, there was confusion and little sense of the sure path to prevention. Although tooth-cleaning powders, pastes, and brushes were available, most Americans did not include toothbrushing in their daily regime until after World War II. Dentists in the early decades of the twentieth century focused primarily on treatment of already diseased or decayed teeth.

This was a good thing for patients, who surely benefited from the development of alternatives to the traditional yank with a pair of pliers. But as the century progressed, the truly deplorable state of the nation's teeth was becoming more and more evident. By the mid-1930s, leading dental experts were worrying that dentistry was at risk of becoming irrelevant. Warned one ADA official: "If the dental profession is to stand in the future on its ability and cleverness in repairing the loss of human structure due to disease, and if it does not make any concerted effort or sacrifice to discover the cause of dental disease, the future of the profession is not very bright."[16]

But then in the 1950s, the future of dentistry started looking much brighter. The discovery that fluoride added to the water supply could strengthen tooth enamel and prevent cavities promised to revolutionize dental health and revitalize the profession of dentistry. Since the early 1900s, researchers had been puzzled by the brown, mottled appearance of children's teeth in certain communities. In 1931, a chemist discovered that the cause was naturally occurring fluoride in the water. Fluoride is toxic at high levels; the tooth discoloration was a symptom of excess fluoride (some would say fluoride poisoning) called "dental fluorosis."* The researchers also noticed that the discolored teeth were surprisingly strong and resistant to decay. Dr. H. Trendley Dean, head of the National Institute of Dental Research, began investigating how much fluoride in the water caused the symptoms of fluorosis. By the late 1930s, Dean had determined that levels of 1 ppm (part per million) in drinking water did not cause any tooth discoloration in most people. Dean got to thinking: if

---

*Fluoridation proponents claim that tooth discoloration caused by excess fluoride is merely cosmetic. Critics argue that dental fluorosis is in fact a symptom of damage to the dental matrix and should be viewed as in a continuum with more severe forms of fluoride toxicity including skeletal fluorosis and other forms of organ damage.

naturally occurring fluoride in water was protective, and 1 ppm was safe, then it would seem to make sense to add fluoride to drinking water as a preventive measure. It was a radical suggestion—after all, he was proposing deliberately adding a potentially toxic mineral to public drinking-water supplies. But public health officials were confident that such low levels of fluoride would not cause any harm, and they were eager to embrace what seemed to be a dramatic and simple solution to the pressing problem of tooth decay. In 1945, Grand Rapids, Michigan, volunteered to test the theory, becoming the first city in the world to fluoridate its water supply.[17] That same year, the ADA Research Commission confidently predicted that widespread adoption of community fluoridation would "prove of great value to coming generations."[18]

Dentists looking for a solution to the nation's dental health crisis were not the only ones glad to promote the cavity-fighting powers of fluoride. The Sugar Research Foundation also had a keen interest in any approach to dental decay that did not involve restricting the amount of sugar in the diet. When fluoride started to look promising, the foundation began quietly funneling funds to researchers working to prove the efficacy of fluoride in preventing cavities, as well as publicizing in their periodic research bulletins studies that supported fluoridation.[19] This must be included among the major ironies of the twentieth century: at the same time the sugar industry was funding studies to investigate the toxicity of cyclamate and sponsoring advertisements attacking relatively benign cyclamate as an unnatural and possibly dangerous chemical added to the food supply, it was funding and promoting research that would support the addition of a known toxin to the nation's water supplies, albeit at what was believed to be safe levels.*

---

*The EPA maximum contaminant level (MCL) goal for fluoride is 4 ppm; the EPA warns that "some people who drink water containing fluoride in excess

The official position of both the sugar refiners and the candy manufacturers was that cavities were mysterious things that might have many causes. Robert Hockett, the scientific director of the Sugar Research Foundation, reassured the assembled confectioners at the 1946 NCA meeting that reducing sugar was no solution to the problem of dental disease. First off, Hockett pointed out, people liked sugar too much to make sugar reduction a realistic approach to preventing dental decay. And second, Hockett suggested the theory that sugar caused decay didn't even make sense because "tooth decay was prevalent long before the introduction of sugar into our diets."[20] The real problem, as far as Hockett and the Sugar Research Foundation were concerned, was not an excess of sugar but a deficiency of fluoride. The candy makers cheered: if dental decay were indeed a deficiency disease akin to rickets or beriberi, then candy was blameless for rotten teeth and dentures. Better still, tooth decay could be conquered the easy modern way, with chemicals.

In 1950, the U.S. Public Health Service endorsed adding fluoride to public water sources, despite the fact that controlled studies on the effects of adding fluoride to community water systems had yet to be carried out. The American Dental Association and the American Medical Association added their blessing. Fluoridation proved controversial at first, especially in small communities where residents worried about dangers ranging from environmental contamination to Communist infiltration, but the program was widely embraced by authoritative and influential figures including scientists, dentists, and government health officials. By the end of the 1960s, 43 percent of the population

of the MCL over many years could get bone disease (including pain and tenderness of the bones)." Four ppm is only four times the typical level of municipal fluoridation. (EPA, "Basic Information About Fluoride in Drinking Water," http://water.epa.gov/drink/contaminants/basicinformation/fluoride.cfm#four.)

was drinking fluoridated water. Today nearly three-quarters of Americans are drinking from fluoridated community water supplies and the Centers for Disease Control and Prevention calls fluoridation "one of 10 great public health achievements of the twentieth century." (Although in 2011 the Department of Health and Human Services announced that it would reduce the recommended level of fluoridation due to concerns about the potential toxicity of excess fluoride consumption.)[21]

It is a little surprising that fluoride was so enthusiastically received at a time when Americans were becoming more and more wary of chemicals in the food supply and the environment. Fluorine is an extremely reactive element that in nature is found bonded to other minerals or metallic ore, creating various fluoride compounds. Naturally occurring fluoride may be found in trace amounts in some water supplies, and therefore in food, but until fluoride supplementation, most humans were consuming minuscule amounts or perhaps none at all. When in 1931 high levels of fluoride were identified in a natural water source for the first time at the Alcoa laboratory in Pennsylvania, the chief chemist insisted it was a mistake: "Whoever heard of fluorides in water," he exclaimed to his lab assistant. "You have contaminated the sample. Rush another specimen."[22] It took another round of painstaking photospectrographic analysis to convince everyone that there really was fluoride in the water.

One reason fluoridation was so appealing was the power of the vitamin metaphor. Americans had embraced vitamins in the 1930s and 1940s as the secret to health, vitality, and vigor. Public health officials also saw vitamin supplementation as the solution to the health problems caused by poverty and poor nutrition. The fact that fluoride appeared to reduce dental disease fit easily into this framework: fluoride was just another kind of vitamin, and if you didn't get enough of it, you would get sick (even today, my daughter's dentist refers to her topical fluoride treatment as "tooth vitamins"). Unwittingly, fluoridation advocates like

Dr. Dean Fisher of the Maine Health Department echoed the Sugar Research Foundation's position when they explained to their constituents that "tooth decay is a result of nutritional deficiency" and that "the average person needs one milligram of fluoride per day."[23] In the 1968 revision of the Recommended Dietary Allowances, fluoride was included for the first time as an "essential nutrient."[24] This put fluoride on a par with calcium and iron, minerals that contribute to the substance and function of bones and blood. The implication was that without fluoride supplementation, America's teeth would be in serious trouble.

Fluoridation was heralded as a "major breakthrough, the first, in the prevention of a major dental disease,"[25] but tooth decay continued to be a serious public health problem. In 1967 national expenditures for dental care amounted to $4.7 billion per year, $2 billion of which was spent on the repair of decayed teeth. Yet even with that vast expenditure, only 40 percent of the population was receiving dental care.[26] The National Institutes of Health estimated that in 1970 there were still eight hundred million untreated cavities in America's two hundred million mouths.[27] Clearly, fluoridation was only a partial solution.

Many people believed that fluoride would soon be followed by some drug or chemical that would eradicate decay. But while researchers looked for this magic bullet, dentists turned to more concrete techniques for prevention: hygiene and nutrition. The American Dental Association aligned with toothpaste manufacturers to encourage daily toothbrushing with fluoridated toothpastes and regular professional teeth cleaning. At the same time, researchers struggled to understand how particular foods interacted with bacteria in the mouth to promote decay. Some investigators believed carbohydrates (including starches) to be the primary culprit, but more and more attention was zeroing in on sucrose specifically.

A 1953 overview and summary of research findings collated by the ADA concluded with a firm advisory linking sugar to cavities (called "caries" in the medical literature): "The dental profession and other interested agencies have a responsibility to warn the public of the cariogenic property of sugars and their solutions (i.e. sweetened beverages and fruit juices) and to point out that many of these products contain no highly important nutritional factors."[28] Further studies in the 1950s and 1960s supported this warning; in 1969, Dr. Ernest Newbrun summed up the position of dentists on sugar with the wittily titled article "Sucrose: The Arch Criminal of Dental Caries."[29]

Newbrun called for eliminating all sucrose-containing foods in order to conquer decay, but not everyone was willing to go so far. There was a growing body of research that implicated one particular kind of sugar consumption: candy, especially eating candy as a snack between meals. There were also all kinds of studies that found quite the opposite, or found that some other aspect of the diet was to blame, or even found that diet had nothing to do with decay. But in the popular accounts summarizing dental research, the studies that showed sugar—and especially candy—to be the worst tended to get more attention.[30] Frequently cited evidence included the work of Albert H. Trithart and Robert L. Weiss, who had studied the diets and health of more than two thousand pre-school-age children and found "a direct relationship" between the number of bad teeth and "the number of confections eaten regularly between meals."[31]

Even more compelling to many experts were the results published in 1954 of a study carried out at a mental hospital in Sweden, which found that more "retentive" sweets (i.e., where sugar stays in the mouth longer) were worse, and that the frequency of consumption of sweets between meals was also a factor.[32] It was the Swedish study that provided the most direct evidence for the damaging effects of candy on the teeth. But although the conclusions became widely known, the circumstances of the research were veiled in secrecy. It was a chilling human experiment, one in which researchers designed a "nutrition study" with the intent to harm.

Vipeholm Hospital was Sweden's largest facility for the long-term care of the mentally handicapped. At Vipeholm, researchers could easily monitor and control patients' food intake as well as their other activities. Without the patients' consent or any form of ethical oversight, researchers set about inducing dental decay in the hospital's residents. During the most troubling phase of the study, carried out between 1947 and 1949, researchers subjected the patients to extreme conditions of carbohydrate consumption, either in very sticky bread taken at meals or in the form of a between-meal snack of six toffees taken four times a day (twenty-four in all). The toffees were not ordinary candy but a special formula created to adhere to the teeth for the longest time possible. While it was certainly useful to discover, as the study did, that the effect of the twenty-four between-meal toffees was far worse than bread eaten with meals, the price was high: by the time researchers discontinued the sticky toffee rations in 1949, 50 of the 660 patients had completely ruined teeth.[33]

As a controlled human experiment, the Vipeholm study was the only one of its kind, and the ability of the researchers to control every aspect of the experiment made the findings especially valuable. Vipeholm was the basis for what became conventional wisdom in the 1970s: eating candy between meals causes cavities. But those who took the trouble to actually examine the Vipeholm study with a more skeptical eye were not entirely convinced that this was the whole story. "The role of diet in dental caries etiology is quite complex," insisted Dr. Stephen N. Kreitzman of the Emory University School of Dentistry in a 1980 essay in the *Journal of Preventive Dentistry*. "Perhaps we can say with conviction 'Don't feed twenty-four extra large and extra sticky toffees to mental patients, who can practice no oral hygiene, every day for a period of three years.' Beyond that there are still many questions."[34] Even at Vipeholm, the results were not quite so unequivocal. Twenty percent of the patients had no cavities at all. And there was also evidence that for some patients, bread

could be as damaging as some kinds of candy (although nothing approached the daily dose of twenty-four sticky toffees for
tooth-rotting capability).[35]

By the late 1960s, dentists were describing tooth decay as "the
most prevalent nutritional problem in the United States."[36] Dentists and oral health experts were making regular appearances at
congressional hearings concerning nutrition, school lunches,
and food advertising in order to explain the connection between
diet and dental health. Dr. Abraham Nizel of the Tufts University School of Dental Medicine was one of several experts to
testify in 1972 congressional hearings considering the state of
national nutrition education. Nizel described three prongs in the
battle against tooth decay: fluoridation, tooth cleaning, and nutrition. While dentists and the public had made important progress in the first two, the role of nutrition education had, in Nizel's
view, been dangerously neglected. Americans needed to understand that "the frequent eating of even minute amounts of sugar
confections or sugar sweetened drinks between meals [is the]
most important" dietary factor in causing cavities.[37] Nizel's summary of the current state of knowledge regarding the relation of
sugar and cavities was applauded by his colleagues as "a good
example of the unanimity there is within this field on this subject" and reflected the same ideas that were being repeated by
experts in other congressional hearings and reports.[38]

Nizel's warning of the pernicious effects of between-meal indulgence in candy and sweets was in large part informed by the
Vipeholm research. But his recommendations for U.S. policy
were quite different from the course pursued in Sweden. In 1959,
when all phases of the nutritional research had been concluded,
the Swedish government decided to implement a national dental
health campaign. In an interesting twist on "candy rots your
teeth," the government actually encouraged its citizens to eat
candy. The new slogan was, "All the sweets you like, but only once
a week." Swedes embraced the new tradition of *lördagsgodis* or

"Saturday Candy."[39] To this day, Saturday is celebrated in Sweden with a trip to the store to load up on "pick what you like" candy mixes, without any guilt, worry, or remorse.

In contrast to the Swedish approach, which recognized and allowed for candy pleasure, Dr. Nizel encouraged Congress to take a page from the recent tobacco experience. Just as mounting evidence for the pathological effects of tobacco had led to legislation requiring warning labels, so Dr. Nizel suggested the FTC should mandate health warning labels on "every package of sugar-sweetened life savers, cough drops, breath mints, candies, chewing gum and soft drinks with a statement warning the user that excessive frequent daily use of these products can produce significant amounts of dental plaque and dental decay."[40] No dental association went so far as to advocate actual warning labels on food. Even so, it was a measure of how far candy had fallen that in 1972, serious, credible, mainstream experts were suggesting that candy might need to be regulated in the same manner as cigarettes.

12 ⊙ Treat or Trick?

Around the same time dentists were warning Congress about candy's dental villainy, stories were surfacing of an evil trickery afoot at Halloween. Lethal poisons like heroin and cyanide were showing up in children's trick-or-treat candy. In 1975, *Newsweek* warned parents of the horrors to be expected: "If this year's Halloween follows form, a few children will return home with something more than an upset tummy: in recent years, several children have died and hundreds have narrowly escaped injury from razor blades, sewing needles and shards of glass purposefully put into their goodies by adults."[1] This was a tragic turn for Halloween fun; since the 1930s, kids had been enjoying the thrill of trick-or-treating. And then suddenly the fun turned treacherous. It was poison candy, all over again.[2]

Before Candy

Halloween, with its attendant binge of mass candy consumption, has become perhaps the most universal American holiday. It proposes no national identity or allegiance, nor any specific religious affiliations. Ninety-three percent of children surveyed by the candy industry said they planned to go trick-or-treating in 2009. Each one of those children could expect a substantial payoff; according to popular Halloween lore, the average jack-o'-lantern bucket holds about 250 pieces of candy, amounting to about nine thousand calories and three pounds of sugar.[3]

This annual sugar-fueled ritual is so deeply ingrained in the American calendar that it's hard to imagine that a hundred years ago, Halloween looked quite different. There was no candy debauch, for starters. There were jack-o'-lanterns, but there were no jack-o'-lantern buckets: trick-or-treating hadn't been invented yet. Descriptions of Halloween fun from the first two decades of the twentieth century don't mention anything resembling trick-or-treating. In her 1919 *Book of Halloween*, Massachusetts writer Ruth Edna Kelley describes traditions that include various pranks and festivities in public, and indoor merrymaking in private homes: "It is a night of ghostly and merry revelry. Mischievous spirits choose it for carrying off gates and other objects, and hiding them or putting them out of reach . . . Bags filled with flour sprinkle the passers-by. Door-bells are rung and mysterious raps sounded on doors, things thrown into halls, and knobs stolen . . . Hallowe'en parties are the real survival of the ancient merrymakings."[4]

What was particular about Halloween in those days, and what set that holiday apart from all the other festive occasions of the year, was mischief. Halloween was the one night a year when communities would tolerate broken gates and upended outhouses. Today Halloween pranks tend to be tame and predictable: smashed pumpkins, toilet-paper-festooned trees, eggs plastered on parked cars. These are but a pale ghost of pranks of old, like those described by an 1895 writer: "Country boys and those in small towns reveled in throwing corn, cabbage heads, and decayed vegetables at the windows and doors of all good residents. The ubiquitous tick-tack was set up at many an old maid's or crusty bachelor's window and worked from a safe distance by the mischievous small boy."[5]

Rotten pumpkins and even the "ubiquitous tick-tack" were pretty straightforward (tick-tack is a setup with a hard object attached to a long string dangling over a window or door; the prankster pulls the string to create an annoying tapping noise). Pranks could also be quite elaborate. Residents at a teachers' boardinghouse on Long Island woke up the morning after Halloween in 1900 "to find their house surrounded by what appeared to be a graveyard," as a reporter recounted in *The New York Times* two days later. "Their screams of horror turned to laughter as they realized they must have been the target of a Halloween prank. Tombstones had been mysteriously transported during the night from a nearby marble yard. The owner of the marble yard, who spent the day carting the stones back to their rightful place, was not so amused."[6]

The warden of Sing Sing prison had a scare on Halloween night in 1915 when reports arrived of an escaped prisoner on the loose. Within minutes, guards captured Louis Minker, eighteen years old. Minker pleaded for lenience, claiming that he was only intending to celebrate Halloween. He had found the castoff prison garb and thought it would make an appropriate costume. The warden threatened to throw him in a cell in retribution, but the judge let him off with a stern talking-to.[7]

Sometimes, the fun could go sour. In 1905, ten boys were fined for soaping the trolley rails on the steepest hill in Greenwich, Connecticut, causing several cars to careen down the hill and dump their passengers. The newspaper reporter who recounted this story seemed sympathetic to the boys' prank, noting that they "thought it a great joke" and had "only considered the fun." The judge, too, took a lenient view, telling the boys that "if the offense had happened on any other night but Hallowe'en he would have sent them to jail."[8]

While the hooligans were out wreaking havoc, the more

genteel would celebrate with parties. The menus and décor for these early Halloween festivities emphasized seasonal fruits. A harvest theme would set the mood, with cornstalks, pumpkins, and apples. Then as today, Halloween parties have always had a place for candy. But the kinds of candy, and the role of candy in the festivities, have changed dramatically.

The American Girls Handy Book (1887) includes a full chapter on celebrating "All-Hallow-Eve." Candy features briefly, in the form of a bubbling candy pot:

> Putting aside conventionality and dignity as we laid aside our wraps, ready for any fun or mischief that might be on hand, we proceeded down-stairs and into the kitchen, where a large pot of candy was found bubbling over the fire. This candy, poured into plates half-full of nuts, was eaten at intervals during the evening, and served to keep up the spirits of those who were inclined to be cast down by the less pleasing of Fortune's decrees.[9]

Ideas for a Halloween party in 1894 published in *American Agriculturalist* included these proposals for refreshments: nut cake, popcorn, molasses candy, and "as many more goodies as one cares to provide."[10] The children's magazine *St. Nicholas* describes in detail the decorations, refreshments, games, and entertainments for a children's celebration of Halloween in 1905. Candy makes one brief appearance as part of the décor: "The dining-table was set with a group of carrot candlesticks and bowlfuls of apples, nuts, grapes, and candy."[11] But candy was definitely not the main attraction; a picture illustrating a sample table arrangement features apples, grapes, nuts, and pumpkins but nary a morsel of candy in sight. If candy was included in a party, it was almost always homemade and not particularly associated with Halloween.

Where purchased candy was incorporated into the party, it

was not necessarily any special kind. For example, in 1917, the Kansas chapter of Phi Gamma Delta fraternity reported, "On October 20 the annual tacky party was given. Arriving in a hayrack, the guests entered the house by way of the kitchen door. The rooms were decorated with corn and witches in true Halloween fashion. Popcorn, apples, penny candy sticks, doughnuts, pie, and cider were served. The party was one of the most successful in the chapter's history."[12]

When candy makers in the 1910s and 1920s looked for ways to grow their fall sales, Halloween barely registered as a potential marketing opportunity, even though retail stores were using other holidays as opportunities to sell seasonal confections. Christmas and Easter were big candy events, already established by 1900: boxed chocolates and hard candies for Christmas, jelly eggs and molded chocolate bunnies for Easter. Lagging not far behind in importance on the candy holiday calendar was Washington's Birthday, celebrated with special marzipan cherries and cocoa-dusted logs. A few forward-thinking retailers might dress up their shop windows for Halloween, but the holiday hadn't yet acquired its array of consumer opportunities like store-bought decorations, costumes, and greeting cards.

Even candy corn, the unofficial candy mascot of Halloween, has not always been so closely tied to the holiday. A Brach's magazine ad from 1957, for example, featured candy corn as one of "Brach's Summertime Candies," alongside circus peanuts, orange slices, and jelly beans. In 1951, a local Virginia drugstore ad celebrated candy corn as "the candy all children love to nibble on all year long."[13] Today Brach's and Jelly Belly (formerly Goelitz) are the only national brands of candy corn, but throughout the twentieth century many major candy companies included candy corn in their offerings. I've found references to candy corn in the 1940s, 1950s, and 1960s, in such diverse sources as children's stories, math textbooks, psychology experiments, party-planning handbooks, and baking and decorating books.

George Renninger, a candy maker at the Wunderle Candy Company, produced the original "butter cream" in Philadelphia in 1888.[14] This soft candy was perfectly suited for molding into all sorts of shapes. Renninger's molded buttercreams were inspired by nature: chestnuts, turnips, peas in a pod, and cloverleaves. But with candy corn, Renninger's fancy went even further, to include not only a corn-kernel shape but also the layering of three colors. This made it taxing to produce (all those colors had to be poured by hand), but it also made it novel and visually exciting.

In the early days, not everybody called it "candy corn." Some people called it "chicken feed." Goelitz's packaging from the 1920s features a proud rooster scratching around in the candy bits and the motto "King of the Candy Corn Fields." Corn wasn't something Americans ate much of before World War I. There were no sweet hybrids in those days. Corn was coarse and cheap and not very tasty: good food for pigs and chickens. Corn bread was a popular staple in the South, but it wasn't until wartime wheat shortages in 1917 that corn gained wider acceptance. Candy corn, on the other hand, quickly became one of America's favorite treats.

As Halloween became more and more dominated by candy beginning in the 1950s, candy corn's yellow and orange colors and harvest associations made the already popular candy an obvious choice. There was a dramatic spike in October advertising of candy corn beginning in the 1950s. Other kinds of candy were advertised for Halloween too, but they were advertised just as heavily during the rest of the year, and the more people thought of candy corn as a special Halloween treat, the less likely they were to consider it for ordinary eating at other times. Today, it's hard to find traditional candy corn any other time of year.

Trick-or-Treat Gangsters

The origins of trick-or-treating are murky and controversial. Its contemporary incarnation resembles older traditions as practiced in distant lands—each potential origin story has its fierce national partisans. There have been annual festivals in many European societies since the Middle Ages, during which certain classes of people were permitted and expected to beg. Trick-or-treating today most closely resembles the English and Irish custom of "souling," the ritual begging for alms and "soul cakes" on Hallowmas (November 1), in return for a promise of prayers for the dead on All Souls' Day (November 2). Other potential sources of influence include traditions of begging for Guy Fawkes Day, Scottish guising (masquerading), and various medieval European traditions of masked ritual solicitation associated with Christmas and other holidays on the Christian calendar. But resemblance is not descent: while immigrants from many of these countries established communities in colonial America, their holiday begging traditions did not automatically translate into what we now know as Halloween.

One of the earliest descriptions of trick or treat as we know it today comes from a newspaper article from Alberta, Canada, in 1927: "Hallowe'en provided an opportunity for real strenuous fun. No real damage was done except to the temper of some who had to hunt for wagon wheels, gates, wagons, barrels, etc., much of which decorated the front street. The youthful tormentors were at back door and front demanding edible plunder by the word 'trick-or-treat' to which the inmates gladly responded and sent the robbers away rejoicing."[15]

Over the next decade, stories describing (and sometimes decrying) trick or treat appeared in papers from western and middle states—the references are infrequent but remarkably similar.[16] The 1930s brought tales of manhunts and shoot-outs into the daily papers, and Hollywood filled movie screens with images of gangster attitudes and styles. Early accounts of trick or treat used the language of gangsterism to describe the activity as a playful version of much more dangerous crimes. From Oregon in 1934 came an account of "young goblins and ghosts, employing modern

Halloween trick-or-treaters, Saint Paul, Minnesota, 1934.
(Courtesy of the Minnesota Historical Society)

shakedown methods, [who] successfully worked the 'trick-or-treat'
system in all parts of the city."[17] In Washington in 1939, a journalist wrote that "pranksters were bought off when oldsters complied
with their 'trick-or-treat' demand."[18] And from Nevada in 1938, a
writer explained that " 'trick-or-treat' was the slogan employed by
Halloween pranksters who successfully extracted candy and fruit
from Reno residents. In return the youngsters offered protection
against window soaping and other forms of annoyance."[19]

Contemporary reports of Halloween encounters in the 1930s
make it clear that sometimes "trick or treat" could be truly menacing. A Reno resident complained in 1938 of being besieged by
a group of six or eight boys and girls and unable to answer the
doorbell. The children consulted among themselves: "If they
don't open up, let's give them the works." Thereupon the garbage

can was emptied, its contents strewn about, and the can dragged down the road.[20] A 1934 newspaper account from Montana puts the playful gangster reference in a more dangerous light: "Pretty Boy John Doe rang the door bells and his gang waited his signal. It was his plan to proceed cautiously at first and give a citizen every opportunity to comply with his demands before pulling any rough stuff. 'Madam, we are here for the usual purpose, "trick-or-treat."'"[21] The "gang" described in this article consisted of older, physically intimidating youths, two boys and a girl, fifteen or sixteen years old. According to the author, when a woman refused their demands for treats or money, they retaliated by smashing an expensive birdbath in front of her house.

"Pretty Boy John Doe" is a reference to the nationally notorious gangster figure Charles "Pretty Boy" Floyd. After a multiyear crime spree that landed him at the top of the nation's most-wanted list, Floyd was killed in a shoot-out on October 22, 1934, two weeks before the article was published. The author presents this scene as a prelude to more serious crimes of theft and gun violence; as the headline puts it, these teenage trick-or-treaters are "The Gangsters of Tomorrow."

Despite the alarm sounded by some that gangster-style trick or treat was a gateway to a criminal future, most of the descriptions of early trick-or-treating were more bemused than alarmed. On the morning after Halloween 1938 in Reno, the newspaper reported that "residents who refused to pay tribute found their lights turned off, their windows soaped, or toothpicks in their doorbells."[22] The pranks were mild and tolerable, and the writer implied that the victimized residents had it coming.

A 1938 *Los Angeles Times* article gives a fuller description of children's trick-or-treat activities: "From house to house the boys and girls will travel, punching doorbells with nerve-jangling peals. 'Trick-or-treat!' is the terse command as the householder peeks warily around the door. 'If you don't give us something, we'll play a trick on you . . .' So the diminutive Halloween goon squads are bought off with cookies, candy, [toy] alarm clocks or the price of an ice cream cone." The writer warned that if readers didn't come up with the goods, they could expect to suffer the consequences: "For those without treats, the boys and girls threaten, 'You wouldn't want your porch littered with paper, or your windows soaped, or a smelly roll of burning film left around, would you?'" None of it was particularly vicious, and the writer considered it all to be in good fun, waving off adults who wouldn't play along as "grumpy citizen[s]."[23]

There were a few of those grumpy citizens in the early days of trick or treat, adults who were vehemently opposed to the idea that kids should be able to annoy their neighbors by ringing their doorbells and demanding a prize. One was Brooklyn high school principal Dr. Gabriel R. Mason. On Halloween night 1952, Dr. Mason's neighborhood was overrun with gangs of rowdy boys who were overturning trash cans and ringing doorbells. Meanwhile, on the other side of the street, Richard Wanderman, age ten, asked his mother for permission to join some friends for a "trick-or-treat tour." As Mrs. Wanderman explained in the subsequent court proceedings, she gave her permission and suggested the boys start at Dr. Mason's house—after all, she reasoned, he was a school principal and therefore sure to give them something.

Richard and his friends rang Dr. Mason's bell. But Dr. Mason was at his wits' end and felt extremely aggrieved by what he perceived as the boys' ungentlemanly demand for treats. Instead of candy, he offered a five-minute lecture on the evils of begging and why little boys should not run about demanding tribute and behaving like gangsters. Richard and crew were not so easily edified. As recounted in the court transcript, Richard stepped up, put his fist in Dr. Mason's face, and growled, "Hand it over, or else!" At which point Dr. Mason did hand it over in a sense: a back of the hand to little Richard's face. Dr. Mason got a charge of assault in the third degree and a court summons. In his defense, he noted, "I did not know it was a neighbor's child."[24]

Sweet Treats

By the late 1940s, trick or treat was firmly established as an American custom. It was recognized and discussed in national publications like *Jack and Jill* (1947) and *American Home* (1947), and featured in Halloween radio broadcasts including *The Jack Benny Show* (1948) and *The Adventures of Ozzie and Harriet* (1948). Halloween vandalism was on the decline, and in 1950 a reporter in Hartford, Connecticut, ventured that it was the "quietest of Halloweens."[25]

As Halloween was becoming less unruly, the emphasis in trick-or-treating was clearly shifting: fewer tricks, more treats. Kids ringing a stranger's doorbell in the early days of trick or treat received all sorts of tribute: coins, nuts, fruit, cookies, cakes, and toys were as likely as candy. In a scene in Frank Capra's *Arsenic and Old Lace* (filmed in 1941, released in 1944), there's a glimpse of a very early version of trick or treat. About twenty-four minutes into the film, the murderous but adorable aunties retire to the kitchen. Dashing Cary Grant follows, and we see some very strange action around the back door. A swarm of masked children are hollering and shouting and holding out their arms, and the aunties are passing them goodies: two big pumpkin jack-o'-lanterns and one pie.

Treats were mostly homespun in the 1940s, but by the 1950s food manufacturers and retailers were figuring out ways to cash in with commercial foods. Local retail stores were the first to emphasize Halloween uses for candy in their weekly newspaper advertising. Kresge's Market in New London, Connecticut, ran an ad in 1951 featuring "Hallowe'en Candy for Parties and 'Trick or Treat' Callers." Among the proposed "Trick or Treat Favors" were M&M's (by the half-pound bag), small Baby Ruth and Butterfinger bars at two cents apiece, and assorted penny candies and gum. The sketch accompanying the ad depicts an elegant 1950s housewife holding a plate of dainties for a tiny clown and a cat.

The ad reminds readers that handing out candy is a way to "be ready to make friends with your little neighbors" and is evidence of how tame trick or treat had become. The boisterous and mischievous gangsters have become three-foot-tall "callers," and the candy is not so much extorted as offered freely in a gesture of hospitality and friendliness.

Only a few candy manufacturers were big enough to afford national advertising campaigns. In the October 26, 1953, issue of *Life* magazine, Fleer Dubble Bubble ran an ad encouraging mothers to "Treat the Kids this Halloween with Dubble Bubble." The accompanying drawing features a trim brunette with a little black cat at her feet, handing gum to a pack of costumed kids. Mars, Inc. was also among the first manufacturers promoting candy for trick or treat. The October 25, 1954, issue of *Life* features an ad for Milky Way bars promoting the "Haunting Flavor" of its "three layer treat," with an image of a ghost eating a Milky Way. Fleer Dubble Bubble ran an ad in the same issue with a masked trick-or-treater ringing a doorbell, a clever visual reference to the early "gangster" origins of trick or treat.

But candy advertised around Halloween might not even make a reference to the holiday. In the October 25, 1954, issue of *Life*, Brach's ran an ad for chocolate peanuts that made no mention of the season or the holiday; likewise, an ad for the Mars bar in the October, 29, 1956, issue. Other products also took up the trick-or-treat theme in their advertising, no matter how far-fetched. The October 25, 1954, issue of *Life* included a Kellogg's ad for cereal Snack-Paks that reads, "Sweet treats for little kids!" and shows a woman handing a box of Frosted Flakes to the trick-or-treaters. In 1959, an October issue featured trick-or-treat-themed ads for Hawaiian Punch ("treats for thirsty tricksters"), Kool-Aid ("loot for the trick or treaters"), and my own favorite for weird Halloween tie-in, Dutch Masters Cigars (costumed kids hold a cigar box out to dad: "No trick . . . all treat").

Anything could be a Halloween treat in theory, but it was

Fleer Dubble Bubble chewing gum ad, 1954

during the 1950s that candy began to make decisive inroads in dominating Halloween. The rise of trick-or-treating made the holiday the perfect occasion for marketing a product associated with children and fun. The push from candy sellers was met with equally enthusiastic demand. Candy was easy to buy and easy to distribute, making it a convenient choice for Halloween hosts. And as the numbers of trick-or-treaters swelled, it was also economical. Small, inexpensive candies became popular, and major manufacturers began making smaller candy bars or treat-sized bags of candy corn and other small candies.

Through the 1950s and 1960s, candy jostled with other goods and treats for place in the trick-or-treat sack. It wasn't until the 1970s that candy came to be seen as the only legitimate treat. The candy industry certainly reaped the benefits, and much of the credit for elbowing out all other possible goodies surely is due to the substantial marketing budgets of confectionery giants like Hershey and Mars. But along with the positive encouragement of advertising, there was a more malevolent and fearsome force at work, which drove terrified parents to reject the old-fashioned goodness of homemade cookies and popcorn balls, and rush to embrace the new era of factory-sealed and factory-made candy treats.

Halloween Killers

In 1959, California dentist Dr. William Shyne (another of those "grumpy citizens") decided to treat the local children with a trick of his own. Shyne distributed over 450 candy-coated laxative tablets to the neighborhood children on Halloween; thirty ate the "candy" and became violently ill. Shyne was charged with "outrage of public decency" and "unlawful dispensing of drugs."[26] Fortunately, the children's injuries were fleeting. Not so fleeting was the image of the "Halloween sadist" that emerged out of Shyne's malicious act.

In the following years, stories began surfacing of children victimized by poisoned candy handed out as a Halloween treat. A few days before Halloween 1970, *The New York Times* published an article alerting readers to the alarming fact that incidents involving poisoning of treats had been growing rapidly over the past five years and specifying some of the potential dangers: "That plump red apple . . . may have a razor blade hidden inside . . . the bubble gum may be sprinkled with lye, the popcorn balls may be coated with camphor, the candy may turn out to be packets containing sleeping pills."[27] Newspapers and magazines began routinely warning parents to be on the lookout for deadly dangers lurking in the Halloween booty. In an effort to stem the apparent epidemic, cities passed laws criminalizing candy tampering, schools began training students in candy inspection, and some communities even tried to ban trick-or-treating.[28] Parents started clamping down to shield their children from abusive strangers and questionable treats. By the early 1980s, it was widely accepted as a fact of life that at Halloween, random crazy strangers would attempt to poison little children with razor-blade-studded apples and tainted candy.

When the sociologist Joel Best decided in 1984 to try to quantify just how bad the poison Halloween candy threat actually was, he discovered something surprising: it was all rumor and fabulation. Best investigated seventy-six press accounts of what he called "Halloween sadism" published between 1958 and 1983. He concluded that "there was simply no basis for *Newsweek*'s claim that 'several children have died.'"[29] Not a single case that Best could discover fit the pattern of an anonymous maniac arbitrarily attacking children by tampering with Halloween treats.

There were two candy-related deaths that Best was able to verify. These cases were examples not of random stranger danger, however, but of calculated manipulation and cover-up. In 1970, five-year-old Kevin Toston went into a coma and died; the initial reports claimed he had eaten candy sticks sprinkled with heroin. Only later did it come out that Kevin had actually swallowed a capsule of the drug. A subsequent investigation led police to believe someone had doctored the candy after Kevin ate the heroin, possibly to deflect suspicion.

The other Halloween death by poisoning was worse: premeditated murder. Eight-year-old Timothy O'Bryan died in 1974 after eating a cyanide-laced Pixy Stix. Investigators discovered that none of the houses Timothy visited for trick-or-treating that year had handed out Pixy Stix candy. According to the prosecution, it was his father who had put the toxic treat in Timothy's sack, on the expectation of a generous life insurance settlement on his son. Ronald O'Bryan was convicted in 1975 and executed in 1984.[30]

And what of the rest of it, the broken wrappers and needles in candy bars and rat-poison-coated jelly beans? Joel Best concluded that "the vast majority were fabrications."[31] Where an actual morsel of dangerous candy was produced, it invariably turned out that the kids themselves were the perpetrators. In an interview, Best explained that "kids—after years of hearing similar stories—[inserted] needles or razor blades into fruit, not realizing (or maybe realizing) how much they frightened their whole town."[32] He recounted how one kid brought a half-eaten candy bar to his parents complaining it was covered in ant poison; it was, but only on the end he hadn't bitten. In another story, a boy claimed to have found a pin in his Tootsie Roll. His parents blamed a neighbor, and relations were frosty for years. Twenty years later, the boy (now grown) confessed that he had planted the pin himself.[33]

In 1982, the NCA made a deliberate effort to defuse some of the negative publicity with a report on candy tampering. The report revealed that "more than 95 percent of the 270 potential Halloween 1982 candy adulterations analyzed by the Food and Drug Administration have shown no tampering, which has led one FDA official to characterize the period as one of 'psychosomatic mass hysteria.'"[34] Best's own conclusion was that the candy-tampering stories were urban legends that, although superficially false, expressed real felt "fears about the safety of children, the danger of crime, and other sources of social strain."[35]

No doubt there is much truth in the idea that the legends of Halloween poisoning reflected broader social ills. The late 1960s and 1970s were a time of social upheaval and transformation. Long-simmering racial conflicts were erupting in the streets.

Young people were clashing with cops in antiwar protests. Women were fleeing suburban housewifery and declaring sexual emancipation. Rapid change and visible social conflicts created anxiety and confusion about who could be trusted, who was a benevolent neighbor, and who was a dangerous stranger.

Fears of murderous Halloween maniacs also fit in with a broader sense that children were becoming especially weak and vulnerable to danger. Historians of childhood have documented a general shift in the postwar period toward securing, protecting, and controlling children. As Howard Chudacoff has noted, children's play became increasingly confined and controlled after the 1950s as parents worked to keep their children safe from all manner of harm, both real and imaginary.[36] The rapid transformation of trick or treat exemplifies this trend. After 1960, parents moved quickly to protect children from Halloween dangers, severely curtailing their after-dark movements, imposing supervision where children previously would have been left alone, and claiming the prerogative to examine and confiscate any "suspect" treats or candies. Through the 1970s and 1980s, no Halloween was complete without dire warnings of what might befall a child who enjoyed Halloween without the proper adult protection.

The Halloween sadist legends are not only about children and strangers, though. They're also about candy. It is not accidental that the warnings about poisons hiding in innocent candies at Halloween in the 1970s and 1980s sound a lot like the warnings about poison and adulteration in the 1890s and 1900s. The persistence of poison candy stories in the era of the "pure food" reform movement reflected a larger context of rapid changes in the way food was being manufactured and sold. Industrial candy was the most visible form of a new kind of manufactured, artificial food that might or might not be safe. When children suffered harm, candy was an easy scapegoat.

Some of the Halloween candy–poisoning cases from the 1980s and 1990s seem to repeat point for point the NCA's investigations from a century before. For example, in 1991 a thirty-one-year-old man died after sampling some of his kid's candy loot. Neighborhood parents rushed to dump all their childrens' candy. It turned out he had died of an ordinary heart attack. In another case, a three-year-old Connecticut boy arrived at the hospital suffering from cocaine poisoning. Halloween candy took the fall, although a subsequent analysis of the leftover candy revealed no traces of the drug.[37] As in the earlier period, no matter the complexity of circumstances, candy was presumed guilty from the start.

Stories of tampered-with treats bolstered the value and desirability of name-brand packaged candies in the 1970s and afterward. Loose, casual, cheap wrappers, the kind of wrappers one might find on locally produced candies or non-brand-name candies, were frequently interpreted as evidence that the candy was somehow suspicious. The close, tight factory wrapper promised protection from tampering strangers. And the recognized brand name on the wrapper lent a reassuring aura of corporate responsibility and accountability. The homemade cookies and popcorn balls that were standard in the 1950s came to seem in later decades to be inherently inferior to the factory product, and also inherently dangerous.

The broader food context probably also played a part in the persistence and popularity of the Halloween sadist legends. By the 1970s, the rise of convenience foods and fast foods that had begun after the Second World War was having a dramatic impact on what, when, and how people were eating. More and more food came in convenient packages, just like candy. And more and more food was being designed and promoted to be enjoyed like candy, as fun and pleasurable. Just as poison candy stories in the 1900s had reflected an underlying worry about the wholesomeness of manufactured food, so the resurgence of poison candy stories in the 1970s coincided with a rising worry about just what it was that people—including children—were eating. Was it food? Or was it junk?

13 ⊚ Junk-Food Junkies

By 1970, Americans were familiar with a whole new vocabulary of previously undreamed-of comestibles. Sleekly packaged brands from Tang and Velveeta to Cup-a-Soup and Minute Rice conjured up the convenience and efficiency of modern living. From Breakfast Squares and Pop-Tarts in the morning to frozen pizzas and TV dinners at night, eating at home had never been easier: just open the box. For items requiring more preparation, "cooking" could usually be accomplished by adding a little hot water.

But as alluring as instant mashed potatoes and gravy from a packet might have been, there were greater temptations just down the road. Away from home it was becoming ever easier to find on-the-go offerings like burgers and hot dogs (McDonald's and In-N-Out Burger opened their first restaurants in 1948, Jack in the Box in 1950, Burger King in 1954, Carl's Jr. and Sonic in 1956); fried chicken (1952 saw Church's and Kentucky Fried); and pizza (Pizza Hut opened in 1958, Little Caesars in 1959, and Domino's in 1961). On the sweet side, there were donuts (Winchell's in 1949, Dunkin' Donuts in 1950) and ice cream (Baskin-Robbins, Tastee Freeze, Dairy Queen, Carvel, all of which began franchising their brands after the war). If none of these were handy, there were vending machines in parks, schools, ballparks, office buildings, bus stops, or anywhere else you might be. Anytime, anyplace, some tempting food was sure to be on offer, in a convenient package and easy to eat on the go.[1]

Along with changes in food came dramatic changes in eating. Most people still believed in three square meals as an ideal. But researchers for the food industry were learning that breakfast, lunch, and dinner were becoming more the exception than the rule. A 1974 study grabbed the headlines: "20 Partials, Not 'Three Squares.'" In lieu of sitting down to a balanced meal, more and more Americans were opting for a constant stream of snacking. The researcher Dr. Paul Fine described a typical day: skipped breakfast, midmorning coffee, lunch or not, and all accompanied by a "perpetual replenishing of the snack larder." Even sleep would provide no respite; Fine found that the "midnight snack" was increasingly punctuating the dark hours with yet more opportunities to munch. Mainstream consumers appeared to be surviving on diets filled with "Oreos, peanut butter, Crisco, TV dinners, cake mix, macaroni and cheese, Pepsi and Coke, pizzas, Jell-O, hamburgers, Rice-A-Roni, Spaghetti-O's, pork and beans, Heinz [ketchup] and instant coffee." Fine calculated that Americans were averaging twenty separate "food contacts" per day, with little reference to traditional meal patterns.[2]

Social critics worried about the apparent collapse of the traditional family meal, which seemed to be a symptom of a whole array of new social dysfunctions: mothers working and not coming home to cook, fathers coming home late or not coming home at all, divorce, latchkey kids with no one watching to be sure they ate their vegetables. Mary Goodwin, a Maryland county nutritionist who frequently lectured and testified before Congress, warned in 1972 that "a harried family life style and too much reliance on convenience foods" were contributing to poor nutritional health, especially among the nation's teenagers. Organized meals, and the social routines they supported, were being shoved aside for "piecemeal," "unplanned" eating. It was teenagers who were most likely to be eating "from vending machines, at ball parks and movies," where they would be offered "nothing but junk food with no nutrition." She was pointing the finger at snack foods, at soft drinks, and of course at the staple of vending machines everywhere, candy.[3]

Snacking wasn't just a fad. The decline of meals, the expectation of convenience, the demand for efficiency in all things including eating, and the preference for foods that didn't require furniture or utensils and could be consumed on the go were trends that had been set in motion by the explosive growth of food processing and technology after World War II, and there were no signs of turning back the clock. Candy makers had long been worried about how to make sure nickels and dimes landed in their own pockets and not in the pockets of competitors making potato chips, cookies, cakes, animal crackers, cheese crackers, and the like, all of which were also packaged in five-cent wrappers in the 1930s. As early as 1937, an Indiana candy store owner had noticed a change: "Men used to come in here and buy candy bars. Now many of them buy a five cent pie, five cent cake or some other type of food."[4] The war had put candy back on solid footing for a time, but by the end of the 1960s the new era of snacking—and the rapid emergence of entirely new forms of snack foods—was setting off new rumbles of concern in candy companies.

Candy technologists of the late 1960s raced to develop new kinds of snacks that originated in candy but branched farther and farther afield. These began with simple items like chocolate- or sugar-coated wafer bars and pretzels, or caramel-glazed popcorn with nuts, formulas that innovated by adding a candy coating or filling to a more traditional food. Other ideas for snack products seemed to push the very boundaries of candy. Golden Chips was a flour-based cookie baked in an oven but with "the feel and flavor of a chocolate covered nut roll." Kit Kat even boasted of its perplexing hybridity in magazine ads: "Introducing the cookie bar. Or is it a candy bar? . . . Whatever it is, it's delicious."[5] *Candy Industry*, the trade journal that had inherited the mantle of industry bellwether from the venerable *Confectioners Journal*, rebranded itself as *Candy and Snack Industry* in 1971, "covering the manufacture of candy, chocolate, cough drops, chewing gum, nuts, biscuits, crackers, pretzels and other snacks." An editorial announcing the change explained the new environment: "One of the major trends of the past decade which started slowly, but has assumed explosive proportions during the past few years, has been the convergence of baked snacks with candy. Actually, candy is the original snack and, as such, it proved to be a most natural marriage partner for baked snacks."[6]

All of this innovation was fun for the consumer but confusing for those whose jobs depended on telling the difference between candy and other things. In New York State in the 1960s, there was a sales tax applied to candy but not to baked goods. A reporter asked the tax commissioner in 1968 how the state would treat snack innovations like Golden Crisps and Kit Kats. The commissioner replied, "When confronted with one of the many borderline items, the questions the state asks are: 'how is the product being represented by the seller and what does the consumer feel he is buying?'"[7] The justification for taxes on candy, which had been proposed and imposed at various times through the twentieth century, was that candy was not like other foods because it was not a necessity. If candy was a nonessential good, then an additional tax would not be an undue burden. Efforts on the part of candy manufacturers to persuade legislators to avoid or eliminate taxes on candy hinged on convincing them that candy was in fact a food like any other sort of food, and therefore necessary. These arguments did not always prevail, although candy makers were generally quite successful in the first part of the century at holding the line on what they called "discriminatory" candy taxes.

In the legal definitions that were applied to candy in order to impose excise or sales taxes, legislators had to make a definitive distinction between candy and food. Through the first part of the century, candy taxes were generally applied based on a 1919 Internal Revenue Service ruling:

> Candy within the meaning of the act includes chocolate creams, bonbons, gum drops, jelly drops, jelly beans, imperials, caramels, stick candy, lozenges, taffies, candy kisses, wafers, fudges or Italian creams, nougats, peanut brittle, sugared almonds, chocolate covered fruits and nuts, glacé or candied fruits and nuts, popcorn and other cereals or cereal products mixed with or covered with molasses, sugar or other sweetening agent, hard candies, plain and chocolate covered marshmallows, candy cough drops and sweetened licorice not taxed as cough drops, sweet chocolate and sweet milk chocolate whether plain or mixed with fruit or nuts; and all similar articles however designated.[8]

Although this list is long, the effort to enumerate the kinds of candy suggested that the list was not infinite. The addition of "similar articles however designated" admits that some specific candies may not have made the list, but their similarity to the named candies is sufficiently evident as to resolve the matter. This approach worked well for fifty years, as candy makers produced candy while other kinds of food manufacturers produced cookies or frozen pizzas or ice cream. But by the late 1960s, new products like Golden Crisps were confounding this once clear line between traditional candies and other foods.

Through the 1970s, the line grew fuzzier, as candy makers brainstormed ways to make their products more foodlike. Food manufacturers were making food that was more and more like candy. And while the counterculture and food reformers were aligning their attacks on processed food monstrosities, which included candy, mainstream nutritional authorities were embracing the idea of "fortification" as a way of turning anything edible into nutritious food.

When the lines of definition and distinction start getting blurry, perceptions matter. By the 1968 New York State tax commissioner's reckoning, candy was in the eye of the beholder. If a retailer was selling his product as candy, it was candy. If the buyer was buying it as candy, it was candy. But representation and interpretation are notoriously slippery. What if, say, a candy bar doesn't call itself a candy bar? What if it calls itself something else, like a "fistful of peanuts" or a "glass of milk"?

When Is a Candy Bar Not a Candy Bar?

Why is Milky Way called Milky Way? I always thought it had to something to do with the galaxy—meant to imply that the candy was so fantastically out of this world that the only way to describe it was with entities measured on the scale of light-years. Milky Way, however, is named for its *milkiness*; but if you weren't around before 1970, you probably don't immediately make an association between a Milky Way bar and fresh dairy products. In 1970, the FTC demanded that Mars, Inc. stop implying that its blockbuster candy bar was the nutritional equivalent of a wholesome serving of fresh milk.

We don't know the exact formula for the original candy bar, and the role of milk is a bit mysterious. The earliest wrappers specify that the candy is "made with malted milk." By 1925, Mars was claiming that it was "adding to the food value and eating qualities" of the bar by increasing the malted milk; now Milky Way had "more malted milk content than a soda fountain double malted milk."[9] This may in fact have been true, but it's nonetheless misleading. Milky Way was dreamed up as the candy answer to the popular fountain drink chocolate malt. As one version of the story goes, young Forrest Mars was sitting in a soda shop with his father, Frank, one day in 1923 and mused aloud, "Why don't you put this chocolate malted drink in a candy bar?"[10] The main ingredients in a chocolate malt are typically ice cream and milk, so that sounds pretty milky. Notice, though, that Mars claims more *malted milk* content.

Malted milk is not milk but a nutritive food supplement invented in the 1870s by James Horlick, a pharmacist seeking a better formula for infant feeding. It is made with malted barley, wheat flour, and whole milk evaporated to form a lightweight, nonperishable powder. In a chocolate malt, malted milk is not the milk but the flavoring; a chocolate malt has just enough malted milk powder to give it the distinctive yeasty taste. When Mars described the confection as "malted milk in a candy bar," or emphasized the "food value" of Milky Way by promoting its increased use of malted milk, it's hard not to conclude that the advertising team was taking advantage of a potential source of confusion. Surely many must have thought that a Milky Way had as much *milk* as a soda fountain malted milk.

By the 1960s, malted milk was out of fashion. After decades of emphasizing its malted milk flavor, Milky Way made a decisive shift to drop the malt and focus on the milk. In a television ad broadcast in the 1960s, Milky Way relaunched the idea of candy as good food by visually transforming fresh farm products into a candy bar. The ad features a towheaded boy swinging from a fence in a wholesome-looking farmyard, surrounded by cows and fields. He's enjoying a Milky Way bar, and the voice-over explains that even though the Milky Way seems like candy, it's really something else: "A Milky Way bar can fool you. It tastes like chewy creamy candy. But it's really good food, that's good for you. A Milky Way is loaded with farm fresh milk [milk pours from a milking can] and the whipped-up whites of country eggs [clucking chickens]. And syrup from fresh picked corn like this [a basket of fresh corn ears]. And that's why we call Milky Way the good food candy bar."[11]

Milk, eggs, and corn: what could be better? Of course, by the time the milk, eggs, and corn arrive at the factory to be incorporated into the candy bar, they are likely powdered, pulverized, and enzymatically transformed beyond recognition. And while some of what is in a Milky Way might have started out as milk and eggs and corn, the whole point of the candy bar is that it's mostly sugar and chocolate, two ingredients the ad conveniently omits, perhaps because both—with their troubled histories of tropical colonialism and slave labor—are so far from the wholesome (and mostly imaginary) American farm where Milky Way bars metaphorically grow from the soil. So the ad isn't exactly a lie, but it isn't exactly the truth, either. As the voice-over puts it with perhaps unintended irony, "A Milky Way bar can fool you."

Not everybody was happy with Milky Way's claims. By the late 1960s, consumer advocates like Ralph Nader were increasingly taking aim at advertising that seemed designed to dupe the gullible. A 1969 report issued by Nader's Raiders, a scrappy band of law school students, sharply criticized the FTC for failing to adequately protect American consumers from the venalities of corporate advertising.[12] The ensuing publicity and controversy ultimately pressured President Nixon to reinvigorate the FTC and to encourage more aggressive regulation of advertising. One of the first targets of the more robust agency was none other than Milky Way candy bars.

The offending ad singled out by the FTC for censure featured a "fanciful visual representation" that showed a glass of milk turning into a Milky Way bar. It's a simple trick, the first special effect in the arsenal of any moviemaker: film the milk, stop the camera, replace the milk with the candy bar. But in the opinion of a newly vigilant commission, Mars had taken the magic of television too far. The FTC concluded that the image of milk turning into candy implied that the candy bar was the nutritional equivalent of a glass of milk, and that the candy "can and should be substituted for milk or milk products," both implications patently false. Under the terms of the consent order filed by the FTC, Mars did not admit to violating any law but agreed to discontinue the alleged misrepresentations of the Milky Way bar.[13]

Despite the FTC's stamp of disapproval, the food-into-candy trick of Milky Way proved too effective to abandon. After the hand slap, Mars went on to air ads for Snickers using a virtually identical technique. Snickers television ads of the early 1970s concluded with an open hand loaded with peanuts that transformed into a Snickers bar. With such a magical image to reinforce the message, how could anyone forget that Snickers packed "a fist-full of peanuts in every bar"?

Candy for Breakfast

Snickers and Milky Way downplayed their candy origins in favor of looking a little bit more like foods from the farm and field, but even the magic of television couldn't hide their form. On the other hand, being a candy bar in the new era of snacking wasn't such a bad thing. Candy bars were a top choice for the vending machines that were springing up everywhere. And what about Snickers and Milky Way, anyway? What with all that milky, corny, nutty goodness, it was no wonder more and more people were reaching for candy bars any time of day. Except breakfast, of course. There was, however, a special kind of candy that was manufactured and marketed as the perfect breakfast. It wasn't called candy, though. It was called cereal.

Sugar Pops in 1950, Sugar Frosted Flakes in 1952, Sugar Smacks in 1953—this was the dawn of a new breakfast era.[14] By the 1960s, the ever-increasing number of presweetened cereals jostling for space in the grocery shelves did little to disguise the fact that they were covered in sugar—some of the cereals sold in the 1960s were more than 50 percent sugar. Ready-to-eat breakfast cereals had been available since the early 1900s, but postwar innovations like Cap'n Crunch and Froot Loops bore little resemblance to their forebears, spartan and bran-full bowls that might be enhanced with a sprinkling of sugar at the table. But as different as they were, these new foods still carried the tattered remains of a more nutritionally illustrious past. Despite the presence of sugar as the number-one ingredient, presweetened cereal was still cereal. This provided a convenient rationale to the millions of mothers who purchased several boxes a week of whatever favorite their offspring were clamoring for. After all, cereal was made from corn and wheat and rice; who could dispute that this was food? Cold cereal was great for Mom: it was convenient, quick, and easy, so easy that Junior could make it for himself. And Mom got an extra push to buy from Junior, whose TV-advertising-inspired whining and begging ensured that boxes of his favorites were tossed into the grocery cart each week.

The cereal preparations sold in the 1890s were not convenience foods so much as health foods, armaments in the battle against constipation and "autointoxication." They were developed by health reformers like Dr. John Harvey Kellogg to combat the ills and ailments of modern lifestyle and diet. Around 1880, Dr. Kellogg developed a crumbly mixture of wheat flour, cornmeal, and oatmeal to serve to patients at his sanitarium in Battle Creek, Michigan. The breakfast innovation was popular, and by 1889 Kellogg was selling two tons of Granola each week. Another early Kellogg product was Granose Flakes, which he began selling after he figured out how to transform wheat kernels into flakes. His brother Will took over the cereal business in the late 1890s, which expanded in 1898 to include Sanitas Toasted Corn Flakes. These early dry cereals were tough and unappetizing; Kellogg was a firm believer in the restorative powers of bran. So too was Kellogg's major competitor in the cereal market,

C. W. Post. Post's Grape-Nuts, a crumbly mixture of bran and molasses, was sold as a health booster that would cure every ailment
from constipation and loose teeth to malaria and appendicitis.

In keeping with their image as a food that promoted good
health and digestion, cereals in the first half of the twentieth century were plain affairs, basic staples like corn flakes, puffed rice,
shredded wheat, and oatmeal. Despite the mania for sweetening
that was afflicting all manner of American foods in this era, the
cereal manufacturers were reluctant to add sugar to their product. The Quaker Oats Company produced a candy-coated cereal
puff for the 1904 Saint Louis World's Fair but never brought the
product to a wider market. Sweetened cereal was a novelty, and as
Scott Bruce and Bill Crawford, the authors of *Cerealizing America:
The Unsweetened Story of American Breakfast Cereal*, explain, the
company believed that "America's sweet tooth was a passing fad."[15]

In retrospect, this turned out to be a serious miscalculation,
but at the time it made sense. Candy-coated popcorn was a popular snack food at this time, with Cracker Jack the top competitor among several other brands. Candy-coated cereal puffs would
have looked more like Cracker Jack than like breakfast food to a
visitor to the 1904 World's Fair. At the same time, consumers who
were faced with bland and basically flavorless grains were taking
matters into their own hands, applying great heaping spoonfuls
of sugar in the privacy of their homes. A 1918 study had found
that households accounted for 70 percent of total sugar use; undoubtedly, much of this sugar was being zestfully applied to the
breakfast cereal bowl.[16]

It was the spectacle of this breakfast table sugar storm that,
according to Bruce and Crawford, in 1939 inspired Jim Rex to
invent the first presweetened cereal.[17] Noticing how his kids
poured the sugar over their plain puffs, Rex figured that a puff
that was already sugared would be a sure hit. Ranger Joe was a
puffed cereal with a coating of honey and corn syrup. Rex's kids
liked it, but it had the unfortunate tendency to congeal into a

solid brick after just a few days on the shelf. Not a recipe for retail success.

The idea of an already sweetened cereal languished for a few years, then around 1948 the big cereal company Post started experiments of its own. There was some controversy among insiders about whether adding a sugary coating to their wholesome cereal products was really a good idea. But advocates for producing a sweetened cereal came up with some pretty compelling arguments. Number one, it would sell. That alone was probably the deal cincher. But executives also insisted that selling the cereal as presweetened was in fact a nutritional advantage, because the factory would add less sugar than the amount people were pouring on at home. One Post executive even went so far as to conclude that the sugar didn't really matter at all, since "you're trading off sugar carbohydrates for grain carbohydrates—and sugar and starch are metabolized in exactly the same way."[18]

At the birth of presweetened cereals, the justification for making cereal more like candy sounded like the justification for selling candy as food: sugar equals starch equals carbohydrate, and all carbohydrates equal energy, and all energy is good. When Post called its first product Happy Jax, it seemed intent on keeping the line between cereal and candy a little fuzzy. Happy Jax was a play on the popular candy-coated popcorn confection Cracker Jack, and the name was meant to suggest that Happy Jax could do double duty as breakfast food and ballpark snack.[19] By this time, such a possibility did not seem as outrageous as it had back in 1904 when Quaker Oats abandoned a similar product.

Happy Jax was reborn as Sugar Crisp in 1949. The novelty of presweetened cereals combined with their similarity to candy-coated popcorn snacks made it easy to promote Sugar Crisp as much more than a breakfast food. Three bears, named Candy, Dandy, and Handy, were dreamed up to sell the cereal. Animated TV spots featured the trio, and at the end of each escapade the announcer would remind viewers: "As a cereal it's Dandy. For snacks it's so Handy. Or eat it like Candy." The same slogan appeared in a variety of print ads as well (plate 15).[20] To propose eating Sugar Crisp either for breakfast or "like candy" seems scandalous today. Yet as this commercial slogan suggests, in the early days of presweetened cereals, manufacturers were quite unself-conscious about the fact that they were making candy meant to be eaten as a breakfast food.

The production of sweetened cereals owed much to candy flavors and candy-making techniques, a fact that was flaunted rather than disguised. Post's next launch, hard on the success of Sugar Crisp, was called Krinkles, a "candy-kissed rice" cereal. The caramel-coated puffed rice took direct aim at their competitor Kellogg's popular Rice Krispies. If Rice Krispies were good, then obviously Rice Krispies covered in candy were even better. In 1951, Post again caught Kellogg by surprise with a sweetened corn flake called Corn-fetti. Efforts to use the sugar coating to keep the corn flake crispy went too far. According to Bruce and Crawford, one of the men involved in the launch described the "clear-candy coating" as being "so insoluble, it would cut your mouth all up like glass."[21] Corn-fetti was soon pulled off the shelves for further testing. But the world of ready-to-eat cereals had, in a few short years, been totally transformed. While candy manufacturers and cereal manufacturers remained separate and distinct, in the business of cereal it was clear that sugar coatings based on candy techniques and candy flavors were the key to successful new product launches.

The new cereals were sweet. Even sweeter was candy-coated cereal mixed with pieces of candy. Marbits, the industry term for those crunchy marshmallow pieces in many sweetened cereals, made their first appearance in 1960. Bruce and Crawford call the introduction of marbits "a move that brought the cereal bowl even closer to the candy dish."[22] Post was the first to introduce marbits in a product called Huckle Flakes. Perhaps due to the obscurity of huckleberries, Huckle Flakes was a flop. But competitor

General Mills wasn't discouraged by Post's failure. Lucky Charms, with its hearts, moons, and clovers, captured market share right away, and soon marbits were popping up in breakfast bowls everywhere. Taking the "candy in the cereal box" idea to its logical conclusion, in 1964 Post Sugar Sparkled Rice Krinkles included a full-size bar of Bonomo Turkish Taffy in the box, and a full-size ad for the taffy bar on the back.[23]

Even cereals that didn't include candy bits were looking more and more like things you'd find at the candy store. General Mills led the way in the late 1960s and early 1970s with Count Chocula, Franken Berry, Boo Berry, Fruit Brute, Baron Von Redberry, and Sir Grapefellow. For General Mills, making cereal out of corn was a lot like making candy: the basic extruded corn puff could be modified with flavors, colors, and shapes to create enormous superficial variety. As Bruce and Crawford explain, "General Mills essentially made new cereals out of old, altering the look, taste, color and packaging of existing brands just enough to make them seem different."[24] Perhaps unknowingly, General Mills's product development followed the path first blazed by candy makers in the early 1900s, who understood that novelty was the secret to capturing consumers' candy pennies.

With their enormous quantities of sugar, lurid colors, surprising flavors, and added candy bits, the presweetened cereals of the 1960s seemed to have abandoned any pretense of the health promises of Grape-Nuts and Granola. This was candy, but candy with an alibi. After all, it was still called cereal, still eaten as a breakfast food, still made from wholesome grains (albeit grains that had been processed almost beyond recognition). Millions of American families were buying and eating the stuff, believing that a breakfast of marbits and candy-coated corn puffs was the modern, nutritious way to start the day.

Robert Choate called cereal's bluff. Choate had started out as a civil engineer, but in the 1960s he turned his attention to food activism and reform. His contributions to the 1969 White House

Conference on Food, Nutrition and Health included recommendations for policies to address malnutrition, hunger, and nutritional illiteracy. Much to his distress, the conference report was
having no effect on either government policy or food industry
practice. So he decided to take his crusade directly to Congress.
In July 1970, he appeared before the Senate Subcommittee on
Consumer Protection of the Committee on Commerce to testify
about the nutritional content of dry breakfast cereals.

Choate assigned each of the sixty cereals currently on the
market a score based on the percentage of the recommended
daily allowance of nine nutrients found in each cereal, according
to manufacturers' data. A few cereals stood out at the top of the
ranking: Kellogg's Product 19 and General Mills's Kaboom
and Total. But the vast majority of cereals, from sugar bombs
like Cap'n Crunch and Alpha-Bits to the more sober varieties
like Puffed Rice and Corn Flakes, clustered at the bottom. On a
scale where 900 represented "optimal nutrition content," forty of
the sixty cereals on the market scored less than 100. In response
to Choate's findings, Subcommittee chairman Senator Frank
Moss warned American consumers, "No longer can mothers
blithely send their children off to school after serving them a
bowl of their favorite cereal confident that they are full of nutritious body-building food. The 'breakfast of champions' or Tony
the Tiger's favorite cereal may be letting us down."[25]

Choate had an impressive array of charts, graphs, and video-
tapes to demonstrate his point. But just as persuasive was a witness who wasn't on the official docket: Choate's five-year-old
son, Rufus. Spotting an unattended microphone, Rufus leapt to
the stand and started belting out TV cereal jingles. It was a
graphic reminder of the insidious power of TV ads to colonize
children's minds. When a reporter asked Rufus about his favorite cereal, he named Cheerios, "but Mom won't let me eat them."
"What do we call it?" his mother prompted. Rufus gave the
answer: "A junk cereal."[26] In the senior Choate's analysis,

Cheerios and similarly low-nutrient cereals were "empty calories" that "fatten but do little to prevent malnutrition."[27] Little
Rufus gave a more vivid name to this kind of food that could fill
you up and still leave you nutritionally empty: junk.

Choate's attack on the nutritional vapidity of breakfast cereals was quickly countered by the major cereal manufacturers
General Foods (Post), General Mills, and Kellogg. Their first line
of defense was denial, obfuscation, and a personal attack on
Choate's qualifications. Kellogg's director of research, Dr. John
Hooper, attempted to defuse Choate's assault by demeaning his
research and sneering that "civil engineer Choate's theories and
so-called formula might be meaningful if you are digging a
mineshaft, but they are completely valueless as a yardstick for
measuring the nutritional values of any type of food." A Kellogg
Company press release called ready-to-eat cereals "among the
best bargains in nutrition" and insisted they gave consumers
what they wanted: "convenience, high nutritive value, palatabil-
ity, and attractive appearance." General Foods pointed out that
Choate had ignored the taste factor: "You cannot force a young-
ster to eat a breakfast food he does not like no matter how loaded
it might be with nutrients."[28]

Of course, the breakfast foods at issue were not so much
loaded with nutrients as they were loaded with sugar—that, after
all, was what cereal makers were talking about when they
pointed to the "taste factor" that gave cereal so much "palatabil-
ity." Dr. Jean Mayer, one of the nation's leading nutritionists,
charged the presweetened cereals with having "more sugar in
them than [they have] cereals. Properly speaking, they ought to
be called cereal-flavored candy rather than sugar-covered cereals."[29] Even the cereal manufacturers recognized that they were
treading a thin line; a former General Mills executive recollected
of the heyday of sweetened cereals, "There was always the question of where was the limit on how much sugar you can put in
before it becomes a confection."[30]

To explain how something so near a confection was ending up on the breakfast table, Choate had come to testify armed with a twenty-seven-minute video showcasing cereal ads targeted at the millions of two- to eleven-year-old children glued to their TV sets every Saturday morning for a two-hour block of cartoons and kiddie shows. This was the first time many of the adults watching Choate's compilation had seen what sort of persuasive arts were being visited on their offspring. "That was very entertaining but distressing," Senator Moss admitted when the video was done.[31] Choate listed the key words that appeared over and over in the cereal ads: "sugar, energy, sweetness, chocolate, vigor, frostedness, action, alertness and prizes." In Choate's view, a child consuming a steady diet of such commercial messages could not help but conclude that "cereals with sugar are great energy sources, that energy and action are equivalent to happiness, and that ability and health are a product of eating ready-to-eat, preferably sweet, cereal."[32] The advertising message of energy and health, Choate suggested, was not at all consistent with the nutritional near zeros that marched across his summary charts.

The romping children and energetic athletes who were selling sugar cereal as "energy food" in the 1960s looked a lot like the heroic aviators and mountaineers of the 1910s and 1920s who extolled the energy-restoring virtues of candy. But the caloric virtues of candy and sugar had, by 1970, been turned on their heads. With no vitamins, minerals, fiber, or anything else, sugar seemed the epitome of the "empty calorie." And, as Choate reminded his audience, empty calories had no nutritional function whatsoever except to "fatten."

Newspapers announced Choate's findings with attention-grabbing headlines like "Snap, Crackle, Flop" and "Breakfast of Fatties." As the hearings wound down, Choate's top-rated choices (Total, Special K, and Kaboom) started flying off grocery shelves.[33] The cereal makers got the message. While they continued publicly to defend their wares, behind the scenes they were trying to figure out how to defuse the rising tide of criticism. Choate had ranked the cereals based on nutrient content. In his testimony, he provided a road map for advancing in the rankings: more nutrients. Sugar was not in itself nutritious. But in Choate's view the difference between the good, nutritious cereals and the bad, empty-calorie cereals was not how much sugar they contained. The difference was how many of the additional nutrients they offered. This approach to nutrition opened a huge loophole for the cereal makers; not surprisingly, they marched right through. Advances in food chemistry allowed every cereal to be easily improved without any change in formula, or character, or sweetness. The solution was fortification.

By adding vitamins and minerals to the mix, "cereal-flavored candy" was elevated to the status of nutritious food. Two years after Choate's exposé, he returned to the congressional hearing room to report that thirty-six of the forty nutritionally inadequate cereals he had analyzed had been "reformulated as to be really different products. The 36 that have shown nutritional improvements have been improved in the vitamin and mineral areas. They have been synthetically augmented or fortified so that they are now of some nutritional worth."[34] By 1984, 92 percent of all ready-to-eat cereals were fortified with synthetic vitamins and minerals.[35] So now instead of cereal-flavored candy for breakfast, kids could feast on cereal-flavored candy sprinkled with vitamin dust.

In a postwar landscape where calories were no longer synonymous with good nutrition, it was the presence or absence of vitamins that could tip the balance. But did people really need extra vitamins in their breakfast cereals? With the possible exception of extremely impoverished enclaves, vitamin deficiency conditions were all but unheard of by the latter half of the twentieth century. The sad fact was that the true vitamin needs of children mattered little in the decision to fortify cereal. What mattered was that adding vitamins enabled manufacturers to sell their product as a "nutritious breakfast." They saw vitamin fortification as a way to make their product stand out in a crowded field. For many consumers, the real risk, recognized early in the fortification stampede, was not so much vitamin lack as vitamin overdose. Yet even with such flimsy justification, the addition of vitamins took hold as the all-important distinction between cereal as candy and cereal as food.

Fortification of candy-flavored cereals proved a lasting strategy to ensure that dry cereals would continue their reign as the nation's favorite breakfast food. Today you can buy Reese's Puffs, a cereal meant to evoke the flavors and fun of beloved Reese's Peanut Butter Cups. The TV ads wink at the ambivalent distinction: "Candy for breakfast?" says one recent television ad. "No! Reese's Puffs!" Granted, every bite of puffs is "like a Reese's cup," but no worries: according to the General Mills website, Reese's Puffs are chock-full of "whole grains," eleven vitamins and minerals, and a "good source" of calcium and vitamin D.[36] Reese's Puffs was ranked "least healthy" among breakfast cereals by a team of Oxford University scientists. At the same time, by the bizarre logic whereby the presence of key nutrients transforms junk into food, Reese's Puffs can still boast that it is part of a "delicious and nutritious breakfast."[37]

Minimal Nutrition

Once children had survived the sugar-laden breakfast table gauntlet, even more dietary challenges awaited on the school grounds. For the 22.6 million children participating in the national school lunch program in the early 1970s, there was likely to be a "Type A" lunch consisting of milk, bread, butter or margarine, some kind of fruit or vegetable (canned or cooked or fresh), and a protein, either meat, eggs, or legumes. (Today, the federal school lunch program operates in more than one hundred thousand schools and feeds more than thirty-one million students each day.)[38] In theory, a school lunch could be delicious. In practice, it often was not. But there was another choice in most schools, and its name was candy.

School lunches became federal government business in 1946, with the passage of the National School Lunch Act. The government would help local schools provide free or subsidized meals to economically disadvantaged children. Federal assistance came in two forms: money and food. When some farm product was in surplus, the government would buy it up in order to prop up the price and protect farm income. But the government didn't have much need for mountains of cheese or lakes of butter. School lunches were the solution: a captive market for all those surplus commodities. Kitchens were obliged to fashion meals that conformed with federal nutrition mandates out of whatever agricultural surplus landed on their doorstep—apricots this year, olives the next—making it difficult to plan ahead or to take into account kids' needs or preferences.[39]

As a result, when kids were given the choice to buy foods sold outside the national lunch program, many were opting out of "nutritious" school lunches and making a beeline for the snack bars and vending machines. As one Texas cafeteria worker said, "What troubles me most is that we give the low-income children free and reduced lunches because they are not supposed to be able to afford the lunch. Then they go through the line and get their tray and throw all or most of it away and go to the machines and buy junk food for their lunch."[40] A Memphis, Tennessee, eighth grader explained the problem in 1979: "The school lunch is over-priced and raunchy tasting. So we buy potato chips and nutty bars, but it's not by choice. If the Memphis board would get some cooks that could cook, we would eat the food."[41]

Selling candy to schoolchildren was in fact an old and venerable tradition, going back to the very beginnings of mass-manufactured candy. In 1909, one observer celebrated the beginning of the school year as a time of opportunity: "This is the time when the little store around the corner from the school house is laying in stock to fill the show case and shelves which have been empty all summer . . . School confectionery is better and cheaper than it used to be . . . the little shops patronized by the children increase in numbers and generally thrive on a demand which grows better every year."[42] Such "little shops" encompassed a wide range of formal and informal candy outlets, from real shops on commercial streets with glass displays and accounting books, to a nook in a local woman's parlor, just around the corner from the schoolhouse, with a jumble of licorice pipes and candy watches. It wasn't always necessary to leave school to find some candy, either. Even before the First World War, many schools were beginning to provide meal service, and frequently school lunch counters sold candy as well. These school meal services were locally organized and unregulated; schools were free to serve or sell whatever sorts of foods they chose.

With the passage of the School Lunch Act in 1946, what children were eating at school became a national issue. For many years, the federal government did not interfere in local decisions about what else could be sold alongside the official meal. But with the changing view of candy and other sugary treats in the 1970s, pressure was building to enact federal regulations to limit children's access to candy, soda, and other so-called competitive foods in schools.*

The Child Nutrition Act of 1966, which renewed and extended the 1946 law, had originally contained language restricting the sale of candy, soda, and other competitive foods; lobbyists sprang into action to rally the opposition, and by the time President

---

*"Competitive food" is not necessarily synonymous with junk food; any sort of food could in theory be sold in competition with the offerings of the national lunch. In practice, though, competitive food was most frequently just the sort of thing kids were likely to prefer to a nutritious, federally approved balanced meal, e.g., candy, soda, chips, snack cakes, and the like.

Nixon signed the final version in 1972, the law omitted that restriction. The 1972 regulations allowed the profits from all competitive food sales to go to the school or student groups. From the point of view of school administrators, competitive food was a win-win: kids got the choices they demanded, and the school got band uniforms, basketballs, or a new podium for the debating team. Vending machine operators and confectioners were very happy with the new status quo, but nutritionists and public health experts were increasingly alarmed that kids were opting out of nutritious food choices in favor of fast and easy treats.

Between 1972 and 1979, the role of competitive foods in the school lunch program was a constant topic of controversy and debate. Michael Jacobson, a microbiologist turned activist who was gaining attention for his outspoken criticisms of the food industry, urged Congress in 1976 to ban "nonnutritious foods, such as soda pop, candy and fruit drinks," from schools and to make the school food program "society's model for good nutrition."[43] Faith Gravenmier, the director of School Food Services for West Virginia, also testified before Congress against junk foods. In 1975, West Virginia had barred the sale of soft drinks, candy, chewing gum, and frozen ice bars in public schools. Gravenmier explained that the elimination of these foods was necessary because the board of education "felt they could not teach nutrition in the classroom, and then down the hall be collecting money from the children for foods which are detrimental or of no value to their health."[44]

On the other side, speaking in support of the vending machines and candy bars, NCA president James Mack ominously warned that if schools wouldn't provide kids with candy, the kids would find other, more dangerous sources. When confections are prohibited, he told Congress, children "merely leave the school grounds to obtain them. In many, if not most, instances this involves traffic hazards; and while the children may leave the school premises with the sole intention of purchasing harmless, enjoyable confections, they may be exposed to various temptations, such as tobacco, alcohol, or drugs, which are very harmful to children."[45] So schools that provided candy on-site were actually protecting children from everything from errant automobiles to predatory drug dealers. Not surprisingly, congressional committee members were not entirely persuaded by this line of reasoning, nor were they completely convinced by Mack's arguments that candy was in fact a wholesome nutritious food that could be favorably compared to raisins, apples, and nuts.

Traffic hazards notwithstanding, momentum was building for a more restrictive rule on competitive foods. But what should be the boundary between allowed foods and disallowed foods? Junk food, after all, was a subjective and elastic term. An initial 1978 USDA proposal would have limited the sale of what Assistant Agriculture Secretary Carol Foreman described as "junk foods of minimal nutritional value," specifically candies, soda waters, frozen desserts, and chewing gum.[46] Other snack and dessert foods, including ice cream, cookies, cakes, and potato chips, would not be restricted.

In response, letters from parents poured into the USDA offices "objecting to the infringement of their children's 'right to have candy,'" while members of the candy industry cried foul, saying that this "discriminated against ingredients cooked on top of the stove, even as it gave approval to those same ingredients when baked in an oven."[47] They had a point: Were Twinkies really any less junky than Tootsie Rolls? So the USDA worked out a different approach, focusing not on the form of the food (cookies or candy) but on its nutritional content.

Under the new standards announced in July 1979, schools participating in the federal school nutrition program would be prohibited from offering foods of "minimal nutritional value" until after the final lunch period. In principle, it sounded like a win for good nutrition: students in the lunchroom would have

the choice of only those foods exceeding the nutritional minimum. Many did not see it that way, though. Mimi Sheraton, re-
porting on the new rule for *The New York Times*, noted that
critics were not appeased by what, on closer inspection, appeared
to be "just one more example of a government agency trying to
improve its public image without really offending private industry."[48] The "minimal nutritional value" that would be required
for school meal foods was in fact astonishingly minimal: a one-
hundred-calorie portion must contain at least 5 percent of the
recommended daily allowance of any one of eight basic nutrients: vitamin A, vitamin C, protein, niacin, riboflavin, thiamine,
calcium, iron. If a food met this requirement, it could be sold
anytime: before school, before and after lunch, even during
lunch.

This was, in the words of Michael Jacobson, "a total cave-in
to the snack food industry."[49] Activists like Jacobson joined nutritionists, school food service administrators, and the national
PTA in attacking the loophole. The bar was ridiculously low; as
everybody could see, any sort of foodstuff could be tinkered with
so that it would meet the 5 percent RDA values. "If a candy bar
has only one nut in it, we feel it is above our minimal nutrient
standards," explained Jodie Levin-Epstein, Foreman's assistant
at the USDA.[50] Dr. Joan Gussow of Columbia University's Teachers College complained, "They are really banning nothing—not
even jelly beans—when you consider how cheap and easy it is to
fortify any food with a little vitamin C and so qualify." The ar-
chitects of the rule admitted as much. Foreman conceded that
any candy bar maker or soda manufacturer could fortify its
product "and so have the product declared minimally nutritious." Jacobson was only slightly exaggerating when he charged
that the standard would allow the sale of anything, even "sugar-
coated grease balls."[51]

The ruling amounted to a federally sanctioned definition of
junk food that sidestepped the difficult question of just what it

was about those processed and packaged foods that made them seem so very junky, and lobbed the ball back into the court of what some nutritionists were beginning to call "nutrification."* Synthetic vitamins or other nutrients added to any edible stuff at sufficient levels would transform "junk" into "food." In later years, as the nutritional tide turned away from vitamin fortification and became more concerned with excess fat, salt, or sugar, the model would be inverted: removing a certain amount of fat, salt, or sugar from any edible stuff would emerge as a way to transform all sorts of processed comestible into "healthy food." By this logic, the difference between junk and food was not one of kind but of quantity: too little of some nutrients, too much of others. Nutritionism could keep candy out of the lunchroom, but just barely.

Sugar-Coated Grease Balls

A day after the announcement of the new rule, the Junk Food Hall of Shame opened its doors at Ralph Nader's Public Citizen Visitors Center in Washington, DC. There weren't any sugar-coated grease balls to view, but there were plenty of other items that would curdle a food reformer's stomach. The exhibit was the brainchild of Nader and Michael Jacobson, who had worked at Nader's Center for Study of Responsive Law before he left to found the Center for Science in the Public Interest in 1971. In a museumlike display, the Hall of Shame featured products high

---

*The term *nutrification* was used in the 1960s to describe the result of excessive nutrients in water, usually as a result of sewage or fertilizer runoff. In 1972, Rutgers University professor of food science Paul Lachance was the first to appropriate the term to describe the process of adding nutrients to food. The use of the same word to describe the pollution of water and the fortification of food probably seems a lot more ironic today than it did then. See P. A. Lachance, "Nutrification: A Concept for Assuring Nutritional Quality by Primary Intervention in Feeding Systems, *Journal of Agriculture and Food Chemistry* 20 (1972): 522–25.

in sugar, high in cost, and low in nutritional value: Pop Rocks, Coca-Cola, Froot Loops, Jell-O, Dream Whip, Lucky Charms, Frosted Flakes, Kool-Aid. "This display describes how the fruits of food factories are shortchanging consumers' health and weekly budgets," Nader explained. "This is the kind of menu the larger corporations are peddling in this country under the guise of good nutrition, good taste, good coloring, etc., but it's pretty fraudulent."[52]

The timing of Nader and Jacobson's splashy attack on big food was meant to shame the USDA for taking such a weak position on "minimal nutrition." But not everyone agreed. Perfectly respectable nutrition scientists were insisting that there was no such thing as junk food, and that the "fruits of food factories" were the best kinds of fruit. Dr. Fredrick Stare, chairman of Harvard's nutrition department, admonished Americans to "eat your additives, they're good for you!" His book *Panic in the Pantry* (written with Elizabeth Whelan) aimed to debunk the popular prejudice against food processed with dyes, flavors, preservatives, emulsifiers, and the rest of the gamut of technological enhancements by extolling the wonders of processed food that was nutrient rich, bacteria-free, palatable, colorful, and flavorful: "The use of additives gives us the opportunity to have a tremendous variety of foods. Compare the selection available at your local market and those on display in Healthfoodland. No wonder even the most dedicated of faddists 'supplement' their diet with forbidden industrial goodies."[53]

In a more sober vein, Dr. F. M. Clydesdale of the University of Massachusetts Department of Food Science and Nutrition explained at a 1975 NCA convention why junk food is a myth: "Food is a material which contains chemicals. Humans are materials which contain chemicals. The only, and I repeat the only, scientific reason for eating is to replace chemicals in the human with chemicals from food. In this process energy is supplied, some tissue is utilized and other tissue is built. Certain chemicals are supplied by food in order to facilitate these processes. Therefore, we must conclude that scientifically the term 'junk food' cannot and does not exist."[54]

For the food processors whose products were coming under fire, the equations that transformed both food and human bodies into equivalent vats of chemicals were quite appealing. For the chemist, protein was protein and vitamin C was vitamin C, no matter whether they came from cows and oranges or from test tubes and beakers. If all food was really chemicals, then there was no reason to shun processed foods. Indeed, the very term the government had adopted to describe the worst kinds of food, foods of "minimal nutritional value," preserved the idea that even these had some nutritional value greater than zero. Which, from the point of view of food as chemicals, is true: even a jelly bean or soda pop has nutrients in the form of carbohydrates.

Even if junk food was as junky as the food reformers insisted it was, many people were outraged that anyone would presume to tell them what they could or couldn't eat. It was a declaration of American independence at the snack bar, in the spirit of "Eat free or die!" One outraged Alabama citizen fumed, "Who does Ralph Nader think he is . . . telling us we can't eat junk food if we want to?"[55] A young student wrote to the USDA to share a similar sentiment: "I think the government should leave the so-called junk food alone because if we want to get rotten teeth or stomach aches . . . I think they should let us. We are old enough to know better."[56]

This was the dilemma for food reformers: people wanted, loved, even craved their junk foods. The market success of Oreos, Pringles, McDonald's hamburgers, and Doritos wasn't due simply to enormous advertising budgets and the power of suggestion. Junk foods were engineered to taste good, so good that people would keep eating and eating. Health-food staples like azuki beans and spelt might be cooked up into all manner of tasty dishes from the *Moosewood Cookbook*, but accompanying the tofu casseroles and the carob cookies was a side dish of culinary ascetism: one would suffer and sacrifice for the higher virtues of dietary purity and wholesomeness. Meanwhile, the food technologists were wizarding up ever more powerful ways to stimulate those salty/sweet/fatty pleasure centers that start lighting up whenever you break into a bag of Crunch 'n Munch. As one processed potato product boasted, "Once you pop, you can't stop." No wonder some people were beginning to think the stuff was addictive.[57]

The 1976 top-ten song "Junk Food Junkie" gave a voice to all those snackers trapped in deep ambivalence about their relation to these new strangely appealing yet obviously unwholesome foods: "In the daytime I'm Mr. Natural / Just as healthy as I can be / But at night I'm a junk food junkie / Good lord have pity on me." The catchy tune bought the singer/songwriter Larry Groce his requisite fifteen minutes of fame. He called it a "satire" written "to poke fun at both the junk food culture and the health food culture."[58] The song features a Jekyll and Hyde character whose daytime fervor for plain yogurt, brown rice, and carrot sticks gives way to nighttime binges: Fritos, Dr Pepper, Moon-Pie, Big Macs, Pringles, Ding Dongs, and of course that crème filled, cakelike treat that came to define a genre of shelf-stable snacks, the Hostess Twinkie. Groce's song captured something of the split personality of the time: all the virtue was on the side of Mr. Natural, and all the fun and pleasure in the lair of the junk-food junkie. Americans wanted it both ways: natural, wholesome virtue but also goopy, sticky, greasy, sweet, crunchy mouthfuls.

And what if you didn't have to choose? What if Fritos could be every bit as nutritious as broccoli? What if lollipops had all the wholesome goodness of carrot sticks? For Mr. Natural, this was an impossible and grotesque question. The qualitative difference between factory and nature needed no further explanation: artificial foods could only ever be artificial, and artificial was by definition inferior to natural. But the science of food technology admitted no essential difference between candy and snacks that came from the factory, and fruits and grains that grew in the fields. If one was nutritionally inferior to the other, it was only because the food technologists had failed to do their job.

The optimistic spirit of technological possibility in the face of deteriorating nutrition was captured by the 1969 report of the White House Conference on Food, Nutrition and Health. The report's solution to rising poverty and malnutrition ran directly through the nation's food laboratories and factories: "American science possesses the knowledge necessary to attack malnutrition, and American food technology has the means of converting that knowledge into attractive and highly nutritious foods in the marketplace."[59] No food was irredeemable in this rosy-eyed view. The very same food technologies that had manipulated the basic molecules of matter to create the monstrous "junk food" could be put to use making "healthy snacks" and "good-for-you" processed foods.

For food chemists, the only important differences between foods were quantitative, numbers that could describe the portions of various nutrients. Once nutrition was handed over to science and technology, the food itself was just packaging. In a language that weirdly echoed the civil rights movement, the White House Report declared all foods equal under the banner of being "nutritional carriers": "No one type of food should be preferred over another as a nutritional carrier, and therefore fortification of any food should not be prohibited. The consumer should be free to select, in the marketplace, any fortified food of her choice, whether of completely natural or completely synthetic origin or some combination."[60] No more would brown foods be preferred over white foods, fresh foods over frozen, natural foods over synthetic. Every food could be a carrier for nutrients.

Once food is redefined as nutritional carrier, there remains little practical difference among candy, snack, and meal. Whatever nutrient you need, whether as between-meal snack or as meal substitute, candy can be the nutritional carrier. And as a nutritional carrier, candy had a real advantage: as the NCA had boasted in one of its industry promotions, "Remember, Everybody Likes Candy!" Candy was tasty, portable, convenient, and universally loved. As *Candy Industry* observed, there was a big potential market in "mothers who want to get more nutrition into their children's diets by using the lure of candy."[61] No wonder, then, that by the early 1970s leading candy technologists had begun to imagine a powerful convergence of candy and food.

Dr. Sherman of the Candy Corporation of America confidently predicted that "five years from now I would expect candy to be more in keeping with a general food."[62] A Knechtel Laboratories scientist working to develop new candy formulations explained current research trends that definitively pointed in that direction: "Candy, particularly the candy bar, is becoming regarded more and more as a snack food or as a replacement for a light meal. Because of this trend, more attention has been paid to its composition in relation to balanced nutritional value." He suggested milk protein, nut and soya flour, and soya protein isolates as potential additives "to improve the value of candy as a nutritive snack food [and] to reduce the carbohydrate and increase the protein content."[63] And inside candy labs, researchers were thinking quite specifically about giving candy the starring role at mealtime. An insider told *Candy Industry* that candy firms were "very very interested in the snack business, especially in high protein foods that will serve as a complete breakfast."[64] Meanwhile, a developer at Guittard chocolate was encouraging his colleagues, "Let's go for real pocket lunches, so to speak, pleasurable foods, more pleasurable eating than any other type of snack food there is, and it can be balanced nutritionally. We have something here that lends itself to extremely good nutritional balance compared to many other snack foods."[65]

Candy for breakfast? But of course! And for lunch and dinner too. Just one little thing, if you please: don't call it "candy."

14 ◎ Candification

"What will the world taste like tomorrow?" asks a 1970s trade ad from the British flavor manufacturer Norda International. The accompanying picture is familiar: above a foregrounded moon-scape floats an orb, a direct echo of that great blue marble Earth as seen from space by the crew of *Apollo 17* in 1972. But here it is flattened into a disc, wrapped in cellophane, and mounted on a stick: Earth as a giant orbiting lollipop. The world of tomorrow, implies the ad, will taste like candy.

Space Food

The dawn of the space age raised serious questions: Will the United States be the first to land a man on the moon? Will we colonize Mars someday? And most pressingly, When we're living in space, what will we eat for dinner?

The unique requirements of extended travel in a confined, weightless environment called for a new kind of food: it would have to be nutritionally adequate, calorically dense, and tasty, while also being easy to transport, unwrap, and eat. Candy seemed to fit the bill perfectly, but when commercial candies were tested in space simulators, they did not fare well. M&M's shattered, gumdrops stuck together and oozed, caramels collapsed, and stray particles of sugar and candy floated around and risked clogging the instruments or choking the astronauts.

For the long-duration Gemini space flights of the early 1960s, NASA worked with Nestlé to develop a special space candy with a base of nonfat dry milk powder, sugar, palm oil, and lecithin, flavored with fruits and nuts and pressed into three-quarter-inch molds.[1] With 12 to 20 percent of the calories coming from protein, these candies were formulated to provide nutrition as well as taste. Candy cubes in apricot, pineapple, strawberry, and peanut flavors enhanced a menu dominated by freeze-dried, gelatine-coated "bites" of beef, chicken, bacon, and meat or cheese sandwiches. Reviews of the first generation of space food were mixed; one critic who sampled the foil-wrapped meals circa 1965 for readers of the *St. Petersburg Times* described a bite-size piece as "quite a mouthful and felt like a hunk of wood." In contrast, the sweets were especially appealing: "delicious and the taste comes through almost immediately."[2]

The first generation of space candies provided the groundwork for the next leap forward in artificial food technology. In 1969, the Apollo astronauts were accompanied by a new kind of food: a high-calorie, soft, chewy nougat containing about 15 percent of its calories from protein, 30 percent from fat, and 55 percent from carbohydrates. Pillsbury released a modified version for the mainstream consumer market called Space Food Sticks.

Space Food Sticks were individually wrapped rods about the size of an old-fashioned peppermint stick. The shape was the result of another unique demand of space feeding. As Pillsbury explained in its introductory advertisements, the astronauts' helmets had a small port in the visor for emergency access. The food stick was designed to fit through the hole, a feature that ensured that even a busy space walker need never suffer the pangs of hunger. Nor would the astronaut be required to sacrifice pleasure for convenience; the artificial food came in chocolate, peanut butter, and caramel flavors. Space Food Sticks were soft and sweet, with a chewy and slightly grainy texture. Organoleptically speaking, eating a chocolate Space Food Stick was not so far from eating a Tootsie Roll. Advertisements boasted "lasting energy, complete protein and balanced nutrition fully equal to the food men could live on in outer space." Compared to the "empty calories" of cookies and candy and chips, a Space Food Stick was "healthier but still tastes snack-y." In fact, they were "tasty enough so that children think they are candy."[3]

Space Food Sticks might have looked like the food of the future, but once the excitement of landing on the moon wore off, they disappeared from grocery shelves. The chewy rods were but one of about a hundred space-friendly foods developed by Pillsbury in collaboration with the space program, foods that included solid sandwiches, dehydrated stews, nonspoiling meat, and "pickle relish in dry, chewy slices." Unlike the food technologies developed for military use in World War II, most of the innovations designed to nourish in deep space had fewer civilian applications. The one exception was the successor to the Space Food Stick: the meal bar.

The first meal-size food bar was a modification of the formula Pillsbury had developed for the food sticks. These two-ounce bars, measuring two by four inches, were first used in the Skylab in 1973. The astronauts could choose bars with chocolate chip, crispy, and flake centers, coated with chocolate, vanilla, or strawberry. In size, flavor, and texture, they resembled nothing so much as candy bars. But with a balanced nutritional profile and three hundred calories apiece, these bars were much more. NASA added 392 of them to the ration for the eighty-five-day Skylab mission that launched on November 10, 1973. The bars were to be consumed in rotation with normal Skylab foods.[4]

A meal in a bar was a good solution for the cramped, gravity-

free confines of a space capsule. But it was an even better solution for the meal-skipping lifestyles of 1970s Americans. A 1975
study by the Market Research Corp. of America found that
nearly 40 percent of eighteen- to forty-four-year-olds were skip-
ping breakfast, and nearly 20 percent were passing on lunch.
Nutritionists and traditionalists wrung their hands at the
"national dietary deficit," but food manufacturers perked up:
"The possibilities for appropriate candy and snack products to
fill the gaps in the nation's increasingly sporadic eating pattern
would seem to hold a great number of unexploited marketing
opportunities for the industry," enthused a 1976 *Candy and Snack
Industry* editorial.[5]

In some ways, the idea of a meal in a bar wasn't new at all.
Back in the 1920s, the candy bar, with its hefty dose of calories,
had made a bid for lunchtime star billing. But by the 1970s,
consumers knew that all those candy calories were empty, the
antithesis of nutrition, and couldn't take the place of a meal. Nevertheless, food manufacturers were well aware that to sell energy
bars in the snack aisle, it wasn't enough to pack in the nutrition.
The product would need to taste good. This usually meant that a
"meal bar" tasted suspiciously like candy.

Carnation's Breakfast Bars, introduced in the mid-1970s,
were chocolate-coated bars in candy bar shapes and sizes, with
crunchy mixed fillings like chocolate chip and peanut butter
crunch. Breakfast Bars were sold in the cereal aisle alongside
corn flakes and oatmeal. As their name implied, they were meant
to be eaten as an on-the-go substitute for an actual sit-down
breakfast. Print ads made the claim that "with a glass of milk"
one bar had as much nourishment as a breakfast of bacon, fried
egg, toast, and juice. General Mills's competing product, Breakfast Squares, boasted "a complete meal in two frosted bars." But
even the promise of "high protein" couldn't keep this confection
out of Ralph Nader's Junk Food Hall of Shame in 1975.

The appeal of Breakfast Bars and Breakfast Squares was

convenience: they replaced the hassle of a full meal with the ease of ripping open a pouch and eating behind the wheel of the car on your way to work. But what if you weren't so much trying to replace a meal as skip it altogether? In the late 1970s, dieting was on the rise again as a perpetual lifestyle for many women. The new meal bars seized on this opportunity beginning around 1980. Figurines, a Pillsbury product that looked and tasted like a crunchy chocolate bar, published magazine ads in 1982 promising "the protein, vitamins and minerals of a sensible meal— without the meal." Carnation offered Slender, a chocolate-coated bar in chocolate chip, chocolate fudge, or chocolate caramel nut flavors. Slender magazine ads in 1980 teased: "They taste like you're cheating, but you're not!" It was the decades-old dream of "eat candy, lose weight," but with a twist: this candy bar didn't have to be called candy.

There were some snack bars that didn't directly imitate candy flavors. General Mills introduced Nature Valley Granola Bars in 1975. This was the first of the granola bars, a compressed version of the ready-to-eat granola cereal General Mills began producing in 1973. Nature Valley was aimed at the "all-natural" market, a "wholesome snack bar" with the convenience of a candy bar. Advertising emphasized "no additives" and "no preservatives": "100% natural." Flavors were named to evoke health food more than candy: Oats 'n Honey, Cinnamon, Coconut. General Mills got the bar onto candy counters at drug and convenience stores, where they were incredibly successful with consumers eager for more natural-seeming snack products. General Mills promoted these novelties nationally, including packaging nine million boxes of Cheerios cereal with free full-size pouches of Nature Valley Granola Bars in 1981.[6]

Natural or not, the granola bars were high in fat and sugar, and not a significant departure from the candy bars they supplanted. Before long, General Mills was tweaking its formula. In 1980, the dry Nature Valley Bars evolved into Granola Clusters, with a center of nougat and chewy caramel rolled in honey granola. They were touted as "Granola's answer to candy."

Candy industry insiders looked on these developments in the grocery aisles with a combination of awe and dismay. Business consultant James Echeandia called these new products "closet candy bars" that "covertly promise the same kicks [as candy], but in an 'approved' vehicle."[7] Sometimes the promise of candy pleasure was overt, as in the 1979 debut ad for Figurines Double Chocolate Bar: "Now you can satisfy your sweet tooth. And still keep your sweet shape" (plate 16). Breakfast Bars and Granola Clusters were candy without the baggage. They were portable, convenient, delicious, and satisfying. But they were cloaked in the guise of real food—granola, honey, nuts—and they were advertised as healthy and nutritious, natural and wholesome, perhaps even slenderizing. They were everything candy presumably was not. Don Gussow, who had been following the industry for more than thirty years as publisher of the trade newspaper *Candy and Snack Industry*, commented wryly, "A good candy bar is a superb example of how special candy really is. The cereal manufacturers are proving it right now."[8]

Some candy manufacturers tried to hold their ground by playing down the candy nature of their product. Mars's popular Snickers bar was especially successful in distancing itself from its category with an advertising campaign that ran from 1979 to 1995, featuring the theme "packed with peanuts, Snickers really satisfies." This campaign was a direct response to the rise of the alternative snack bars. As supermarket consultant Phil Lempert explained to *Advertising Age* in 2010, "What Snickers did really intelligently was position itself as being satisfying and really separating itself out as not being a candy bar but more nourishing, more of a food."[9] But food hunger was only one aspect of Snickers's appeal. The brilliance of the candy's marketing in the 1980s was to play on the multiple meanings of "Snickers satisfies": consumers were invited to imagine the many moods and desires

"When he comes home from school hungry, there's only one way to satisfy him. And me."

When my kids come home from football practice, or band or just knocking around, I know it's time for SNICKERS. Because a SNICKERS Bar does more than satisfy my family's hunger between meals. It also satisfies my desire to give them something good.

SNICKERS has no preservatives. That's important to me. It's packed with fresh peanuts, peanut butter nougat, caramel and milk chocolate. And like many good foods, each SNICKERS is freshness dated.

So when they come home hungry, I give them something they love. And I like. SNICKERS.

Packed with peanuts, SNICKERS really satisfies.

Snickers candy bar ad, 1984

that a Snickers bar might answer. Innuendo was an inevitable part of the game, as in a 1984 print ad that juxtaposed the mother's desire for good food to offer her family with her teenage son's desire for a tasty snack: "When he comes home hungry, there's only one way to satisfy him. And me." Snickers brings mother and son together in a hair-tousling embrace; everyone gets some satisfaction.

Snickers notwithstanding, cereal manufacturers did indeed come to dominate the market for "closet candy bars." New products leveraging the names of popular breakfast cereals proliferated in the 1990s and 2000s. While the names sound like breakfast, the resemblances to candy are striking. Kashi's chewy bars with frosting and chocolate chips are rendered virtuous by an "all-natural" aura (and helped along by the fact that few consumers know Kashi is owned by Kellogg); Kellogg's Nutri-Grain bars allude to nutritious grains even if they taste more like jam-filled cake; General Mills's Milk 'n Cereal Bars put a new spin on the old controversies over ready-to-eat cereal by putting what appeared to be frosting in between two layers of sugary cereal; Kellogg's Special K Protein Meal Bars and FiberPlus Bars taste like sweet dessert (and not at all like conventional sources of protein and fiber like chicken breasts and carrots) but promise all the healthy food benefits to busy dieters and office workers.

Today the snack bar market is growing at three times the rate of the overall packaged food sector, and sales are in the neighborhood of $6 billion. Clif Bar, General Mills, and Kellogg are the market leaders.[10] Snack bars today go by many names—cereal bars, granola bars, breakfast bars, energy bars, sport bars, diet bars—as well as various nutritional bars that promote specific health values, including fiber, superfoods, protein, and other nutritional enhancements.

So what makes something a snack bar and not candy? Marketing expert Jerry Hunt says that "what defines a snack bar is its status as a nutritious product," not any specific ingredient or nutritional profile. "[Snack bars] have wide appeal and a perception of being healthier than candy," says Kevin Weiner, president of LBM Sales. "There may be the same amount of sugar, the same amount of calories, and even more salt, but the perception is they're better for you."[11] And even though consumers seek snack bars for nutrition, Hunt points out that "the ones that sell are chocolate, caramel and fudge." All of which seems to suggest that the difference between candy bars and snack bars is smoke and mirrors. It is a bit tautological to define a snack bar as "a nutritious product" when what makes the snack bar nutritious seems to be nothing other than the fact that it's called a snack bar.

But aren't these snack bars better than candy? After all, they do have more "natural ingredients," more protein, less sugar, more fiber. Well, not always. As they say, read the label. Asking whether snack bars are better than candy is really the wrong question. Snack bars are exhibit number one in the phenomenon I like to call "candification." They taste and look and feel just like candy but promise all the virtues of food. The trick is nutritionism: by promoting food as nutrients rather than food as whole foodstuffs, snack bars pass themselves off as more wholesome and nutritious than the candy they so clearly and closely resemble. The real question is whether candified snack bars are better than (or at least as good as) real food.

The snack bar makers would certainly like people to think so. The most illuminating example I've come across is a 2011 television ad for Fiber One cereal bars.[12] This is one of the new "high-fiber" foods made with inulin, a starch-derived carbohydrate that is not absorbed by the intestine. Inulin is found naturally in certain high-starch root vegetables, but only in the food-processing lab can it be isolated as a separate food component. The Fiber One bars actually avoid the word "inulin" and instead list "chicory root extract" on the ingredients list, a more natural-sounding term for the same thing. Whether artificially enhanced "high-fiber" foods have the same benefits as fruits and vegetables naturally high in fibrous matter is hotly debated. But most consumers in the twenty-first century have heard the message that "fiber is good" and conclude that whatever claims to be "high fiber" must be healthy.

The premise of the advertising campaign that introduced this product is that Fiber One bars are so much like candy that you won't even realize you're eating something good for you. In a television spot, a woman is unpacking groceries in her sunny kitchen and has paused to take a bite of her Fiber One bar. Her husband pokes around in the groceries and wonders whether she's bought anything good at the store:

> WOMAN: Sweetie, I think you need a little extra fiber in your diet.
>
> MAN: Oh Carol, fiber makes me . . . sad.
>
> WOMAN: Oh, come on. I dare you to taste one hint of fiber in Fiber One.
>
> MAN: Oh, I'd be able to tell. Why not just eat . . . [lifts green vegetable from paper grocery sack, drops it] this bag. And how can you talk to me about fiber when you are eating [snatches bar] a *candy bar*. [He takes a bite.]
>
> WOMAN: You enjoy that.
>
> MAN: Oh yeah [moaning and chewing].
>
> TAGLINE: *Fiber beyond recognition.*

The ad plays on the popular perception of fiber as dietary penance (might as well eat this bag). The man in the scene seems to be comparing the taste of the green vegetables to the paper bag. The unstated but implicit message is that you can eat Fiber One instead of those unappealing green things. We aren't quite in the terrain of vegetables turning into a candy bar, but we're pretty close. This is why Fiber One is "fiber beyond recognition": as the ad suggests, you can't trust your senses to tell you the truth about what Fiber One really is. The man can't recognize the true fibrous virtue of Fiber One, so he mistakes it for a candy bar.

The irony of this ad is that the man's supposed mistake— "you are eating a candy bar"—in fact speaks the truth: when we scrape away the magical layer of marketing, Fiber One is much closer to a candy bar than it is to anything green and leafy. But in the new nutritional world of ads like these, candy bars have become food, and you can eat them with the smug knowledge that now you don't have to eat your broccoli.

Healthy Snacking

"Meal replacement" bars might be one of the few food items on the market that explicitly broadcast their intention of taking the place of that good old-fashioned experience of actual dining. But there are signs that traditional meals and food categories are on the way out, and the future will be all about "replacements." Bruce Horovitz, author of a 2011 report on future food in *USA Today*, calls it the "eat-what-I-want-when-I-want-it" trend: McDonald's is selling 20 percent of all its cookies and pies at breakfast time, while Kellogg has found that 30 percent of cereal is eaten at times other than breakfast. Dunkin' Donuts sells chicken salad sandwiches in the early morning, and one-fifth of Stonyfield yogurt's customers are cracking open a plastic tub for dinner. Research firm Technomic reports that only 5 percent of all consumers eat three meals a day. Food manufacturers and fast-food restaurants sense big opportunities in the new all-snack menu. As Horovitz reports, "Most have turned their new product labs and test kitchens on their heads. It's no longer about inventing the next big meal, but about concocting the next big snack."[13]

The difference between meal and snack, or between meal food and snack food, doesn't hold up in the land of "anytime, anywhere, anyhow" eating. Which might not be such a problem, except that most of what ends up in the hand and the mouth is likely to be of somewhat compromised nutritional merit. A USDA analysis of recent data on food consumption confirms that we are a nation of junk-food junkies: nearly 40 percent of total calories, and fully one-half of all snacking calories are empty calories from added sugars, fats, and alcohols.[14]

The nutrition researcher Barry Popkin has spent many years trying to understand the role of snacking in the American diet. His research finds a strong correlation between the sharp increase in the number of calories consumed and the growing number of meals and snacks—"eating occasions"—in the daily diet. His findings "suggest that efforts to prevent obesity among U.S. adults (and among adults in other developed countries) should focus on reducing the number of meals and snacks people consume during the day."[15]

On the other hand, some nutritionists and dietitians think that more frequent, smaller meals work better than the traditional pattern of three main meals a day. Dietitian Megan Porter recommends eating "consistent amounts throughout the day with mini meals" to improve health and reduce weight.[16] The Cleveland Clinic advises its patients that "eating small, frequent meals/snacks throughout the day" can "have a positive impact on your weight and cholesterol."[17] "To snack or not to snack: that is the question" just about sums up the contradictory state of nutritional advice and is the title of an online continuing education course for nutritionists led by James J. Kenney. He concludes his review with this ambivalent bottom line: "More research is needed to further clarify the metabolic impact of snacking or increasing meal frequency on weight control and overall health."[18]

What to do? Fortunately, despite the lack of professional consensus on whether people should be eating three square meals or more frequent snacks and meals, there is an underlying common ground. Those who decry the excess of snacking focus on the junk-food predilections of most snackers. And those who advocate more frequent, smaller repasts emphasize that each "minimeal" should consist of wholesome, nutritious foods. What everyone seems to agree on is this: if you are going to snack, you should choose "healthy" snacks. Here's advice to teens, from Kidshealth.org: "Even if you take time to eat three meals a day, you may still feel hungry at times. What's the answer? Healthy snacks."[19] The American Heart Association joins in the snack chorus, with a seeming desire to repeat "health" as many times as possible: "Snacking isn't 'bad' if you do it in moderation and make healthy choices. Healthy, good-for-you snacks can be a part of a healthy diet—which you need to do to live healthfully."[20]

It seems like an easy solution to the derangement of modern eating habits and the dangers of bad food. Just choose healthy snacks. The only problem is figuring out what counts as "healthy." Apple slices and carrot sticks, sure, but what else? Seeking healthy "snack-spiration," *The Huffington Post* asked ten nutritionists about the snacks they choose for their own families. Their answers ranged from raw vegetables, hard-boiled eggs, and plain yogurt with honey to a handful of nuts: basically whole or minimally processed food.[21] But in the era of eat-what-I-want-when-I-want-it, such fresh and fragile foods have obvious limitations. Most require planning and preparation; there's little chance of finding a ripe avocado on a midnight run to the drive-thru.

So while nutritionists and "real food" advocates may have some good ideas for healthy snack choices, in practical terms the real action is in the food labs where technologists and innovators are looking for ways to cash in on the new "healthy snacking" trend. Raw almonds can hardly compete with the brand-name buzz or the highly engineered taste of the hundreds of processed food products designed to exploit the growing market for foods promoting wellness and health. Front-of-the-box graphics that boast "whole grains," "no GMOs," "gluten free," "trans fat free," "no artificial colors," and "all natural" point consumers toward processed foods that promise to be "better for you." How about Baked! Cheetos, not only baked, which is good, but in a one-hundred-calorie pack to boot? You can always eat two packs if you're still hungry. Nabisco 100% Whole Grain Fig Newtons have whole grain, which everybody knows we're supposed to be eating. WebMD's nutritionist Elaine Magee is partial to South Beach Living Fiber Fit Double Chocolate Chunk or Oatmeal Chocolate Chunk cookies.[22] It looks like a cookie, but it is made healthier with a dose of whole-grain wheat flour and oat fiber sweetened with maltitol (a sugar alcohol that causes gastric dis-

tress in some people), sucralose (Splenda), and acesulfame potassium. Yum.

The theme of healthy snack foods is out with the bad stuff, in
with the good: more fiber, more whole grains, baked instead of
fried, less sugar, fewer calories, lower fat. It's basic nutritionism,
that powerful marketing tool that translates ultraprocessed food
products into healthy and wholesome food choices. But emphasizing nutrients rather than foods opens the door to some interesting propositions. Just visit the website for Pepsi subsidiary
Frito-Lay, where you can learn all about "sensible snacking," and
how Frito-Lay products like potato chips and Tostitos can give
you "less of the bad, more of the good."[23] And let's not forget that
come-on for Fiber One: it looks like a candy bar, but it's really
just as good for you as a bunch of leafy greens. If that's not
healthy, then what is?

Michele Simon, a public health attorney and author of *Appetite for Profit*, calls the food industry's embrace of healthy food
and wellness "nutriwashing": as people begin to scrutinize the
unhealthy products of the food industry, it responds by adding
more "nutrition" and "good for you" to its products. But are these
"healthy snacks" really making us healthier? As Simon points
out, "whatever 'health'-oriented innovations they dream up, the
major packaged-food companies must continue—on pain of
going out of business—to sell the American public a steady diet of
highly processed products full of some combination of fat, sugar
and salt."[24] Tinkering around the edges of highly processed food
products may change the words on the box, but it doesn't really
change what's inside. The new mantra of "healthy snacking"
might remind some to stock up on dried edamame and steel-cut
oatmeal, but it's also a great way to get people to eat more of the
kind of "healthy snacks" that come wrapped in cellophane and
Mylar, packaged in individual servings or one-hundred-calorie
pouches, festooned with heavily advertised logos and pictorial
allusions to farms, sunlight, and trees.

And what about candy? If current trends continue, it's hard to see much future in the stuff. On the other hand, candy seems to serve an important function in organizing food into vice and virtue. After all, good-for-you processed snack foods like Funky Monkey: Fruit that Crunches! ("100% Real Fruit, 100% Fat Free, No Sugar Added, Gluten Free") or American Bounty's Berries & Cherries Crunch Fiber Enriched ("Gluten Free, GMO Free, Vegan") seem especially "good for you" when you compare them with things like Swedish Fish and Starburst, candies that don't apologize for their allegiance to several kinds of refined sugar, artificial colors, and flavors.

This dichotomy can lead to food decisions that contradict logic and the facts of nutrition. Take, for example, health-conscious parents who wouldn't dream of tossing a bag of jelly beans into children's lunch boxes, or of offering them gumdrops as an after-school snack. What they might offer instead, as a healthy alternative, is a pouch of fruit snacks.

Fruit Snacks

Today, fruit snacks in the form of flat roll-ups or molded morsels are on the product lineup of breakfast behemoths like General Mills and Kellogg, fruit brands like Mott's and Welch's, and specialty companies with names that promise healthier processed food, like Florida's Natural and Annie's Homegrown. They are so familiar that it's easy to forget that once upon a time "fruit snack" actually referred to a piece of fresh fruit. General Mills's Fruit Roll-Ups, introduced in 1983, were the first product to suggest that a processed food could also be a "fruit snack." Fruit no longer had to be that fragile, bruised, perishable stuff from the produce aisle; now fruit was something you could carry in your pocket, unroll, peel, and chew. The new fruit snacks weren't just convenient—even better, they were fun, a point brought home by a 1985 Sunkist branded jelly-bean-like fruit snack that grabbed for the high ground with the name Fun Fruits. "We turned real fruit into real fun for kids," Sunkist explained in its introductory magazine ad (plate 17). Meaning, of course, that real fruit was the ultimate in un-fun.

Although manufacturers are required to label ingredients accurately, "fruit snack" is not a legally regulated category. Most fruit snacks get their sweetness from white grape juice and apple juice. Fruit juices, purees, and fruit pectins enhance the fruit content boasted on the package of many brands. But even if all the ingredients started out as fruit, what the fruit snack primarily delivers is sugar. Sugar from fruit, sugar from cane, sugar from corn—no matter where it comes from, sugar is sugar. Fruit snacks resemble nothing so much as soft gummy candies (and many are actually manufactured in candy factories), but packages plastered with fruit bouquets and boasting fruit juices and purees give this category a powerful aura of virtue.

General Mills's product was inspired by a small-scale confectioner named Louis Shalhoub, who had developed an apricot-puree-based candy sold as Joray Fruit Rolls in the 1970s. Tart and grainy, sold in specialty and natural food shops, Joray Fruit Roll was more likely to be found in a hiker's backpack than in a kid's lunch box.[25] General Mills's revision of the fruit roll was sweet, smooth, and designed to appeal to kids with a taste for Starburst and Skittles. Backed with the promotional and distributional resources of a major food processor, the Fruit Roll-Up leapt from the specialty shops to the aisles of every grocery store, where it sat happily alongside Lucky Charms and Frosted Flakes as a mainstream food item.

Shortly after the new Fruit Roll-Ups appeared on grocery shelves, the *Deseret News* in Salt Lake City put the product to a taste test with a panel of local women, many of them mothers. Alice Ross compared the strawberry flavor to strawberry jam. Dawn Russell said the snacks were "sweeter than we had imagined" and her children "ended up with sticky hands." Janet

Thomas took the snacks to her office, where her coworkers reported liking the fact that the roll-ups used "real fruit" and said they would like the roll-ups "as a substitute for candy." Janet compared the price of the roll-ups favorably with the price of a candy bar. Shirley Mills, on the other hand, compared the roll-ups to her own family's version of fruit leather and thought that the roll-ups were "a bit on the expensive side for us since we raise a lot of our own fruit." For these taste testers, the Fruit Roll-Ups seemed a lot like candy: sweet, sticky, comparable to a candy bar. But at the same time, none of them doubted that this was a product with all the goodness of an actual piece of fruit. Shirley, maker of fruit leathers, a mom who knew the difference between homegrown fruit and the grocers' shoddy produce, was the one who best expressed the magic spell of the fruit snack: "A mother feels good about children enjoying a fruit snack instead of cookies or cakes or other sweets."[26]

There it is: a mother feels good about giving her children fruit—even in the tenuous form of the processed fruit snack. And it isn't just that she feels good about giving the fruit snack, but also that she feels better about the fruit snack than about those other sweet snacks, cookies and cakes and candy. The brilliance of fruit snacks as a marketing ploy was—and is—crossing the line from candy to fruit in a way that lets a mother feel good about giving candy to her children. As long as it isn't called candy.

Since General Mills first staked out a claim to the category, fruit snacks have proliferated and mutated into a dizzying array of products. Variations on the roll-up theme remain popular, with violent colors and "tongue tattoo" effects lending an exciting edge to a somewhat dull product. And if rolling and unrolling isn't your thing, there are many other options. Major brands found in every grocery store offer a variety of chewy, squirty, and filmy variations on the fruit jelly theme. Scooby-Doo and Disney princesses lend their star power to some varieties, enticing kids with their celebrity aura. For a more serious approach to fruit snacking, moms can turn to brands associated with natural, organic, or healthy processed foods like Clif and Annie's Homegrown, both of which offer an array of fruit-juice-based gummy snacks. The most popular brands are sold in boxes containing multiple single-serve packages, perfect for kids' lunch boxes and for stashing in the minivan to quiet whining on the way to soccer practice. Sweet candy, happy kids. Fruit on the box, happy moms.

General Mills's Betty Crocker–branded fruit snack products—including Fruit Roll-Ups, Fruit by the Foot, Fruit Gushers, and Fruit Shapes—are among the least fruitlike of all the products: whatever fruit-derived substances these products contain, calling them "fruit snacks" seems blatantly misleading, even if not impermissible by regulatory standards. The ingredient list for Strawberry Fruit Roll-Ups, for example, omits strawberries entirely and rapidly devolves from "Pears from Concentrate" (aka sugar) to "Corn Syrup, Dried Corn Syrup, Sugar, Partially Hydrogenated Cottonseed Oil, Citric Acid, Sodium Citrate, Acetylated Monoglycerides, Fruit Pectin, Dextrose, Malic Acid, Vitamin C (ascorbic acid), Natural Flavor, Color (red 40, yellows 5 & 6, blue 1)." Such a brazen attempt to pass off serious junk as good food should not go unchallenged, and indeed a 2011 class-action suit was mounted against General Mills, alleging that its fruit snacks make misleading health claims. The suit argues that General Mills "is conveying an overall message of a healthful snack product to parents when, in fact, the products contain dangerous, non-nutritious, unhealthy partially hydrogenated oil, large amounts of sugar, and potentially harmful artificial dyes."[27] The suit further accuses General Mills of using misleading packaging and marketing in order to "deceptively convey the message that its products are nutritious and healthful."

Behind this lawsuit is the Center for Science in the Public Interest, the nation's most powerful nutritional advocacy group. The complaint sets the groundwork for a wider argument with much higher stakes: when foodlike sugar-filled fruit snacks promote selective nutritional claims like "low fat," "gluten free," or "100% of the daily allowance of Vitamin C," the message is that the food is healthful and nutritious. Even if, taken singly, the claims are true, the lawsuit aims to prove that the packaging and marketing are essentially deceptive. Whatever the outcome of this particular lawsuit, it points the way for a new strategy in consumer food advocacy that might make it more difficult for ultraprocessed foods to hide their true nature behind a smoke screen of "good for you" words and pictures.

The year 2011 also brought the debut of Mott's for Tots Fruit Snacks. Although this product was not named in the class-action lawsuit, it represents the very worst of fruit snack marketing abuses. Mott's for Tots Fruit Snacks is a smaller, softer fruit bite with a mild flavor, touted as "easier for tots to enjoy."[28] The Mott's for Tots line of products is a brand extension of the venerable Mott Company, which got its start in 1842 with cider and now, as Mott's LLP, produces a full line of fruit and vegetable juices and other products. The "for Tots" version of Mott's juice is a "reduced sugar" apple juice for toddlers—thrifty moms can achieve the same effect by diluting regular juice with water. The Mott's for Tots Fruit Snack also contains reduced sugar: eleven grams per twenty-six-gram pouch in "for Tots" vs. fifteen grams in the same serving of regular Mott's Fruit Snacks. But reducing the sugar from fifteen to eleven grams doesn't change the nature of the snack. What we have here, when we peel away all the lingo, is the world's first candy created just for toddlers. Candy training pants, if you will. Which wouldn't be so bad if we were training them to have a sensible relationship to candy. But that's not the point of Mott's for Tots, since it insists that it *isn't* candy. No, Mott's for Tots is preparing children for a lifetime of snacking on processed sugar–laden foodlike substances that wave the magic wand of "fruit" to avoid the stigma of "candy."

The magical power of the word *fruit* to decandify candy was demonstrated in 2011 by a team of researchers who were curious about how names affect our perceptions of what we eat.[29] In one part of the study, undergraduates were handed a bowl of something resembling jelly beans to snack on while they watched a video. The researchers gave the students a questionnaire to test their "dieting tendency" and sorted the participants into dieters and nondieters. All of the students—dieters and nondieters alike—thought the jelly beans were very tasty when they were told that they were eating "fruit chews." But when they were told that the same jelly beans were "candy chews," the students with a high "dieting tendency" suddenly lost their taste for the treat.

But even worse, when the beans were called "fruit chews," dieting students ended up eating 25 percent more. For the dieting students in this study, calling candy a "fruit chew" made it more appealing, and presumably less fattening. Of course, it was really no different from the "candy chew." As a matter of fact, all the participants saw the ingredient list before they ate the jelly beans—the same ingredient list whether they were told the item was fruit chews or candy chews. But even with the knowledge that the so-called fruit chews contained no fruit whatsoever, college students who were diet-conscious thought that these were somehow healthier or better. For some people—especially those who might be inclined to think of candy as unhealthy and fattening—names matter, and the study demonstrates this impressively. If you want to sell more candy, just call it fruit.

Beyond the narrow category of fruit snacks, fruit juice has become the ultimate better-for-you ingredient in nonchocolate candies, especially in gummies and jellies. Mintel, a market research firm, asked consumers in 2010 what ingredients or qualities were most important to them when they were considering a candy purchase. "Made with real fruit juice" was at the top of the list, ahead of benefits like reduced calorie or low fat.[30] So shoppers can choose Starburst Fruit Chews "made with real fruit juice, so they have a real fruit taste,"[31] or Wonka Sluggles Gummies from Wonka's Edible Garden with "25% Real Fruit Juice," or perhaps jelly beans like Gimbal's Sour Lovers, "Made with Real Fruit Juice, High in Antioxidant Vitamin C." It's like your mother used to tell you: fruit is nature's candy.

And when it comes to better-for-you candies, fruit juice is just the beginning. Snap Infusion brand Supercandy jelly beans, gummies, caramels, and tart tablets are "infused with six B vitamins for energy, vitamins C & E for antioxidant value, and key electrolytes—magnesium, potassium and calcium—for fluid balance."[32] From Quest Nutrition comes Quest Cravings Peanut Butter Cups, a high-protein, low-carb Reese's alternative. Gummy Owls from Neuliven Health contain a "yam super fiber" believed to promote weight loss: "People like to eat something sweet and delicious," says Tom Gardner, Neuliven's director of marketing. "With gummies, you can put them in your pocket and carry them around with you, so it's really a convenient, delicious form of weight loss."[33]

Gummy Owls teeter on the line between functional food and dietary supplement: Is it a candy that has an added benefit, or a supplement that tastes as good as candy? The difference may matter more to the FDA than it does to consumers. Diet and supplement company Hero Nutritionals manufactures a "multivitamin dark chocolate supplement" as part of the Healthy Indulgence line of chocolates. It contains 60 percent cacao solids dark chocolate, with a multivitamin thrown in the mix. "Our goal was to develop the most premium supplement for women that makes taking vitamins enjoyable and satisfies chocolate cravings without guilt," founder and CEO Jennifer Hodges explains. The chocolate squares are "completely natural and utterly indulgent."[34]

As for the proliferation of gummy vitamins and calcium chews that weigh down the vitamin shelves at drugstore chains, there are now too many to name. These supplements take Mary Poppins's notion of a "spoonful of sugar" to a whole new level: with the chewy gummy goodness of One A Day VitaCraves and Gummy Sour Powers, you might even forget that you're taking your vitamins. A suburban mom going by the name of Victoria B gave a reporter for *Time Out New York Kids* her proven trick for getting her distracted preschooler out the door: "I stand at the door with a Gummy Vitamin. That gets him going. He thinks it's candy. But it's really good for him."[35] There's little difference between this pill and a gummy bear, but with the magic of vitamins, Victoria can pretend that she's not luring her child outside with candy.

Chocolate Fruit

While many traditional candies are being reshaped for the wellness market, there's one candy that can bask in the glow of newly discovered dietary virtue. I'm referring, of course, to chocolate.

Over the past decade, the news media has eagerly reported on numerous studies purporting to prove a plethora of health miracles that can be attributed to chocolate, including reduced risk of stroke and heart attack, weight loss, reduced cavities, improved math scores, and better cognitive function among the elderly.[36] Chocolate is now being included among the "superfoods," those natural sources of powerful micronutrients that hold the secret to longevity and vitality.

The way the chocolate story gets spun, it's pretty easy to conclude that nibbling on a chocolate bar is tantamount to eating your fruits and vegetables. As a 2011 article in *Candy Industry* explains, "Because chocolate is a plant-based food it contains many of the same nutrients as other plant-based foods."[37] In popular chocolate promotions, tantalizing pictures of cacao trees and bean pods draw an appealing connection between the fruit in its unprocessed state and our favorite foil-wrapped indulgence. For "healthy snacking," it seems that applesauce and a Hershey bar might serve equally well.

The good-news chocolate stories don't always disclose the source of funding for most of these studies (drumroll, please):

chocolate manufacturers. And a quickie sound bite is unlikely to explain the limitations of research on the dietary effects of chocolate—limitations that are common to any research that tries to tease out the health effects of an isolated nutrient or food factor. Many of the studies that measured direct effects were based on small sample sizes, and it's never certain whether the results of a small study will hold up in larger groups. This is especially true when the small group is also a homogeneous group, as, for example, is the case with researchers' favorite subjects: college students. Population studies, which do include more people, are by necessity observational: people report what they eat, and researchers measure whatever health effect they are interested in. One problem, however, is that people often forget what they eat, or they lie. Another problem with all such studies is that they can show correlation but not causation: the fact that people who eat chocolate are less likely to have a stroke does not prove that chocolate prevents strokes. There might be all kinds of other explanations—maybe chocolate eaters are also nonsmokers, or maybe the "liking chocolate" gene is linked to the "lower stroke risk" gene. It's possible![38]

Beyond the inherent limitations of any scientific claim that appears to link a specific aspect of diet to broad health outcomes, there is another problem specific to chocolate research: many of the studies that seem to support the "healthy chocolate" message actually didn't study chocolate at all. In laboratory research, the substance that is most frequently used is a special cocoa compound manufactured by Mars, Inc. called Cocoapro, usually mixed up in a dairy-based drink. Mars points to "over 140 peer-reviewed scientific papers on cocoa flavanols" published by its own scientists and independent labs that use Mars Cocoapro.[39] Unlike your average cup of Swiss Miss, Cocoapro contains very high levels of a plant substance called flavanols, which turn out to be the secret behind whatever health benefits might be found in chocolate.

Mars's scientists discovered cocoa flavanols in the mid-1990s. Early test-tube experiments suggested that flavanols might have an effect on the cells that line blood vessels, causing them to relax and thus improve the flow of blood. Subsequent studies in independent labs, many of them funded by Mars, have led many researchers to believe that cocoa flavanols may increase blood flow to the brain, decrease blood pressure, reduce the tendency of blood to clot, and increase arterial flexibility. These are beneficial effects, to be sure. The problem is that while the cocoa bean is a rich source of flavanols, chocolate is not.[40]

It is quite a long way from cocoa beans to chocolate candy bars—almost as far as it is from fruit to fruit snacks. Cocoa beans are harvested from a pulpy pod; in their raw state, they are bitter and inedible. A long process of drying, fermentation, roasting, and processing with alkali brings out the more pleasing flavors of the beans, but it also destroys the flavanols. Chocolate suitable for eating as candy is the result of further processing of cocoa butter, chocolate liquor, and cocoa powder, all derived from the beans, with the addition of sugar and other ingredients, including emulsifiers and milk products. By the time the candy bar falls off the assembly line, there's little left of the active compounds of the fresh cocoa bean.

Good-for-you chocolate stories don't usually mention the significant difference between high-flavanol cocoa and the chocolate bars on sale at Walmart and Safeway. Mars does sell a consumer version of its high-flavanol cocoa on the Internet as a dietary supplement under the brand name CocoaVia, but despite over a decade of research, Mars has not brought a high-flavanol eating chocolate to the regular market. Flavanols are not so easy to use for confectionery purposes. In addition to being destroyed by conventional processing methods, they don't taste very good. Good-tasting chocolate is almost by definition low in flavanols. This means you'd have to eat a lot of chocolate to get the levels of flavanols that resemble anything near the levels typical in

laboratory research. Some recent studies of the effects of flavanols on blood pressure that do use the kind of chocolate sold for
eating as candy have been feeding subjects one hundred grams
of chocolate a day; that's five hundred extra calories, and a lot of
candy.[41] It seems counterproductive—if the whole point is to improve cardiovascular health, wouldn't it be better just to not eat
one hundred grams of chocolate every day?

Major chocolate manufacturers are working hard to insert a
health message into chocolate promotion. The National Confectioners Association publishes a pamphlet called *Taking Chocolate to Heart: For Pleasure and Health* that includes an overview
of recent cocoa research. The message: "As one of life's little
pleasures, chocolate and cocoa products do more than provide
enjoyment and satisfaction to eating—emerging science suggests
they may also support overall health and well-being when included in a balanced diet and healthy lifestyle."[42] And Hershey's
website features a tutorial on chocolate science: "It's more than
wishful thinking—chocolate can be good for you. Studies show
that eating chocolate, primarily dark chocolate, may contribute
to improved cardiovascular health. A source of natural flavanol
antioxidants, dark chocolate and cocoa sit in the same good-for-
you category as green tea and blueberries."[43]

It's a nice idea: chocolate bars and blueberries nestled together in the healthy foods basket. It's an idea that makes nutritionists crazy. "The industry would have us believe that chocolate
candy is right up there with fruits and vegetables," Bonnie Lieb-
man, director of nutrition at the Center for Science in the Public
Interest, fumes. "But chocolate is not a health food. If people
are eating chocolate candy for their health rather than for pleasure, they're fooling themselves."[44] Unprocessed cocoa beans
may be just as wholesome as fresh blueberries, but that's not what
we're eating. Once cocoa beans have made their way through the
food-processing wringer, the chocolate bar that comes out the
other end is yet another species of ultraprocessed food.

Here's a not-so-radical thought: fruit is not candy, and candy is not fruit. Under the spell of nutritionism, chocolate flavanols and fruit snacks and fiber bars blur the distinction between food and technology, substituting nutrients and food factors for whole foods. But candy is not a healthy snack, no matter how it's disguised or how much it's crammed full of probiotics or fiber or omega-3s or vitamins or flavanols or fruit juice. And if you think of real food as the fresh, minimally processed stuff that people ate once upon a time, then despite how delicious it might be, candy is not even food. Candy isn't "good for you," it isn't "healthy," it isn't food at all. So if it's as bad as all that, maybe we should just get rid of it.

15 ⊙ In Defense of Candy

And yet . . . I love candy. I'll never say no to a Kraft caramel or a Snickers bar. I know all the places in my neighborhood to find Haribo gummies and licorice Allsorts. A box of See's chocolates is the first thing I buy when I travel to California to visit family. I even like processed fruit snacks. I suspect I'm not alone in my wish to enjoy the pleasures of candy without feeling so guilty about it—without feeling like it might give me some dread disease, or, worse, harm my daughter.

I have at least one reliable ally in my quest to make America safe for candy lovers: the National Confectioners Association. Here's how they imagined the role of candy in 2012: "It is important to remember that candy and chocolate are treats, snacks or desserts. The key to maintaining a balanced diet and appropriate weight with confections, as with all foods, is to consume them in moderation, as part of an active lifestyle."[1] I totally agree, at least with the part about candy being a treat. The NCA gave up a long time ago trying to persuade people that candy was "good food." The official position for the twenty-first century is that candy is not food. It's a treat, and treats are okay, as long as you eat them as treats and not as food. This seems to me to be an eminently sensible position.

The real question is not whether candy is a treat but what to eat the rest of the time. This is where things get more complicated. We hear that we should eat a "balanced diet." But just what is a balanced diet? The *New York Times* Health Guide defines it as "getting the right types and amounts of foods and drinks to supply nutrition and energy for maintaining body cells, tissues, and organs, and for supporting normal growth and development."[2] According to this definition, a balanced diet doesn't have anything to do with what food looks or tastes like, or where it came from, or how it's prepared. A balanced diet provides the correct nutrients for energy and growth: protein, carbohydrate, and fat. And we know we're eating a balanced diet when we choose our foods from the food groups, currently five: fruits, vegetables, grains, proteins, and dairy.

These food groups are not always helpful out in the real world, though: Where do you put lasagna? And should cottage cheese be in the dairy category with ice cream, or in the protein category with chicken? The fact is, the food groups have very little to do with food as we actually eat it. The food groups are yet another manifestation of nutritionism, the view that food can be broken down into its individual nutrients. Nutritionism has been on shaky ground for a while. In this book I've revealed many occasions in the history of candy when the language of nutritionism—and especially the view of candy as carbohydrates—was put to use in order to promote questionable ends.

In any case, we don't eat nutrients; we eat food. And it is in relation to actual food that the limitations of nutritionism seem most glaring. Researchers attempt to separate nutrients and study the effects of each in isolation, but that's not how food works. (As I write this, the latest nutrition flip-flop arrives in my news feed: "Eating fish high in omega-3 fatty acids slightly reduces the risk for stroke, a large review of studies has found, but taking supplements of omega-3 fatty acids does not have the same effect."[3] Toss out that bottle of pills. Score: minus one for nutritionism.) Not only do we eat complex foods that are made up of countless nutrients (new ones are discovered daily, and who knows if we'll ever have a full picture of just what it is that is in food), but we eat many foods each day, and our patterns of eating various foods develop over time. Each person reacts to the same food a little differently. And no wonder: among food, body, diet, and lifestyle, the consequences of eating anything are always part of a complicated system.

What's more, nutritionism seems deaf to the differences in the quality of foods, or where they come from. Nutritionism makes no distinction between the industrial meat product in an Arby's roast beef sandwich and the grass-fed, locally sourced roast that you spent Sunday afternoon cooking. Nutritionism is indifferent to whether the loaf of whole-wheat bread came from Mom's oven or from Mom's Oven™. Nutritionism is just as happy with the bagged romaine salad at Safeway as with the slug-infested, spindly lettuce plant growing in your kitchen garden.[4]

And it's not really clear that nutritionism has done much to help us toward better eating. Since the 1970s, the official dietary recommendations have encouraged us to avoid or reduce our consumption of specific nutritive substances believed to contribute to chronic disease. There is not always a consensus about what these substances might be; today, the antisugar crowd is gaining ground fast over the well-established low-fat advocates. Singling out one particular component or ingredient of food as the dietary demon, whether it's saturated fat or white flour or refined sugar or fructose, might lead us to healthier eating. But it might not. What it definitely has done is give food manufacturers an incredible marketing tool for promoting the superiority of new and improved food products that promise to eliminate the bad stuff and increase the good stuff—whatever that might be.

Food manufacturers react quickly to changing nutrition fashions, so today's research "breakthrough" is likely to appear in a box of something on tomorrow's grocery shelves. We saw examples of this as vitamins and other nutrients were added to enhance what would otherwise be recognized as "junk foods," and as new kinds of candylike products were developed to deliver popular nutritional enhancements. Whole, fresh foods don't have nutrition labels or encouraging claims on the front of the box to draw your attention. And whole foods don't bend to the whims of shifting nutritional orthodoxies. An avocado is still mostly fat, whether you think that fat is clogging your arteries or boosting your "good" cholesterol levels. Whole food advocates like Michael Pollan think this is a good thing. If, as he puts it, "they can't put oat bran in a banana or omega-3s in a peach," all the more reason to eat more bananas and peaches.[5]

Candy is about as far as you can get from what Pollan and others such as the *New York Times* food columnist Mark Bittman and the food advocate and writer Nina Planck call "real food," wholesome farm fare like fresh milk and braised chard.[6] But does that mean candy is food's opposite, poison? Obviously I don't think so, despite the long history of accusations against candy. For one thing, as we have seen, the evil of candy has proved quite mutable. Over the past century, some have worried about public health, like the pure food reformers who railed against adulterated candy. Some have worried about morals, like the temperance reformers who preached that candy temptation was the beginning of a slide into vice. And others have emphasized more scientific perspectives on candy's potential harmfulness, like the 1970s activists who blamed sugary treats for cavities and other physical ailments. On closer scrutiny, these alarmist views never really held up to the facts. Even where there was actual harm, for instance a demonstrable link between certain kinds of sugar consumption and an increased risk of dental disease, the causes have always been more diverse and complicated than just candy. Then and now, candy alarms have been less about the facts and more about using candy as a scapegoat. And as long as we have that scapegoat, we can go on eating whatever else we desire.

The candy creations of yesteryear provoked all sorts of fears about what harm might come from fake foodstuffs. Today, the plenitude and variety of candy is overwhelmed by the stunning array of ultraprocessed foods that stock grocery and convenience stores, fast-food restaurants, and vending machines everywhere. And in the case of both candy and more recent ultraprocessed food forms, the variety is entirely superficial. In the early years of industrial candy, variety was achieved by applying ever more creative effects to a narrow range of ingredients: primarily sugar, corn syrup, egg whites, milk, and chocolate. Out of these basic elements thousands of candies were born. Now go look at the cereal aisle in your local supermarket: Os, nuggets, squares, flakes, bars, and more, all variations on corn, sugar, and wheat. Or head over to frozen dinners: aside from the window dressing of a few peas or a stray carrot, what you'll mostly find is ever more clever ways of transforming soy and corn.

The fact that candy is mostly sugar and corn syrup is no surprise to anyone. But food civilians (including me, before I started looking behind the curtain) have little comprehension of the enormous volume of corn- and soy-derived ingredients and additives in packaged and processed foods, even those that seem quite benign. There's nothing inherently wrong with corn or soy; corn on the cob and edamame are in my opinion delicious and satisfying foods. The problem is that when corn and soy are manipulated and reconstructed in laboratories and factories, it gets more and more difficult to recognize them for what they are, or to know what it is that we're really eating.

One reason for our ignorance of the true sources of our food is that many of the items listed in the ingredients of even your basic loaf of bread have so many syllables that it's impossible to tell what they might be unless you're a food chemist. For example, did you know that both lecithin and texturized vegetable protein come from soy? And what about mono- and diglycerides? Unless you take the time to do a little Googling, you'll never guess they come from soy oil.

The superficial resemblance of many processed foods to something more homespun is also confusing. My recipe for cupcakes is less than a page long, and I have all the ingredients in my cupboard. On the other hand, the making of a processed snack cake like a Hostess Twinkie is so arcane and complex that author Steve Ettlinger devoted an entire book to demystifying its thirty-seven or so ingredients. The basic food materials of a Twinkie are the same "raw materials" of the full panoply of processed foods: wheat, sugar, soybeans, corn. But as Ettlinger reveals, the journey from these raw materials to the finished product leads through chemistry labs, mineral mines, fertilizer plants, and even the defense industry (artificial emulsifier polysorbate 60 was invented when the chemicals bakers had been using previously were diverted to munitions plants during World War II to make the explosive nitroglycerine).[7]

In a brilliant demonstration of the illusion of variety in ultraprocessed foods, Michael Pollan reports on the proportion of corn-derived matter in each item in a McDonald's meal. The molecular analysis reveals the presence of corn everywhere, derived directly from corn sweeteners, emulsifiers, binders, and fillers, and also indirectly from corn fed to animals and converted into meat:

- soda: 100 percent corn
- milk shake: 78 percent corn
- salad dressing: 65 percent corn
- chicken nuggets: 56 percent corn
- cheeseburger: 52 percent corn
- french fries: 23 percent corn[8]

What is stunning about this molecular breakdown is that no matter the appearance, or even the taste, of these ultraprocessed foodstuffs, underneath they are all remarkably similar. As public health attorney Michele Simon puts it, "Food companies like Kraft, McDonald's, and Coca-Cola maximize profit by taking raw materials such as wheat, potatoes, salt, and sugar, pulverizing them and combining them with a chemical soup of additives; at the other end of the factory, out comes a wide array of 'consumer products.'"[9] Like candy, the full array of ultraprocessed foods is produced by enacting machine and chemical transformations on a narrow palette of raw materials—raw materials, it should be added, that have little going for them nutritionwise beyond dense calories.

The way I see it, candy is no worse than any of those other ultraprocessed industrial foods. In fact, I'd argue that a lot of times it's much better. When I read the ingredient list on a package of Swedish Fish, I recognize every one of the nine substances. Sure, that includes tiny amounts of artificial color and food-grade wax (for shine—it's on apples too). But at least with candy, I know that I'm getting what I expect.

My friends, especially the ones with kids, start growing a little nervous at this point in the conversation. I try to be reassuring: I'm not suggesting that a candy diet is the way to go. It is candy, after all. To which the relieved response is often something along the lines of, "I guess the best solution is 'everything in moderation.'" It sounds a lot like the official advice on the NCA website. Moderation is the way we've learned to live with our vices: not too much, and you'll be fine. However, the advice to eat candy "in moderation" suggests that there is some ideal amount of candy eating that is safe and appropriate. That's how we talk about drinking: one beer is "moderation," one six-pack is excess. But I'm not sure this is the right way to think about eating candy.

Asking whether candy is good or bad, or whether it's okay to eat it, makes it sound like eating candy is separate from all the other eating that happens during the course of the day or week. But it's not. One person is eating Eggo waffles for breakfast and Stouffer's macaroni and cheese for dinner, while another is eating kale salad and poached chicken. For these two eaters, who choose their foods from opposite ends of the fresh to ultraprocessed food spectrum, adding candy to the mix is quite a different proposition. "How much candy" makes sense only in relation to what else gets eaten. Because the Eggo breakfast and Stouffer's dinner are each already just about as wholesome as candy; add candy, you're just adding more of the same. The risk of moderation is that when we eat moderate amounts of Sara Lee bran muffins, Froot Loops, Hot Pockets, and Big Macs (or, if you prefer, Earth's Best Organic Blueberry Mini Waffles, Applegate Farms Chicken Pot Pie, and Amy's Organic Soy Cheeze Frozen Pizza), and toss in moderate amounts of candy, chips, and soda (even the organic "all-natural fruit juice" kinds), it doesn't add up to moderation.

All of it is, to be blunt, fake food. And whether it's brown or red or green, sweet or savory, chewy or crunchy, it still isn't real food. It may have calories and protein and vitamins, it may even be organic and "natural" and GMO free, but that doesn't change the fact that foodstuffs that pass through the wringer of factory processing are essentially different from real food. There is real food on one side—fresh or minimally processed for storage or preparation—and on the other side are the "edible foodlike substances" that are the products of technology and chemistry: candy and all the rest. Candy isn't food, at least not by any definition of food that I'd like to live by. But candy isn't poison, either. That little jelly bean is just a jelly bean: it won't rot your teeth, or make you fat, or drive you to drink, or give you cancer. Candy is just candy, a sweet morsel without any supernatural powers.

I say, let candy be candy. Call it what it is and know when you're eating it. Choose the most delicious candy and let yourself enjoy it. Worry less about what's "good" and what's "bad." It isn't so complicated: eat real food. And then, have a few jelly beans.

Notes

1: Evil or Just Misunderstood?

1. Dionne Searcy, "Just Say No . . . to Smarties? Faux Smoking Has Parents Fuming," *Wall Street Journal*, March 20, 2009.
2. Examples of drunken gummy bear stories at www.kmvt.com/news/re gional/Kids-turning-to-gummy-bears-to-get-drunk-131404838.html, and www.clickondetroit.com/video/29384556/index.html.
3. Tom Dalzell, ed., *The Routledge Dictionary of Modern American Slang and Unconventional English* (New York: Routledge, 2008), p. 165.
4. Amanda Ferris, "You Can Now Buy 'Breaking Bad' Blue Meth Candy," August 22, 2012, http://thefw.com/breaking-bad-blue-meth-candy/.
5. A. Gearhardt et al., "Neural Correlates of Food Addiction," *Archives of General Psychiatry* 68, no. 8 (2011): 808–16.
6. Kathleen Sebelius, speech delivered at the Weight of the Nation Conference, Washington, DC, May 7, 2012; transcript at www.hhs.gov/secretary /about/speeches/sp20120507.html.
7. David Benton, "The Plausibility of Sugar Addiction and Its Role in Obesity and Eating Disorders," *Clinical Nutrition* 29, no. 3 (June 2010): 288–303.
8. Michael Moss, "Can Food Be as Addictive as a Drug?" *New York Times*, October 2, 2011.
9. Tara Parker-Pope, "Craving an Ice Cream Fix," Well column, September 20, 2012, *New York Times Blogs*, http://well.blogs.nytimes.com/2012/09/20 /craving-an-ice-cream-fix/.

10. Laura Sanders, "Junk Food Turns Rats into Addicts," *Science News* 176, no. 11 (November 21, 2009): 8.

11. Kessler, *End of Overeating*, p. 91.

12. E. J. Schultz, "Snickers Surging to Top of Global Candy Race," *Advertising Age*, September 20, 2012.

13. Global Candy & Chocolate Manufacturing Market Research Report, *IBISWorld*, June 2012, www.ibisworld.com/industry/global/global-candy-chocolate-manufacturing.html.

14. Mark Garrison, "Why Snickers Is Poised to Rule the World," *Marketplace* (American Public Media), September 21, 2012; Lauren Alix Brown, "The World's Candy Land Is Now Flat," *Quartz*, November 1, 2012; Ruona Agbroko, "European Dominance in Cocoa Challenged," *Financial Times*, October 29, 2012.

15. Quoted in Ellen Jean Hurst, "Halloween Candy Sales to Reach $2.4 Billion," *Chicago Tribune*, October 31, 2012.

16. Cybele May, personal communication; my summary and paraphrase.

17. Gary Taubes, "Sweet and Vicious: The Case Against Sugar," *New York Times Magazine*, April 17, 2011.

18. For more on the "fat hypothesis" and the "carbohydrate hypothesis," see Taubes, *Good Calories, Bad Calories*.

19. The most recent data on the contribution of candy to total added sugars in the U.S. diet is from the 2005–2006 National Health and Nutrition Examination Survey (NHANES). See U.S. National Institutes of Health, National Cancer Institute, "Risk Factor Monitoring and Methods: Diet: Food Sources," Table 5a: "Mean Intake of Added Sugars & Percentage Contribution of Various Foods Among U.S. Population, by Age, NHANES 2005–06," http://riskfactor.cancer.gov/diet/foodsources/added_sugars/table5a.html. Overall, candy is only about half sugar by weight; chocolate, milk, other fats, nuts, and other ingredients make up the balance.

20. Robert Bradfield, "Kentucky Cows Chow Down on Candy," CNN Money, October 10, 2012; Aaron Smith, "Cash-Strapped Farmers Feed Candy to Cows," CNN Money Online, October 10, 2012, http://money.cnn.com/2012/10/10/news/economy/farmers-cows-candy-feed/index.html.

21. Pollan acknowledges Gyorgy Scrinis as the first to coin the word *nutritionism* to name the idea that "we should understand and engage with food and our bodies in terms of their nutritional and chemical constituents and requirements." In his writings, Scrinis is developing a more fully elaborated critique of nutritionism; however, to the extent the concept has passed into a wider discussion, it is largely due to Pollan's lucid and persuasive explication. Scrinis, "Sorry Marge," *Meanjin* 61, no. 4

(2002): 108–16, quoted in Pollan, *Defense of Food*, p. 27. See also Gyorgy Scrinis, "On the Ideology of Nutritionism," *Gastronomica: The Journal of Food and Culture* 8, no. 1 (2008): 39–48.

22. Hooker, *Food and Drink*, p. 251.

23. Richardson, *Sweets*, p. 53.

24. Woloson, *Refined Tastes*, p. 3. Sidney Mintz was the first to examine the relation between the economic value of sugar and the growth and spread of sugar-sweetened foods; see *Sweetness and Power*.

25. Katy Able, "Child Abduction: What Every Parent Needs to Know," http://life.familyeducation.com/stranger-safety/safety/36556.html#ixzz2Ef2G5qhx.

26. "Eat Candy, Escape a Jag," *Chicago Tribune*, August 7, 1907.

27. C. Monteiro, "The Big Issue Is Ultra-Processing," *World Nutrition* 1, no. 6 (November 2010): 238, www.wphna.org.

28. Julia Moskin, "Candy: Evil, or Just Misunderstood?," *New York Times*, October 29, 2010.

2: The Machine Candy Revolution

1. All details in this account are drawn from "Brooklyn Leads Country in Candy Export," *Brooklyn Daily Eagle*, March 17, 1908.

2. Hooker, *Food and Drink*, p. 33.

3. Descriptions of the goods offered by Dutch bakers and early American confectioners from Gott, *All About Candy*, pp. 14–15.

4. A. T. Hayward, "Confectionery Trade in America," *Encyclopedia Americana*, Vol. 5, 1904.

5. Early candy industry statistics are compiled in Gott, *All About Candy*, pp. 22, 25.

6. Per capita consumption is only a rough measure of the amount of candy anyone actually ate in any given year. The figure is the "total shipments plus imports minus exports divided by population," as reported by the U.S. Commerce Department each year after 1923 (prior to that year, the numbers are unofficial estimates). The figure is higher than actual consumption, since there is no account for loss, waste, or spoilage. Also, early calculations did not include imports or exports, although industry observers believed these more or less balanced out. But as imprecise as the figure may be for any single year, the numbers are relatively comparable year to year. This means that looking at changes in per capita consumption over time gives us a pretty good idea of how the volume of candy has grown or shrunk relative to the population.

7. Department of Agriculture, Economic Research Service Food Availability Data Sets, www.ers.usda.gov/Data/FoodConsumption/#table.

8. Useful accounts of sugar production and the sugar trade can be found in Mintz, *Sweetness and Power*, and Abbott, *Sugar*.

9. Woloson, *Refined Tastes*, p. 26.

10. Ibid., pp. 27–28.

11. On traditional methods of comfit making, see Mason, *Sugar-Plums and Sherbet*, pp. 121–28.

12. Untermeyer, *A Century of Candymaking*, pp. 10–11.

13. For descriptions of early candy machines and the Great Exposition, see Hayward, "Confectionery Trade in America"; Untermeyer, *A Century of Candymaking*, p. 80; Gott, *All About Candy*, p. 16.

14. Henry Weatherly, *Treatise on the Art of Boiling Sugar* (London, 1864), cited in Richardson, *Sweets*, p. 14.

15. Frank H. Page, "Candy Machines Have Revolutionized the Candy Industry," *Confectioners Journal*, December 1924, p. 128.

16. Gott, *All About Candy*, p. 22; Ellwood B. Chapman, *The Candy Making Industry in Philadelphia*, Educational Pamphlet no. 6, Philadelphia Chamber of Commerce, 1917, p. 9.

17. J. D. Waite, "A Review of the Processes and Incidental Hazards Involved in the Manufacture of Candy—The Moral Hazard Light," in *Live Articles on Special Hazards: A Series of Articles Reprinted from the Monthly Fire Insurance Supplement of "The Weekly Underwriter," 1909–1910* (New York: Underwriter Printing and Publishing Company, 1910), p. 50; David J. Price, "Dust Explosions: Cause, Effect and Prevention," *Engineering News Record* 86, no. 15 (April 14, 1921): 634–36.

18. "Dipping," *Wages of Women in the Candy Factories of Massachusetts*, Commonwealth of Massachusetts Minimum Wage Commission Bulletin no. 4, October 1914, pp. 14–17; "Chocolate Dipping," *Confectioners' and Bakers' Gazette* 30 (June 10, 1909): 27.

19. Ad for Confectioners' Machinery & Manufacturing Company, *Confectioners' and Bakers' Gazette* 30 (June 10, 1909): 39.

20. On women's labor in confectionery manufacture, see Cooper, "Love, War, and Chocolate," pp. 82–83. For wages, see "Analysis of the Wage Situation," *Wages of Women in the Candy Factories of Massachusetts*, p. 20.

21. "Lessons on Common Things," *Ohio Journal of Education*, May 1857, p. 159.

22. *Confectioners Journal*, June 1911, p. 83, quoting from the *Philadelphia North American*, May 6, 1911.

23. "Alfalfa Candy," *International Confectioner*, April 1915, p. 55; "Horse-radish Bonbons," *Confectioners Journal*, November 1915, p. 106; "Candy from Cottonseed," *Confectioners Journal*, December 1915, p. 69.

24. "Cactus Candy in Louisiana," *American Food Journal*, June 1918, p. 341.

25. Don White, "The Variety Craze," *Confectioners Journal*, January 1915, p. 80.

26. Eflorose Sugar Company ad, *Confectioners Journal*, November 1918, p. 13.

27. Acarose ad, American Cereal Syrup Company, *Confectioners Journal*, January 1920, p. 95.

28. J. P. Booker, service manager, Numoline Co., "Adapting a New Sugar to a New Use in Candy Making," *Confectioners Journal*, July 1926, p. 104.

29. H. S. Paine, "Constructive Chemistry in Relation to Confectionery Manufacture," *Industrial and Engineering Chemistry* 16, no. 5 (May 1924): 513; see also "Chemistry and Confectionery Manufacture," *Confectioners Journal*, June 1924, p. 88.

30. Edwin O. Blomquist, E. J. Brach & Sons, "History of Candy," *Candy Industry*, January 1, 1952, p. 8.

3: Fake Sweets and Fake Food

1. Quoted in Mary and Lewis Theiss, "Fake Sweets and Soft Drinks to Be Dodged," *Pearson's Magazine*, July 1911, p. 82.

2. Root and de Rochemont, *Eating in America*, pp. 152–53.

3. Smith, *Eating History*, pp. 86–89.

4. Root and de Rochemont, *Eating in America*, p. 190.

5. Ibid., pp. 190–91; Smith, *Eating History*, pp. 69–70.

6. On Pasteur, Lister, and the development of chemical preservatives, see Young, *Pure Food*, p. 111.

7. Ibid.

8. For useful accounts of food fraud in the nineteenth century, see Wilson, *Swindled*, and Young, *Pure Food*.

9. Alexander Wedderburn, *A Popular Treatise on the Extent and Character of Food Adulterations*, U.S. Department of Agriculture, Division of Chemistry, bulletin 25, 1890, p. 10.

10. The oleo controversy is recounted in detail in Young, *Pure Food*, pp. 71–95, and Okun, *Fair Play*, pp. 251–86.

11. This account of Mège-Mouriès and oleomargarine is based on details in Young, *Pure Food*, pp. 71–72.

12. Ibid., pp. 72–74.

13. Robert M. La Follette, 1886, quoted ibid., p. 66.

14. Kamps, *What's Cooking, Uncle Sam?*, pp. 28–29.

15. Mancelia Folsom, president of New York State Dairymen's Association, 1880, quoted in Okun, *Fair Play*, p. 257.

16. Young, *Pure Food*, p. 88.

17. Okun, *Fair Play*, p. 224; Young, *Pure Food*, p. 66.

18. *Report on Glucose, Prepared by the National Academy of Sciences, in Response to a Request Made by the Commissioner of Internal Revenue*, Washington, DC, 1884, quoted in Young, *Pure Food*, p. 70.

19. Ibid.

20. *Facts: A Compilation of Various Newspaper Reports on the Subject of Supposed Poisoning by Candy and Investigations of the Circumstances by Our Association*, National Confectioners Association of the United States, 1907, pp. 67, 84.

21. Cleveland Moffett, "Cassidy and the Food Poisoners," *Hampton's Magazine*, February 1911, p. 146.

22. "The Corn Syrup Controversy Settled," *American Food Journal*, February 15, 1908, pp. 2, 5.

23. Young, *Pure Food*, p. 67.

24. Woloson, *Refined Tastes*, p. 6.

25. McGee, *On Food and Cooking*, pp. 686–87.

26. An account of the Kirchmaier correspondence is in *Facts*, p. 72; see also "A Crotchety Chemist," *Confectioners Journal*, October 1895.

27. Theiss, "Fake Sweets and Soft Drinks to Be Dodged," pp. 79–86.

28. Burton Hendrick, "Eight Years of the Pure Food Law," *McClure's Magazine*, March 1915, pp. 59–70.

29. Ibid., pp. 59, 60–62.

30. "Adulterated Confectionery: The Poisonous Compounds That Are Sold in Cheap Shops for Candy," *New York Times*, December 8, 1877; all quotations in this paragraph are from this article.

31. Vincent L. Price, report to NCA convention, June 1911, reported in *Confectioners Journal*, July 1911, p. 105.

32. "Wife Released in Poison Candy Plot," *New York Times*, December 11, 1925; "Free Richmond Woman," *New York Times*, April 15, 1920; "Sent Poison Candy to Self," *New York Times*, March 19, 1904.

33. Theiss, "Fake Sweets and Soft Drinks," p. 79.

34. *Foods and Food Adulterants*, U.S. Department of Agriculture, Division of Chemistry Bulletin 13, 1887, p. 741.

35. Young, *Pure Food*, p. 141.

36. Seventh Annual Report of the Dairy and Food Commissioner of the State of Michigan, 1900, p. 31.

37. Fourth Annual Report of the State Food Commissioner of Illinois, 1903 (Springfield: Phillips Bros., 1904), p. 85.

38. Quoted in *Facts*, p. 178.

39. "No Poison Candy," *Spatula*, April 1908, p. 476.

40. *Foods and Food Adulterants*, p. 736.

41. "The Corn Syrup Controversy Settled," *American Food Journal*, February 15, 1908, p. 8.

42. Robert Moses testimony, Hearings on Pure Food Bills, House Committee on Interstate and Foreign Commerce, 57th Cong., 1st sess., 1901–1902, p. 66.

43. Wilson, *Swindled*, p. 232.

44. For these and other examples, and a more extended discussion of the regulation of imitation foods, see ibid., pp. 225–32.

45. The account of a shift in food standards and the role of breaded shrimp comes from Suzanne White Junod, "The Rise and Fall of Federal Food Standards in the United States: The Case of the Peanut Butter and Jelly Sandwich," in *The Food and Drug Administration*, ed. Meredith A. Hickmann, pp. 35–48 (New York: Nova Science Publishers, 2003); see also Wilson, *Swindled*, pp. 232–33.

46. Judge Robert W. Sweet, *Pelman v. McDonald's Corp.*, 237 F. Supp. 2d 512 (S.D.N.Y. 2003), quoted in Pollan, *Omnivore's Dilemma*, p. 112.

4: Demon Candy, Demon Rum

1. "Snappy Recitation," *Pennsylvania School Journal* 48, no. 12 (June 1900): 548.

2. James W. Redfield, *Comparative Physiognomy; or, Resemblances Between Men and Animals* (New York: Redfield, 1852), pp. 271–72.

3. Sara Tyson Rorer, "Why Sweets Are Not Good for Children," *Ladies' Home Journal*, March 1906, p. 38, quoted in Woloson, *Refined Tastes*, p. 62.

4. "A Crusade Against Candy," *Confectioners Journal*, June 1893, quoted in *Facts*, p. 42.

5. Okrent, *Last Call*, pp. 7–8.

6. John Bartholomew Gough, ca. 1845, quoted ibid., p. 10.

7. The terrifying consequences attributed to drink are described in Whorton, *Crusaders*, p. 39.

8. Ibid., p. 75.

9. Smith, *Eating History*, p. 30.

10. Ibid., p. 32.

11. Bonnie Slotnik, "Sylvester Graham," in Smith, *Oxford Companion*, p. 263.

12. Whorton, *Crusaders*, pp. 48–49.

13. Smith, *Eating History*, pp. 31–33.

14. Whorton, *Crusaders*, pp. 48–49.

15. Sylvester Graham, *Lectures on the Science of Human Life*, 1854, p. 547, quoted in Chen, *Taste of Sweet*, p. 106.

16. John Harvey Kellogg, *Plain Facts for Old and Young: Embracing the Natural History and Hygiene of Organic Life*, 1888, p. 245, quoted in Woloson, *Refined Tastes*, p. 139.

17. Slotnik, "Sylvester Graham," p. 263.

18. Letter from Mrs. E. Frances Lord to Mr. A. J. Walter, January 19, 1898, in *Facts*, p. 137; "Toddy, Maybe, in Goldman's Candy," *New York Journal*, January 10, 1898; "Children Affected by Whiskey Drops: Mystery of the Drowsiness of Grammar School Pupils Is Explained and a Candy Seller Is Arrested," *New York Herald*, January 10, 1898.

19. *Facts*, p. 104; the original story appeared in *Confectioners Journal*, February 1897.

20. "Eat Candy, Escape a Jag," *Chicago Tribune*, August 7, 1907; "Candy Same as Alcohol," *Meridian Morning Record*, August 13, 1907.

21. "Eat Candy, Escape a Jag."

22. "Eat More Candy," *International Confectioner*, July 1916, p. 68.

23. "Oh! Doctor!," *International Confectioner*, July 1916, p. 40.

24. "Down on Candy," *Confectioners Journal*, November 1915, p. 69.

25. "Candy a Cure for Drunkenness," *Confectioners Journal*, May 1908, p. 70.

26. "The Virtues of Candy: Eat Candy and Give Up the Booze," *International Confectioner*, October 1914, p. 74.

27. Okrent, *Last Call*, p. 373.

28. Ibid., p. 208.

29. Pinkham's Vegetable Compound ad, *Salt Lake Weekly Herald*, December 8, 1881.

30. Okrent, *Last Call*, p. 194.

31. J. Ruth Dempsey, "Lydia Pinkham 'For the female discomforts,'" www.heliograph.com/trmgs/trmgs4/pinkham.shtml.

32. Quoted ibid.

33. "New York's Sweet Tooth," *New York Times*, February 26, 1899.

34. My account of Ella Kellogg and her leadership in the women's health reform movement is based on Goodwin, *Pure Food Crusaders*, esp. pp. 27–29.

35. Ibid., p. 123.

36. Kellogg published a series of her lectures under the title "Health Talks" in several issues of the *Union Sentinel* in 1883 and 1884; the contents are summarized in Goodwin, *Pure Food Crusaders*, p. 28.

37. "Ye Gods! What Have We Here?," *Confectioners Journal*, September 1924, p. 130.

38. "Roundabouts," *American Stationer*, November 22, 1888, p. 1234.

39. Sanford Bell, "The Psychology of Foods," 1904, quoted in Woloson, *Refined Tastes*, p. 58.

40. L. U. Snead, "A Little Child Shall Lead Them," *The Bible Students' Cyclopaedia*, 1900, p. 203.

41. "The Corrupting ? Candy Cigar," *Confectioners Journal*, February 1923, p. 80.

42. Ibid.

43. Hershey Chocolate cigarettes in McMahon, *Built on Chocolate*.

5: Becoming Food

1. The energy balance model is based on a nineteeth-century idea of the body as a fuel-burning machine. However, there is considerable evidence that the body's mechanisms for metabolizing different kinds of foods, and the relationship of metabolism to fat storage, are substantially more complex. See especially Taubes, *Why We Get Fat*, for an alternative hypothesis of obesity as a fat-storage disorder triggered by insulin resistance, which in turn may be caused by excessive sugar consumption.

2. Whorton, *Inner Hygiene*, p. 168.

3. For an extensive discussion of the transformation of food into numerical measurements, see Mudry, *Measured Meals*.

4. "Nourishing Stuff Is Candy, if Real," *New York Times*, February 20, 1910. The chocolate cream diet is expounded in "Pure Candy Is Healthful—Sound the Slogan," *Confectioners Journal*, October 1916, p. 86.

5. The description of food protests is based on Levenstein, *Revolution*, p. 109.

6. Ibid., pp. 112–13.

7. Dr. Charles F. Boldman, New York City Department of Health, "Fuel Values of Foods: The Bill of Fare of the Future, Pricing Each Item in Calories as Well as Cash," *Scientific American*, July 28, 1917, p. 62.

8. Walter Hughes, *The Story of Candy*, National Confectioners Association, 1926, p. 24.

9. "Candy as Food," *Literary Digest*, May 31, 1919, p. 30.

10. Dr. Ruth Wheeler, "The Children's Food," in *The Day's Food in War and Peace*, U.S. Food Administration, 1919, p. 190.

11. "Candy and Calories," *Journal of the American Medical Association*, May 3, 1919, p. 1297.

12. Hughes, *Story of Candy*, p. 24.

13. Viedt ad, *Confectioners Journal*, October 1916, p. 83.

14. Biographical information on Abel from Levenstein, *Revolution*, chap. 4, "New England Kitchen," esp. pp. 48, 54–55, and Shapiro, *Perfection Salad*, pp. 143–47.

15. Mary Hinman Abel, *Sugar as Food*, USDA Farmers' Bulletin no. 93, 1906, p. 17.

16. Ibid.

17. Ibid., p. 18.

18. Ibid., p. 19.

19. "Confectionery in Army Rations," *Scientific American*, January 6, 1900, p. 6.

20. "Brooklyn Leads Country in Candy Export," *Brooklyn Daily Eagle*, March 7, 1908.

21. "Aviators 5 Days on Wreckage Lived on a Piece of Chocolate," *New York Times*, June 2, 1917; "War Chocolate," *International Confectioner*, August 1917, p. 57.

22. "Chocolate in New Army Ration," *Confectioners Journal*, October 1918, p. 86.

23. Roland Isker, Col., U.S.A., Ret., "For That Extra Effort: The Values of Candy in Military Rations," in Gott, *All About Candy*, p. 101.

24. "Preparedness," *International Confectioner*, June 1916, p. 39.

25. "Candy in the Army," *Literary Digest*, April 5, 1919, p. 28.

26. *Confectioners Journal*, July 1917, p. 59.

27. Abel, *Sugar as Food*, p. 25.

28. Judy Putnam, Jane Allshouse, and Linda Scott Kantor, "U.S. Per Capita Food Supply Trends," *FoodReview* 25, no. 3 (Winter 2002), Figure 1: "Calories from the U.S. Per Capita Food Supply," p. 3.

29. Woloson, *Refined Tastes*, p. 6.

30. Department of Commerce estimate cited in "America's Sweet Tooth," *Confectioners Journal*, May 1922, p. 117.

31. Abel, *Sugar as Food*, p. 25.

32. Ibid., p. 19.

33. Ibid.

34. Ibid., p. 21.

35. Marion Harris Neil, *Candies and Bonbons and How to Make Them* (Philadelphia: D. McKay, 1913), p. 20.

36. Leonard Keene Hirshberg, M.D., "New Discoveries About Sugar," *Confectioners Journal*, May 1914, p. 111.

37. Woods Hutchinson, A.M., M.D., "The Sweet Tooth; and Why It Is So Keen," *Confectioners Journal*, November 1909, p. 81.

38. Hirshberg, "New Discoveries."

39. Captain J. Alcock, D.S.C., "Alcock and Brown Fly Across Atlantic: Captain Alcock's Own Narrative of His Flight from Newfoundland to Ireland," by special cable to *The New York Times*, June 16, 1919; "Chocolate as a Food for Endurance," *Confectioners Journal*, July 1919, p. 102.

40. "Candy Diet Helped Mountain Climbers," *New York Times*, January 21, 1923.

41. Peck biography at "Annie Smith Peck," www.ric.edu/faculty/rpotter /smithpeck.html; "To Counteract Fatigue," *New York Times*, March 26, 1916; "Miss Annie Peck, Noted Mountain Climber Finds 25 Cents Ample Sum for Daily Menu," *Milwaukee Sentinel*, March 31, 1915.

42. "Sugar Gave Ritchie His 'Punch,'" *Confectioners Journal*, September 1914, p. 64; "Sugar Fine Food for Athletes," *Confectioners Journal*, May 1916, p. 83; Brady quoted in Hughes, *Story of Candy*, p. 25.

43. C. Houston Goudiss, *The Strength We Get from Sweets: How Sugar—One of the Chief Sources of Heat and Energy—Serves Man at Every Age* (New York: privately printed, 1921), p. 7.

44. History of the Food Administration and war food policy is based on William Mullendore, *History of the United States Food Administration, 1917–1919* (Stanford: Stanford University Press, 1941).

45. "Hoover May Order Rationing of Candy," *New York Times*, October 17, 1917.

46. The account of Hughes and the impact of the NCA on sugar policy is based on Walter Hughes, "Highlights of 20 Years as Secretary, the National Confectioners Association," *Confectioners Journal*, June 1933, pp. 117–26.

47. The results of the study are summarized ibid., pp. 121–22.

48. "Food Board Orders Sugar Supply Cut," *New York Times*, June 25, 1918.

49. "Plan Strict Check on Sales of Sugar," *New York Times*, July 27, 1918.

50. Letter quoted in Hughes, "Highlights," p. 122.

51. Undated letter, archived at Nebraska State Historical Society, www.ne braskahistory.org/publish/publicat/timeline/wwi_sugar_shortage.htm.

52. J. W. Vogan, "Truth About Candy," *Confectioners Journal*, September 1918, p. 59.

53. "Food Value of Candy Booklets," *Confectioners Journal*, March 1918, p. 71.

54. "A Fair Outlook for 1918," *Confectioners Journal*, January 1918, p. 60.

55. Walter Hughes, "Candy and Its Relation to the Food Problem," *Confectioners Journal*, March 1918, pp. 70–71.

56. "War Special" candies ad, George Close Co., *Confectioners Journal*, January 1918.

57. White-Stokes ad, *Confectioners Journal*, March 1918, p. 44.

58. Touraine Confectionery Co. ad, *Confectioners Journal*, March 1918, p. 51.

59. Walter Hughes, "Let Us Sit Down and Talk It Over," *Confectioners Journal*, March 1918, p. 69.

60. "Food Value of Candy Booklets," p. 71.

61. "Candy Is a Food," *Confectioners Journal*, February 1919, p. 64.

62. Mason, Au and Magenheimer Confectionery ad, *Confectioners Journal*, March 1919.

63. "Candy Becomes a Food," *Printers' Ink* editorial, quoted in *Confectioners Journal*, April 1920, p. 170.

64. Candy Manufacturers of Oregon, "The Story of a Chocolate Cream," *The Truth About Candy* no. 6, reproduced in *Confectioners Journal*, October 1918, p. 70.

6: In the Kitchen

1. George V. Frye, *How to Make Candy: Comprising Receipts for the Finest Home-Made Candies, Especially Adapted for Manufacture in the American Kitchen* (Chicago: Morrill, Higgins, 1892), p. 3, cited in Dusselier, "Bonbons," p. 16.

2. Shapiro, *Perfection Salad*, pp. 35–36.

3. Laura Shapiro recounts the role of Ellen Richards in the beginnings of the domestic science movement ibid., pp. 36–38.

4. For a more extended discussion of the role of Fannie Farmer and her cookbooks in the domestic science movement, see Smith, *Eating History*, pp. 134–37.

5. Dona MacKenzie Snyder, *The Art of Candy Making Fully Explained, with 105 Recipes for the Home* (Dayton, OH: Health Publishing Co., 1915), p. 4.

6. Elizabeth Du Bois Bache and Louise Franklin Bache, *When Mother Lets Us Make Candy* (New York: Moffat, Yard, 1915), preface.

7. Mary M. Wright, *Candy-Making at Home: Two Hundred Ways to Make Candy with Home Flavor and Professional Finish* (Philadelphia: Penn Publishing, 1915), p. 13.

8. Mrs. Helen Armstrong and Janet M. Hill, *Karo Recipes for Cooking and Candy Making* (New York: Corn Products Refining Co., 1908), p. 1.

9. Shapiro, *Perfection Salad*, p. 191.

10. Mary Elizabeth [Evans], *My Candy Secrets* (New York: Frederick A. Stokes, 1919), p. 8.

11. Mary Elizabeth Hall, *Candy-Making Revolutionized: Confectionery from Vegetables* (New York: Sturgis & Walton, 1912), p. viii.

12. Jessica Seinfeld, *Deceptively Delicious: Simple Secrets to Get Your Kids Eating Good Food* (New York: Harper, 2008); Missy Chase Lapine at sneakychef.com.

13. See Hooker, *Food and Drink*, p. 228.

14. Levenstein, *Revolution*, p. 57.

15. Hall, *Candy-Making Revolutionized*, p. vi.

16. Amy L. Waterman, *A Little Candy Book for a Little Girl* (Boston: Colonial Press, 1918), pp. 10, 11, 13.

17. Bache and Bache, *When Mother Lets Us Make Candy*, p. 13.

18. On the banishing of sugary treats from school parties, see, for example, Susan Dominus, "Mother's Fight Against Junk Food Puts a School on Edge," *New York Times*, June 16, 2009.

19. Barbara Allen, "Christmas Confections," *Everyday Housekeeping: A Magazine for Practical Housekeepers*, December 1895, pp. 142–43.

20. Ellye Howell Glover, *"Dame Curtsey's" Book of Candy Making* (Chicago: A.C. McClurg, 1920), foreword.

21. Woman's World Magazine, *The Candy Calendar* (Chicago: Woman's World Magazine Co., 1923), inside front cover; Glover, *"Dame Curtsey's,"* p. 11.

22. Woloson, *Refined Tastes*, p. 198.

23. On the growth of Ora Snyder's candy business, see Shannon Perich, "Chocolate Dipped," http://blog.americanhistory.si.edu/osaycanyousee/2009/03/chocolate-dipped.html; and Alice K. Fallows, "Christmas Candies from a Famous Maker," *Ladies' Home Journal*, December 1922, p. 146.

24. Cooper, "Love, War, and Chocolate," p. 80.

25. "Hymneal: Deitz-Nuss," *Confectioners Journal*, July 1923, p. 108; John C. Hover et al., *Memoirs of the Miami Valley*, 3 vols. (Chicago: Robert O. Law, 1920), 3:425.

26. *Candy Calendar*, inside cover.

27. *Hood's Practical Cook's Book: For the Average Household* (Lowell, MA: C.I. Hood, 1897), p. 323.

28. Mary Annable Fanton, "Mary Elizabeth's Plan," *Success Magazine*, February 1906, pp. 110–11; Wyndham Martin, "Mary Elizabeth," *Pearson's Magazine*, September 1915, pp. 297–301.

29. Mary Elizabeth [Evans], *Mary Elizabeth's War Time Recipes* (New York: Frederick A. Stokes, 1918), p. vi; see also Virginia Hunt, "Mary Elizabeth's Wartime Candies," *Ladies' Home Journal*, December 1917, p. 64.

30. Martin, "Mary Elizabeth," p. 301.
31. Sarah Tyson Rorer, *Home Candy Making* (Philadelphia: Arnold and Co., 1889), p. 10.
32. Ibid.
33. Ibid., p. 9.
34. For a more detailed discussion of daintiness in the context of scientific cooking, see Shapiro, *Perfection Salad*, pp. 86–94.
35. Barbara Allen, "Christmas Confections," *Everyday Housekeeping: A Magazine for Practical Housekeepers*, December 1895, pp. 142–43.
36. "Home Candy Making Outfit" ad, *The Boston Cooking School Magazine of Culinary Science and Domestic Economics*, December 1917, p. 404.
37. "Those Silly Sunday Pages," *Confectioners Journal*, February 1915, p. 62.
38. "'Lasses Candy," *Confectioners Journal*, April 1916, p. 78.
39. Pennsylvania Department of Agriculture, Dairy and Food Division Bulletin no. 216, *Cheap Confectionery*, 1911, p. 50.
40. "Sea Girt Plays Croquet," *New York Times*, August 1, 1908.
41. "Allenhurst: Keen Interest Shown in the Tennis Contest for Club Cup," *New York Times*, August 20, 1911.
42. "Pow-Wow Department," *Boys' Life*, July 1924, p. 43.
43. On white sauce and scientific cooking, see Shapiro, *Perfection Salad*, pp. 86–89.
44. Ibid., pp. 193–94.
45. Ibid., p. 194.
46. Sylvia Lovegren, *Fashionable Foods: Seven Decades of Food Fads* (New York: Macmillan, 1995), p. 43.
47. Mary D. Chambers, *One-Piece Dinners* (Boston: Little, Brown, 1924), cited in Levenstein, *Revolution*, p. 157.
48. Eva Alice Miller, "Marshmallow Mixtures," *Table Talk*, February 1913, p. 93.
49. Lesley Porcelli, "How Sweet It Is," *Saveur* 142 (November 2011): 43.
50. Campfire ad, *Confectioners Journal*, February 1920, p. 11.
51. "Changing a Confectionery into a Staple Article of Cooking," *Printers' Ink*, January 27, 1921, pp. 97–100.
52. "Making a Candy into a Food," *Confectioners Journal*, March 1921, p. 123.

7: A Nourishing Lunch

1. Kimmerle, *Candy*, p. 150; Goo Goo company history at www.googoo.com/our-story/history/.
2. New England Confectionery Company ad announcing consumer campaign, *Confectioners Journal*, April 1916, p. 55.

3. Excellent sources for the story of Milton Hershey and his invention of milk chocolate can be found in Brenner, *Emperors*, pp. 101–09, and McMahon, *Built on Chocolate*, pp. 38–42.

4. On Hershey's marketing innovations, see Brenner, *Emperors*, pp. 109–10.

5. On early chocolate and candy bars, see Gott, *All About Candy*, pp. 18, 25.

6. Ibid., p. 25.

7. James Somerville Jr., American trade commissioner, London, "English Dislike Eating in Public," *Confectioners Journal*, October 1929, p. 74.

8. M. B. Thornton, "What's in a Name?," *Confectioners Journal*, November 1926, p. 78.

9. Smith, "Snack Foods," *Encyclopedia of Junk Food*, p. 245.

10. For the history of lunch in America, see Andrew Smith, "Meal Patterns," *Oxford Companion*, pp. 372–73.

11. Knickerbocker Chocolate Company trade ad, *International Confectioner*, June 1916.

12. U.S. Patent Office, Serial Number 75,705 Lunch Bar logo, filed February 5, 1914; undated Klein's advertising poster.

13. U.S. Department of Agriculture, Notices of Judgment Under the Food and Drugs Act, Issue 5101, Part 6000: Number 5435. Adulteration and Misbranding of "Milk Chocolate Lunch Bars." *U.S. v. Klein Chocolate Co., Inc.*, a corporation. Plea of nolo contendere. Fine, $10. F. & D. No 8022 I.S. No. 4543-1, 1917.

14. Kimmerle, *Candy*, p. 151; Broekel, *Chocolate Chronicles*, p. 37.

15. Waleco Sandwich Bar, undated advertising poster.

16. Chicken Dinner trade ad, *Confectioners Journal*, February 1924.

17. These and many other candy bars long gone are documented in Broekel, *Chocolate Chronicles*.

18. Ibid., p. 22.

19. Forrest Mars quoted in Brenner, *Emperors*, p. 55.

20. Don Gussow, "A Bicentennial Recollection of an Era That Shaped Today's Candy Business," *Candy and Snack Industry*, August 1976, pp. 26–28.

21. Joseph Nathan Kane, "Foreign Candy Likes and Dislikes," *Confectioners Journal*, June 1928, p. 83.

22. "Otto Schnering, 61, of Curtiss Candy," *New York Times*, January 12, 1953; http://encyclopedia.chicagohistory.org/pages/2638.html; see also Samantha Chmelik's full biographical entry, "Otto Y. Schnering (1891-1953)," in *Immigrant Entrepreneurship: German-American Business Biographies 1720 to the Present*, www.immigrantentrepreneurship .org/entry.php?rec=111.

23. Curtiss Candy trade ad, *Confectioners Journal*, December 1920, p. 52.

24. Ray Broekel, "Otto Schnering Is My Name, Advertising Is My Game," *Great American Candy Bar Book*, p. 22.

25. Patrick O'Hara, "The Great Baby Ruth Debate—Resolved," October 2011, americanpopularculture.com/sports.htm; Broekel, *Great American Candy Bar Book*, p. 23; Richard Sandomir, "Baseball Adopts Baby Ruth, Whomever It's Named After," *New York Times*, June 6, 2006.

26. Trial transcript, transcribed by Patrick O'Hara, "The Great Baby Ruth Debate—Resolved."

27. On Williamson and the beginnings of oh Henry!, see Smith, *Peanuts*, pp. 82–83; Broekel, *Great American Candy Bar Book*, pp. 99–100.

28. *Williamson Candy Co. v. Ucanco Candy Co.*, Delaware District Court, 1925; 3F.2d 156 (1925).

29. Williamson Candy ad, *Confectioners Journal*, November 1926, p. 30.

30. For examples and a more extended discussion of the use of female figures in early 1900s candy advertising, see Dusselier, "Bonbons," pp. 17–22.

31. Williamson trade ad, *Confectioners Journal*, March 1926, p. 31.

32. Oh Henry! ad, *Ladies' Home Journal*, February 26, 1926, p. 108.

33. Williamson trade ad, *Confectioners Journal*, March 1926, p. 31.

34. Fred G. Taylor of the Sugar Institute, "Sugar Institute Program to Teach Public Confidence in Sweets," *Confectioners Journal*, July 1929, pp. 55–57.

8: Fattening

1. Karl J. Smith, *Mathematics: Its Power and Utility* (Belmont, CA: Cengage Learning, 2012), p. 399; see also Norman O. Dahl, *Practical Reason, Aristotle, and Weakness of the Will* (Minneapolis: University of Minnesota Press, 1984), p. 175.

2. "Eat Candy and Be Warm," *Monthly Bulletin of the Dairy and Food Division of the Pennsylvania Department of Agriculture* 10, nos. 11–12 (December 1912–January 1913): 5.

3. "The 'Chocolate Cure,'" *Confectioners Journal*, January 1914, p. 97.

4. Levenstein, *Paradox*, p. 166.

5. Carl Malmberg, *Diet and Die* (New York: Hillman-Curl, 1935), p. 7.

6. Quoted in Fraser, *Losing It*, p. 33. On the evolution and adoption of the personal scale, see Schwartz, *Never Satisfied*, chap. 6, "The Measured Body."

7. On changing ideals of female beauty, see Fraser, *Losing It*, chap. 1, "The Inner Corset."

8. Examples from Schwartz, *Never Satisfied*, p. 181; see also Malmberg, *Diet and Die*, chap. 5, "Quack Remedies."

9. Schwartz, *Never Satisfied*, p. 179. On dangerous diet remedies, see also Yager, *Hundred Year Diet*, pp. 48–49, and Malmberg, *Diet and Die*, pp. 114–16.

10. Quoted in Schwartz, *Never Satisfied*, p. 183. On fad diets and the dire consequences, see Malmberg, *Diet and Die*, pp. 16–18, 104.

11. Yager, *Hundred Year Diet*, p. 19.

12. Lulu Hunt Peters, *Diet and Health with Key to the Calories*, 2nd ed. (Chicago: Reilly & Britton, 1919), p. 13.

13. Schwartz, *Never Satisfied*, p. 175.

14. Ibid.

15. Peters, *Diet and Health*, p. 84.

16. Ibid., p. 24.

17. Ibid., p. 21.

18. Ibid., p. 22.

19. Ibid., p. 37.

20. Ibid., p. 17.

21. All quotations in this paragraph are from Peters's syndicated column "Diet and Health" that appeared in the *Los Angeles Times* and other papers around the country; the quotes are from columns dated May 12, 1928, and December 19, 1925.

22. Ibid., August 25, 1926.

23. Ibid., January 27, 1925, and November 10, 1927.

24. Peters, *Diet and Health*, p. 13.

25. Brumberg, *Fasting Girls*, p. 241.

26. Peters, *Diet and Health*, p. 94.

27. C. J. Nadherny, "For Health's Sake, Eat Candy. Dietetic Value of Carbohydrates to Feature New Advertising Policy of NCA," *Confectioners Journal*, September 1928, p. 69.

28. The candy-vs.-cigarette wars are described in Gott, *All About Candy*, pp. 176–78, and Brandt, *Cigarette Century*, pp. 71–75. See also Philip Wagner, "Candy vs. Cigarettes," *New Republic*, February 13, 1929, pp. 343–45; Kenneth M. Goode, "Lucky Strike Advertising Tosses Bombs Among the Bonbons," *Advertising and Selling*, November 14, 1928, pp. 19–20; Eugene Pharo, "When Thin Women Smoke Confections and Fat Men Eat Cigarettes," *Confectioners Journal*, December 1928, pp. 45–47; Eugene Pharo, "A Hopeful Call on George W. Hill," *Confectioners Journal*, January 1929, pp. 49–50.

29. Gott, *All About Candy*, p. 176.

30. Pharo, "A Hopeful Call," p. 49.

31. "Demand the Proof," *Confectioners Journal*, February 1929, p. 46.

32. Allen Ridgway, "Who Says Candy Is Fattening?," *Confectioners Journal*, February 1929, pp. 55–56.

33. Pharo, "When Thin Women Smoke Confections," p. 45.

34. Brandt, *Cigarette Century*, p. 43.

35. McMahon, *Built on Chocolate*, p. 146.

36. Brandt, *Cigarette Century*, p. 59; see pp. 54, 70 for advertising expenditures.

37. Ibid., p. 70.

38. Ibid., p. 71.

39. Wagner, "Candy vs. Cigarettes," p. 344.

40. Gott, *All About Candy*, p. 177.

41. All quotations in this paragraph are from the United States of America Before Trade Commission, in the Matter of American Tobacco Company, a Corporation, File No. 1-4989, Stipulation as to the Facts, November 13, 1929, http://legacy.library.ucsf.edu/tid/gkf41a00.

42. Meyer Bodansky, "Weight Reduction and Candy," *JAMA* 927 (February 16, 1929): 579.

43. Burgess Gordon and E. von Stanley, "The Use of Dextrose in the Treatment of Obesity: With Special Reference to the Reduction of the Body Weight Without Markedly Lowering the Daily Caloric Intake," *American Journal of Medical Sciences* 175 (January 1928): 37–43, publicized to the candy trade in "Physician Describes Use of Candy as Part of 'Reducing' Diet," *Confectioners Journal*, January 1929, pp. 61–62.

44. "How Facts About Candy Are Spread," *Confectioners Journal*, July 1929, p. 62.

45. Bundesen's contributions to Chicago public health are recounted in Donald Dye et al., "Maternity and Infant Care Services in Chicago Retrospectus," in *Historical Review and Recent Advances in Neonatal and Perinatal Medicine*, ed. George F. Smith (Glenview, IL: Mead Johnson Nutritional Division, 1980).

46. Herman N. Bundesen, *The New Knowledge of Candy* (Chicago: National Confectioners Association, 1929), p. 8.

47. NCA press release, "New Study Finds Candy Consumption Not Associated with Negative Health Outcomes," April 29, 2009; "Association of Candy Consumption with Body Weight Measures, Risk Factors for Cardiovascular Disease, and Diet Quality in U.S. Adults: NHANES 1999–2004," *Nutrition Research* 31 (2011): 122–30.

48. "Sugar Institute Sets an Example," *Confectioners Journal*, March 1929, p. 66a.

49. All examples are ibid.

50. "Energy Value of Confectionery Proved by Psychologist," *Confectioners Journal*, August 1929, pp. 60–61.

9: A Fighting Food

1. Dr. Meyers's story and the NCA's response are recounted in "President Chapman Rushes to Defense of Candy," *Confectioners Journal*, September 1938, p. 31.

2. A more detailed account of McCollum and the "newer knowledge of nutrition" can be found in Levenstein, *Revolution*, pp. 147–48, and Levenstein, *Fear*, pp. 79–86.

3. "Rats Put to Use to Help Mankind," *New York Times*, August 26, 1923.

4. Eunice Fuller Barnard, "In Food Also, a New Fashion Is Here," *New York Times Magazine*, May 4, 1930.

5. "Over 100,000 Attend Philadelphia Candy Show," *Confectioners Journal*, December 1939, p. 39; "More than 35,000 Attend Chicago Candy Club Show," *Confectioners Journal*, October 1939, p. 38; "60,000 Nearly Mob Candy Show Held in Boston MA," *Confectioners Journal*, May 1939, p. 40.

6. "National Confectioners Association Unlimbers Advertising Guns!," *Confectioners Journal*, April 1938, p. 11.

7. "News and Notes of the Advertising Field," *New York Times*, April 11, 1938.

8. "Corn Products Sponsors Nation-Wide Campaign," *Confectioners Journal*, May 1938, p. 40.

9. The Corn Products Refining Company now goes by the name Ingredion; history of Corn Products at www.ingredion.com/about-us/history/.

10. Cerelose ad, *Confectioners Journal*, March 1937, p. 25.

11. "Food Act Ruling to Get Court Test," *New York Times*, March 31, 1940.

12. For the history of the AMA's Council on Foods, and the 1937 decision to discontinue the endorsement of candy, see "Council on Foods," *JAMA* 108, no. 22 (1937): 1891; see also "Council on Foods," *JAMA* 107, no. 5 (1936): 355.

13. Gott, *All About Candy*, pp. 182–83; "NCA Educational Bureau Procures Publicity for Candy," *Confectioners Journal*, September 1938, p. 32.

14. Eugene Pharo, "Somebody Else Is Helping Candy," *Confectioners Journal*, July 1940, p. 24.

15. Col. M. Moffett, "There's Enough Corn Syrup—but That's Not the Point," *Confectioners Journal*, August 1941, p. 12.

16. Dextrose ad, *Life*, September 9, 1942.

17. Dextrose ad, *Life*, June 1, 1942.

18. Quoted in Levenstein, *Fear*, p. 88.

19. Ibid., p. 89.

20. "Observations on Induced Thiamine (Vitamin B₁) Deficiency in Man," *Archives of Internal Medicine* 66, no. 4 (October 1940): 785–99, cited in Levenstein, *Fear*, p. 98.

21. "Vitamins for War," *JAMA* 115 (October 5, 1940): 1198, cited in Levenstein, *Fear*, p. 99.

22. "Enriched Flour Is Celebrating Its Sixth Birthday Anniversary," *Milwaukee Journal*, January 23, 1947; "Bake Bread with Enriched Flour," *San Jose News*, September 12, 1941; "Enrich Health Through Enriched Flour and Bread," Extension Bulletin 605, Oregon State System of Higher Education, Federal Cooperative Extension Service, Oregon State College, Corvallis, September 1942.

23. Dextrose ad, *Life*, January 20, 1941.

24. Quoted in "Glucose Ousting Sugar," *Confectioners Journal*, January 1942, p. 8.

25. "Hints on Diet and Health," *New London Day*, January 6, 1939.

26. For an account of the emergence of the concept of "hidden hunger," see Levenstein, *Fear*, chap. 7, " 'Hidden Hunger' Stalks the Land."

27. Ibid., p. 96.

28. Levenstein, *Paradox*, p. 67.

29. Paul V. McNutt, *Boys' Life*, October 1941, p. 16.

30. Levenstein, *Paradox*, p. 66.

31. Apple, *Vitamania*, pp. 77–78; Levenstein, *Paradox*, p. 69.

32. Levenstein, *Paradox*, p. 69.

33. Apple, *Vitamania*, p. 31.

34. FDA statement of policy, *Federal Register*, July 3, 1943, quoted in "About Enriching Foods by Adding Vitamins," *Confectioners Journal*, August 1943, p. 23.

35. *Washington Reports on Rationing*, NBC radio weekly broadcasts 1942–1944.

36. Philip Gott, "Take All Necessary Measures to Know What We Are Doing," *Confectioners Journal*, July 1941, p. 28.

37. "Candy Goes with the Army," *New York Times*, November 15, 1942.

38. "Hard Candy to Replace Field Ration Chocolate," *New York Times*, September 3, 1941.

39. "Candy Goes with the Army."

40. "50 Pounds of Candy Per Year Per Soldier," *Confectioners Journal*, November 1943, p. 39.

41. *Wall Street Journal*, February 5, 1943, quoted in "Candy's War Program Told in *Wall Street Journal*," *Confectioners Journal*, March 1943, p. 32.

42. *Food for Victory* (Chicago: National Confectioners Association, 1943).

43. "To Allot Candy Supply," *New York Times*, February 5, 1943.

44. Curtiss Candy ad, *Boys' Life*, October 1943.

45. "Civilian Sweet Tooth Left Unfilled by Army and War Plant Candy Orders," *New York Times*, February 6, 1943.

46. Judith Klein, "A Fond Farewell to Penny Candy," *Washington Post*, October 27, 1946.

47. George Mooney, "Lauds War Effort of Confectioners," *New York Times*, June 14, 1942.

48. Curtiss Candy ad, *Life*, January 25, 1943.

49. Philip Gott, "VE Day Will Not Bring Relief to Consumer Appetites," *Confectioners Journal*, October 1944, p. 43.

50. "Five Cent Candy Items Must Be Set Aside for Government Order," *Confectioners Journal*, November 1944, p. 52.

51. Gott, "VE Day."

52. "Fliers Test Candy Diet 5 Days on Raft at Sea," *New York Times*, September 11, 1944.

53. Franz A. Koehler, "Special Rations for the Armed Forces, 1946–53," QMC Historical Studies, Series II, no. 6, Historical Branch, Office of the Quartermaster General, Washington, DC, 1958, www.qmfound.com/army _rations_historical_background.htm.

54. Gott, *All About Candy*, p. 106.

55. "Ration D Bars," Hershey Community Archives, www.hersheyarchives .org/essay/details.aspx?EssayId=26.

56. Ibid.; D'Antonio, *Hershey*, pp. 233–34.

57. Letter from Colonel R. A. Isker, May 2, 1945, "Possible Use for Excess Type D Rations," quoted in Koehler, "Special Rations."

58. Council on Candy ad, *Life*, August 14, 1944.

59. For conflicting accounts of the origins of M&M's, see Brenner, *Emperors*, pp. 147–53.

60. On postwar food and its relation to war technologies, see Shapiro, *Something from the Oven*, p. 8.

61. "Experiment with Formulas for Making New Candy Bar," *Billboard*, October 13, 1945, p. 86; Matthew Berman, "Candy Research," *Confectioners Journal*, July 1944, p. 5.

62. "5,000 to Attend NCA Confab," *Billboard*, June 4, 1949, p. 100.

63. "Candy Bar to Equal Well Balanced Diet Seen in Near Future," *Candy Industry*, July 17, 1951, p. 3.

10: Sugar Free

1. "TV Show to Promote Candy as Food," *Confectioners Journal*, December 1951, p. 27.
2. William L. Laurence, "Obesity Is Called Drag on Life Span," *New York Times*, October 24, 1952.
3. "The Plague of Overweight," *Life*, March 8, 1954, pp. 120–24.
4. de la Peña, *Empty Pleasures*, pp. 23–25.
5. Whelan and Stare, *Panic in the Pantry*, p. 151.
6. de la Peña, *Empty Pleasures*, pp. 76–98.
7. Ronald M. Whitfield, "Cyclamates: The Triumph of Hysteria over Science," 2010, p. 2, www.flexiblevinylalliance.com/uploads/FVA_Abott_Labs_Cylclamates_-_Hysteria_Over_Science_10-2010.pdf.
8. Smith, "Diet Soda," *Encyclopedia of Junk Food*, p. 72.
9. de la Peña, *Empty Pleasures*, pp. 105–31.
10. Sucaryl ad, *Life*, December 5, 1955.
11. Tillie Lewis quoted in de la Peña, *Empty Pleasures*, p. 106.
12. Domino Sugar ad, *Life*, April 20, 1953.
13. Domino Sugar ad, *Life*, October 3, 1955.
14. Domino Sugar ad to the trade, *Confectioners Journal*, April 1955, p. 9.
15. "Memo to Dieters," *Confectioners Journal*, July 1954, p. 32.
16. Albert Lambert, "Artificial Sweeteners—The Challenges and Opportunities," *Candy Industry*, July 8, 1969, p. 7.
17. Sugar Information ads, *Life*, January 10 and July 17, 1964.
18. Whelan and Stare, *Panic in the Pantry*, p. 159.
19. P. O. Nees and Philip Derse, "Effect of Feeding Calcium Cyclamate to Rats," *Nature*, March 25, 1967.
20. Yudkin, *Sweet and Dangerous*, p. 182.
21. Letter from J. C. Lowey of Abbott, September 26, 1967, quoted in de la Peña, *Empty Pleasures*, p. 240.
22. Whelan and Stare, *Panic in the Pantry*, pp. 155–57.
23. "Scientist Scores Cyclamates Ban; Says His Research Did Not Justify F.D.A. Action," *New York Times*, July 12, 1975.
24. "Discoverer of Cyclamate Suggests Sugar Lobbying," *Lewiston Morning Tribune*, October 20, 1969.
25. "Sugar Futures Make Sharp Gains," *New York Times*, October 21, 1969; "Discoverer of Cyclamate Suggests Sugar Lobbying."
26. Yudkin, *Sweet and Dangerous*, p. 183.
27. Belasco, *Appetite for Change*, p. 72.
28. White House panel quoted in Levenstein, *Paradox*, p. 165.

29. Ibid., pp. 164–65; see also Belasco, *Appetite for Change*, p. 180.

30. All quotations in this paragraph are from Davis, *Let's Eat Right to Keep Fit*, pp. 17, 44–46.

31. Ibid., p. 47.

32. The term *sugar-phobia* is Harvey Levenstein's, *Paradox*, p. 191.

33. Yudkin, *Sweet and Dangerous*, p. 176.

34. On Yudkin and the heart disease debate, see Taubes, *Good Calories, Bad Calories*, pp. 119–21.

35. "Dietary Fat and Its Relation to Heart Attacks and Strokes," *JAMA* 175 (February 4, 1961): 389–91; "The Fat of the Land," *Time*, January 13, 1961.

36. Taubes, *Good Calories, Bad Calories*, p. 120.

37. Levenstein, *Fear*, pp. 147–48.

38. Taubes, *Good Calories, Bad Calories*, p. 120.

39. Yudkin, *Sweet and Dangerous*, p. 3.

40. Ibid., p. 175.

41. Leverton and Briggs quoted in Virginia Lee Warren, "Sugar—The Question Is, Do We Need It at All?," *New York Times*, July 4, 1972.

42. Richard Lyons, "Ban on Sugary-Cereal TV Ads Urged," *New York Times*, March 6, 1973.

43. All quotations in this paragraph are from Whelan and Stare, *Panic in the Pantry*, pp. 180–82.

11: Cavities

1. CBS broadcast and NCA response in "Candy Promotion Not Good Enough," *Candy Industry*, March 8, 1966, pp. 58–59.

2. Sir Walter Raleigh, "Instructions to His Son, and to Posterity" (1632).

3. Sylvester Graham, *A Treatise on Bread and Bread-Making* (Boston: Light & Stearns, 1837), p. 18.

4. Sylvester Graham, *A Lecture to Young Men on Chastity*, 4th ed. (Boston: G. W. Light, 1838), p. 114.

5. James Hart, *Klinike, or the Diet of the Diseased* (1633).

6. "Things Pleasant and Otherwise," *Ballou's Monthly Magazine* 50 (1879): 497.

7. For a summary of the 1890s state of the art concerning tooth decay, see J. Leon Williams, "The Degeneration of Human Teeth; Its Cause and Its Cure," *New Review* (London), 1892, p. 474.

8. Weston A. Price, *Nutrition and Physical Degeneration: A Comparison of Primitive and Modern Diets and Their Effects* (1939; La Mesa, CA: Price-Pottenger Nutrition, 2008).

9. Eugene Talbot, "Developmental Pathology and Tooth Decay," *Dental Digest* 11 (1905): 1073–82.

10. Ibid., p. 1073.

11. "Bad Teeth Traced to 'Sweet Tooth,'" *Philadelphia Record*, February 4, 1937.

12. "Prove Vitamin D Halts Tooth Decay," *New York Times*, December 7, 1932.

13. "Urges Vitamin C in Babies' Bottles," *New York Times*, April 18, 1941.

14. "Prove Vitamin D Halts Tooth Decay."

15. Dorothea F. Radusch, *Diet and Dental Health* (Chicago: American Dental Association, Bureau of Publications, 1945), pp. 8–9.

16. Robert W. McCluggage, *A History of the American Dental Association: A Century of Health Service* (Chicago: American Dental Association, 1959), p. 401.

17. This account of the discovery of fluoride's effect on teeth is based on National Institute of Dental and Craniofacial Research, "The Story of Fluoridation," www.nidcr.nih.gov/oralhealth/topics/fluoride/thestoryoffluoridation.htm.

18. McCluggage, *History of the ADA*, p. 436.

19. "Scientist Lays Tooth Decay to Varied Causes—Not Candy," *Billboard*, July 6, 1946, p. 109.

20. Ibid.

21. Centers for Disease Control and Prevention, "Ten Great Public Health Achievements," *Morbidity and Mortality Weekly Report* 48, no. 12 (April 2, 1999): 241–43; CDC 2010 Water Fluoridation Statistics; "U.S. Says Too Much Fluoride in Water," *USAToday*, January 7, 2011. See also a discussion of mainstream researchers who are reversing or qualifying their positions on fluoridation in Dan Fagin, "Second Thoughts on Fluoride," *Scientific American*, December 16, 2007.

22. "The Story of Fluoridation."

23. "Fluoridation Facts Outlined to Kiwanis," *Lewiston Daily Sun*, June 9, 1960.

24. National Research Council Food and Nutrition Board, *Recommended Dietary Allowances: A Report*, 7th rev. ed. (Washington, DC: National Academy of Sciences, 1968).

25. McCluggage, *History of the ADA*, p. 433.

26. Hearings Before the Senate Select Committee on Nutrition and Human Needs, 92nd Cong., 2nd sess., Nutrition Education—1972, 276, 277 (hereafter cited as *Nutrition Education*).

27. "Halt in Tooth Decay Within the Decade," *New York Times*, February 8, 1970.

28. Joint report of the Council on Dental Health and the Council on Dental Therapeutics of the American Dental Association, "Sugar and Dental Caries: The Effect on the Teeth of Sweetened Beverages and Other Sugar-Containing Substances," *Journal of the American Dental Association* 47 (October 1953): 415.

29. Ernest Newbrun, "Sucrose: The Arch Criminal of Dental Caries," *ASDC Journal of Dentistry for Children* 36 (1969): 239–48.

30. A survey of some of the frequently contradictory research that has investigated the link between carbohydrates and cavities can be found in Informatics Incorporated, *Scientific Literature Reviews on Generally Recognized as Safe (GRAS) Food Ingredients: Dental Caries and Carbohydrates*, prepared for the Food and Drug Administration (National Technical Information Service, 1974), and M. V. Landow, ed., *Trends in Dietary Carbohydrate Research* (Hauppauge, NY: Nova Science, 2006).

31. Robert L. Weiss and Albert H. Trithart, "Between-Meal Eating Habits and Dental Caries Experience in Preschool Children," *American Journal of Public Health* 50 (1960): 1097; see also summary of studies cited in Informatics, *Scientific Literature Reviews*, p. 6.

32. B. E. Gustafsson et al., "The Vipeholm Dental Caries Study," 1954, cited in *Nutrition Education*, p. 278.

33. Bo Krasse, "The Vipeholm Dental Caries Study: Recollections and Reflections 50 Years Later," *Journal of Dental Research* 80, no. 9 (2001): 1785–88; Elin Bommenel, thesis summary, www.innovations-report.de /html/berichte/medizin_gesundheit/bericht-57360.html; thanks to Anna Lundh for bringing the full story of the Vipeholm research to my attention.

34. S. N. Kreitzman, "Carbohydrates and Dental Caries: An Examination of the Evidence." *Journal of Preventive Dentistry* 6 (1980): 11.

35. Krasse, "Vipeholm," p. 1786.

36. *Nutrition Education*, p. 276.

37. *Nutrition Education*, p. 280.

38. Ibid., p. 283.

39. Krasse, "Vipeholm," p. 1787.

40. *Nutrition Education*, p. 281.

12: Treat or Trick?

1. "The Goblins Will Getcha . . . ," *Newsweek*, November 3, 1975, p. 28.

2. This chapter is based on material previously published as Samira Kawash, "Gangsters, Pranksters, and the Invention of Trick-or-Treating, 1930–1960," *American Journal of Play* 4, no. 2 (Fall 2011): 150–75.

3. The candy contents of the jack-o'-lantern are widely cited on the Internet, although no one takes credit for doing the math.

4. Ruth Edna Kelley, *The Book of Halloween* (Boston: Lothrop, Lee & Shepard, 1919), pp. 154–55.

5. "Halloween Fun and Mischief," *New York Times*, November 1, 1895.

6. "Gruesome Halloween Joke," *New York Times*, November 2, 1900.

7. "Masked in Sing Sing Suit," *New York Times*, October 31, 1915.

8. "Soaped the Trolley Tracks," *New York Times*, November 3, 1905.

9. Lina Beard and Adelia B. Beard, *How to Amuse Yourself and Others: The American Girls Handy Book* (New York: Scribner, 1887), p. 190.

10. "Our Young Folk," *American Agriculturalist, Middle Edition* 27 (October 1894): 271.

11. Isabel Gordon Curtis, "A Children's Celebration of Hallowe'en," *St. Nicholas*, October 1905, p. 1124.

12. "Chapter Notes," *Phi Gamma Delta* 40, no. 3 (December 1917): 264.

13. Brach's ad, *Life*, May 13, 1957; People's Service Drug Store ad, *Fredericksburg Free-Lance Star*, October 4, 1951.

14. Frank Burke, "Not How Cheap but—How Good," interview with Fred and Horace Wunderle, sons of founder Philip Wunderle, *Confectioners Journal*, September 1946, p. 40.

15. "'Trick-or-Treat' Is Demand," *Lethbridge Herald* (Alberta, Canada), November 4, 1927.

16. Early newspaper accounts were located by searching "trick or treat," "tricks or treat," "tricks and treat" at ancestry.com, Google News Archive, ProQuest; see also Gary Martin, "Trick-or-Treat," *The Phrase Finder*, www.phrases.org.uk/meanings/trick-or-treat.html, and the entry on "Trick-or-treating," *Wikipedia*, http://en.wikipedia.org/wiki/Trick-or-treating.

17. "Halloween Pranks Keep Police on Hop," *Oregon Journal*, November 1, 1934.

18. *Centralia (WA) Daily Chronicle*, November 1, 1939.

19. "Youngsters Shake Down Residents," *Reno Evening Gazette*, November 1, 1938.

20. "Halloween Pranks Draw Objections," letters to the editor, *Reno Evening Gazette*, October 29, 1938.

21. "The Gangsters of Tomorrow," *Montana Herald-Record*, November 2, 1934.

22. "Youngsters Shake Down Residents."

23. "Getting in Practice for Night of Fun: Halloween Pranks Plotted by Youngsters of Southland," *Los Angeles Times*, October 30, 1938.

24. "Trick-or-Treat Seeker Gets Neither: Mother Says Principal Slapped the Boy," *New York Times*, November 4, 1952; "Everyone Regrets Halloween

Slap," *New York Times*, November 11, 1952. The case was dismissed when the ruling magistrate persuaded Dr. Mason to apologize, and Mrs. Wanderman agreed to drop the charges.

25. "15,000 Enjoy Quietest of Halloweens," *Hartford Courant*, November 1, 1950; "Gay Throngs End Annual Siege of City by Witches; Halloween Passes with Little Damage," *Washington Post*, November 1, 1950.

26. "Coast Dentist Hunted: Wanted in Halloween 'Treat' That Made Children Ill," *New York Times*, November 4, 1959.

27. Judy Klemesrud, "Those Treats May Be Tricks," *New York Times*, October 28, 1970.

28. Joel Best and Gerald T. Horiuchi, "The Razor Blade in the Apple: The Social Construction of Urban Legends," *Social Problems* 32, no. 5 (June 1985): 488–99.

29. Ibid., p. 490.

30. Ibid.; see also Barbara Mikkelson, "Halloween Poisonings," www.snopes.com/horrors/poison/halloween.asp.

31. Best and Horiuchi, "Razor Blade," p. 490.

32. Joel Best interview, *Los Angeles Times*, November 9, 1989, quoted in Mikkelson, "Halloween Poisonings."

33. Needle in the Tootsie Roll story as told by "Dan" at http://candyprofessor.com/2009/10/30/laxatives-and-the-end-of-trick-or-treating/.

34. "Halloween 1982: An Overview," National Confectioners Association, Chocolate Manufacturers Association, and National Candy Wholesalers Association, n.d., quoted in Best and Horiuchi, "Razor Blade," p. 491.

35. Best and Horiuchi, "Razor Blade," p. 488.

36. Howard Chudacoff, *Children at Play: An American History* (New York: New York University Press, 2007), pp. 163–64.

37. These and many more edifying examples of false or fabricated Halloween poison candy stories have been gathered by Barbara Mikkelson in "Halloween Poisonings" at the legend-busting website snopes.com.

13: Junk-Food Junkies

1. For a romp through fast-food history, see Smith, *Encyclopedia of Junk Food*.

2. John Hess, "The Unbalanced American's Diet: 20 Partials, Not 'Three Squares,'" *New York Times*, January 3, 1974.

3. "Snacks and Busy Families Blamed for Much Poor Nutrition Among Youths," *New York Times*, March 13, 1972.

4. W. C. Dickmeyer, "8 Cents Gives Bakers Edge in Competing for Nickels," *Confectioners Journal*, June 1937, p. 60.

5. Myron Lench, "Fences Being Torn Down Between Candy and Baked Goods," *Candy Industry*, March 16, 1968, p. 1.

6. "We Are Changing—With a Changing Candy Industry—Adding Baked Snacks, editorial, *Candy and Snack Industry*, January 1971, p. 21.

7. Lench, "Fences," p. 1.

8. Report of the 36th Annual NCA Convention, Springfield, Illinois, May 14–16, 1919, published in *Confectioners Journal*, June 1919, pp. 94–108. The court decision in which this opinion appeared was *Malley v. Baker* (1st Cir., May 17, 1922).

9. Milky Way ad, *Confectioners Journal*, June 1925, p. 48.

10. Brenner, *Emperors of Chocolate*, p. 54.

11. 1960s Milky Way television ad, www.youtube.com/watch?v=eAq7a1HG-rY.

12. Edward Finch Cox, Robert C. Fellmeth, and John E. Schultz, *Nader's Raiders: Report on the Federal Trade Commission* (New York: Grove Press, 1969).

13. "Mars Agrees to Soften Ads for Milky Way Bars," *Wall Street Journal*, August 26, 1970; Mars, Incorporated, consent order, 77 F.T.C. 1435, 1436, October 22, 1970.

14. My account of the history of ready-to-eat cereals in this and following paragraphs is drawn from Bruce and Crawford, *Cerealizing America*.

15. Ibid., p. 214.

16. Walter Hughes, "Highlights of 20 Years as Secretary, the National Confectioners Association," *Confectioners Journal*, June 1933, pp. 121–22.

17. Bruce and Crawford, *Cerealizing America*, pp. 103–05.

18. Post executive Kent Mitchell, quoted ibid., p. 106.

19. Ibid.

20. Ibid., p. 150.

21. Ibid., p. 107.

22. Ibid., p. 209.

23. Untitled news item, *Candy Industry*, May 5, 1964, p. 4.

24. Bruce and Crawford, *Cerealizing America*, p. 111.

25. Hearings Before the Senate Subcommittee on Consumer Protection of the Committee on Commerce, Dry Cereals, 91st Cong., 2nd sess., July 23, August 4–5, 1970, p. 1 (hereafter cited as *Dry Cereals*).

26. "Nutrition Specialist's Son Loves His 'Junk Cereals,'" *Washington Evening Star*, July 24, 1970, reproduced ibid., p. 184.

27. Ibid., p. 3.

28. "Cereal Makers Deny Nutritionist's Charges," *Dry Cereals*, p. 185; Kellogg press release, *Dry Cereals*, p. 28; General Foods press release, *Dry Cereals*, p. 29.

29. Jean Mayer, testimony, *Nutrition Education*, p. 18.
30. Quoted in Bruce and Crawford, *Cerealizing America*, p. 225.
31. *Dry Cereals*, p. 9.
32. Ibid., pp. 8–9.
33. Bruce and Crawford, *Cerealizing America*, p. 231.
34. Choate testimony, *Nutrition Education*, p. 37.
35. Nestle, *Food Politics*, p. 305.
36. General Mills website, http://growupstrong.com/kid-cereals/reeses-puffs.
37. Bonnie Rochman, "The Sugary Brands Doing the Most Kid-Chasing," *Time*, October 23, 2009.
38. Levine, *School Lunch Politics*; Gordon W. Gunderson, "The National School Lunch Program: Background and Development, USDA Food and Nutrition Service, February 12, 2012, www.fns.usda.gov/cnd/lunch/AboutLunch /ProgramHistory_5.htm; USDA, "National School Lunch Program Fact Sheet," www.fns.usda.gov/cnd/lunch/aboutlunch/NSLPFactSheet.pdf.
39. The relationship between agricultural politics and school lunches is explained in Levine, *School Lunch Politics*, pp. 93–94.
40. "Health Care," *Southern Changes* 1, no. 5 (1979): 23.
41. Ibid.
42. "When the Schools Open," *Confectioners Journal*, September 1909, p. 65.
43. Oversight Hearings on the School Lunch Program, House Committee on Education and Labor, Subcommittee on Elementary, Secondary, and Vocational Education, 94th Cong., 2nd sess., 1976, p. 486.
44. Ibid., p. 12.
45. Ibid., p. 508.
46. "U.S.: Limit School Junk Food Sale," *Pittsburgh Post-Gazette*, April 22, 1978.
47. Mimi Sheraton, "'Junk Food' Plan Widely Criticized," *New York Times*, July 13, 1979.
48. Ibid.
49. "Consumer Groups Blast School Junk Food Rule," *St. Petersburg Times*, July 7, 1979.
50. "Hall of Shame for Junk Food Opened," *Lodi News-Sentinel*, July 7, 1979.
51. "Consumer Groups Blast School Junk Food Rule."
52. Sheraton, "Junk Food."
53. Whelan and Stare, *Panic in the Pantry*, p. 122.
54. F. M. Clydesdale, "Let's Dispel the Junk Food Myth," *Candy and Snack Industry*, August 1975, p. 57.
55. "Hall of Shame," *Florence (AL) Times Daily*, July 8, 1979.
56. "Health Care," *Southern Changes* 1, no. 5 (1979): 23.

57. The view of junk food expressed in this paragraph owes its inspiration to David Kessler, *The End of Overeating*. See also George Dvorsky, "How Flavor Chemists Make Your Food So Addictively Good," http://io9.com/5958880/how-flavor-chemists-make-your-food-so-addictively-good.

58. Groce quoted in Bruce Nash and Allan Zullo, *The Wacky Top 40* (Avon, MA: Adams Media Corp., 1993).

59. White House Conference on Food, Nutrition and Health, final report, 1969, section 3, p. 118.

60. Ibid., p. 123.

61. "Candy Firms Looking to Nearby Snack Field," *Candy Industry*, May 12, 1970, pp. 3, 6.

62. "The Shape of Candy's Future—The Scientist's View," *Candy Industry*, August 19, 1969, pp. 75–76.

63. Bernard W. Minifie, "Balance of Ingredients Can Be Changed to Fortify Candy," *Candy and Snack Industry*, February 1973, p. 25.

64. "Candy Firms Looking to Nearby Snack Field."

65. "The Shape of Candy's Future."

14: Candification

1. Arthur W. Anti, "Considerations Different for Space Candies," *Candy Industry*, December 13, 1966, pp. 55–56, 59.

2. William J. Cromie, "Space Food Isn't Altogether Delicious," *St. Petersburg Times*, August 19, 1965.

3. Pillsbury full-page advertorial, "Snack Food Now Available as a High-Energy Snack," *Pittsburgh Press*, December 3, 1969.

4. NASA press release 73–143, November 6, 1973.

5. Mike Lench, "Filling the Nutritional Gap," *Candy and Snack Industry*, January 1976, p. 86.

6. "Newsletter," *Candy and Snack Industry*, May 1981, p. 8.

7. James Echeandia, "Snack Bars Emerging as Formidable Candy Competitors," *Candy and Snack Industry*, November 1979, p. 56.

8. Don Gussow, "Wondering About the Challenges of Health Food, Breakfast Bars?," *Candy and Snack Industry*, April 15, 1977, p. 12.

9. Emily Bryson York, "Snickers Uses Humor to Satisfy Generations of Hunger," AdAge.com, March 29, 2010.

10. "U.S. Snack Bar Market Continues Growth," *Candy and Snack Today*, October 2012, p. 26.

11. "Segment Report: Raising the Bar," *Candy and Snack Today*, January/February 2010, pp. 34–38.

12. Fiber One television ad, 2011, www.youtube.com/watch?v=s18TtmNmioQ.

13. Bruce Horovitz, "Marketers Adapt Menus to Eat-What-I-Want-When-I-Want Trend," *USA Today*, November 21, 2011.

14. R. S. Sebastian, C. Wilkinson Enns, and J. D. Goldman, *MyPyramid Intakes and Snacking Patterns of U.S. Adults: What We Eat in America, NHANES 2007–2008*, Food Surveys Research Group Dietary Data Brief no. 5, June 2011, http://ars.usda.gov/Services/docs.htm?docid=19476.

15. Anne Harding, "Snacking, Not Portion Size, Largely Driving U.S. Overeating," CNNHealth, June 30, 2011; Kiyah Duffey and Barry Popkin, "Energy Density, Portion Size, and Eating Occasions: Contributions to Increased Energy Intake in the United States, 1977–2006," *PLoS Medicine*, June 2011; B. M. Popkin and K. J. Duffey, "Does Hunger and Satiety Drive Eating Anymore? Increasing Eating Occasions and Decreasing Time Between Eating Occasions in the United States," *American Journal of Clinical Nutrition* 91 (2009): 1–6.

16. Megan Porter, RD, "Eating Smaller, More Frequent Meals," www.caloriesperhour.com/news_051130.php_.

17. "Small Meals and Cholesterol," http://my.clevelandclinic.org/heart/prevention/askdietician/ask4_02.aspx.

18. James J. Kenney, "To Snack or Not to Snack, That Is the Question," Food and Health Communications, http://foodandhealth.com/cpecourses/snack.php.

19. Nemours Foundation, "Smart Snacking," http://kidshealth.org/teen/food_fitness/nutrition/healthy_snacks.html.

20. American Heart Association, "Healthy Snacking," www.heart.org/HEARTORG/GettingHealthy/NutritionCenter/HealthyCooking/Healthy-Snacking_UCM_301489_Article.jsp.

21. "Healthy Snacking: What Do Nutritionists Eat Between Meals?," "Huffpost Healthy Living," November 13, 2012, www.huffingtonpost.com/2012/11/12/healthiest-snacks-nutritionists-food_n_2119332.html?ir=Healthy+Living#slide=more262802.

22. Elaine Magee, "The Best Healthy Snacks in Your Supermarket," www.webmd.com/food-recipes/features/the-best-healthy-snacks-in-your-supermarket.

23. "Sensible Snacking," www.fritolay.com/your-health/sensible-snacking.html.

24. Simon, *Appetite for Profit*, p. 113.

25. Joray company history at www.joraycandy.com/?view=About; "Joseph Shalhoub & Son, Inc.," *New York Press*, October 19, 2004.

26. "Fruit Roll-Ups: Fun, Flavorful Snack-Time Treat," *Deseret News*, March 30, 1983.

27. "General Mills Facing Class Action Lawsuit over 'Fruit Snacks' Full of Sugars, Partially Hydrogenated Oil, & Dyes," Center for Science in the Public Interest press release, October 14, 2011; *Lam v. General Mills*, Case No. 11-5056-SC, United States District Court, N.D. California (October 14, 2011).

28. "New Mott's for Tots Brings Natural Goodness Down to Size," Mott Company press release, May 27, 2011.

29. Caglar Irmak, Beth Vallen, and Stefanie Rosen Robinson, "The Impact of Product Name on Dieters' and Nondieters' Food Evaluations and Consumption," *Journal of Consumer Research* 38, no. 2 (August 2011): 390–405.

30. Grace Weitz, "A Healthy Duo: Fruits and Functional Ingredients," *Candy Industry*, March 2011, p. 24.

31. Walmart product description, www.walmart.com/ip/Starburst-Original -Fruit-Chews-41-oz/10452953.

32. Supercandy information at http://snapinfusion.com/faq.

33. Kawther Albader, "Multi-Tasking Treats," *Candy Industry*, July 20, 2012.

34. Rita Mu, "Hero Launches First Multivitamin Dark Chocolate Supplement," *Food Magazine*, November 16, 2010.

35. This quote appeared in an article on parenting tricks in *Time Out New York Kids* in 2009. I carried it around in my backpack for months while I was mulling over what my candy book might look like. Alas, the exact citation has disappeared from my notes. With such inadequate documentation, I thought about leaving it out. But I just couldn't.

36. Jake Heller, "11 Reasons Chocolate Is Good for Your Health," *Daily Beast*, March 28, 2012; James Meek, "Chocolate Is Good for You (or How Mars Tried to Sell Us This as Health Food)," *Guardian*, December 23, 2002.

37. Weitz, "A Healthy Duo," p. 25.

38. Elena Conis, "Science Picks Through the Chocolate Nuggets," *Los Angeles Times*, May 31, 2010; Gary Taubes, "Chocolate and Red Meat Can Be Bad for Your Science: Why Many Nutrition Studies Are All Wrong," *Discover Magazine Blog*, "The Crux," April 5, 2012, http://blogs.discover magazine.com/crux/2012/04/05/chocolate-red-meat-can-be-bad-for -your-science-why-many-nutrition-studies-are-all-wrong/.

39. Mars research at www.healthycocoa.com, a Mars-affiliated website.

40. See Jon Gertner, "Eat Chocolate, Live Longer?," *New York Times*, October 10, 2004, for an inside look at the Mars cocoa research program.

41. Michelle Castillo, "Flavanol-Rich Dark Chocolate May Help Reduce Blood Pressure," CBS News, August 16, 2012.

42. National Confectioners Association, *Taking Chocolate to Heart*, www
.thestoryofchocolate.com/About/content.cfm?ItemNumber-3730.

43. "Chocolate 101: Antioxidants," www.thehersheycompany.com/nutrition
-and-wellness/chocolate-101/antioxidants.aspx.

44. "Chocolate: Exploding the Myths," Center for Science in the Public Interest press release, February 26, 2001.

15: In Defense of Candy

1. National Confectioners Association, "Science and Nutrition," 2012, www
.candyusa.com/FunStuff/Science.cfm?navItemNumber=2792.

2. *New York Times* Health Guide, http://health.nytimes.com/health/guides
/nutrition/balanced-diet/overview.html.

3. Nicholas Bakalar, "For Omega-3s, Fish May Beat Pills," *New York Times*, November 5, 2012.

4. My discussion of nutritionism and its limitations is indebted to Michael Pollan, especially *Defense of Food*, pp. 19–81, and also Ross Hume Hall's *Food for Nought*, published nearly forty years ago. Hall was an early critic of the "food is chemicals" framework. Although long out of print and largely forgotten, *Food for Nought* remains relevant and informative.

5. Pollan, *Defense of Food*, p. 38.

6. For a persuasive and inspiring account of the pleasure and necessity of real food, see Planck, *Real Food*. See also Mark Bittman, "Real Food," *Men's Health*, September 2009.

7. Ettlinger, *Twinkie*, pp. 188–89.

8. Pollan, *Omnivore's Dilemma*, p. 117.

9. Simon, *Appetite for Profit*, p. 6.

Selected Bibliography

This bibliography includes full publication information for secondary sources and recent books cited in the text. Primary and historic sources are cited in full in the notes.

Candy

Almond, Steve. *Candyfreak: A Journey Through the Chocolate Underbelly of America*. Chapel Hill, NC: Algonquin Books, 2004.

Brenner, Joël Glenn. *Emperors of Chocolate: Inside the Secret World of Hershey and Mars*. New York: Random House, 1999.

Broekel, Ray. *The Chocolate Chronicles*. Lombard, IL: Wallace-Homestead, 1985.

———. *The Great American Candy Bar Book*. Boston: Houghton Mifflin, 1982.

Cooper, Gail. "Love, War, and Chocolate: Gender and the American Candy Industry, 1890–1930." In *His and Hers: Gender, Consumption, and Technology*, ed. Roger Horowitz and Arwen Mohun, pp. 67–94. Charlottesville: University of Virginia Press, 1998.

D'Antonio, Michael. *Hershey: Milton S. Hershey's Extraordinary Life of Wealth, Empire, and Utopian Dreams*. New York: Simon & Schuster, 2006.

Dusselier, Jane. "Bonbons, Lemon Drops, and Oh Henry! Bars: Candy, Consumer Culture, and the Construction of Gender, 1895–1920." In *Kitchen*

Culture in America: Popular Representations of Food, Gender, and Race, ed. Sherrie A. Inness, pp. 13–49. Philadelphia: University of Pennsylvania Press, 2001.

Goddard, Leslie. *Chicago's Sweet Candy History*. Charleston, SC: Arcadia Publishing, 2012.

Gott, Philip. *All About Candy and Chocolate. A Comprehensive Study of the Candy and Chocolate Industries*. Washington, DC: National Confectioners Association, 1958.

Kimmerle, Beth. *Candy: The Sweet History*. Portland, OR: Collectors Press, 2007.

Mason, Laura. *Sugar-Plums and Sherbet: The Prehistory of Sweets*. Totnes, Devon, UK: Prospect Books, 2004.

McMahon, James D., Jr. *Built on Chocolate: The Story of the Hershey Chocolate Company*. Hershey, PA: Hershey Foods Corporation, 1998.

Richardson, Tim. *Sweets: A History of Candy*. New York: Bloomsbury, 2002.

Untermeyer, Louis. *A Century of Candymaking, 1847–1947: The Story of the Origin and Growth of the New England Confectionery Company*. Revere, MA: New England Confectionery Company, 1947.

Woloson, Wendy A. *Refined Tastes: Sugar, Confectionery, and Consumers in Nineteenth-Century America*. Baltimore: Johns Hopkins University Press, 2002.

Food: History and Politics

Belasco, Warren. *Appetite for Change: How the Counterculture Took on the Food Industry*. Ithaca: Cornell University Press, 2006.

Bruce, Scott, and Bill Crawford. *Cerealizing America: The Unsweetened Story of American Breakfast Cereal*. New York: Faber and Faber, 1995.

Chen, Joanne. *The Taste of Sweet: Our Complicated Love Affair with Our Favorite Treats*. New York: Crown, 2008.

Ettlinger, Steve. *Twinkie, Deconstructed*. New York: Hudson Street Press, 2007.

Goodwin, Lorine Swainston. *The Pure Food, Drink and Drug Crusaders, 1879–1914*. Jefferson, NC: McFarland, 1999.

Hall, Ross Hume. *Food for Nought: The Decline in Nutrition*. New York: Vintage Books, 1976.

Hooker, Richard J. *Food and Drink in America: A History*. Indianapolis: Bobbs-Merrill, 1981.

Kamps, Alice D. *What's Cooking, Uncle Sam? The Government's Effect on the*

American Diet. Washington, DC: Foundation for the National Archives, 2011.

Levenstein, Harvey. *Fear of Food: A History of Why We Worry About What We Eat.* Chicago: University of Chicago Press, 2012.

———. *Paradox of Plenty: A Social History of Eating in Modern America.* Rev. ed. Berkeley: University of California Press, 2003.

———. *Revolution at the Table: The Transformation of the American Diet.* Berkeley: University of California Press, 2003.

Levine, Susan. *School Lunch Politics: The Surprising History of America's Favorite Welfare Program.* Princeton: Princeton University Press, 2008.

McGee, Harold. *On Food and Cooking: The Science and Lore of the Kitchen.* New York: Scribner, 2004.

Nestle, Marion. *Food Politics: How the Food Industry Influences Nutrition and Health.* Rev. ed. Berkeley: University of California Press, 2007.

Okun, Mitchell. *Fair Play in the Marketplace: The First Battle for Pure Food and Drugs.* DeKalb: Northern Illinois University Press, 1986.

Planck, Nina. *Real Food: What to Eat and Why.* New York: Bloomsbury, 2006.

Pollan, Michael. *In Defense of Food: An Eater's Manifesto.* New York: Penguin, 2008.

———. *The Omnivore's Dilemma: A Natural History of Four Meals.* New York: Penguin, 2006.

Root, Waverley, and Richard de Rochemont. *Eating in America: A History.* New York: William Morrow, 1976.

Shapiro, Laura. *Perfection Salad: Women and Cooking at the Turn of the Century.* Berkeley: University of California Press, 2008.

———. *Something from the Oven: Reinventing Dinner in 1950s America.* New York: Penguin, 2004.

Simon, Michele. *Appetite for Profit: How the Food Industry Undermines Our Health and How to Fight Back.* New York: Nation Books, 2006.

Smith, Andrew F. *Eating History: 30 Turning Points in the Making of American Cuisine.* New York: Columbia University Press, 2009.

———. *Encyclopedia of Junk Food and Fast Food.* Westport, CT: Greenwood Press, 2006.

———, ed. *The Oxford Companion to American Food and Drink.* New York: Oxford University Press, 2007.

———. *Peanuts: The Illustrious History of the Goober Pea.* Urbana: University of Illinois Press, 2002.

———. *Popped Culture: A Social History of Popcorn in America.* Columbia: University of South Carolina Press, 1999.

Whelan, Elizabeth M., and Fredrick J. Stare. *Panic in the Pantry: Food Facts, Fads, and Fallacies.* New York: Atheneum, 1975.

Wilson, Bee. *Swindled: The Dark History of Food Fraud, from Poisoned Candy to Counterfeit Coffee.* Princeton: Princeton University Press, 2008.

Young, James Harvey. *Pure Food: Securing the Federal Food and Drugs Act of 1906.* Princeton: Princeton University Press, 1989.

Diet and Health

Brumberg, Joan Jacobs. *Fasting Girls: A History of Anorexia Nervosa.* New York: Vintage Books, 2000.

Davis, Adelle. *Let's Eat Right to Keep Fit.* New York: Harcourt, Brace, 1954.

Fraser, Laura. *Losing It: America's Obsession with Weight and the Industry that Feeds on It.* New York: Dutton, 1997.

Kessler, David A. *The End of Overeating: Taking Control of the Insatiable American Diet.* Emmaus, PA: Rodale, 2009.

Mudry, Jessica J. *Measured Meals: Nutrition in America.* Albany: State University of New York Press, 2009.

Schwartz, Hillel. *Never Satisfied: A Cultural History of Diets, Fantasies, and Fat.* New York: Free Press, 1986.

Taubes, Gary. *Good Calories, Bad Calories: Fats, Carbs, and the Controversial Science of Diet and Health.* New York: Anchor Books, 2008.

———. *Why We Get Fat and What to Do About It.* New York: Knopf, 2011.

Whorton, James C. *Crusaders for Fitness: The History of American Health Reformers.* Princeton: Princeton University Press, 1982.

———. *Inner Hygiene: Constipation and the Pursuit of Health in Modern Society.* New York: Oxford University Press, 2000.

Yager, Susan. *The Hundred Year Diet: America's Voracious Appetite for Losing Weight.* New York: Rodale, 2010.

Yudkin, John. *Sweet and Dangerous: The New Facts About the Sugar You Eat as a Cause of Heart Disease, Diabetes, and Other Killers.* New York: Peter H. Wyden, 1972.

Other

Abbott, Elizabeth. *Sugar: A Bittersweet History.* Woodstock, NY: Overlook, 2010.

Apple, Rima. *Vitamania: Vitamins in American Culture.* New Brunswick, NJ: Rutgers University Press, 1996.

Brandt, Allan M. *The Cigarette Century: The Rise, Fall, and Deadly Persistence of the Product That Defined America*. New York: Basic Books, 2007.

de la Peña, Carolyn. *Empty Pleasures: The Story of Artificial Sweeteners from Saccharin to Splenda*. Chapel Hill: University of North Carolina Press, 2010.

Mintz, Sidney W. *Sweetness and Power: The Place of Sugar in Modern History*. New York: Viking, 1985.

Okrent, Daniel. *Last Call: The Rise and Fall of Prohibition*. New York: Scribner, 2010.

Acknowledgments

Although the research and writing of this book have been relatively solitary activities, such work could never bear fruit without the many hands that have lifted me up and propelled me forward from the glimmer of an idea to a completed book. First, thanks to friends who listened patiently to my earliest candy ravings: Betsy Beier, who got me thinking about how to leverage ideas into something more tangible; Tina Fallon, a force of nature whose early enthusiasm and encouragement helped tip the project from fantasy into action; and Kristin Ordahl, ever ready with tea, sympathy, and marzipan. The final stretches were sweetened by Leilani Rapaport, whose good cheer and computer wizardry were equally appreciated, and by the Levy-Lyons family, who don't eat candy but love me anyway.

CandyProfessor.com, a blog I launched in 2009 to begin recording my findings, was made easy and elegant thanks to the technology wizards at Word Press. Fellow bloggers Cybele May (candyblog.net), Patti Woods (candyyum yum.com), and Mark Doby (sugarpressure.com) were a constant source of inspiration and fellowship as I jump-started the blogging engine. CandyProfessor.com readers have been a wonderful community of virtual friends who encouraged me from the start to dig ever deeper in the candy archives. I also benefited from conversations and contacts with many professionals and experts in the business of making and selling candy today, especially Tomi Holt at Jelly Belly and Liz Dee at Smarties Candy Company.

Along the way, I have been lucky to meet writers and other professionals who provided crucial advice, mentoring, and inspiration: Julia Moskin of *The New York Times*, a great writer with an eye for a good story, who helped me ask the right questions and who provided ongoing support; Dan Fromson of TheAtlantic.com, who helped me connect with a broader audience; Steven Schmidt, a fellow enthusiast of all things old and sugary, who understood why CandyProfessor was so much fun; novelist Katharine Weber (*True Confections*) and culinary historian Jeri Quinzio (*Of Sugar and Snow*), who in person and in their books were just the sort of role models I was looking for; Brooklyn writers Jenny Egan and Laura Kriska, who were generous with advice and hand-holding when I really needed it; *American Journal of Play* editor Scott Eberle, who encouraged my research and provided an ideal venue for publishing work that straddled the academic and the popular. Special thanks to Kirby Kim, my agent at William Morris Endeavor, whose enthusiasm and curiosity helped propel this project from idea to proposal to book; and to Faber and Faber editor Chantal Clarke, who found me before I found her, and whose smart, funny, creative work editing this book has made it all the better.

Given the elusive and ephemeral nature of many aspects of candy's past, my research would have been impossible without digital full-text searches of books, newspapers, and other publications. I am tremendously grateful to the generations of inventors and investors who have given us the technology to bring the universal library that much closer to reality. But what Google giveth, Google (and copyright law) taketh away; this project has convinced me of the necessity of publicly funded and publicly controlled digital archives that can accommodate full access for research and scholarship. Make it so!

The invisible heroes of this book are the librarians and archivists: both those who generously helped me find and retrieve obscure, heavy, dusty volumes, and all those others, yesterday and today, who worked invisibly, anonymously, and often thanklessly to collect, catalog, preserve, and store items of seemingly dubious value on the theory that someday, someone might want to know. I especially benefited from the hospitality and assistance of librarians and staff at the research divisions of the New York Public Library, particularly the Stephen A. Schwarzman Building and the Science, Industry and Business Library; the Brooklyn Public Library, especially the Brooklyn Collection and the Business and Career Library; Rutgers University Libraries; the New York Academy of Medicine Library; Baker Library Historical Collections at the Harvard Business School; the Francis A. Countway Library of Medicine at Harvard Medical School; and the Public Library of Cincinnati and Hamilton County. Curator Alice D. Kamps and the rest of the staff of the National Archives also deserve special mention; many of the images in this book were first exhibited in the National Archives Experience 2011 exhibit "What's Cooking, Uncle Sam?"

My deepest debts of gratitude are to my family. My mother, Alice, trained me early in vital research skills by insisting that the correct answer to every question is, "Look it up." Sabri, my father, taught me to be curious about everything and also gave me the gift of deep skepticism. Illia inspired this book with her generous jelly-bean baby ways; she has grown to become an enthusiastic and invaluable assistant in the CandyProfessor laboratory and test kitchen, where her good cheer and can-do spirit constantly buoy me up. And finally, unending gratitude to my husband and companion, Roger Cooper, who gave me the courage to step boldly into the unknown. His support and encouragement have kept me going through bad days and made the good days so much better. I count myself exceedingly fortunate to have spent so much of my life in his thoughtful, kind, and loving company.

Index

Page numbers in *italics* refer to illustrations.

A Note About the Author

Samira Kawash holds a Ph.D. in literary studies from Duke University and is a professor emerita at Rutgers University. She is the author of *Dislocating the Color Line* (Stanford University Press, 1997) and the founder of the website CandyProfessor.com. She lives in Brooklyn, New York.